CHOOSING TO SUCCEED: LAND USE LAW & CLIMATE CONTROL

John R. Nolon

ENVIRONMENTAL LAW INSTITUTE
Washington, D.C.

1730 M Street NW, Washington, DC 20036

Cover design by Natalia Arango, www.renoleum.com.

Published April 2021.

Printed in the United States of America
ISBN 978-1-58576-229-3

Praise for *Choosing to Succeed: Land Use Law & Climate Control*

I often have conversations with friends who are deeply concerned about climate change and who are concerned that their individual efforts (bicycling to work, flying less) aren't enough, yet uncertain about how to more productively contribute. Professor Nolon's book has an answer, providing a blueprint for how every person can work within their community to mitigate and adapt to climate change. The book is comprehensive yet nuanced, simultaneously accessible to those outside of the climate policy space and enlightening to those within it. Professor Nolon's book gives productive, concrete advice every American willing to choose to succeed in meeting the climate change challenge.

—Katrina Fischer Kuh, Distinguished Professor of Environmental Law,
Pace University Elisabeth Haub School of Law

Leave it to John Nolon, the prime mover of environmental land use law, to serve as our optimistic guide to the complex challenges that climate change, pandemics, and natural disasters pose to local officials and others on the front lines of government response. This comprehensive volume provides real-world examples of effective, responsive, 21st century zoning and planning regulations that serve as valuable guideposts for communities engaged in the struggle to craft and implement mitigation and resilience strategies.

—Michael Allan Wolf, Richard E. Nelson Eminent Scholar Chair in Local
Government, University of Florida Levin College of Law

Despite numerous attempts to increase state and federal involvement, land use regulation remains primarily a function of local governments. John Nolon's masterful book embraces local land use authority and highlights numerous opportunities for local governments to use their authority to plan for and mitigate the consequences of climate change. In that sense, this book truly does provide local officials with knowledge needed to Choose to Succeed.

—Ashira Pelman Ostrow, Peter Kalikow Distinguished Professor in
Real Estate and Land Use Law and Executive Director of the
Breslin Center for Real Estate Studies, Maurice A. Deane
School of Lawat Hofstra University

This is the hopeful, comprehensive, solution-oriented book that the climate crisis has long demanded. Professor Nolon—the leading U.S. voice on land use law and sustainability—expertly pinpoints local governments as the locus for both climate impacts and solutions, exploring local and collaborative pathways for mitigating and adapting to a rapidly changing climate.

—Hannah Wiseman, Professor of Law, Professor and Wilson Faculty
Fellow in the College of Earth and Mineral Sciences, and
Institutes of Energy and the Environment Co-funded
Faculty Member, Penn State Law School

Table of Contents

About the Author

John R. Nolon is Distinguished Professor of Law at the Elisabeth Haub School of Law at Pace University where he teaches property, land use, dispute resolution, and sustainable development law courses and is Counsel to the Law School's Land Use Law Center, which he founded in 1993. He served as Adjunct Professor of land use law and policy at the Yale School of Forestry and Environmental Studies from 2001-2016.

Professor Nolon served on President Carter's Council on Development Choices for the 1980's, President Clinton's Council on Sustainable Development, New York Governor George Pataki's Transition Team, and Governor Elliot Spitzer's Transition Team. In 2009, he received the National Leadership Award for a Planning Advocate by the American Planning Association; in 2014, the International City/County Management Association presented him its Honorary Membership Award, its highest honor for a person outside the city management profession for his exemplary service to local government. The NY Planning Federation presented him its Lifetime Achievement Award in 2018. He is on the advisory boards of the Sustainable Development Code, the NY Planning Federation, and the Westchester/Fairfield chapter of the Urban Land Institute.

Professor Nolon received a Fulbright Scholarship to develop a framework law for sustainable development in Argentina where he worked from 1994 through 1996. A collection of articles produced as a result of this work appeared in a symposium edition of the *Pace Environmental Law Review.* He has produced five books published by the Environmental Law Institute on the topics of land use law, open space protection, local environmental law, and the mitigation of damage caused by natural disasters. A prolific writer, he published nearly 50 articles in the *New York Law Journal* and over 60 law review articles on various aspects of land use and sustainable development law. Professor Nolon is also co-author of the nation's oldest casebook on land use law: *Land Use and Sustainable Development Law: Cases and Materials,* currently in its ninth edition.

Acknowledgments

Choosing to Succeed contains over 1,200 footnotes citing important sources of information that support its positions. Its chapters refer to over 80 cases that chart the trajectory of judicial decisions regarding climate change and the use of the land.

I can't count how many students contributed to this volume, but it is an important number. Dozens of Haub Law School students over the past three years wrote papers for me in classes and seminars, did small research papers on individual topics, and helped me prepare for law school workshops, symposia, and conferences. They found and briefed the 80 cases and they found, explained, and cited the 1,200 sources.

In the last year, two outstanding research assistants helped me organize all of this into eight chapters for this nearly 300-page book. I am indebted to Haley Brescia and Jessica Roberts for this partnership. Whenever I asked them to help me with a task, they said "of course" or "sure thing" and delivered soon and expertly. Their positive attitude was shared by the dozens of students who contributed to this book: they have chosen to succeed and, if their attitude is contagious enough, we will.

It is during these students' time as practicing lawyers that we must mitigate the causes and adapt to the consequences of climate change. Having learned so much from creating *Choosing to Succeed*, they join me in hoping that this book will help its readers learn how to use the law to foster meaningful and much needed change.

John R. Nolon
Distinguished Professor
Counsel to the Land Use Law Center
Elisabeth Haub School of Law
Pace University

Foreword
Bubble Trouble

In late August 2017, the outer bands of Hurricane Harvey were still wringing out the last of 50 inches of rain on downtown Houston when—with up to one-third of the city still underwater—an investigative piece in the *The Washington Post* suggested the real target of blame for the deluge that would become the most expensive storm in U.S. history. The fault lay not in our stars or the wanting response of an under-sourced FEMA. The real villain, according to the *Post*, was *bad planning*—or as the headline put it, "Houston's 'Wild West' Growth." One can hardly disagree. The largest U.S. city to have no zoning laws had indisputably courted fate, steering sprawled neighborhoods into flood plains and paving over the last postage-stamp lots of absorbent soil. It turns out that Houston residents—so far-flung and so often trapped in traffic congestion—were also among the most ardent emitters of greenhouse gases (per capita) on earth.

It seems the nation's "Space City," a vibrant symbol of American progress, had been swiveling on a bubble. And before anyone knew it, that bubble popped—to the tune of 68 lives lost and $125 billion in damage. I say, "before anyone knew it," but that's just an expression. The trouble with bubbles is not that you don't know you're on one, but that you don't want to do anything about it yet—not while the bubble is floating so high and expanding so much. Not while its iridescence is so mesmerizing to people on the surface.

As John Nolon points out in this wonderfully informative and highly readable book, millions of us around the country are also living on bubbles that, as in Houston, are just waiting to burst. The reasons are many, related to increased flooding, sooty air, heat stress, water scarcity, shrinking biodiversity, and more. The climate crisis backlights almost all of this. We've heard the warnings: our climate system is quickly unraveling. The breakdown can be traced to a primary human cause: the release of greenhouse gases, most notably, carbon dioxide emitted from burning fossil fuels. Thus the world we inhabit is getting hotter, drier, wetter, and weirder. Our coastlands are sinking. Forests are bursting into flame. Droughts and heat waves are getting worse. Rain patterns are see-sawing across the continent and in many other parts of the world. We've heard this from a consensus of the world's climate scientists, from farmers whose families have plowed land for generations, from U.S. federal courts and judicial tribunals abroad. We hear this from the Pope. And we know that, absent some ambitious intervention, the climate's Great Unraveling will accelerate.

What you might not know is that an essential key to the intervention we need sits in the lap of your local government. Whether learning to cope with more fires and storm or deploying green energy to cut carbon pollution, much of the action is at the municipal level. There are a few reasons for this. First, the physical infrastructure involved is often dependent on internal planning rules and the characteristics of local geography. Second, it's generally easier to rally public support for projects that deliver tangible benefits at the local scale than those that do not. Finally, opening inclusive channels for public discussion, participation, and leadership is much easier on the ground floor.

That said, local government planning is almost always a frustrating exercise. The costs come early, the benefits late. In the case of climate change, it is sometimes hard to know exactly what you are planning for. Will the storms be more intense, or more frequent, or both? Are we talking two feet of sea level rise or eight? Will the atmospheric rivers propelling West Texas windfarms continue unabated or peter out as warming air currents realign? Add to this the paradoxical fact that politicians seem to get more credit for *responding to* climatic disruptions than actually avoiding them. After all, emergency response implies leadership and action. Prophylactic planning comes mostly in the form of restrictions and denials—attacks on basic freedom. But it shouldn't be seen that way. There is freedom in having a home to return to when the floodwaters drain, or a road that is passable when you need an ambulance. There is freedom in flipping a switch and having the lights come on.

Championing such freedom is what Professor Nolon calls "choosing to succeed." Part of that means harnessing municipal governing structures to abate carbon pollution by retooling transportation systems and greening the grid. But Nolon makes clear we need to reach *beyond* cutting carbon, toward a basic goal of *climate resilience.* That means being able to "bounce back" from the climate disasters we can't avoid. Or as an expert might say, managing and recovering from a climate impact in a way that allows a community to learn, adapt, and *thrive.*

Over the last 30 years, most strategies to address climate change did not fully embrace resilience, focusing much more on reducing greenhouse gas emissions. There were reasons for this. Because greenhouse gas emissions were the cause of the problem, it seemed to many that it was more important to attack that problem first. Girding ourselves for the leftover risk could come later. A second reason was that, as compared to climate resilience, the transition from fossil fuels to renewable energy made for a more straightforward conversation. Replacing dirty energy with clean energy turns out to be a complicated problem when you dig into it; but the focus is pretty clear: changing the way we produce energy. Climate resilience, on the other hand, involves nearly everything: infrastructure; wildlife management; disaster response; agriculture; public health; and more. Squeezing that subject into a manageable size was like trying to fold an octopus into a box.

Finally—and this is a big point—years ago a lot of environmentalists saw climate resilience as a drooping white flag. They thought that talk about elevating homes and expanding drainpipes was admitting defeat or, worse, giving Big Oil permission to do nothing and say the risks were manageable. In his 1992 best-seller, *Earth in the Balance*, Al Gore even called efforts to adapt to climate impacts a "kind of laziness." (Gore later reversed that characterization, but not until 2013.) For years, resilience efforts were seen as the "poor cousin" of the richer, meatier work of carbon reduction.

Fortunately, things have changed. Today climate action takes two distinct priorities—curbing greenhouse gases to fend off worst-case consequences and boosting community resilience to cope with the impacts already mounting. Or to put it another way, climate action now seeks to *avoid* the harm we can't *manage* and to *manage* the harm we can't *avoid*.

As it turns out, preparing for climate stress not only makes moral sense (some people are getting slammed *now*), but economic sense too. Preventing climate-based damage is almost always a bargain. Studies, for instance, show that every dollar spent on complying with a better building code saves four dollars of future loss. Grants that help homeowners improve storm resilience pay for themselves six times over.

As the examples of building codes and residential grants suggest, the local vision is key. There is no one better than Professor Nolon to develop this theme. He has pioneered many advances in local environmental law. Professor Nolon, it can be said, practically invented the field. Since the 1990s he has identified the ways local governments influence environmental protection, how they have obtained the power to do it, and followed that with theories of how local players can coordinate with one another and collaborate with large scales of power. Integrating those ideas into a book focused on the climate crisis is a crowning achievement.

Though comprehensive, this book meets readers where they are, laying out the basics of local government law and land use, then pivoting to the questions at the heart of climate action: How do we reach push-through politics and get people to care more? How do we make plans that provide stability, but that are flexible enough to handle surprises? How do we involve and address disadvantaged communities that already bear the brunt of environmental risk?

Some innovations addressed are technological, but the meat of this book involves governance and social cooperation—what experts in the United States and abroad consistently say is most lacking in addressing the effects of climate breakdown. Professor Nolon reminds us that in addition to making good personal choices like avoiding flood plains or installing a green roof, we all have a duty to make sure our governments and business leaders are up to the task. That means getting involved in local decisionmaking, voting, advocating for smart policies, and discussing climate resilience with colleagues, family, and friends.

The takeaway here is that grappling with the climate is not a fad, like *sous-vide* cooking or axe throwing. It is the *new normal*. People will be reading and talking about global warming and climate bubbles for decades to come. This book is meant to start readers on that journey, whether they are new to the issue, already familiar, or have some professional stake in it. Remember, throwing up your hands in despair is not an option when there is action to be taken. The opposite of despair is courage.

Robert Verchick
Gauthier-St. Martin Eminent Scholar
and Chair in Environmental Law,
Loyola University New Orleans
College of Law

Preface: Choosing to Succeed

By sheer happenstance, I became a land use law professor. Pace, a highly ranked environmental law school, needed a real estate professor who could also teach land use law. All my experience involved representing clients at the local level. They were real estate clients who needed land use permits to develop their properties, or neighbors who opposed the issuance of such permits, or the municipalities themselves who needed counsel to ensure they followed legislated procedures and did not violate constitutionally protected property rights. I experienced land use law as it concerned property owners' rights and local governments' authority to limit those rights. The focus of my engagement was local law.

My environmental law colleagues, of course, taught federal environmental law, including how states implement standards contained in federal regulations. They were concerned about the use of state and federal lands and how point source pollution is controlled at the local level by state permitting systems. Local law was outside the circumference of what they taught. Environmental law, at the outset, was outside mine as well.

Gradually, things changed. My environmentally sensitive land use students found that local governments were adopting local laws to protect environmental values. Urban sprawl precipitated great interest in open space protection to maintain community character and property values. Soon, local laws became focused on the ecosystems that open space harbored: habitats; wetlands; and locally threatened species. Watershed and source water protection laws began to proliferate as local stakeholders learned that federal law was not seriously engaged in stemming nonpoint source pollution or protecting groundwater. My land use students helped me write articles and books about "local environmental law."

Around 1990, my students and I found that zoning and other land use regulations moved toward sustainability as they embraced green construction standards, transit-oriented development, the transfer of development rights, and renewable energy. We responded by writing about "local sustainable development law." Over the past decade, we learned that land use planning and regulation could be an instrument for managing climate change, both by promoting resilience and mitigating carbon emissions through the proper design and construction of human settlements. We called this "low-carbon land use law" and wrote about this emerging framework of local laws. As this book goes to press, city officials and their professional advisors are exploring how zoning, building codes, and municipal budgets can create safe buildings and densities to stem the flight of urban dwellers to the suburbs: a response to the coronavirus—COVID-19. Failing in this task means that the ability of cities and urban villages to mitigate climate change will be greatly diminished.

This personal journey is the story told by this book. It starts with a shocking look at the escalating economic costs of untethered climate change, focusing on damage at the local level where municipal officials are the first to respond and where people and property are the most vulnerable. We call these "climate change bubbles" and show that when combined, they dwarf the housing bubble of 2008. The book then backtracks more than a century and explores the evolution of land use law from a system focused on civil engineering, traffic management, home construction, and the ridged separation of land uses to one that became nimble and flexible enough to meet the changing needs of society, to protect ecosystems, promote sustainability, and mitigate climate change.

The story continues with an exploration of the limitations that federal takings jurisprudence places on local power to retreat from sea-level rise, storm surges, and constant flooding. It then looks at side-stepping these limitations through local, nonregulatory strategies that can sharpen investor due diligence and discourage investments in these dangerous zones. Next, the need for governmental cooperation along the legal system's vertical axis is illustrated by the wise integration of local comprehensive planning into state and federal hazard mitigation planning to anticipate, mitigate, and recover from the extreme natural disasters. Then, the fragmented state of the federal and state water law system is disclosed along with grass-roots driven actions that can integrate and leverage local, state, and federal resources. The book ends with a reflection on how municipalities can hone the local land use system's tools and techniques, leveraged by state and federal assistance, to create safer buildings and places, including low-income neighborhoods, where a public health emergency has existed for decades.

This book is dedicated to my environmental colleagues at Pace and partner law schools, and, especially, to my students. The circumferences of what we professors teach have truly begun to overlap and all of us are buoyed by the optimism and curiosity of our students.

John R. Nolon
Distinguished Professor
Counsel to the Land Use Law Center
Elisabeth Haub School of Law
Pace University

Chapter One
Climate Change Bubbles

Land use climate bubbles are popping up throughout the nation at a rapid rate. As they burst, they are creating an economic crisis that will be more damaging than that of the housing bubble of 2008. The costs to ecosystems and low- and moderate-income households are equally severe. These bubbles, where land and building values are declining, provide extensive, objective evidence that climate change is real and must be dealt with on the ground. It sidelines the ideological battles over the political response and focuses, laser-like, on the practical question: what can we do to respond? Local leaders understand the urgency of the crisis and are highly motivated to learn how to prevent and mitigate its consequences. This chapter describes how the local land use legal system can leverage state and local assistance to reduce per capita carbon emissions as an important and now recognized component of global efforts to manage climate change. The tools and techniques presented in the remaining chapters of the book are available to the nation's 40,000 local governments, if led by courageous leaders choosing to succeed in this epic battle.

I. Cities on the Bubble

In numerous communities in every state, property values are declining because of repeated flooding, damaging storm surges, sustained high temperatures, constant fear of wildfires, water scarcity, and potential mudslides. Cumulatively, these changes are causing a reverse economic bubble associated with land use that mirrors the effect of the infamous housing bubble of 2008 but is potentially much more harmful to the economy and environment.[1]

1. *See* Henry M. Paulson Jr., *The Coming Climate Crash: Lessons for Climate Change in the 2008 Recession*, N.Y. TIMES, June 21, 2014, www.nytimes.com/2014/06/22/opinion/sunday/lessons-for-climate-change-in-the-2008-recession.html (where Henry M. Paulson, Secretary of the Treasury during the housing bubble era, wrote that "[w]e're making the same mistake today with climate change. We're staring down a climate bubble that poses enormous risks to both our environment *and* economy"). *See also* John Nolon, *Land Use and the Climate Bubble*, GREENLAW PACE ENVTL. L. PROGRAMS BLOG (Feb. 3, 2014), http://greenlaw.blogs.law.pace.edu/2014/02/03/land-use-and-the-climate-bubble/:

This chapter begins this book with a description of countless new bubbles, which are forming and are attributable to the consequences of climate change.[2] Imagine that you are a real estate broker showing a house in Spicewood Beach, Texas, listed for $225,000. When you arrive at the house with your prospective buyer, there is a water truck at the curb, filling a cistern. The client asks: "What's happening?" The house is in a neighborhood near Lake Travis, in one of the state's largest lake-based real estate markets.[3] Investor interest in lakefront real estate, tourism, and local businesses tends to rise and fall with the lake's water level. Frequent droughts take a toll on the lake's ability to meet residential needs for potable water.[4] For over a year, water was imported into Spicewood Beach to satisfy the community's potable water needs.[5] As a broker, you picked a bad time to show this house. A climate change bubble had popped, and the price of a house, with a water truck in front, tanked along with the lake community's economy.

Land use climate bubbles are popping up across the nation at a rapid rate.[6] These bubbles, where land and building values are declining due to conse-

---

Real estate prices in many parts of the country are beginning to fall due to the real and perceived effects of climate change on land use. What is happening on the land is an indicator that a climate bubble is forming . . . . Under the age-old concept of *caveat emptor*, buyers may soon enough learn not to invest in properties in threatened places. If they don't the bursting of the climate bubble will certainly change their minds.

2. The notion of a climate bubble first surfaced in a different context: the over-investment in high carbon assets in the coal, oil, and gas industries. The specter of climate change and the threat of regulating these industries might create a reservoir of unburnable carbon reserves and cause a decline in such investments. There is a finite capacity of the atmosphere to absorb carbon without reaching a tipping point in global warming from which we cannot return. This, in turn, will diminish the investment value of much of the world's carbon assets.
3. Brian Rash, *Report Names Lake Travis as Biggest Lake-Based Real Estate Market in Texas*, CMTY. IMPACT NEWSPAPER, Aug. 2, 2019, https://communityimpact.com/lake-travis-westlake/housing-real-estate/2019/08/02/report-names-lake-travis-as-biggest-lake-based-real-estate-market-in-texas/.
4. Asher Price, *Central Texas Drought Persists, With October Flows Into Lakes Travis and Buchanan Among Lowest on Record*, STATESMAN, Sept. 26, 2016, https://www.statesman.com/news/20160926/central-texas-drought-persists-with-october-flows-into-lakes-travis-and-buchanan-among-lowest-on-record; Mary Huber, *Rice Farmers Relying on Water From Highland Lakes Amid Absent Rains*, STATESMAN, Sept. 2, 2018, https://www.statesman.com/news/20180902/rice-farmers-relying-on-water-from-highland-lakes-amid-absent-rains/1.
5. Manny Fernandez, *Texas Drought Forces a Town to Sip From a Truck*, N.Y. TIMES, Feb. 3, 2012, https://www.nytimes.com/2012/02/04/us/texas-drought-forces-town-to-haul-in-water-by-truck.html; Holly Heinrich, *Texas Community Without Water Still Waiting for a Solution*, NPR STATE IMPACT (June 24, 2013), https://stateimpact.npr.org/texas/2013/06/24/texas-community-without-water-still-waiting-for-a-solution/.
6. *See* Andrew Freedman, *Climate Change Could Cost the U.S. Up to 10.5 Percent of Its GDP by 2100, Study Finds*, WASH. POST, Aug, 19, 2019, https://www.washingtonpost.com/weather/2019/08/19/climate-change-could-cost-us-up-percent-its-gdp-by-study-finds/ (stating that if greenhouse gas (GHG) emissions in the United States continue without mitigation or diminution, "the country could see a 10.5 percent cut in real income by 2100."); *see* David Hone, *The Climate Bubble Reality Check*, HUFFINGTON POST, Mar. 5, 2013, www.huffingtonpost.co.uk/david-hone/climate-bubble-climate-change_b_3204677.html.

quences associated with climate change, provide extensive, objective evidence that climate change is real and must be dealt with on the ground.[7] Reinforcing this imperative is the dramatic local evidence of climate change's extensive costs. Climate change has been added to the list of issues that pose the greatest risks to the U.S. taxpayer because of its far-reaching economic impacts on coastal infrastructure, agriculture, energy consumption, and many other aspects of the economy.[8] As a result, there is a developing urgency to understand these impacts and to learn how to prevent and mitigate them.[9]

These climate-caused consequences are indiscriminate: they pop up everywhere. Natural disasters are increasing in intensity and becoming more frequent, causing much economic stress.[10] Severe droughts in the West have caused some communities to seek external sources of water and minimize their use.[11] Wildfires raging through western states have compromised property values and forced residents to move.[12] Extreme heat, even in northern states, has challenged the health of vulnerable populations, making life in some cities difficult.[13] Mortgages and casualty insurance are becoming harder to get, without which most prospective buyers cannot afford housing. Real estate prices in many parts of the country are falling due to the real and perceived effects of climate change on land use.[14]

---

7. *See* John R. Nolon, *Land Use and Climate Change Bubbles: Resilience, Retreat, and Due Diligence*, 39 Wm. & Mary Envtl. L. & Pol'y Rev. 321 (2015); *see also* John R. Nolon & Patricia Salkin, Climate Change and Sustainable Development Law in a Nutshell (2010).
8. U.S. Gov't Accountability Off., Climate Change: Information on Potential Economic Effects Could Help Guide Federal Efforts to Reduce Fiscal Exposure 2-3 (2017) (GAO-17-720); *see* U.S. Gov't Accountability Off., High Risk Series: Substantial Efforts Needed to Achieve Greater Progress on High-Risk Areas 110-22 (2019) (GAO-19-157SP); *see also* Neil Irwin, *Climate Change's Giant Impacts on the Economy: 4 Key Issues*, N.Y. Times, Jan. 17, 2019, https://www.nytimes.com/2019/01/17/upshot/how-to-think-about-the-costs-of-climate-change.html.
9. *See* Risky Business, The Economic Risks of Climate Change in the United States (2014) (supporting an independent economic analysis to quantify the range of likely costs of climate-driven impacts on everyday weather, natural disasters, and the economy of nine specific regions of the United States); *see also* Danielle Kurtzleben, *Rep. Alexandria Ocasio-Cortez Releases Green New Deal Outline*, NPR (Feb. 7, 2019), https://www.npr.org/2019/02/07/691997301/rep-alexandria-ocasio-cortez-releases-green-new-deal-outline (delineating potential federal strategy to mitigate climate change effects.).
10. Adam B. Smith, *2018's Billion Dollar Disasters in Context*, Nat'l Oceanic & Atmospheric Admin. (NOAA) (Feb. 7, 2019), https://www.climate.gov/news-features/blogs/beyond-data/2018s-billion-dollar-disasters-context.
11. U.S. Global Change Research Program, Fourth National Climate Assessment Vol. II, at 149-51 (2018) (discussing that droughts are intensifying because of unpredictable rainfall and increasing temperatures. Compared to droughts in the 20th century, modern droughts are "extraordinary"); *see supra* notes 3-5 and accompanying text.
12. *See infra* notes 58-65.
13. *See infra* notes 66-72.
14. *See* Kaysen, *infra* note 56.

II. Why Read This Book? Choosing to Succeed

The book's title answers this question. Its chapters are full of information and strategies available to people at the local level: tools to plan for and mitigate the consequences of climate change—a global phenomenon. We can choose to succeed in our battle against this awful menace.

The book does not minimize the need for strong and effective action at the state, federal, and global level, about which much is written and debated. Often ignored in the literature and discussions, however, is the powerful role that local leaders and officials can play at the grass-roots level. The debates that occur locally are not ideological, not about whether climate change is happening or whether governmental action is needed. Rather, they are about what we can do in our neighborhoods and cities to solve real problems that are happening now. The bubbles are talismans: real warnings about consequences that we must confront.

What can be done by locals about such a formidable global crisis? The chapters of this book explain:

Chapter Two discusses the evolution of local land use law and the incredible legal power that local governments have to shape human settlements: to produce sustainable neighborhoods, promote green buildings, sequester open spaces, and create walkable, livable communities.

Low-carbon land use is explored in Chapter Three. It catalogues the many methods of using local land use authority to mitigate climate change by reducing energy use and carbon emissions from vehicle travel and expand the carbon sequestering natural environment. It demonstrates that local land use tools affect about 70% of carbon emissions, which constitute 80% of greenhouse gases (GHGs).

Chapter Four confronts the iron grip of a single U.S. Supreme Court case that seriously obstructs strategies to retreat from danger. *Lucas v. South Carolina Coastal Commission*[15] limits our ability to direct development away from areas vulnerable to natural disasters, the frequency and ferocity of which are compounded by climate change. In Chapter Four is a blueprint for using the local process of reviewing and approving proposed land developments to discourage investment in vulnerable areas, those subject to flooding, sea-level rise, storm surges, and other consequences of climate change. Its goal is to prevent more bubbles from forming.

15. 505 U.S. 1003 (1992).

In Chapter Five, the focus is on these natural disasters, showing the way to the extreme adaptation that is required by presenting many case studies of innovative local action plans aimed at this fearful reality.

Chapter Six demonstrates how local land use law fills major gaps in the national system of protecting water supplies; there are stories about local leaders inventing strategies to ensure adequate water for residential, commercial, and agricultural use. Who knew that the Clean Water Act and federal government do not address effectively nonpoint source pollution—the primary cause of water degradation—or the protection of groundwater? Perplexingly, that power does not exist at the federal level; in most states, it has been delegated to towns, cities, boroughs, counties, and villages.

Chapter Seven is aspirational. It concludes the book with a discussion of how societies can choose to succeed in the face of existential crises. The tools that the law gives local leaders to employ against the consequences of climate change are many and readily available. Their successful use by serious, committed people—champions of change—will send signals to state and federal leaders that the problem is present and real, that it must and can be confronted, and that these local efforts need their help. Powerful signals from the grass-roots groups can realign and strengthen top-down policy and programs. The chapter concludes by showing that this aspiration is supported by the findings and recommendations of respected scholars in many fields of study.

Chapter Eight looks ahead at the effect of the pandemic which is causing the flight of middle- and higher income residents from low-carbon cities to the suburbs, a trend that could cripple cities' ability to mitigate climate change. The chapter builds on what we know from earlier chapters about the breadth of local land use power and how this system can use public health strategies to create safe buildings and safe density in order to win this newest battle with suburban and exurban communities. While on the subject of public health emergencies, it discusses systemic racism and how zoning and other governmental actions are complicit in causing climate change-related health problems in low-income, minority neighborhoods. The chapter ends with an examination of how far governmental regulation can go without violating private property rights protected by the U.S. Constitution. Efforts to respond to climate change and pandemics will inevitably limit what property and business owners can do with what they own.

III. Bubbles, Bubbles Everywhere

A. *Drought*

1. Kansas

In Kansas, agriculture is a cornerstone of everyday life and the economy.[16] In Morton County, the southwestern-most county of the state, about 85% of land is devoted to agricultural use and over one-third of the county's jobs are related to agriculture.[17] Successfully growing crops depends on a stable water source and planting on critical days of a growing season.[18] While the region sits atop the Ogallala Aquifer, prolonged droughts, consistently less rainfall, and a lowering water table have destabilized this water source and challenged the success of raising crops. Without action to preserve the aquifer, total depletion in decades ahead is likely.[19] With warmer temperatures, farmers are finding it difficult to know when to plant, how long the growing season will be, and what type of crop to plant. Corn is struggling to produce where it used to flourish.[20] In Morton County, more than 80% of farm acres are used to grow corn.[21] The decrease in water and increase in temperature are working against the future of the crop in Kansas; there is evidence that the optimal growing area for corn is moving rapidly to the north, causing economic disruption in its wake.[22] In the short term, impacts of climate change

16. *Corn*, Kansas Dep't of Agric. (2019), https://agriculture.ks.gov/docs/default-source/ag-growth-summit/january-2018-documents/corn-sector.pdf?sfvrsn=3e3c80c1_20.
17. National Agric. Statistics Serv., U.S. Dep't of Agric. (USDA), 2017 Census of Agriculture: County Profile of Morton County, Kansas (2017) (data of Morton County land area used for corn production of 32,877 acres used to calculate percent of total land used for the crop); *Quick Facts: Morton County, Kansas*, U.S. Census Bureau, https://www.census.gov/quickfacts/fact/table/mortoncountykansas/LND110210#LND110210 (last visited Aug. 21, 2020) (data of Morton County total land area of 730 square miles used to calculate percent of land used for corn production); Kansas Dep't of Agric., Morton County: Estimated Economic Contribution of Agriculture, Food, and Food Processing Sectors (June 27, 2019).
18. *See* Leah Burrows, *Changing Temperatures Are Helping Corn Production in U.S—For Now*, Harv. John A. Paulson Sch. of Eng'g & Applied Sci. (Nov. 5, 2018), https://www.seas.harvard.edu/news/2018/11/changing-temperatures-are-helping-corn-production-us-now.
19. Roxana Hegeman, *Kansas Water Office's 50-Year Plan Says Ogallala Aquifer Will Be 70% Depleted*, Topeka Cap.-J., July 1, 2014, https://www.cjonline.com/news/2014-07-01/kansas-water-offices-50-year-plan-says-ogallala-aquifer-will-be-70-percent-depleted?v= [http://perma.cc/GF8F-CTHR]; *see* Michon Scott, *National Climate Assessment: Great Plains' Ogallala Aquifer Drying Out*, NOAA (Feb. 19, 2019), https://www.climate.gov/news-features/featured-images/national-climate-assessment-great-plains%E2%80%99-ogallala-aquifer-drying-out.
20. *See infra* Coulter, note 22.
21. *See* National Agric. Statistics Serv., *supra* note 17.
22. Phyllis Coulter, *Corn Belt Moves North as Planting Practices Shift*, Ill. Farmer Today, Dec. 10, 2018, https://www.agupdate.com/illinoisfarmertoday/news/crop/corn-belt-moves-north-as-planting-practices-shift/article_da2df746-f994-11e8-ba1d-c3a39c0a4c35.html.

are lowering crop production, increasing the cost of crop insurance, and lowering the sales price of farmland in the region.[23] In the foreseeable future, areas at the southern border of corn's growing range like Morton County will no longer be able to grow the crop but instead have to shift their economy to other crops or industries, if they are viable.[24]

2. Oregon

Drought is also testing the water needs of agriculture in the Northwest. In Harney County, Oregon, agriculture remains strong despite severe water scarcity.[25] In the region, 97% of groundwater is used for irrigation, including agricultural uses.[26] Residents and farmers are seeing a dramatic decrease in water resources, requiring them to dig deeper into groundwater aquifers. Much of the water being funneled up through wells is contaminated with arsenic, rendering it useless without elaborate and costly filtering. If the local farming industry dries up, so will the region's tax base, weakening public infrastructure and creating issues that extend beyond water access. The continual dwindling of water in Harney County is causing competing users to work together to seek local solutions that will most benefit the economy and environment.

3. The Southwest

The threat of water scarcity extends well beyond agricultural communities. The continual warming and drought conditions of western states along the Colorado River are causing shifting precipitation patterns, increasing evaporation rates, and lowering water levels.[27] Many of these states rely on the stability of water levels to run hydroelectric dams to provide electricity to

23. Brian Grimmett, *Climate Change Will Affect Infrastructure, Agriculture and Health of Kansas*, KCUR (May 13, 2019), https://www.kcur.org/post/climate-change-will-affect-infrastructure-agriculture-and-health-kansans#stream/0; ANDREW CRANE-DROESCH ET AL., USDA ECON. RES. SERV., CLIMATE CHANGE AND AGRICULTURAL RISK MANAGEMENT INTO THE 21ST CENTURY 20 (2019); *see* Sarah Schafer, *Slow and Steady Decline for Kansas Farmland Values*, AGWEB FARM J., June 1, 2018, https://www.agweb.com/article/slow-and-steady-decline-for-kansas-farmland-values.

24. *See* DROESCH ET AL., *supra* note 23.

25. *See* NATIONAL AGRIC. STATISTICS SERV., USDA, 2017 CENSUS OF AGRICULTURE: COUNTY PROFILE OF HARNEY COUNTY, OREGON (2017); Emily Cureton, *The Search for Solutions to Harney County's Water Crisis*, OPB (Jan. 2, 2020), https://www.opb.org/news/article/oregon-harney-county-water-crisis-hay-farming/.

26. Cureton, *supra* note 25.

27. P.C.D. Milly & K.A. Dunne, *Colorado River Flow Dwindles as Warming-Driven Loss of Reflective Snow Energizes Evaporation*, 367 SCIENCE 1252 (2020), https://science.sciencemag.org/content/sci/367/6483/1252.full.pdf.

their residents.[28] The Colorado River powers the turbines of 260 dams with electricity output reaching residents from Denver to San Diego.[29] If these turbines have less water to use, the electricity provided to 40 million people will be reduced and leave many communities, and the economy, in the dark. The demand for power in conjunction with lower water levels in rivers will have major financial impacts on property values and tax revenues.

B. *Sea-Level Rise*

1. Louisiana

Isle de Jean Charles is a small community on an island in Terrebonne Parish, Louisiana.[30] The broader region of southern Louisiana is exceptionally vulnerable to sea-level rise, coastal erosion, and hurricanes.[31] Severe flooding and storm surges put most of the island under water and damaged homes beyond repair.[32] Ninety-eight percent of the island has disappeared since 1955. The loss of land to sea-level rise has destroyed the local economy due to the loss of farmland, inability to raise livestock and crops, and the periodic inability to use the road connecting the island to mainland Louisiana. Currently, just two dozen families occupy the vanishing island and are resisting efforts to uproot and resettle on higher ground. In 2016, the U.S. Department of Housing awarded the state of Louisiana $48 million to resettle the community of Isle de Jean Charles to a 515-acre inland parcel.[33] While infrastructure may be restored upon resettlement, many residents who belong to the Biloxi-Chitimacha-Choctaw Indian Tribe fear the loss of their culture in separation from their land.[34] In having to relocate an entire community

28. *See Western U.S. Hydro Generation Profile, 2013*, NAT'L HYDROPOWER ASS'N, https://www.hydro.org/waterpower/why-hydro/available/hydro-in-the-states/west/ (last visited Aug. 28, 2020).
29. Allen Best, *The Future of the Dammed*, AM. PLAN. ASS'N. (Nov. 2018), https://www.planning.org/planning/2018/nov/futureofthedammed/.
30. ISLE DE JEAN CHARLES, www.isledejeancharles.com/island (last visited Aug. 28, 2020).
31. *Storms and Sea-Level Rise*, NAT'L PARK SERV., https://www.nps.gov/articles/storms-and-sea-level-rise.htm (last updated June 26, 2019).
32. Robynne Boyd, *The People of the Isle de Jean Charles Are Louisiana's First Climate Refugees—but They Won't Be the Last*, NRDC (Sept. 13, 2019), https://www.nrdc.org/stories/people-isle-jean-charles-are-louisianas-first-climate-refugees-they-wont-be-last.
33. Press Release, Isle de Jean Charles Biloxi-Chitimacha-Choctaw Tribe and Tribal Council, The Isle de Jean Charles Tribal Resettlement: A Tribal-Driven, Whole Community Process (Jan. 15, 2019), https://static1.squarespace.com/static/5672cfb1d82d5e366e753691/t/5c425ac4c74c507d878e696a/1547852484564/IDJC+Press+release+1-18-19.pdf. *See Resettlement Plan*, ISLE DE JEAN CHARLES RESETTLEMENT PROGRAM, STATE OF LA., http://isledejeancharles.la.gov/resettlement-plan (last visited Aug. 28, 2020).
34. Coral Davenport & Campbell Robertson, *Resettling the First American "Climate Refugees,"* N.Y. TIMES, May 2, 2016, https://www.nytimes.com/2016/05/03/us/resettling-the-first-american-climate-refugees.html.

several miles away, the immense cultural and economic value of their former land is lost.[35] The people of Isle de Jean Charles may become the first climate refugees in America, and perhaps foreshadow the fates of countless communities dotting our nation's coasts.

2. Florida

Miami-Dade, Florida, is a low-lying coastal county along the Atlantic Coast in southern Florida that faces severe challenges due to sea-level rise, storm surges, and high winds.[36] Because many residents live less than four feet above a rising sea level, flooding and associated impacts critically threaten the county's infrastructure.[37] The taking of freshwater by various industries like agriculture only exacerbates the issue, leaving depleted aquifers more vulnerable to saltwater intrusion.[38] For Floridians, 90% of potable water is sourced from aquifers.[39] The risk of saltwater intrusion and groundwater contamination affects the property values of shoreline and inland residences and businesses.[40] It is expected that the value of homes susceptible to flooding can

35. In a 2018 letter to the U.S. Department of Housing & Urban Development, Chief Albert White Buffalo Naquin wrote that the resettlement plan no longer met "the goals and objectives set out by the residents and IDJC [Isle de Jean Charles] Tribe." Alaska Inst. for Just., Rights of Indigenous People in Addressing Climate-Forced Displacement app. E (Jan. 15, 2020). Chief Naquin expressed strong concern that the relocation under the plan required Isle de Jean Charles (IDJC) residents to "sign away the legacy from their ancestors." *Id.* at 29. In 2019, the IDJC tribe learned, through a press release, that "the state purchased land for the resettlement site." After negotiation attempts, "IDJC Tribe-led resettlement plans have been suspended because of the state's refusal to allocate funds to IDJC to implement the Tribe's plan as originally described in the National Disaster Resilience Competition grant application. The state continues its own planning without consultation with the Tribe." *Id.* at 30.

36. Daniel Cusick, *Miami Is the "Most Vulnerable" Coastal City Worldwide*, Sci. Am., Feb. 4, 2020, https://www.scientificamerican.com/article/miami-is-the-most-vulnerable-coastal-city-worldwide/.

37. Forbes Tompkins & Christina DeConcini, World Res. Inst., Sea-Level Rise and Its Impact on Miami-Dade County 3 (2014); Jess Nelson, *Sea-Level Rise in Miami-Dade Could Cost $3.2 Billion by 2040*, Miami New Times, June 20, 2019, https://www.miaminewtimes.com/news/climate-change-study-says-sea-level-rise-could-cost-miami-dade-32-billion-for-seawall-construction-11201008.

38. Scott T. Prinos et al., U.S. Dep't of the Interior & U.S. Geological Surv., Origins and Delineation of Satlwater Intrusion in the Biscayne Aquifer and Changes in the Distribution of Saltwater in Miami-Dade County, Florida 1 (2014):

> Prior to development, much of Miami-Dade County was covered by the shallow marshes of the Everglades. Beginning in the early 20th century to provide land for urban development, flood control, irrigation, and agriculture, a large part of the Everglades in this county was drained by a network of uncontrolled or inadequately controlled canals that extended to the bays and the ocean. This drainage and subsequent water-supply withdrawals reduced water levels in the aquifer. These water-level declines were exacerbated during droughts and allowed saltwater to intrude some water-supply wells and municipal well fields in Miami-Dade County. (Citations omitted.)

39. *Groundwater Modeling*, South Fla. Water Mgmt. Dist., https://www.sfwmd.gov/science-data/gw-modeling (last visited Feb. 9, 2020).

40. Tompkins & DeConcini, *supra* note 37.

depreciate by 5 to 15% in the coming decade, severely impacting the real estate and insurance markets in Miami-Dade.[41] Although property values continue to increase, they are increasing at lesser rates because of investment risks associated with climate change.[42] Community leaders are acutely aware of the potential climate bubble consequences in the near term and have begun strategizing. Some strategies include developing climate-adaptive zoning, prioritizing restoration projects, educating residents on the importance of natural land in mitigating climate effects, and sharing climate hazard data.[43]

3. Hudson Valley—New York

The Hudson River, the artery of the broader New York City region, is rising.[44] Storms that feed on the river are becoming stronger.[45] The steady increase in high tides and storm intensity endangers not only this metropolis but the numerous communities, businesses, and ecosystems dependent on the river's stability. The spreading reach of tides threatens more than 9,000 riverfront acres.[46] This area is expected to increase dramatically and jeopardize property values. In addition to harboring low-lying residences, businesses, and fishing and tourist establishments, the estuary serves as a critical riverine habit and sanctuary for biodiversity.

C. Thin Ice: Alaska

Generations of Alaskans have depended on ice.[47] Its use for fishing, hunting, driving, and dogsled racing is deeply ingrained in Alaskan culture and

41. Alex Harris, *As Seas Rise, Your Coastal Home in Florida Could Lose Value. One Report Says 15% by 2030*, Miami Herald, Jan. 16, 2020, https://www.miamiherald.com/news/business/real-estate-news/article239344973.html.
42. Alex Harris, *Your Coastal Property Has Already Lost Value to Sea Rise. This Site Can Tell You How Much*, Miami Herald, July 25, 2018, https://www.miamiherald.com/news/local/environment/article215421425.html.
43. *Adapting to Sea-Level Rise in Miami-Dade County, Florida*, NOAA, https://coast.noaa.gov/digitalcoast/stories/slr-miamidade.html (last visited Aug. 28, 2020).
44. Mark Fischetti, *Sea Level Could Rise 5 Feet in New York City by 2100*, Sci. Am., June 1, 2013, https://www.scientificamerican.com/article/fischetti-sea-level-could-rise-five-feet-new-york-city-nyc-2100/; Bobby Magill, *New York Prepares for Up to 6 Feet of Sea Level Rise*, Climate Ctr. (Nov. 2, 2015), https://www.climatecentral.org/news/new-york-prepares-sea-level-rise-19629.
45. *How Climate Change Makes Hurricanes More Destructive*, Envtl. Def. Fund, https://www.edf.org/climate/how-climate-change-makes-hurricanes-more-destructive (last visited Aug. 28, 2020).
46. *Sea-Level Rise*, Scenic Hudson, https://www.scenichudson.org/our-work/climate/sea-level-rise/ (last visited Feb. 9, 2020).
47. Kristin Hettermann, *Iceless in Alaska*, Sci. Am., Nov. 18, 2019, https://blogs.scientificamerican.com/observations/iceless-in-alaska/.

economy.[48] The melting of permafrost and sea ice also threatens the security of physical infrastructure, like roads, dams, and reservoirs.[49] In tracking the seasonal "break up" of ice, communities are adjusting; they now need to know when it is safe to walk atop or when to avoid ice for fear of falling through. Premature ice melt in 2019 led to several deaths due to the instability of the formerly dependable ice sheets.[50] Food sources like fish, walrus, and seal have become more difficult to hunt on unstable ice.[51] For rural Alaska, ice connects people to important resources: without ice, many communities are essentially stranded.[52] With earlier seasonal melting of ice and weaker ground to hunt or drive on, local economies will collapse, and communities will have to adapt, perhaps having to retreat inland and reorganize their activities away from the ice.

D. *Natural Disasters*

1. Tennessee

Nashville, a vibrant city known for its music culture, has experienced numerous natural disasters. In 1998, tornadoes tore through the city; in 2010, the city was flooded; in 2020, several tornadoes seriously damaged or destroyed more than 500 buildings and claimed at least 24 lives.[53] In the wake of disasters cycling through Nashville, the city's people and culture are now vulnerable both environmentally and economically. After the 2010 flood, lower income families struggled to rebuild, while developers bought and flipped the damaged homes.[54] This practice "supplant[ed] families who had been

---

48. Julia O'Malley, *Alaska Relies on Ice. What Happens When It Can't Be Trusted?*, N.Y. Times, Apr. 10, 2019, https://www.nytimes.com/2019/04/10/us/alaska-ice-melting.html; *see* U.S. Global Change Res. Program, Fourth National Climate Assessment Vol II, ch. 26: Alaska (2018), https://nca2018.globalchange.gov/chapter/26/ [hereinafter Fourth Nat'l Climate Assessment: Alaska].
49. Fourth Nat'l Climate Assessment: Alaska, *supra* note 48.
50. Sarah Kaplan, *One of Alaska's Warmest Springs on Record Is Causing a Dangerous Thaw*, Wash. Post, Apr. 19, 2019, https://www.washingtonpost.com/science/2019/04/19/one-alaskas-warmest-springs-record-is-causing-dangerous-thaw/; Associated Press, *Melting Alaska Sea Ice Has Residents, Scientists Worried*, N.Y. Post, July 1, 2019, https://nypost.com/2019/07/01/melting-alaska-sea-ice-has-residents-scientists-worried/.
51. Associated Press, *supra* note 50.
52. Jocelyne Zablit, *Climate Change Forcing Alaskans to Hunt for New Ways to Survive*, Yahoo! News (May 3, 2019), https://sg.news.yahoo.com/climate-change-forcing-alaskans-hunt-ways-survive-012049863.html.
53. Adam Tamburin, *Nashville Comes Together After Tornado, But Some Worry Accelerating Gentrification Will Push Them Out*, Nashville Tennessean, Mar. 6, 2020, https://www.tennessean.com/story/news/local/2020/03/06/nashville-worry-tornado-accelerate-gentrification/4953350002/.
54. Jessica Bliss, *"We Need Help": In Tornado Recovery, North Nashville Doesn't Want to Be Forgotten Again*, Nashville Tennessean, Mar. 4, 2020, https://www.tennessean.com/story/news/local/2020/03/04/tornado-recovery-north-nashville-forgotten/4942814002/.

generational staples of the community." In North Nashville, a neighborhood "in the throes of gentrification," activists worry about how the 2020 tornado damage will cause even more displacement.

2. New York/New Jersey

In New York and New Jersey, rebuilding after Hurricane Sandy was delayed.[55] Property values fell in some locations because of the difficulty of collecting on flood insurance, the slow pace of delivering federal assistance, the high cost of elevating new buildings under newly released Federal Emergency Management Agency (FEMA) floodplain maps, the reluctance of lenders to invest, and the fact that many damaged properties are nonconforming uses under local zoning.[56] These factors, coupled with the despair wrought by Sandy, slowed sales and lowered prices in many neighborhoods, giving new meaning to "underwater properties."[57]

E. *Wildfires: California*

In 2018, wildfires set ablaze nearly two million acres of California land. Although wildfires are natural in the western landscape, a combination of drought and high winds strengthens their size and intensity.[58] As suburbia pushes further into the traditional terrain of wildfires, communities

---

55. Michael Powell, *17 Months After Hurricane, Recovery Effort Plods Along*, N.Y. Times, Mar. 24, 2014, http://www.nytimes.com/2014/03/25/nyregion/17-months-after-hurricane-recovery-effort-plods-along.html?_r=0 (discussing that seventeen months after Superstorm Sandy, recovery efforts made very little progress).
56. *See* Rhonda Kaysen, *Back to the Jersey Shore*, N.Y. Times, Apr. 4, 2014, http://www.nytimes.com/2014/04/06/realestate/back-to-the-jersey-shore.html:

    > Rebuilding in a high-hazard area is not cheap. If a house was destroyed or sustained substantial damage, it must be rebuilt to local floodplain requirements, which in the most risky areas can require costly measures like elevating the house on pilings or columns . . . . Homeowners with federally backed mortgages must also buy flood insurance, which can be expensive. Owners who can't afford the flood insurance premiums or who can't afford to rebuild to these standards are selling.

    See also Anthony S. Guardino, *Legal Hurdles for Coastal Residents Rebuilding After Sandy*, 249 N.Y. L.J. 15 (2013).
57. *See* Kaysen, *supra* note 56:

    > Prices for waterfront property in hard-hit areas plunged after the storm, largely because of damage to houses. Suddenly, towns where land was rarely available, like Mantoloking, had listings. Of waterfront homes that sold in the area between November 2012 and June 2013, the median selling price dropped 34 percent from the same time period a year earlier, according to an analysis of listings data by Tom Wissel, Multiple Listing Service coordinator for the Ocean County Board of Realtors.
58. *2018 Incident Archive*, Cal. Fire, State of Cal., https://www.fire.ca.gov/incidents/2018/ (last visited Aug. 28, 2020).

are severely threatened.[59] Residents in Paradise, California, were struck by the Butte County Camp Fire in 2018, which reigns as the deadliest and most destructive fire in the state's history.[60] Not only did this fire claim the lives of 85 people,[61] it destroyed nearly 20,000 structures and caused around $16.5 billion dollars of damage.[62] Around $7 billion of the property damage was uninsured. Six months after the fire raced through Paradise, California, "an estimated 1,000 or more families still [hadn't] secured even temporary housing."[63] The subsequent volume of insurance claims proved so massive that "one of the few insurers that still provided wildfire coverage in the region" became insolvent.[64] According to Ed Mayer, director of the Butte County Housing Authority, the town lost the "ability to produce housing that is affordable to our citizenry."[65] This, he stated, "is the larger tragedy."

F. *Extreme Heat*

1. Illinois

While an unsuspecting culprit, extreme temperatures sustained for several days can be deadly for vulnerable populations.[66] With a sudden increase in electricity usage and overwhelmed electrical grids, a power outage can occur and leave entire communities without working air conditioners and fans.[67] In 1995, a heatwave lasting five days with temperatures soaring above 100 degrees Fahrenheit (100°F) claimed the lives of more than 700 Chicago residents. [68] Of the victims, a majority were elderly or poor who were unable to

59. *The Connection Between Climate Change and Fires*, UNION OF CONCERNED SCIENTISTS, https://www.ucsusa.org/resources/climate-change-and-wildfires (last updated Mar. 11, 2020).
60. Ayrton Braga, *The Economic Impact of the Butte County Camp Fire*, FOUNDER'S GUIDE (Mar 14, 2019), https://foundersguide.com/butte-county-camp-fire/.
61. Megan Cassidy, *Butte County Officials Revise Camp Fire Death Toll From 86 to 85*, S.F. CHRON., Sept. 25, 2019, https://www.sfchronicle.com/california-wildfires/article/Butte-County-officials-revise-Camp-Fire-death-14468583.php.
62. Braga, *supra* note 60.
63. Kirk Siegler, *More Than 1,000 Families Still Searching for Homes 6 Months After the Camp Fire*, NPR (May 8, 2019), https://www.npr.org/2019/05/08/721057281/more-than-1-000-families-still-searching-for-homes-6-months-after-the-camp-fire.
64. Braga, *supra* note 60.
65. Siegler, *supra* note 63.
66. *See* Michael B. Gerrard, *Heat Waves: Legal Adaptation to the Most Lethal Climate Disaster (So Far)*, 40 U. ARK. LITTLE ROCK L. REV. 515, 515-36 (2018) (commenting on the relationship between vulnerable urban populations and the necessity of air conditioning in the context of heatwaves, and also notes the importance of mitigation efforts to reduce negative impacts).
67. Daniel P. Tucker, *As Temperatures Climb, So Does the Risk of Blackouts*, WNYC NEWS (Oct 12, 2014), https://www.wnyc.org/story/nyc-2050-greater-energy-demand/.
68. Bonnie Miller Rubin & Jeremy Gorner, *Fatal Heat Wave 20 Years Ago Changed Chicago's Emergency Response*, CHI. TRIB., July 15, 2015, https://www.chicagotribune.com/news/ct-chicago-heat-wave-20-years-later-met-20150715-story.html.

access generator-powered air-conditioned spaces. As climate change worsens, it is probable heatwaves will become more frequent and perhaps more intense.[69] In conjunction with the urban heat island effect, which causes cities to experience warmer temperatures than surrounding regions, the impacts on vulnerable populations in the hotter months can be alarming.[70] This threat is compounded by the pandemic. As of 2015, around 12% of American households lacked air conditioning.[71] These households are disproportionately composed of lower income or older adults, for whom coronavirus also poses the greatest risk.[72] Before the coronavirus (COVID-19), cooling centers provided much-needed relief for many people during periods of extreme temperatures. Nevertheless, amid a pandemic during which social distancing is an imperative, a crowded cooling center could be a source of greater risk for those already most vulnerable.

2. Long Island

In the Peconic Bay area on Long Island, New York, increasing water temperatures associated with climate change are putting scallops and other marine populations—and the economy they support—at substantial risk.[73] Scallops are sensitive to environmental changes like rising temperatures, impacting their ability to survive until harvest.[74] Within the last 50 years, the number of Peconic Bay scallops has noticeably decreased but is now worrisome as the population nears extinction.[75] Generations of baymen have banked on the harvesting of scallops as careers, but due to the decreasing scallop popula-

69. Justin Carissimo, *Massive Heat Wave Blamed for at Least 6 Deaths*, CBS News, July 20,2019, https://www.cbsnews.com/live-news/heat-wave-2019-extreme-heat-advisory-warning-deaths-latest-weather-forecast-us-nyc-2019-07-20/ (last updated July 21, 2019); *Heat Waves and Climate Change*, Center for Climate & Energy Solutions, https://*www*.c2es.org/content/heat-waves-and-climate-change/ (last visited Aug. 28, 2020).
70. *Heat Island Impacts*, U.S. EPA, https://www.epa.gov/heat-islands/heat-island-impacts (last updated July 29, 2020).
71. David Montgomery, *8 Charts on How Americans Use Air Conditioning*, Bloomberg CityLab (July 10, 2019), https://www.bloomberg.com/news/articles/2019-07-10/why-we-always-fight-over-air-conditioning#:~:text=The%202015%20survey%20found%20that,before%20air%20conditioning%20became%20common.
72. *Id.*; *see also* Ilissa Ocko, *The Coronavirus Crisis Was Already Bad. Extreme Heat Waves Are Making It Worse*, Envtl. Def. Fund (July 17, 2020), https://www.edf.org/blog/2020/07/17/coronavirus-crisis-was-already-bad-extreme-heat-waves-are-making-it-worse.
73. *See* Alec Hamilton, *Rising Water Temperatures in Long Island Sound Brings a Change in Fish*, WNYC News (Aug. 19, 2012), https://www.wnyc.org/story/230693-blog-rising-water-temperatures-sound-brings-change-fish/.
74. Michael Wright, *Mysterious Die-Off of Scallops Seen in Peconics Is Worst Since Infamous "Brown Tides,"* Sag Harbor Express, Nov. 6, 2019, https://sagharborexpress.com/mysterious-die-off-of-scallops-seen-in-peconics-is-worst-since-infamous-brown-tides/.
75. Charity Robey, *The Baymen's Nightmare: All the Scallops Are Dead*, N.Y. Times, Nov. 11, 2019, https://www.nytimes.com/2019/11/07/nyregion/peconic-bay-scallop-season.html.

tion, baymen are now faced with potential job loss and the collapse of their industry.[76] The restaurant and fishing industries dependent on the harvest of scallops will likely endure steep economic hits as long as ocean temperatures remain high.[77]

G. *Weird Weather: Wine Country*

In Napa Valley, California, residents and businesses face myriad climate change effects like wildfires, heatwaves, cold snaps, and droughts.[78] After experiencing a cold snap this past May, many wineries in the region lost nearly half of their grape crops. Unfortunately, much of their industry relies solely on a few types of grapes due to the region's signature cabernet sauvignon and merlot wines. The grapes used are more climate-sensitive than other, hardier varieties, risking the future of wine production in the region.[79]

H. *Increased Rainfall*

1. Washington

Too much water is not always beneficial: constant rain in Oso, Washington, triggered a fatal mudslide in 2014.[80] The mudslide occurred 600 feet above the town of Oso and rolled down to destroy an entire neighborhood.[81] It took six months to reopen the town's main highway to two-way traffic after it

---

76. *Id.*; *see Massive Peconic Bay Die-Off Putting Strain on Scallop Season*, News 12 Long Island (Nov. 6, 2019), http://longisland.news12.com/story/41284069/massive-peconic-bay-dieoff-putting-strain-on-scallop-season.
77. *See* Jay Shah & Desiree D'iorio, *Climate Change May Be Culprit in Long Island Scallop Die-Off*, WSHU Pub. Radio (Nov. 12, 2019), https://www.wshu.org/post/climate-change-may-be-culprit-long-island-scallop-die#stream/0; *see also* Jodi Goldberg, *Scallop Die-Off in Peconic Bay Takes Toll on Local Economy*, Fox 5 New York (Nov. 8, 2019), https://www.fox5ny.com/news/scallop-die-off-in-peconic-bay-takes-toll-on-local-economy.
78. Eric Asimov, *In Napa Valley, Winemakers Fight Climate Change on All Fronts*, N.Y. Times, Oct. 31, 2019, https://www.nytimes.com/2019/10/31/dining/drinks/napa-valley-wine-climate-change.html?searchResultPosition=1.
79. Esther Mobley, *The End of Cabernet in Napa Valley?*, S.F. Chron., Aug. 16, 2019, https://www.sfchronicle.com/wine/article/Napa-wineries-confront-climate-change-by-planting-14308512.php.
80. Chris Winters, *Near-Record Rainfall Gave Oso Mudslide Its Destructive Force, USGS Finds*, Herald-Net (Jan. 12, 2015), https://www.heraldnet.com/news/near-record-rainfall-gave-oso-mudslide-its-destructive-force-usgs-finds/.
81. Kirk Johnson, *Leveled by Landslide, Towns Mull How to Rebuild*, N.Y. Times, Apr. 19, 2014, https://www.nytimes.com/2014/04/20/us/leveled-by-landslide-towns-mull-how-to-rebuild.html?searchResultPosition=1 [http://perma.cc/8AWE-4W2W]; Ken Armstrong et al., *"Unforeseen" Risk of Slide? Warnings Go Back Decades*, Seattle Times, Mar. 25, 2014, https://www.pulitzer.org/files/2015/breaking-news-reporting/seattletimes/05seattletimes2015.pdf.

was damaged and blocked by debris.[82] Experts suggested completely diverting or reinforcing the Stillaguamish River, a landmark feature of the town.[83] Further investigation showed that because the mudslide area was expected to expand with time, any such fix would wash away. Records of consistent mudslides in Oso date back to the 1940s, which should have warned stakeholders to take precautions against enabling present conditions to worsen. The Growth Management Act of 1990 required towns in Washington to affirmatively protect residents in landslide-prone regions, but the town of Oso continued to permit logging and home development projects on the mountain.[84] In the aftermath of the 2014 mudslide, surviving residents claimed that such activity worsened conditions for the disaster and attributed to the magnitude of damage. [85] In 2016, and again in 2018, residents and relatives of survivors settled claims against the state of Washington, receiving some compensation for the collapse of their economic bubble. Imagine trying to sell a home in the shadow of an imposing cliff or hillside in the Northwest after the damage witnessed in the Oso market.

2. Maryland

Old Ellicott City has experienced two flash floods within the last five years.[86] Both disasters required extensive repairs, caused businesses to close their doors, and forced the city's government to consider options for climate change adaptation. The city's main street was not equipped with the infrastructure to handle drainage for such huge storms. Its location in a valley along the downstream routes of several creeks made the community's historical neighborhood especially prone to flooding.[87] Flooding can become more

82. *Mudslide-Ravaged Highway in Oso Reopens After Six Months*, NBC News (Sept. 23, 2014), https://www.nbcnews.com/storyline/deadly-mudslide/mudslide-ravaged-highway-oso-reopens-after-six-months-n209661 [http://perma.cc/V3YL-7C6U].

83. Armstrong et al., *supra* note 81.

84. Editorial, *In Oso Mudslide, Signs That Warnings May Have Been Missed*, Seattle Times, Mar. 30, 2014, https://www.seattletimes.com/opinion/editorial-in-oso-mudslide-signs-that-warnings-may-have-been-missed/ [http://perma.cc/FAH9-9ADL]; *see* Mike Baker et al., *State Allowed Logging on Plateau Above Slope*, Seattle Times, Mar. 25, 2014, https://special.seattletimes.com/o/html/localnews/2023225363_mudslideloggingxml.html [http://perma.cc/QQ4S-ES6M].

85. Hal Bernton, *State Reaches $50M Settlement in Oso Landslide Suit*, Seattle Times, Oct. 9, 2016, https://www.seattletimes.com/seattle-news/50m-settlement-reached-in-oso-landslide-suit/; Gene Johnson, *Second Oso Landslide Lawsuit Settled for $11.5M*, Claims J., July 25, 2018, https://www.claimsjournal.com/news/west/2018/07/25/285920.htm.

86. *After the Water*, NPR (Nov. 7, 2019), http://apps.npr.org/ellicott-city/ (floods devastated the community in 2016 and again in 2018.).

87. Linda Poon, *In a Town Shaped by Water, the River Is Winning*, Bloomberg CityLab (May 24, 2019), https://www.citylab.com/environment/2019/05/ellicott-city-flood-control-historic-downtown-memorial-day/589054/.

likely when increased urbanization transforms the paths of natural drainage systems and blocks surplus water from escaping.[88] The floods have pushed many residents out of Old Ellicott City causing those staying significant anxiety about the costs of recovering their former lives and economy.

3. Louisiana

Among all of the states, the oyster industry in Louisiana consistently supplies the largest quantity of oysters.[89] Unfortunately, Gulf Coast oysters are dying out due to the surplus of freshwater coming down the Mississippi River caused by heavy upland precipitation.[90] When Hurricane Katrina ravaged Louisiana, oyster harvesting was nearly impossible. Oysters are central to Louisiana's culinary culture, threatening the many and varied businesses dependent on their harvesting.[91] Prices of oysters in the area are skyrocketing, making them largely inaccessible and decreasing the revenue of businesses.

I. Effervescence: The Disappearance of Billions of Birds

Birds provide a very colorful conclusion to our bubble story. The continent has lost nearly one-third of its bird population since 1970—nearly three billion birds. Many of them are backyard favorites; collectively, they are a powerful economic asset.[92] Birds are integral to the food production system as pollinators.[93] The value of crops such as fruits, vegetables, seeds, and nuts increase by $15 billion annually because of pollinators' contribution.[94] Factors including climate change, poor land use practices, and pesticide use endanger birds and many other pollinators.[95] The honeybee population in

---

88. Melissa Denchak, *Flooding and Climate Change: Everything You Need to Know*, NRDC (Apr. 10, 2019), https://www.nrdc.org/stories/flooding-and-climate-change-everything-you-need-know#causes.
89. Shawn Stokes et al., Data Research, Louisiana Oyster Industry: Building Competitiveness and Resilience 7 (2014).
90. Travis Lux, *Katrina, BP, 2019 Mississippi River—Oyster Industry Braces for Another Major Disaster*, WWNO New Orleans Pub. Radio (July 2, 2019), https://www.wwno.org/post/katrina-bp-2019-mississippi-river-oyster-industry-braces-another-major-disaster.
91. Brett Anderson, *Gulf Oysters Are Dying, Putting a Southern Tradition at Risk*, N.Y. Times, Nov. 12, 2019, https://www.nytimes.com/2019/11/12/dining/gulf-oysters.html?smid=nytcore-ios-share.
92. Carl Zimmer, *An Ecological "Crisis" as 2.9 Billion Birds Vanish*, N.Y. Times, Sept. 20, 2019.
93. *Animal Pollination*, USDA & U.S. Forest Serv., https://www.fs.fed.us/wildflowers/pollinators/animals/index.shtml (last visited Feb. 9, 2020).
94. *U.S. Pollinator Information*, USDA, https://www.ree.usda.gov/pollinators (last visited Feb. 9, 2020).
95. *See* Daniel Hellerstein et al., USDA, Land Use, Land Cover, and Pollinator Health: A Review and Trend Analysis (2017).

our nation has declined as well: by almost 60% since 1947.[96] The effects of climate change are expected to alter the timing between plant flowering and pollination, resulting in the dwindling of plant and pollinator populations.[97] If these populations continue to spiral downward, economic loss could be severe. All this effervescence forms a growing bubble of serious consequence. It also shows, in a dramatic and memorable way, the interconnections between the economy and biodiversity. The birds are helping us realize and seek to address the causes of these bubbles on all our populations—poor and rich, natural and human—and the economy and environment on which their survival depends.

IV. The Land Use Stabilization Wedge—Tools Close at Hand

The leaders and residents of cities on a bubble are learning firsthand that something is wrong with the climate, that something must be done. This global problem requires global attention, to be sure, but acting locally can help significantly. The tools are close at hand. One way of characterizing them is as a "land use stabilization wedge." First proposed in 2008, this strategy incorporates many of the ways the devices of land use control and zoning can be employed to reduce carbon dioxide (CO_2) emissions.[98] It borrows from and reorganizes five of the seven climate change stabilization wedges introduced by Profs. Stephen Pacala and Robert Socolow in 2004.[99] They are: (1) reduced use of personal vehicles; (2) energy-efficient buildings; (3) CO_2 sequestration in the natural environment; (4) solar power; and (5) wind power.

These five original wedges can be accommodated by the land use stabilization wedge— strategies based on the broad land use powers that the nation's 40,000 municipal governments have been given. Reduced use of vehicles, for example, is accomplished by adopting transit oriented and transportation-efficient plans and zoning,[100] encouraging walking and biking through

96. Aylin Woodward, *Last Year, 40% of Honey-Bee Colonies in the U.S. Died. But Bees Aren't the Only Insects Disappearing in Unprecedented Numbers*, Bus. Insider (June 21, 2019), https://www.businessinsider.com/insects-dying-off-sign-of-6th-mass-extinction-2019-2.

97. Samuel S. Myers et al., *Climate Change and Global Food Systems: Potential Impacts on Food Security and Undernutrition,* 38 Ann. Rev. Pub. Health 259 (2017).

98. John R. Nolon, *The Land Use Stabilization Wedge Strategy: Shifting Ground to Mitigate Climate Change*, 34 Wm. & Mary Envtl. L. Pol'y Rev. 1, 23-26 (2009).

99. Stephen Pacala & Robert Socolow, *Stabilization Wedges: Solving the Climate Problem for the Next 50 Years With Current Technologies*, 305 Science 968, 969, 971, (2004).

100. *See, e.g.*, Palo Alto, Cal. Code §18.34.010(a) (2007) (discussing the purposes of the California Avenue Pedestrian and Transit Oriented Combining District).

site plan standards, and zoning for compact mixed-use developments that use less energy per household.[101] Natural sequestration can be accomplished by adopting local laws that preserve existing open space or require landscape amenities in proposed developments.[102] The use of wind power can be encouraged by adopting special use permit provisions in zoning that allow for small wind turbines on buildings and wind farms on largely undeveloped lands,[103] and by eliminating design and dimensional requirements that discourage the use of both wind farms and solar panels.[104]

In fact, local governments are doing a great deal already with their legal, financial, and program development capacities. As they progress, local governments are adding strategies to the land use stabilization wedge by using innovative techniques and new technologies. Localities may adopt, for example, standards that require buildings to accommodate plug-in vehicles and reduce idling.[105] They can facilitate the use of renewable energy and on-site small power generation facilities through site plan requirements, financial incentives, zoning bonuses, and environmental impact mitigation requirements.[106] Localities may also accommodate the growing, harvesting, and processing of biofuel feedstocks,[107] and increase cooling through water-efficient landscaping and green or reflective roofs.[108] Localities can implement district electricity systems in neighborhoods,[109] as well as building standards that combine heat and power sources in buildings.[110] They can also encour-

101. *See, e.g.*, Bloomington, Minn. Code §19.29(a)(4) (2008):

> The provisions . . . are intended to . . . [r]educe vehicle trips and vehicle miles traveled . . . by allowing residences in close proximity to employment and services, by allowing intense development in close proximity to high frequency transit service, and by encouraging multipurpose trips, walking trips, carpool trips and transit trips[.]

102. *See, e.g.*, Bloomington, Minn. Code §19.29(g)(4)(C)(ii) (2008) ("The plaza or park must include at least 5,000 square feet of contiguous area.").

103. *See* Dana Drugmand & Val Stori, Clean Energy States Alliance, Distributed Wind Energy Zoning and Permitting (Nov. 2017).

104. *See, e.g.*, N.Y. Energy Law §21-106(2) (1990). ("[N]o state department, board, . . . or any agency thereof may require any approval, consent, permit, certificate, statement, report or other condition for the construction or operation of: (a) a co-generation or alternate energy production facility. . . .").

105. *See, e.g.*, Boston, Mass. Zoning Code §37, app. A (one of the building credits for hotels requires "[o]n-site electric charging plug-in stations for plug-ins capable of serving one percent (1%) of the building occupants.").

106. *See* Jessica Bacher & John Nolon, Zoning for Solar Energy: Resource Guide (2015).

107. *See, e.g.*, *Advanced Biofuels*, Mass.Gov., https://www.mass.gov/service-details/advanced-biofuels (last visited Aug. 30, 2020).

108. *See, e.g.*, *Case Study: City of Portland, Oregon Ecoroof Incentive*, Adaptation Clearinghouse (Feb. 23, 2017), https://www.adaptationclearinghouse.org/resources/case-study-city-of-portland-oregon-ecoroof-incentive.html.

109. *See* Jayson Antonoff, *Scandinavia Taps Power District Energy Systems*, Seattle Daily J. of Com. (May 26, 2004), http://www.djc.com/news/ae/11157334.html ("District energy systems have proven to be the most efficient model for generation and distribution of electrical and thermal energy in urban environments.").

110. *See id.* (discussing energy systems in Scandinavia).

age low-impact retrofitting in existing private buildings through efficiency standards and incentives.[111] On an administrative level, local governments can lay the foundation for green development by building the professional infrastructure needed for green development services, verification methods, and weatherization programs through training, certification, and building demand and support for these services. Finally, localities can increase the use of state and federal energy-saving and transportation-enhancement programs, including subsidies, grants, and loans.[112]

The key concept behind the land use stabilization wedge is that there are already adequate land use techniques that can be employed immediately to help control CO_2 emissions.[113] For a complete discussion of low-carbon land use strategies, see Chapter Three, which demonstrates that local land use tools affect about 70% of carbon emissions, which constitute 80% of GHGs. Indeed, important tools are close at hand to prevent local bubbles and help address the global specter of climate change.

---

111. *See, e.g.*, Andrew Stern, *FACTBOX: Incentives to Retrofit Buildings*, REUTERS, Sept. 2, 2009, http://www.reuters.com/article/idUSTRE5817F220090902 (discussing tax incentives and rebate programs to encourage retrofitting of buildings).

112. *See How Are Building Codes Adopted?* OFFICE OF ENERGY EFFICIENCY & RENEWABLE ENERGY (Sept. 19, 2016), https://www.energy.gov/eere/buildings/articles/how-are-building-codes-adopted (energy conservation codes are either adopted by state governments—which typically require local enforcement and allow localities to adopt stricter standards—or by local governments directly).

113. *See* Nolon, *supra* note 98, at 6-8.

Chapter Two
The Evolution of Land Use Law

At its inception at the beginning of the 20th century, zoning was controversial. State courts split over the issue of whether it was constitutional to create zoning districts and limit privately owned land uses to those permitted. It was declared constitutional in *Village of Euclid v. Ambler Realty Co.*,[1] which led to "Euclidian zoning," a ridged system based on geometrically shaped districts and a requirement that land uses, building shapes, and locations be uniform throughout those zones. In the post-World War II period, the environmental and economic damage caused by sprawl and the flight from urban to suburban communities led to a more flexible approach. This neo-Euclidean period allowed "floating zones' and "density bonuses" in exchange for affordable housing, protections for natural resources in "critical environmental areas," and other innovative land uses. Zoning moved toward "smart growth," balancing development and conservation objectives. Around 1990, zoning and other land use regulations moved toward sustainability and embraced green construction standards, transit-oriented development (TOD), the transfer of development rights (TDRs), and renewable energy. Today, we know that land use planning and regulation could be an instrument for managing climate change, both by promoting resilience and mitigating carbon emissions through the proper design and construction of human settlements. As this book goes to press, municipal officials in urban areas are exploring how zoning, building codes, and municipal budgets can create safe buildings and densities to stem the flight of urban dwellers to the suburbs: a response to land use law's latest challenge, COVID-19.

1. 272 U.S. 365 (1926).

I. From Nuisance Law to Uniform Zoning

A. *The Need for Public Regulation of Land Use—The First Comprehensive Zoning Law*[2]

Zoning's progress has been a long and dramatic journey. What was considered the appropriate use of the land when zoning was first adopted in 1916 evolved rapidly as time passed. At its inception, the nation's population was 102 million[3]; land use challenges then differed greatly from today's issues—with over 330 million people.[4] As we celebrated zoning's 100th birthday, households were abandoning rural communities and remote suburbs and moving into denser urban areas seeking livable, transit-oriented neighborhoods.[5] Initially zoning's challenge concerned civil engineering—safe intersections and access for fire-fighting equipment; today, it focuses on all aspects of land development and natural resource conservation in rural, suburban, and urban settings: all challenged by global warming and, now, by the pandemic.

Zoning grew out of the recognized power of local governments to protect residents from nuisance-like land uses and to achieve an appropriate scale of development in selected neighborhoods. Local officials understood that the ponderous process of civil law nuisance suits between individual property owners was not sufficient to protect larger areas within their jurisdictions. Locally legislated height restrictions, for example, were validated in 1909 by the U.S. Supreme Court.[6] In 1915, the Court upheld use restrictions that prohibited downtown riding stables in Little Rock[7] and brick manufacturing in Los Angeles.[8]

These early precedents, however, fell far short of creating comprehensive standards for building cities designed to protect property owners and neighborhoods from incompatible land uses. This changed when the first compre-

---

2. *See* John R. Nolon, *Historical Overview of the American Land Use System: A Diagnostic Approach to Evaluating Governmental Land Use Control*, 23 Pace Envtl. L. Rev. 821 (2006) [hereinafter *Historical Overview*].
3. *Historical National Population Estimates: July 1, 1900 to July 1, 1999*, U.S. Census Bureau, https://www.census.gov/population/estimates/nation/popclockest.txt (last updated June 28, 2000).
4. *U.S. and World Population Clock*, U.S. Census Bureau, http://www.census.gov/popclock/ (last updated July 29 2020).
5. *See Growth in Urban Population Outpaces Rest of Nation*, U.S. Census Bureau (Mar. 26, 2012), https://www.census.gov/newsroom/releases/archives/2010_census/cb12-50.html#:~:text=MARCH%2026%2C%202012-,Growth%20in%20Urban%20Population%20Outpaces%20Rest%20of%20Nation%2C%20Census%20Bureau,to%20the%20U.S.%20Census%20Bureau.
6. Welch v. Swasey, 214 U.S. 91 (1909).
7. Reinman v. City of Little Rock, 237 U.S. 171 (1915).
8. Hadacheck v. Sebastian, 239 U.S. 394 (1915).

hensive zoning law was adopted by New York City. A new subway system, the construction of new high-rise buildings, the rapid expansion of the garment district, and increasing congestion in the streets struck fear into the hearts of building owners and businesses on Wall Street and in the posh Fifth Avenue retail neighborhood. These early precedents called for reform, a study was done, a commission established, hearings held, and on July 25, 1916, the city was ready with an ordinance, that was adopted by the Board of Estimate and Apportionment by a vote of 15 to 1.[9] This was the first zoning ordinance of its kind in the United States regulating land uses and building types in all neighborhoods of the city.

B. *The Delegation of Legal Authority to Adopt Zoning*[10]

Cities are not sovereign entities; they get their legal authority from the state. New York City's zoning law, for example, was enabled by a 1913 act of the state legislature, which amended the city's charter to authorize it to control land use.[11] Following New York City's action, zoning spread quickly. Twenty state legislatures, plus the District of Columbia, followed suit by adopting some form of zoning enabling act by 1921. In other states, many localities rushed to adopt zoning laws in the absence of state authority, risking invalidation due to their lack of legal authority. The need for enabling acts in all states and for a uniform and effective method of delegating control of land use to municipalities led to the promulgation of a model zoning enabling act by a national commission in 1921.[12] By the mid-1920s, over 500 local governments had adopted comprehensive zoning laws.[13] Their authority to do so was granted by enabling acts originally drafted by the federal government and then adopted by their state legislatures. Although the federal government has limited power to regulate local land uses, it has an important role to play in enabling, guiding, and assisting local governments in exercising their delegated power wisely. Zoning's story illustrates the powerful influence that the federal government can wield if it plays this facilitative role strategically. In the case of zoning's adoption, the story involves the U.S. Department of Commerce (DOC).

As Secretary of Commerce under presidents Warren Harding and Calvin Coolidge in the 1920s, Herbert Hoover paved the way for the rapid adoption

9. N.Y.C., N.Y. Building Zone Resolution (July 25, 1916).
10. *Historical Overview*, *supra* note 2.
11. N.Y. Gen. City Law §§19-20 (McKinney 1913) (amended 2003).
12. *See* U.S. Dep't of Commerce (DOC), A Standard State Zoning Enabling Act (1922) [hereinafter A Standard State Zoning Enabling Act].
13. *Historical Overview*, *supra* note 2.

of zoning. Hoover noted: "Our cities [do] not produce their full contribution to the sinews of American life and national character," and these "moral and social issues can only be solved by a new conception of city building."[14] His response was to appoint two advisory committees: one to write a standard building code; and another to draft model zoning and planning statutes to be adopted by the states, in their discretion.

The latter committee was called the Advisory Committee on City Planning and Zoning. It appointed a subcommittee on laws and ordinances, which produced a final draft of a 12- page enabling statute called A Standard State Zoning Enabling Act Under Which Municipalities Can Adopt Zoning Regulations.[15] The draft was issued by DOC in August 1922. It contained nine sections, including the grant of zoning power to local governments; a provision that the local legislature could divide the city into districts or zones; a statement of zoning's purposes; the creation of a zoning board of appeals; and procedures for establishing, waiving, and amending those regulations. By the end of 1927, over half of the states had adopted some form of the Standard Zoning Enabling Act.

The success of the Standard Zoning Enabling Act, which requires that zoning conform to a comprehensive plan, paved the way for another act, a Standard City Planning Enabling Act, intended as a companion to the Standard Zoning Enabling Act.[16] The Standard City Planning Enabling Act was to provide for the creation of such plans and to effect the coordinated and harmonious development of cities. It covered several major topics:

- the adoption of and recommended content of a "master" plan;
- the creation and operation of a planning commission;
- the adoption of a street plan, or official map;
- involvement of the planning commission in approving public improvements;
- planning for the subdivision of land into marketable parcels; and
- the voluntary creation of a regional planning commission and a regional plan.

---

14. Regional Plan of New York and Its Environs, *Plan of New York and Its Environs; the Meeting of May 10, 1922*, at 15, https://babel.hathitrust.org/cgi/pt?id=uc2.ark:/13960/t6qz2g73r&view=1up&seq=7.
15. *See* A STANDARD STATE ZONING ENABLING ACT, *supra* note 12.
16. U.S. DOC, A STANDARD CITY PLANNING ENABLING ACT (1928) [hereinafter A STANDARD CITY PLANNING ENABLING ACT].

After its publication in 1928, the Standard City Planning Enabling Act was not as widely implemented by state legislatures as was the Standard Zoning Enabling Act. Some felt that a city-wide zoning ordinance embodied a sufficient comprehensive plan and that a separate plan was not needed and then, of course, land development and land use planning slowed down significantly during the stock market crash in 1929 to the end of World War II in the mid-1940s.[17]

All 50 states have adopted some form of the Standard Zoning Enabling Act, and most have adopted a version of the Standard City Planning Enabling Act. In many of these states, the initial enabling acts were virtual verbatim versions of DOC drafts, and a surprising number of them retain a significant amount of that original content today. The standard acts recognized the political nature of controlling private land use and the great diversity among municipalities in every state; as a result, their provisions are largely voluntary. Under their terms, zoning and comprehensive plans may be adopted. The American land use system today largely retains this opt-in feature with notable exceptions.

The original approach to zoning and planning raises many questions:

- How can a system of law that relies on localities with limited geographical jurisdictions properly serve the needs of larger regions?;
- Was it wise to separate land uses into prescribed districts, within which standards must be uniform?;
- Did such uniformity unduly constrain the organic process of growth and produce an artificial settlement pattern?;
- How can the flexibility needed to respond to unique market and geographical conditions be realized under such a rigid system of law?;
- Did zoning protect the urban poor and public health by preventing congestion, overcrowding, and blight, or is it overly protective of property investment and values?;
- Was is it prudent to empower locally elected legislators to adopt land use regulations without mandating the adoption of a comprehensive plan prepared by a less political body?, and, of course;

17. F. John Devaney, Tracking the American Dream 50 Years of Housing History From the Census Bureau: 1940 to 1990, at 54 (1994).

- Was the separation of land uses into districts constitutional? Did it violate landowners' due process or equal protection rights, or was it a taking of property without just compensation?

C. *Zoning Was Contagious, but Was It Constitutional?*[18]

There was much to be worked out as zoning entered its second decade in 1926 when the question of zoning's constitutionality reached the Supreme Court. By the mid-1920s, zoning had been challenged in several state courts with split results. A majority of the courts that considered early zoning laws agreed with *State ex rel. Carter v. Harper*,[19] which upheld so-called zoning against takings, equal protection, and due process claims. Several quotes from the case explain this result: In *Harper*, the court established that "[t]he rights preserved to the individual by these constitutional provisions are held in subordination to the rights of society."[20] Further, the case held that "[t]he purpose of the law is to bring about an orderly development of our cities . . . . Everyone who has observed the haphazard development of cities . . . has appreciated the desirability of regulating the growth and development of our urban communities."[21] Ultimately, the court raised a critical question: "When we reflect that one has always been required to use his property so as not to injure his neighbors . . . can it be said that an effort to preserve various sections of a city [from harmful intrusions] is unreasonable?"[22]

Other courts agreed with Judge T. Scott Offutt, who wrote in *Goldman v. Crowther*: "This ordinance at a stroke arrests that process of natural evolution and growth, and substitutes for it an artificial and arbitrary plan of segregation . . . ."[23] He further noted: "[I]t has never been supposed in this state that the police power is a universal solvent by which all constitutional guarantees and limitations can be loosed and set aside, regardless of their clear and plain meaning . . . . [T]hose limits . . . must bear some substantial relation to the public health, morals, safety, comfort or welfare."[24] Thus, "[s]o much of the ordinance as attempts to regulate and restrict the use of property in Baltimore City is void."[25] The court found that the ordinance itself did not contain adequate provisions demonstrating that it was based on legiti-

18. *See* John R. Nolon, *Comprehensive Land Use Planning: Learning How and Where to Grow*, 13 Pace L. Rev. 351 (1993) [hereinafter *Comprehensive Land Use Planning*].
19. 196 N.W. 451 (Wis. 1923).
20. *Id.* at 453.
21. *Id.* at 454-55.
22. *Id.* at 455.
23. Goldman v. Crowther, 128 A. 50, 53 (Md. 1925).
24. *Id.* at 55.
25. *Id.* at 60.

mate public interests. Judge Offutt ruled that the separation of land uses into zones was void in Maryland. Such was the legal background when, one can imagine, the chief executive office of Ambler Realty Co. awoke one morning in the early 1920s to learn from the local newspaper that its 68-acre property in the village of Euclid, Ohio, had been divided into three separate zoning districts under the zoning ordinance adopted by the Village Board of Trustees the previous evening.[26] Outraged by this unprecedented interference with his industrial development plans and the resulting substantial diminution of the value of his property, he brought suit claiming that zoning, on its face, was a deprivation of private property without due process.[27] The affected parcel had been listed and sold for industrial development. It was situated next to a railroad and in the "path of progressive industrial development."[28] Yet, the new zoning law limited its use, in substantial part, to residential and retail purposes at significantly lower market values. The question, wrote the Supreme Court, was whether "the ordinance [is] invalid, in that it violates the constitutional protection 'to the right of property in [Ambler Realty] by attempted regulations under the guise of the police power, which are unreasonable and confiscatory.'"[29]

The Court noted "while the meaning of constitutional guarantees never varies, the scope of their application must expand or contract to meet the new and different conditions which are constantly coming within the field of their operations."[30] Invoking the law of nuisance and the "painstaking considerations" found in the reports of various planning and land use commissions and experts that concur in the view that the segregation of different land uses serve many public interests, the Court found zoning constitutional.[31] It did so by firmly establishing the standard still used today in determining whether a zoning regulation is a valid exercise of local police power: "The reasons [supporting the separation of land uses could not be said to be] clearly arbitrary and unreasonable, having no substantial relation to the public health, safety, morals or general welfare."[32]

In this way, the judicial attitude toward zoning was fixed: courts would presume the constitutional validity of zoning, defer to the findings of local legislatures, and impose on the challenger a heavy burden of proving that zoning was unreasonable and arbitrary. When a property owner, however,

26. Village of Euclid v. Ambler Realty Co., 272 U.S. 365, 380-83 (1926).
27. *Id.* at 384.
28. *Id.* at 383.
29. *Id.* at 386.
30. *Id.* at 387.
31. *Id.* at 394.
32. *Id.* at 395.

challenges zoning not on its face, as in *Euclid*, but rather as applied to a particular parcel, it is somewhat easier to carry this burden of proof. In *Nectow v. City of Cambridge*,[33] the Supreme Court invalidated a zoning ordinance that subjected the petitioner's property to use restrictions that were unreasonable. The petitioner's burden of proof was carried when it demonstrated to the satisfaction of the Court that under the zoning ordinance "no practical use can be made of the land in question," and that the use permitted "would not promote the health, safety, convenience, and general welfare of the inhabitants of that part of the defendant city."[34]

These bookend principles raised countless questions, the answer to which would have to wait more than two decades while land use law essentially slumbered during the Great Depression and World War II. After a decade of post-war development, the consequences of what became known as Euclidean zoning could be assessed. Was the rigid separation of land uses into discrete zones effective or, in Judge Offutt's terms, did it arrest "that process of natural evolution and growth" to the detriment of society?[35]

D. *The Unintended Consequences of Euclidian Zoning*[36]

Following the decision in *Euclid* 1926,[37] land use lawyers and planners celebrated the advent of a new, comprehensive method of shaping human settlements and protecting investments in the built environment. Their excitement, however, was short-lived. In 1929, the stock market crashed, and land development moved at a snail's pace until the end of World War II.[38] The growth rate in housing units increased by 40% in the 1950s over the 1940s, putting much more pressure on the land use regulatory system at mid-century. We had to wait until this growth was absorbed to see what zoning had wrought.

The Standard State Zoning Enabling Act, as adopted by most state legislatures, seemed simple enough.[39] It permitted local governments to separate land uses into use districts or zones within which they may regulate the construction and the use of buildings or land. The Act stipulated that "regulations shall be uniform for each class or kind of buildings throughout [each] district." Existing patterns of land use in 1926 were disorganized and chaotic

33. 277 U.S. 183 (1928).
34. *Id.* at 187.
35. Goldman v. Crowther, 128 A. 50, 53 (Md. 1925).
36. *Comprehensive Land Use Planning*, *supra* note 18.
37. 272 U.S. at 365.
38. F. John Devaney, *supra* note 17, at 8.
39. *See* A Standard State Zoning Enabling Act, *supra* note 12.

in urban areas, a consequence of the unplanned results of countless unguided private-sector land use decisions. Zoning, presumptively, fixed that problem.

What would neighborhoods look like after being filtered through a zoning ordinance that channeled like-kind land uses into geometric-shaped districts, governed by bulk and area standards, limited lot sizes and coverage, and building heights and set-backs: standards that must apply uniformly to all parcels within the district? Much of what concerned zoning in its inception had to do with civil engineering, traffic concerns, such as ensuring fire truck access to buildings during fires; designing streets and driveways to reduce accidents; and limiting house heights to 35 feet, so that they were tucked under the tree canopy of the neighborhood to preserve community character.

Euclidean zoning seemed well named, as lawyers and planners first drew the shapes this law seemed to dictate. The geometry was not flexible, due in part to the adherence of judges to Dillon's Rule, under which courts were obliged to read literally the laws that delegate power to local governments.[40] How much uniformity was optimal; what would the legacy of uniformly regulated neighborhoods be?

After World War II, growth pressures in suburban communities intensified due to the return of soldiers from the battlefields, affordable federal mortgages, and the 1956 Federal Highway Act that allowed city dwellers to abandon cities in record numbers. This migration rapidly revealed the designs that zoning created. Much of the land in developing communities was zoned for single-family housing on relatively large lots, large enough to permit builders to use septic systems and individual wells, thereby reducing the capital infrastructure costs to the municipality. These homes were uniformly sized, and their shape was dictated by zoning's area and bulk requirements.

There was a similarity to many of these emerging neighborhoods. As they expanded outward, commutes lengthened, increasing vehicle miles traveled (VMT) and carbon dioxide (CO_2) emissions; impermeable lot coverage intensified stormwater runoff and flooding; open space shrunk and, with it, wetlands and habitats; housing became less affordable, creating racially imbalanced neighborhoods; the lack of workers repelled employers, reducing jobs and property tax revenues; municipal services became more expensive; and the character of communities changed, not always to the liking of those who lived there. In response, land use lawyers and planners began to tweak the legal framework to achieve more flexibility in permitted development.

40. 1 J. Dillon, Commentaries on the Law of Municipal Corporations §237 (5th ed. 1911).

As the century progressed, zoning's weaker sibling—land use planning—became a larger factor in land use law. The adverse effects of promulgating the Standard City Planning Enabling Act after, instead of before, the Standard State Zoning Enabling Act were better understood. Day-to-day zoning decisions needed to be guided by a vision for the city's or town's future; adopting a comprehensive land use plan gave citizens and local officials a method of accomplishing that in addition to mitigating the unintended consequences of Euclidean zoning. Some states stipulated that the local planning commission or a special advisory committee should formulate and adopt the comprehensive plan, insulating the planning process somewhat from electoral politics and tying zoning's conformance to an apolitical document. Communities that took planning seriously and conformed their zoning to their plan learned that they had protected zoning from a variety of challenges, including due process and ultra vires claims. If a zoning provision furthers a comprehensive plan objective, it is less likely to be invalidated for failing to further a legitimate public objective or failing to be within the legal power of the locality to enact.

That zoning was to reach beyond civil engineering objectives was embedded in the Standard City Planning Enabling Act. As a predicate for zoning, it provided that plans will, "in accordance with present and future needs, best promote health, safety, order, morals, convenience, prosperity, and general welfare as well as efficiency and economy in the process of development . . . ."[41] The purposes of planning were broad. Zoning had to conform. The stage was set for the adoption of flexible zoning and land use strategies that moved beyond the rigid contours of Euclidean zoning.

The neo-Euclidian era began as zoning turned 40, roughly a decade after the post-war experiments with the original model. Its failures led to a variety of legal remedies—all experiments in search of proper development patterns. Courts slowly moved past Dillon's Rule, and some state legislatures changed the law, calling for a liberal interpretation of the strict language of the enabling act, and others delegated new powers to localities to mitigate the cookie-cutter results of the Euclidean era.

E. *The Most Appropriate Use of the Land*[42]

Immediately after World War II, Euclidian zoning was not working for the village of Tarrytown, New York. The village needed workers to attract employ-

41. *See* A Standard City Planning Enabling Act, *supra* note 16.
42. *See* John R. Nolon, *The Law of Sustainable Development: Keeping Pace*, 30 Pace L. Rev. 1246 (2010) [hereinafter *Keeping Pace*].

ers to build its tax base. For political and economic reasons, it decided not to zone large areas for multi-family housing. Instead, in 1947, the village board of trustees created a floating garden apartment zone, which allowed landowners who owned ten acres or more to apply for the floating zone to alight on their property; a unique two-step process that was clearly not within the specific delegated power of the village under the state zoning enabling act.[43] The foundation for this creative zoning technique was laid in the village's comprehensive plan, which identified the need for affordable housing and an effective means to provide it. The village knew that a straightforward rezoning of land to multi-family use would greatly increase its value and adversely affect the desired affordability. Following this enactment, the owner of an eligible parcel successfully applied for rezoning.

In *Rodgers v. Tarrytown*, the plaintiff, who owned six acres nearby, pointed out that nothing in New York's zoning enabling act expressly authorized the village to first create a multi-family zoning district and then, later, apply it to a parcel in a single-family district after consideration of an application made by the parcel's owner.[44] In the view of the Euclideans, zoning districts were to be changed by amendments to the zoning map, adopted at the same time as the provisions regulating land uses were changed.

The state's highest court disagreed with the plaintiff and broadly interpreted the creative authority of local governments. The court noted that "zoning is by no means static . . . [c]hanged or changing conditions call for changed plans." And, further, "[t]he village's zoning aim being clear, the choice of methods to accomplish it lay with the board."[45] With these words, the neo-Euclidean period began.

The dissent in *Rodgers* spoke for the conservative interpretation of the enabling act. It argued that "the device . . . most assuredly is not 'zoning.'"[46] It feared that upholding floating zoning could "well prove to be the opening wedge in the destruction of effective and efficient zoning in this State." The dissent called this an ultra vires act, one that created a nonconforming use in an established zone for the benefit of the owner of a single parcel (also known as "spot" zoning), or gave the legislature the power to grant variances, a power reserved to the zoning board of appeals.[47] For all these reasons, the dissent believed that the creation of a floating zone was not within the delegated authority of the board of trustees.

43. Rodgers v. Village of Tarrytown, 96 N.E.2d 731, 732-33 (N.Y. 1951).
44. *Id.* at 733.
45. *Id.* at 733-34.
46. *Id.* at 736.
47. *Id.* at 736-39.

The rationale of the majority in *Rodgers* was on sound footing. The Standard State Zoning Enabling Act, which was adopted nearly in its entirety by the New York State Legislature, contains this provision: "Such [zoning] regulations shall be made . . . with a view to conserving the value of buildings and encouraging the most appropriate use of land throughout the community."[48] This language was included in most of the zoning enabling acts adopted by state legislatures throughout the country.

If floating zoning was not zoning, in the dissent's view, what was it? Perhaps this 1951 case sufficiently broadened the term zoning so that, over time, it became land use law. Today, we utilize land use law, including floating zones and its many siblings and descendants, to create sustainable neighborhoods, permit community solar facilities, and promote mixed-use developments oriented to transit. Beyond this first flexible tool, the courts and legislatures have added many more to the land use toolbox: special use permits; overlay zoning; planned unit development districts; receiving and sending zones for TOD rights'; growth control ordinances; density bonuses in exchange for affordable housing; and a host of additional neo-Euclidean devices.

As this century progresses, land use law is becoming an essential strategy for mitigating and adapting to climate change. By properly shaping settlement patterns, it can greatly decrease per capita carbon emissions, water use, energy consumption, and impervious coverage, which causes flooding. Today, lawyers practice land use law—not zoning—thanks, in part, to the *Rodgers* holding and similar decisions in other states. Law and planning students go far beyond memorizing and applying the holding in *Euclid* and now study dozens of land use techniques. The practice of land use law today focuses on shaping settlement patterns to achieve "the most appropriate use of the land" in an era fraught with frightful challenges, now including COVID-19.

II. Toward Flexibility: The Challenge of Sprawl and Ecosystem Decline

A. *The Surprising Origins of Smart Growth*[49]

The idea that local land use law can intelligently shape settlement patterns was not a familiar concept in the late 1960s when the town of Ramapo, New York, adopted an ordinance that delayed development permits until the town

48. *See* A Standard State Zoning Enabling Act, *supra* note 12.
49. *See* John R. Nolon, *Golden and Its Emanations: The Surprising Origins of Smart Growth*, Urb. Law., Winter 2003, at 15.

could provide needed infrastructure.[50] Ramapo was experiencing unprecedented growth as one of the closest northern suburbs of New York City. Developers, who in some cases had to wait years for services to their land, sued; they argued that these phased development controls were intended to prohibit subdivisions and restrict population growth, which is not authorized under the state's zoning enabling legislation.

New York's highest court disagreed, holding that "phased growth is well within the ambit of existing enabling legislation."[51] The court found that Ramapo was not acting to close its borders to growth, but was trying to prevent the negative effects of uncontrolled growth.[52] It found that Ramapo's zoning was not in violation of either the U.S. Constitution or the New York State Constitution because a rational basis for phased growth exists where "the existing physical and financial resources of the community are inadequate to furnish the essential services and facilities which a substantial increase in population requires."

Another form of growth control, a strategy that became known as smart growth, was created 25 years later in Maryland, under Gov. Parris Glendenning (D), who became president of the Smart Growth Leadership Institute.[53] He radically changed state budget priorities by investing state infrastructure funds in priority growth areas to foster new development and by acquiring open space in conservation areas to preserve natural resources. This approach controlled growth in order to reign in the ill effects of sprawling land use patterns. Such patterns evolve gradually, as the land use blueprint contained in the municipal zoning ordinance is built out, one project at a time.

Maryland did what the *Ramapo* court suggested that the New York State Legislature should do. "Of course," the New York court wrote, "these problems cannot be solved by Ramapo or any single municipality, but depend upon the accommodation of widely disparate interests for their ultimate resolution. To that end, Statewide or regional control of planning would insure that interests broader than that of the municipality underlie various land use policies."[54]

Governor Glendenning's strategy called for local action. If local governments are to revise their basic blueprint and accomplish smarter growth, how should they proceed? State law provides numerous planning tools for munici-

---

50. Golden v. Planning Bd. of Town of Ramapo, 285 N.E.2d 291, 293-96 (N.Y. 1972).
51. *Id.* at 300.
52. *Id.* at 304-05.
53. *Leadership Institute*, Smart Growth America, http://old.smartgrowthamerica.org/leadership-institute/about (last visited Jul. 29, 2020).
54. *Ramapo*, 285 N.E.2d at 300.

palities to use to accomplish growth and conservation objectives. Principal among these, of course, is the comprehensive plan, the ideal document to account for the rational allocation of land use.

Local plans properly drafted to accomplish smart growth call for the use of a host of land use techniques that are capable of creating smarter, less wasteful, and more economically efficient development patterns. These include, among others, cluster zoning, performance zoning, overlay zoning, floating zones, TOD, traditional neighborhood zoning, planned unit development zoning, the purchase of development rights, the imposition of conservation easements, and TDRs. In addition, comprehensive plans can guide the creation of capital budgets and the funding of water, sewer, roads, lighting, sidewalks, parks, and education infrastructure in areas where denser development is needed. Today, priority growth areas are found in cities and urban villages, which are out-competing suburbs for growth and its benefits. Urban neighborhoods are fueling the economy by spiking construction and retail jobs, increasing real estate sales, brokerage commissions, financing, and title insurance, as well as providing urban amenities to newly formed households looking for lively places to work and live. These efforts in the cities and villages that host colleges, hospitals, affordable housing, restaurants, and entertainment venues make both themselves and development in adjacent communities more viable. Workers and residents, for example, are attracted to a transformed mixed-use office park when they can access the shopping, nightlife, and services available in a nearby, rejuvenating city or village.

"Smart growth" is a popular label for a growth strategy that addresses current concerns about traffic congestion, disappearing open space, nonpoint source pollution, the high cost of housing, increasing local property taxes, longer commutes, excessive fossil fuel and energy consumption, and the diminishing quality of community life. What was barely perceptible in the real estate market two decades ago is rapidly becoming a booming business. Developers make it clear that they will invest in this new market, but only where local mayors and councils are champions of sustainable development, where a clear local vision and conforming zoning are in place, and where the local land use approval process works efficiently. Urban municipalities are doubling down on this strategy as they confront the possibility of the flight of residents from higher density neighborhoods in fear of COVID-19.

States are following Maryland's example, learning how to shape spending policies to influence local action. They are adopting smart-growth infrastructure plans, new energy plans, complete street infrastructure policies, main street programs, climate-smart community initiatives, brownfield spending budgets, and TOD policies and programs. Together, these state efforts create a clear target for local governments and developers to address.

What is smart about these policies and the projects they spawn, in addition to being sensitive to powerful new market trends and utilizing existing infrastructure, is that they also greatly reduce, on a per household basis, water consumption, energy use, building materials used, and the impervious coverage that causes stormwater runoff and flooding. These developments can also be more affordable, particularly where localities offer bonus densities to developers in exchange for workforce housing, bringing office, research, retail, and service workers closer to where they work.

B. *The Advent of Local Environmental Law*[55]

As development progressed into the 1980s, the landscape changed due to the prevalence of sprawl. People became perturbed at the local level, where environmental degradation is painfully obvious. Natural resources were threatened. Open space, wetlands, and habitats—and their obvious local benefits—diminished. Many of these problems were beyond the reach and competence of federal environmental law, with its primary focus on point-source pollution of the air and navigable waters.[56] As these worries deepened, local leaders and their lawyers gradually learned to rely on "local environmental law" as an antidote and, in doing so, greatly expanded the net of land use law.

As land use regulation matured during the 1950s and 1960s, the line between physical, or infrastructure, planning, and natural resource protection blurred. In 1955, for example, rezoning that increased lot sizes in single-family zones to protect drinking water from pollution was upheld in *De Mars v. Zoning Commission of Town of Bolton*.[57] The Connecticut Supreme Court rested its decision, in part, on the fact that one of the purposes of the state zoning enabling act was to promote "the most appropriate use of the land."[58] The National Flood Insurance Program, created in 1968, exerted an early and strong influence on the initiation of local environmental legislation.[59] It required localities to adopt and enforce floodplain zoning restrictions so that local property owners would be eligible for flood disaster insurance and

55. *See* John R. Nolon, *In Praise of Parochialism: The Advent of Local Environmental Law*, 26 Harv. Envtl. L. Rev. 365 (2002).
56. *See* Clean Air Act §§101-618, 42 U.S.C. §§7401-8018 (2012); Clean Water Act §§101-607, 33 U.S.C. §1251-1857 (2012).
57. 115 A.2d 653 (Conn. 1955).
58. *Id.* at 654.
59. 42 U.S.C. §§4001-4128 (2012).

payments.[60] Although originally focused on minimizing property loss and personal injury, flood insurance regulation gradually recognized, and in some cases protected, the ecological services provided by floodplains. This concern for nature gradually grew as local environmental law progressed into the 1990s.

Local land use law, we now understand, dictates how much of the land is covered with impervious surfaces, causing flooding; how many miles of roads are built, fragmenting habitats and watersheds; how many septic systems, sewer plants, and water systems are created, diminishing groundwater and surface water quantity and quality; and where buildings and improvements are located, increasing VMT and air pollution, aggravating climate change. Quite obviously, regulating land development and environmental considerations are intimately linked.

As local environmental perturbations increased, more localities adopted laws that protect natural resources and lessen environmental pollution. These local environmental laws take a number of forms and accomplish an array of objectives. They include local comprehensive plans expressing environmental values, zoning districts created to protect critical environmental areas, environmental standards contained in subdivision and site plan regulations, and stand-alone environmental laws adopted to protect particular natural features such as ridgelines, wetlands, floodplains, stream banks, existing vegetative cover, and forests. Local governments have creatively used a variety of traditional and modern powers that their state legislatures have delegated to them to address locally occurring environmental problems.

Much progress has been made under the authority to encourage the appropriate use of the land through zoning. In some states, however, state legislatures are more explicit. They authorize local governments, for example, to protect the physical and aesthetic environment, control development in floodplains, prevent soil erosion, or require local governments to conduct environmental impact reviews before approving development proposals.

The evolution of this authority is seen in South Carolina. The state constitution authorizes the legislature to provide for "the structure and organization, powers, duties, functions, and responsibilities of the municipalities."[61] The state constitution says that "[t]he provisions of [the] Constitution and all laws concerning local government shall be liberally construed in their favor,"

---

60. *Id.* §4102.
61. S.C. Const. art. VIII, §9.

and that any powers granted local governments by the constitution and laws "shall include those fairly implied and not prohibited by [the] Constitution."[62]

The South Carolina Legislature, through the South Carolina Local Government Planning Enabling Act, which requires local plans to include natural resource components, statutorily implemented this broad grant of local authority.[63] State law requires that all zoning and land use regulations must be in accordance with the comprehensive plan.[64] The Act also authorizes a variety of neo-Euclidian techniques to be used, and makes it clear that "any other planning and zoning techniques may be used."[65] Municipalities are authorized by this state law to consider "the protection of . . . ecologically sensitive areas" in adopting their zoning laws.[66]

We learn two key lessons from this continuing progress toward a robust system of local environmental law. The first is that local legislators, driven by residents animated by environmental degradation, have surprisingly broad powers to protect the environment in many states. This springs from the parochial nature of local land use law, where citizens within constrained borders call for their natural resources to be protected. The second is that environmental resources often transcend those borders and require intermunicipal or regional arrangements to be effectively protected.

C. *Regionalism and "Wistful Hoping"*[67]

We praise the parochial nature of American land use law because it gives power to local people to cure local problems and take advantage of local opportunities that deeply affect them. Nevertheless, in the seminal *Euclid* case, the owners of the property regulated by the village and an entire regional industry were upset by zoning's interruption of the natural evolution of urban development.[68] In *Euclid*, the Court wrote:

> It is said that the Village of Euclid is a mere suburb of the city of Cleveland; that the industrial development of that city has now reached and in some degree extended into the village, and in the obvious course of things will soon absorb the entire area for industrial enterprises . . . . But the village, though

62. *Id.* art. VIII, §17.
63. S.C. Code Ann. §6-29-510(D)(3).
64. *Id.* §6-29-720(B).
65. *Id.* §6-29-720(C).
66. *Id.* §6-29-510(D)(4).
67. *See* John R. Nolon, *Grassroots Regionalism Through Intermunicipal Land Use Compacts*, 73 St. John's L. Rev. 1011 (1999).
68. 272 U.S. at 365.

physically a suburb of Cleveland, is politically a separate municipality, with powers of its own and authority to govern itself as it sees fit . . . .[69]

The flip side of parochial power is that natural resources, nonpoint source pollution, and economic and housing markets transcend local boundaries. They are intermunicipal, regional, and, in some cases, interstate in nature. Critics, including industry, environmental, and fair housing advocates have bemoaned local control and called for its preemption by state or federal regulation, where their particular interests are thwarted.

The case that first validated local control of regional growth recognized the irony of its position. New York's highest court, in *Ramapo*, wrote that "[s]tatewide or regional control of planning would insure that interests broader than that of the municipality underlie various land use policies."[70] The court further noted, however, that local control should not be struck down "in the wistful hope that the efforts of [regional planning] will soon bear fruit."

The dissonance between the regional nature of land use problems and local control is best explained by former U.S. House of Representatives' Speaker, Thomas P. O'Neill Jr. (D-Mass.), who quipped that "all politics is local."[71] State and congressional lawmakers stand for election in essentially local districts where control by remote governmental agencies is anathema.

The quandary can be resolved by searching for regional processes that respect the critical role that local governments play in land use decision making. To be politically palpable, these initiatives must not be perceived as methods of imposing a state or regional body's will on local governments. Rather, they should be viewed as a means of communicating effectively about regional and local needs, balancing those interests, and arriving at mutually beneficial decisions over time.

From its inception, the U.S. land use system has encouraged voluntary, grass-roots approaches to intermunicipal and regional planning. The Standard City Planning Enabling Act provided for regional planning by authorizing local planning commissions to petition the governor to establish a regional planning commission and to prepare a master plan for the region's physical development.[72] Provisions were included in the Act for communication between the regional and municipal planning commissions, with the objective of achieving a certain degree of consistency between local and

69. *Id.* at 389.
70. 285 N.E.2d at 300.
71. *See* Thomas O. Sargentich, *The Future of the Item Veto*, 83 Iowa L. Rev. 79, 135 n.245 (1997) (quoting Thomas P. O'Neill Jr., Man of the House 26 (1987)).
72. *See* A Standard City Planning Enabling Act, *supra* note 16.

regional plans. Regional consciousness has been with us since the early days of American zoning.

Many localities have adopted sustainable development strategies because of encouragement, information, or funding provided by the state or federal government. This observation aligns with research results published in *Urban Affairs Review*, where the authors demonstrate that "more policy making occurs in states with a multilevel governance framework supportive of local sustainability action."[73]

Localities will align their land use plans with commonsense state policies if they receive information and support via state assistance offered in the right way, without a heavy top-down emphasis or requirements that seem like mandates. Correcting the deficiencies in the 100-year-old zoning system is not about taking away local power, but rather should focus on working with localities to build a better system. This suggests that we need to discover and implement methods of using federal and state policies and resources to support, guide, and sustain local initiatives to coordinate land use policy across municipal and state borders.

Regionalism is not at odds with our land use planning tradition. It need not be "wistful hoping" if approached in the right way. We have not, however, developed a consensus on the proper strategy of weaving local control into the broader fabric of society. It takes a clear understanding by federal and state lawmakers and agencies that parochialism has its place. We are still waiting for this insight to seriously shape their efforts to solve regional land use problems.

D. *Mixed Signals: Exclusionary Zoning and Fairness*[74]

After encountering significant "not in my backyard" opposition to the expansion of the Lucasfilm facilities on his land in Marin County, California, film director George Lucas abandoned his plans and proposed to sell his land to affordable housing developers.[75] The backstory involves the Fair Housing Act, various federal grant-in-aid programs, and a Voluntary Cooperation Agreement entered into between Marin County and the U.S. Department of

73. George C. Homsy & Mildred E. Warner, *Cities and Sustainability Polycentric Action and Multilevel Governance*, URB. AFFAIRS REV., January 2015.

74. *See* John R. Nolon & Tiffany Zezula, *Affirmatively Furthering Fair Housing: The Search for Solutions That Are Just Right*, ZONING & PLAN. L. REP., July 2012, at 1; John R. Nolon & Jessica Bacher, *Affordable Housing in the New York Courts: A Case for Legislative Action*, N.Y. PLAN. & PRAC. REP., Nov./Dec. 2008, at 1 [hereinafter *Affordable Housing in New York Courts*].

75. Norimitsu Onishi, *Lucas and Rich Neighbors Agree to Disagree: Part II*, N.Y. TIMES, May 22, 2012, https://www.nytimes.com/2012/05/22/us/george-lucas-retreats-from-battle-with-neighbors.html.

Housing and Urban Development (HUD).[76] After an investigation, HUD required the County to take steps to affirmatively further fair housing opportunities for people of color and other groups that face barriers to housing in the region.

Marin County's minority population is much lower than that of other communities in the San Francisco Bay Area. As a recipient of federal funding, it has an obligation to Affirmatively Further Fair Housing (AFFH), which includes eliminating impediments to fair housing, such as zoning restrictions that cause segregation. The neighbors of Lucas' property are now contemplating a different change in the neighborhood than the one they initially opposed.

Under the Tenth Amendment, the matter of land use control is left to the states, which have delegated that power to local governments.[77] Exclusionary zoning is, in the first instance, a matter of state law. It is based on the Euclidean notion that zoning's purpose is to segregate different land uses into various districts. Zoning is inherently exclusionary. Yet, since land use authority is delegated to localities by the state, there are constitutional limits to excluding growth and affordable housing.

State courts, however, are relatively shy about intruding into the local legislative realm and mandating solutions to affordable and fair housing. State legislatures, because all politics is local, have been equally reticent. Courts in New Jersey and the state legislatures in California and Connecticut, which have aggressively and clearly defined the obligations of local government regarding housing, are outliers.

New York courts are more engaged in the topic than most state court systems, but their holdings fall far short of providing effective guidance to localities regarding their responsibilities to provide affordable housing. In the seminal case *Berenson v. New Castle*, the state's highest court noted:

> [T]he primary goal of a zoning ordinance must be to provide for the development of a balanced, cohesive community which will make efficient use of the town's land . . . . [I]n enacting a zoning ordinance, consideration must be given to regional [housing] needs and requirements . . . . There must be a balancing of the local desire to maintain the status quo within the community and the greater public interest that regional needs be met.[78]

76. *Affordable Housing in the New York Courts*, *supra* note 74.
77. U.S. Const. amend. X.
78. 341 N.E.2d 236, 241 (N.Y. 1975).

The state court held that New Castle's failure to zone land for multi-family housing was exclusionary.[79] Mr. Berenson's land was then rezoned for condominiums that sold for today's equivalent of $500,000.

These abstract judicial utterances, in the few jurisdictions where state courts have entered the fray—coupled with the absence of state legislative guidance—leave localities wondering what their obligations are under state law. Meanwhile, if they receive federal funding or fail to rezone land proposed for multi-family housing, like Marin County, they may be liable for their failure to AFFH. The Fair Housing Act aims to fight racial segregation and thus implicates the very nature of zoning.[80] How can segregation be eliminated if most land in communities is zoned for single-family housing, the ubiquitous result of Euclidean zoning? But what exactly does this mean? What does federal law require?

What we know is that communities that receive federal housing and community development funding must certify that they have analyzed the impediments to AFFH and acted in good faith to eliminate them.[81] They may be liable if they have not, which implicates the zoning that creates a segregative settlement pattern.[82] We also know that the refusal to rezone specific parcels for multi-family housing may result in municipal liability for discrimination if such failure results in disparate impacts or disparate treatment. *Huntington Branch, NAACP v. Town of Huntington* held: "[W]e find that the disproportionate harm to blacks and the segregative impact on the entire community resulting from the refusal to rezone create a strong prima facie showing of discriminatory effect."[83]

In *Texas Department of Housing & Community Affairs v. Inclusive Communities Project, Inc.*, the Court held that "recognition of disparate-impact claims is consistent with the FHA's central purpose."[84] The Court pointed to "zoning laws and other housing restrictions" that it viewed as "unfairly . . . excluding minorities from certain neighborhoods without any sufficient justification." It went on to say that "[g]overnmental or private policies are not contrary to the disparate-impact requirement unless they are 'artificial, arbitrary, and unnecessary barriers.' Courts should avoid interpreting disparate impact liability to be so expansive as to inject racial considerations into every housing decision."[85]

79. *Id.* at 236-43.
80. 42 U.S.C. §3601.
81. *Id.* §3608. *See also* Affirmatively Furthering Fair Housing, 24 C.F.R. §§5, 91, 92 (2015).
82. 42 U.S.C. §3608.
83. 844 F.2d 926, 938 (2d Cir. 1988).
84. 135 S. Ct. 2507, 2511 (2015).
85. *Id.* at 2524.

Municipalities and their attorneys are getting unclear signals in this area of land use law. They may create zoning districts and specify whatever uses they wish. But they must not craft these districts and uses in a way that excludes households in the state in search of housing. Yet, nowhere in nearly all states is the extent of this responsibility defined. There is little guidance on what constitutes "the region" or "regional needs"; localities' "fair share" or their "duty" to actually make housing for such households affordable; or what combination of zoning techniques and housing subsidies (over which there is no local control) municipalities must use. When precisely, under federal law, are localities responsible to affirmatively further fair housing? Is that liability limited to communities that get federal funding and those that deny housing developers multi-family zoning? Or, does it extend to the entire pattern of development created by local zoning if its districts are not integrated racially? Would that be injecting racial considerations into every land use decision that affects housing? In the *Inclusive Communities* case, Supreme Court dicta suggested that such an expansive interpretation of its holding is not required.

Perhaps nowhere in the story of zoning's evolution is the legal system more confused than in this area of fair and affordable housing. It is an inter-jurisdictional mess, begging for sensible reform. But where should this reform begin? State governments are often the appropriate intermediary between federal and local interests. State constitutions give the police power to their legislatures. They have, in turn, delegated it to localities regarding land use without clear guidance as to these critical fairness issues. The resolution of these questions should be a matter of state concern and become state priority, given the importance of these unresolved issues.

E. *The Emergence of the Law of Sustainable Development*[86]

When the Land Use Law Center for Sustainable Development at Pace Law School was created in 1993, there was only a foggy vision of the contours of sustainable development law. We knew that the advent of local environmental law, the origins of smart growth, and zoning for affordable housing traced the outlines of this field of law and practice. These movements in land use law focused on promoting and regulating economic development to meet present needs, providing for equitable community development, and preserv-

86. *See* John R. Nolon, *Shifting Paradigms Transform Environmental and Land Use Law: The Emergence of the Law of Sustainable Development*, 24 Fordham Envtl. L. Rev. 242 (2013); *Keeping Pace*, *supra* note 42.

ing natural resources to meet the needs of future generations: the essential elements of sustainable development as defined in the Rio Accords of 1992.[87]

We did not know then, however, that land use law would progress rapidly over the next one-quarter century to include topics as diverse as green infrastructure and biological sequestration; adaptation to sea-level rise and storm surges; siting and promoting wind and solar facilities; preserving agricultural land through urban food sheds; creating livable neighborhoods through design controls; and regulating hydrofracking to protect the health of local residents.

In 1993, the technology was either nascent or did not exist for achieving high levels of on-site stormwater infiltration; constructing zero-net energy buildings; measuring increases in sequestering vegetation and urban tree canopies; expanding domestic gas and oil exploration through fracking; creating clean energy facilities such as geothermal, combined heat and power, and micro-grids; developing rating systems for sustainable buildings and neighborhoods; identifying neighborhoods where high-energy waste occurs; understanding ecosystem services and their values; creating metrics that identify baselines for carbon emission and measure its increases and decreases; and designing models that project the extent of sea-level rise in coastal areas.

Over the ensuing three decades, as these technologies developed, the law adapted to put them to effective use in promoting sustainability in all of its dimensions. We now know, through examining advances in technology and local law, how to achieve development that uses less material, avoids destroying wetlands or eroding watersheds, consumes less energy, eliminates or shortens vehicle trips, emits less CO_2, lessens stormwater runoff, reduces groundwater and surface water pollution, and creates healthier places for living, working, and recreating.

This body of law is being created mainly by municipalities, which have the principal legal authority to regulate building construction, land use, and the conservation of natural resources at the local level. Increasingly, however, positive federal and state influences are speeding local adoption of sustainable law techniques.

This is evident in federal and state tax credit, spending programs, and technical assistance that promote solar and other clean energy facilities.[88] Similarly, the Sustainable Communities Initiative—a partnership between HUD, the U.S. Department of Transportation, and the U.S. Environmen-

87. U.N. Conference on Environment & Development, *Agenda 21*, §5.3 (June 3-14, 1992).
88. *See, e.g.*, 26 C.F.R. §1.23-1 (1987).

tal Protection Agency (EPA)—once aided local efforts to achieve TOD and reduce VMT.[89] HUD's recent efforts to affirmatively further fair housing guide localities in identifying the impediments to fair and affordable housing.[90] With coastal protection and disaster planning, federal and state efforts are helping localities, as first responders deal with climate-induced hazards.[91] Federal and state transportation spending is directed by federally required metropolitan planning organizations, creating one model of regional planning that involves local elected officials.[92] In the environmental field, EPA's stormwater management program and aligned state efforts have greatly assisted localities to reduce stormwater runoff.[93] EPA has experimented with efforts to cooperate with local land use authorities to reduce nonpoint source pollution to achieve its total maximum daily load objectives for federally impaired waters.[94] These initiatives that exhibit a clear-eyed view of the importance of local land use provide a basis for a fuller integration of local, state, and federal efforts to create rational land use, transportation, and environmental patterns.

The challenge ahead is to scale up the most exemplary of these integration efforts. The patterns of a more coherent framework of sustainable development law can be observed in the operations of each level of government and the close connections between economic development, environmental protection, and the promotion of equitable development.

As these patterns become better understood, the prospect brightens for a robust and integrated system of federal, state, and local laws dedicated to sustainable development and climate change management. The law has always evolved in this way to serve the needs of society. Expect as much progress in law and technology over the next one-quarter century as we have witnessed in the last.

89. HUD, Partnership for Sustainable Communities: Five Years of Learning from Communities and Coordinating Federal Investment 2 (2014), https://www.epa.gov/sites/production/files/2014-08/documents/partnership-accomplishments-report-2014-reduced-size.pdf.

90. *See* Affirmatively Furthering Fair Housing Assessment Tool for States and Insular Areas, 81 Fed. Reg. 12921 (proposed Mar. 11, 2016).

91. *See, e.g.*, Coastal Zone Management Act §§302-319, 16 U.S.C. §§1451-1465 (2012). *See also* Chapter Seven.

92. 23 U.S.C. §134 (2012).

93. *See NPDES Stormwater Program*, U.S. EPA, https://www.epa.gov/npdes/npdes-stormwater-program (last updated Mar. 20, 2020).

94. *See* Chesapeake Bay Total Maximum Daily Load (TMDL), U.S. EPA, https://www.epa.gov/chesapeake-bay-tmdl (last updated June 1, 2020).

III. Memorializing Sustainability

A. *Designing Density*[95]

In land use, there are two things that Americans dislike: one is sprawl, the other is density. This catch-22 can be resolved by mitigating those aspects of urban living associated with density: congestion; bulky buildings; sameness; design incongruities; unsafe streets; inefficiency; and the sense that neighborhoods are not livable and pleasant. These characteristics of density cut against sustainability. They define places that people want to leave as soon as they can. To reduce VMT and carbon emissions, as well as to prevent sprawl, we must create places of enduring value, located next to transit in walkable and sustainable neighborhoods. In the wake of the pandemic, public health needs to play a central role in dealing with the fear of urban buildings, sidewalks, parks, and other open spaces.

When zoning was first adopted a century ago, little attention was paid to design. The focus was on separating incompatible uses and rigidly defining building heights, setbacks, and lot coverage: the ingredients of sameness, often the antithesis of livability. Gradually, over the years, communities addressed this issue by creating architectural review boards (ARBs), landmarks commissions, historic district commissions, and adopting design review standards for individual buildings, whether new, landmarked, or historic. Over time, these initiatives have been supplemented by adopting standards contained in the U.S. Green Building Council's Leadership in Energy and Environmental Design (LEED)-Neighborhood Development rating system and by incorporating into zoning the Congress for the New Urbanism's form-based codes approach to urban design control.[96] Eventually, we may have something akin to LEED-MD, which includes public health facilities, measures, and services into buildings and their environs.

The law in many states expressly supplements traditional zoning by authorizing localities to create boards and commissions and design standards that are either advisory or regulatory. Such locally created commissions and boards can issue certificates of consistency to rehabilitate landmarks or build in historic neighborhoods. Similarly, these laws authorize the creation of ARBs, and the adoption of design guidelines for all buildings within the

95. Pace Land Use Law Center, Technical Guidance Manual for Sustainable Neighborhoods (2013); *Form-Based Codes Defined*, Form Based Codes Inst., http://formbasedcodes.org/definition (last visited July 29, 2020).

96. *Reference Guide for Neighborhood Dev.*, U.S. Green Building Council, https://www.usgbc.org/guide/nd (last visited July 29, 2020).

community, enforced either by the ARB or, with the ARB's advice, by the local planning commission. In the latter case, the planning commission is authorized to require design features in all development it approves through subdivision or site plan review or the issuance of special permits.

The idea is to ensure that individual buildings are consistent with the historic fabric of the locality or are architecturally compatible with the neighborhood. These techniques are not Euclidian zoning, but rather constitute an attempt to mitigate the designs wrought by use separation and area and bulk requirements that are traditionally applied uniformly in zoning districts.

Two relatively recent land use innovations have evolved organically to breathe better design into zoning at the neighborhood scale: the voluntary LEED-Neighborhood Development rating system,[97] promulgated by the U.S. Green Building Council, and form-based codes, developed by the Congress for New Urbanism and the Form-Based Codes Institute.[98]

The LEED-ND rating system was developed by the U.S. Green Building Council in response to criticism of its new construction rating system, which could result in platinum or gold-rated buildings located in agricultural zones or environmentally sensitive areas.[99] These buildings, while internally sustainable, are decidedly not consistent with larger principles of sustainability that emphasize environmental conservation and the reduction of automobile use and VMT. Here, place matters and LEED-ND contains prerequisites and criteria that require rated buildings to be sustainability located as well as built.

Local governments have begun to incorporate LEED-ND standards in their zoning and land use regulations. See, for example, the *Technical Guidance Manual* for local governments developed by the Land Use Law Center for the U.S. Green Building Council. This document includes a step-by-step process for incorporating sustainable neighborhood standards into the local comprehensive plan, zoning, land use regulations, approval processes, and capital budgets.

Finally, form-based codes are beginning to catch on, especially in urban neighborhoods. The unique aspect of such codes is that they deemphasize use, bulk, and area requirements, substituting for them actual physical designs adopted as code that govern development. Diagrams and illustrations become regulations and govern building styles, details, and materials

---

97. *LEED Rating System*, U.S. Green Building Council, http://www.usgbc.org/leed#rating (last visited July 29, 2020).
98. *Library of Codes*, Form-Based Codes Inst., http://formbasedcodes.org/codes/ (last visited July 27, 2020).
99. Technical Guidance Manual, *supra* note 95.

that are permitted, as well as the ways in which they can be incorporated into specific building elements. These regulations reach into the public realm and present in graphic form the width and dimensions of streets, sidewalks, paths, street trees, furniture, and more.

To zoning's credit, design standards fit into the Standard State Zoning Enabling Act, its focus on the appropriate use of the land, and the processes it uses to review and approve specific buildings. We are unaware of any case that has successfully challenged as ultra vires the incorporation of LEED-ND standards or the precepts of form-based codes into local law. And, since historic, landmark, and architectural guidelines are often authorized by discrete state laws, the power of local governments to design density is clear and is becoming an important aspect of sustainable development.

B. *Green Infrastructure*[100]

Green infrastructure has also become a major component of sustainable development. At their inception, comprehensive planning and zoning focused intensely on capital infrastructure: streets and roads, water and sewer, and electric lines and other utilities. These served development parcels with their buildings, driveways, and other hardscapes. Streets and roads were classified by traffic load and function with local streets, secondary streets, collectors, and arterials governing the flow of traffic in the public interest. When viewed from 10,000 feet, this gray infrastructure is clearly visible: a thoughtful pattern of connectivity to serve the built environment. This result was one of the principal objectives of early zoning.

Over time, evolving concerns with flooding, public safety, wetland and watershed protection, the urban heat island effect, and the loss of open space and its ecological services gave rise to mapping and preserving the green infrastructure of a community. These plans connect the natural assets of the community in much the same way that planners design a locality's gray infrastructure. Planners concerned with green infrastructure calculate the current green space coverage and connectivity and then figure out methods of increasing it to a healthy amount of the surface area of the community. This process ensures that an adequate percentage of the land is sheltered and shaded, with its soils held intact and its ability to absorb and retain water preserved, if not enhanced. Water and wildlife, like vehicles and people, need to travel through connected paths and landscapes.

100. *See* John R. Nolon, *Enhancing the Urban Environment Through Green Infrastructure, in* PEOTECTING THE ENVIRONMENT THROUGH LAND USE LAW: STANDING GROUND (Environmental Law Inst. ed., 2014).

The broad view of green infrastructure envisions it as a strategy for adapting to climate change, bettering air quality, lowering heat stress, creating greater biodiversity, conserving energy, providing ecological services, sequestering carbon, preserving and expanding habitats, enhancing aesthetics, increasing property values, and improving the livability of neighborhoods.

The elements of green infrastructure include green roofs; planters; rainwater harvesting; street trees; preserved open space on building sites; natural vegetated corridors and swales; permeable paved areas accented with green features; xeriscaping; private gardens and public parks; detention basins; bioretention ponds and rain gardens; green building facades; and greened medians and edges along streets, paths, and rail lines. Parking lots can be greened by adding trees and using permeable surfaces that allow infiltration and permit vegetative growth. When seen from the air, the community with robust green infrastructure appears more connected naturally; ideally, the green and the gray are complementary.

All of these elements of green infrastructure can be built into local planning, zoning, and land use regulations. Cities can begin green infrastructure planning at the same time they create and implement their plans for building and development to accommodate anticipated increases in population. The local comprehensive plan can be supplemented by the addition of a green infrastructure component that grows out of this planning process. Then, zoning and land use regulations can be amended to implement the green infrastructure component's vision.

An adopted overlay zone can trace the contours of the green infrastructure plan and, within that zone, local review boards can condition approvals, or use zoning incentives, to implement it. Landscaping requirements, along with erosion and sediment controls, can be added to subdivision and site plan regulations. Developers can be required to include green features in, on, and around their buildings. They can also be required to pull development back from floodplains and wetlands and to leave room on their sites for open space. They can pay impact fees where they cause the destruction of vegetated areas, and the proceeds can be used to pay for the greening of nearby public spaces. Local and state capital budgets can support street trees, medians, parks, the greening of publicly owned buildings and sites, and open space preservation.

What the architects of green infrastructure do is use these land use techniques in an integrated fashion; they plan the entire community so that its natural functions are connected and create healthy and livable neighborhoods. In communities that have made green infrastructure a priority, zoning helps achieve objectives that although they were invented 100 years ago, they would not have been fully understood back then.

C. Land Use and Energy Conservation[101]

The private sector is cooperating with land use regulators to dramatically reduce the energy use in buildings; a key, if not essential, strategy for reducing reliance on fossil fuels and mitigating climate change.

Approximately 40% of total U.S. energy consumption and 70% of all electricity consumed domestically are attributed to residential and commercial buildings.[102] Two-thirds of the energy used to produce electricity is wasted as heat escapes into the atmosphere during generation[103] and up to 15-20% of the net energy produced at these plants is lost in transmission.[104]

The following is a laundry list of energy conservation and climate change mitigation techniques that rely on land use law, assembled from real projects on the ground:

- Because of the enormous waste of energy at the point of generation in remote locations, the lowest hanging fruit in the orchard of energy-conserving land use techniques is to permit or require on-site generation, which is now technically and financially possible in many situations. The LEED-ND rating system gives developers credit for on-site generation, and many are earning those points.[105] What LEED recognizes; local governments can make mandatory as part of zoning.
- The principal method of achieving energy efficiency in new building construction and the substantial renovation of buildings is the energy conservation code; promulgated by the International Codes Council, it has been adopted in most states, and is enforced by local governments.[106] This code contains minimum standards for the design, construction, and installation of the building shell or envelope, mechanical

101. *See* John R. Nolon, *Land Use for Energy Conservation and Sustainable Development: A New Path Toward Climate Change Mitigation*, 27 J. Land Use & Envtl. L. 295 (2012) [hereinafter *Land Use for Energy Conservation*].

102. *How Much Energy Is Used in Buildings in the United States?*, U.S. Energy Info. Admin., http://www.eia.gov/tools/faqs/faq.cfm?id= 86&t=1 (last updated June 15, 2020); *Overview*, Alliance to Save Energy, https://www.ase.org/initiatives/buildings (last visited July 29, 2020).

103. E-mail from Thomas Bourgeois, Deputy Dir., Pace Energy & Climate Ctr., to author (June 30, 2011, 21:55 EST) (on file with author).

104. *Id.* (on file with author).

105. *See On-Site Energy Generation*, U.S. Green Building Council, http://www.usgbc.org/articles/getting-know-leed-neighborhood-development (last visited July 29, 2020).

106. *Status of State Energy Code Adoption*, U.S. Dep't of Energy, https://www.energycodes.gov/status-state-energy-code-adoption (last updated June 30, 2020).

systems, and lighting. By vigorously enforcing this code, dramatic progress can be made in energy conservation.

- Land use law in some states allows local governments to enhance the energy code by adopting additional standards aimed at achieving greater energy efficiency. A creative example is found in Marin County, California. The county requires large homes under 4,000 square feet (sq. ft.) to exceed the energy conservation code requirements by 15%.[107] If the home is over 4,000 sq. ft., but less than 5,500 sq. ft., it must exceed the state code in efficiency by 20%. For homes between 5,500 and 6,500 sq. ft., the requirement is 30%. Homes over 7,000 sq. ft. must be "net zero energy" users; a goal that green builders can actually achieve.
- In New York, the town of Greenburgh amended its local code to require that "all new one- or two-family dwelling or multiple single-family dwelling (townhouse) of three stories or less [b]e built to achieve a HERS [Home Energy Rating System] Index of 70 or less on the Residential Services Network (RESNET) Home Energy Rating System (HERS) . . . ."[108]
- The town of Blooming Grove, New York, uses a density bonus to encourage home developers to adopt Energy Star. Energy Star can achieve energy savings in excess of 30% greater than the base energy code. It governs appliances, heating and cooling systems, the thermal envelope, electrical, ventilation, and equipment efficiency.[109] The town awards a 10% increase in the number of homes that can be constructed under local zoning in exchange for making them all Energy Star compliant.[110]
- Local subdivision and site plan regulations can be amended to govern building orientation, layout, or landscaping on sites, which can be used to reduce energy consumption in new buildings. Land use laws can require homes in subdivisions to be clustered and designed to conserve energy or equipped with solar panels (or at least to be wired and built to accommodate them).

---

107. *See* County of Marin, Cal., Ordinance §19.04.100 (2011).
108. Town of Greenburgh, N.Y., Code §100-20 (2011), http://www.ecode360.com/?custId=GR0237.
109. *About Energy Efficiency*, Energy Star, https://www.energystar.gov/about/about_energy_efficiency (last visited July 31, 2020).
110. Blooming Grove, N.Y., Town Code §235-14.1(A)(3) (2011).

- Solar and wind generation facilities can be either frustrated or facilitated by local land use law. On-site solar arrays and rooftop wind turbines can be prohibited by use, setback, and height restrictions found in traditional zoning codes. Amendments to these provisions can designate renewable energy facilities as as-of-right uses, allow them by special permit, or permit them as accessory uses. Bonuses, like those found in Blooming Grove, can be used to incentivize renewables.
- Local land use boards can require developers and their design consultants to follow an integrated design process, where they collaborate during the early stages of the project review process to achieve the greatest possible energy conservation and cost reduction. It is at this stage that decisions can be made about building orientation, form, shading, energy-efficient exterior lighting, window size and location, rooflines and extensions, reflective roofing, height-to-floor ratios, and building features that relate to passive ventilation and cooling.
- Local land use laws can achieve extraordinary energy efficiency by permitting and encouraging the use of combined heat and power (CHP) systems in individual buildings and interconnected energy systems in certain mixed-use districts. By employing CHP—a mechanical system that can be used to produce electricity, heating and cooling in higher density, mixed-use neighborhoods—the potential for energy efficiency, and therefore energy conservation, is remarkably greater than if used on an individual parcel of land.
- To increase the use of district energy systems (DES), the local land use regulatory system can be adjusted to allow, or even to incentivize, them. DES must be made an allowable use under local zoning and site plan regulations, as well as local building and energy codes. They, too, may be encouraged through bonus zoning provisions that provide additional development densities for developers who adopt DES technologies.
- Finally, the number of localities that are adopting TOD zoning ordinances has been growing exponentially over the past 10 years. There are hundreds of examples of new zoning districts that create livable, mixed-use neighborhoods where new buildings are connected to transit systems through design and infrastructure enhancements. In these neighborhoods, per capita CO_2 emissions can be two-thirds less than those in typically zoned neighborhoods in the suburbs.

D. Transit-Oriented Development[111]

TOD is a modern zoning imperative with exceptional potential to reduce GHG emissions. According to the Presidential Climate Action Project, "[t]he greatest potential for reducing greenhouse gas emissions . . . is to reduce vehicle miles traveled (VMT)—the miles Americans drive each year."[112]

TOD land use plans and zoning encourage mixed-use, compact development in transit neighborhoods. They locate housing and jobs near transit stops and significantly reduce the number and distance of vehicle trips. Encouraging land use patterns that house and employ more people in urban, transit-connected areas will cause a significant reduction in VMT, while placing households in smaller, more energy-efficient homes and offices will further reduce fossil fuel consumption and CO_2 emissions.

Transportation Efficient Development (TED) is TOD's country cousin. TOD and TED have many relatives. They bracket a profusion of terms that describe the rapidly increasing focus on reducing VMT through zoning. The terminology used is varied. Some authors write about "transit supportive" or "transit ready" development, or "transportation efficient" land use patterns. Others refer to "transit friendly zoning," "station area planning," "transportation demand management," "traditional neighborhood development," "planned unit development," "development-oriented transit," "transit supportive urban design," "transit station communities," "transit focused development," and "transit villages."

These terms encompass many different geographical contexts, populations, densities, and transportation modalities. Any attempt to describe a single approach is subject to a host of exceptions, but some common principles can be articulated to highlight the legal underpinnings of this important subject and to explain why zoning matters.

When neighborhood density is increased for both residential and commercial uses, the distance between origin and destination is shorter, and walking, bicycling, and mass transit services are more feasible. In order for increased densities to be tolerated, standards requiring attractive building, landscape, and streetscape design must be employed.

The successful development of transit stations and rail and bus lines is dependent upon land use densities and mixed uses. There must be a large enough number of commuters in a relevant area to provide a base level of ridership. In addition, ridership must be sufficiently diverse to ensure that

---

111. *See Land Use for Energy Conservation, supra* note 101.
112. Presidential Climate Action Project, Presidential Climate Action Project Plan §7:6 (2007).

people are traveling to work, to shop, to seek entertainment, and to go home at various times during the day, thereby increasing the cost-efficiency of the transit system.

Local land use plans and zoning, which determine population density and building uses, control how much the population will increase over time in a certain area, and what transportation needs new people will have. This, in turn, dictates the demand for various types of transportation services. Locally, this planning is done at the neighborhood level and should be guided by objectives contained in the city's comprehensive plan. To make transit systems feasible, land use planning among localities in a transportation region must be coordinated with transportation planning and development, which occurs under federal programs in urban areas at the metropolitan-area scale.

Many state enabling statutes require or encourage local governments to include a transportation element in their comprehensive plans. Increasingly, these transportation elements have incorporated planning strategies intended to encourage people to drive less and to walk, bicycle, and use mass transportation more frequently.

Arizona's planning enabling statute, for example, requires cities with more than 50,000 people to prepare a bike transportation element as part of their comprehensive plan.[113] Nevada's enabling legislation supports planning for mass transit, bicycle, and pedestrian infrastructure. This statute encourages local planning to include a transit element that "[s]how[s] a proposed multimodal system of transit lines, including mass transit, streetcar, motorcoach and trolley coach lines, paths for bicycles and pedestrians, satellite parking and related facilities."[114]

Even where communities are not currently served by transit systems, they can create compact, mixed-use neighborhoods that reduce car trips and miles traveled. Zoning controls in TED zones can limit the size of housing units and combine retail, office, and residential land uses, putting services, shops, and jobs in closer proximity to homes. Zoning can also require new construction to meet energy standards and further reduce GHG emissions.

Communities not yet served by transit can design one or more priority growth districts and create overlay zones for them that allow greater densities and more land uses than permitted in the underlying zoning districts. By clustering development strategically, these growing localities position themselves for future service by commuter rail or bus rapid transit, thereby becoming "transit ready."

---

113. Ariz. Rev. Stat. Ann. §94611.05(E)(9) (West 2011).
114. Nev. Rev. Stat. Ann. §278.160(1)(R) (West 2011).

Suburban areas that adopt higher density, mixed-use zoning will find it easier politically to adopt strong environmental protection ordinances applicable to the land outside high-density zones. Where state law permits, density bonuses may be provided in TED zones and cash contributions made by developers in exchange. This money can be used to purchase development rights from landowners in sensitive environmental areas outside the higher density zone, areas that mitigate climate change through sequestration. This balance between development and conservation can be accomplished within TOD areas as well—highlighting again zoning's ability to create sustainable settlement patterns and mitigate climate change.

E. *Zoning for Solar and Clean Energy*[115]

As zoning turned 100, it is showed its age by its failure to specifically permit modern clean energy systems in many communities. At the same time, it is demonstrating its historical resiliency as more and more progressive communities act to reform zoning to permit, require, and incentivize renewable and clean energy facilities. These rapidly evolving systems include building integrated solar systems, ground- and roof-mounted solar arrays, large- and small-scale wind generation, multi-building combined heat and power facilities, micro-grids, on-site electricity generation, and geothermal systems.

For clean energy systems to be constructed, they must be permitted by local zoning and not subject to expensive regulatory barriers that discourage their use and increase their cost. Promoting clean energy systems under local land use regulations is one of the latest efforts on the part of local governments to mitigate climate change, which, in the aggregate, are most impressive.

It is an uphill battle. By analyzing the comprehensive plans and zoning codes of most local governments, it is evident that regulatory barriers to clean energy systems are ubiquitous. These range from the simple failure to define and permit clean energy systems, to excessive height and setback restrictions, to additional or outdated permitting requirements, which greatly increase the costs of systems or discourage their use due to the unpredictability or length and costs of the approval process. The battle is being fought first on the solar front, given the popularity, improved technology, and reduced costs of solar energy systems.

---

115. *See* John R. Nolon, *Mitigating Climate Change by Zoning for Solar Energy Systems: Embracing Clean Energy Technology in Zoning's Centennial Year*, Zoning & Plan. L. Rep., Dec. 2015.

Although both the federal and state levels of government have a strong interest in encouraging the deployment of renewable energy systems, the power to permit small- and intermediate-scale solar energy systems has been delegated by most states to local villages, towns, and cities. Most states are not willing to preempt local control of solar and other clean energy systems; as a result, it is state policy to defer to local discretion in these matters, allowing local policymakers to determine the types of solar and other clean energy systems that will be deployed in the state.

Local officials who want to encourage solar energy systems are adjusting the local land use system first by adding a solar energy component to the comprehensive plan or adopting a special solar energy policy or plan to guide the reform of land use regulations. These local governments are then amending zoning regulations to permit and encourage these systems.

The primary, and most common, barrier to solar energy system implementation occurs when solar energy systems are neither defined nor permitted in one or more zoning districts. Without explicit definitions of solar facilities, they cannot be permitted by reference in the district use provisions of local zoning. In addition, the lack of clear clean energy- or solar- related definitions misses the opportunity for municipalities to send a signal to developers, property owners, and installers that they are "open for clean energy business." Municipalities are beginning to fix this problem by amending their zoning code to include definitions of the different solar energy systems available based on type, size, and/or energy capacity.

Since solar energy systems vary significantly by type, location, size, and energy capacity, zoning definitions generally are based on these factors. Where these characteristics align with the intensity of use or impact of a solar energy system, they justify different land use regulations for each type and guide local planners as to where to allow each type of system to be constructed.

Municipalities chose to permit solar energy systems by designating them as principal, accessory, secondary, or specially permitted uses. They are subjecting them to modified and expedited site plan review, waiving design standards enforced by local ARBs, and providing exemptions from historic district review standards for conforming designs and proper locations.

Solar easements, not recognized by common law in most states, can be created by local government regulation to ensure access to sunlight over the life of the solar system. Typically, these regulations require written and recorded solar easements that define easement dimensions, how the easement will terminate, and compensation for easement maintenance or interference, among other provisions.

Some localities are requiring developers to install solar energy systems or, short of that, make buildings solar-ready. Other communities incentivize, rather that require, these solar facilities, typically by providing density bonuses for solar panels, solar readiness, and solar access easements.

The process for zoning to allow other forms of clean energy follows the pattern set by zoning for solar. First, local comprehensive plans should set forth as a goal furthering clean energy facilities; next, zoning should define each of these clean energy technologies; and finally, district use regulations should be amended to permit them in appropriate locations at appropriate scales. The processes used to regulate and approve such facilities should be streamlined as fully and prudently as possible.

There is a clear need for municipal attorneys, local land use leaders, and state agencies interested in reducing energy costs and harmful fossil fuel emissions to develop model laws and approval processes for all clean energy facilities, in order to further the important objectives that they accomplish. These will all aid zoning in its adaptation to meet yet another contemporary challenge.

IV. Tackling Climate Change

A. *Fracking as an Industrial Use Under Zoning?*[116]

Is there currently a more controversial land use, environmental, and economic issue in America than fracking? Just listen to the ongoing debates:

"Fracking is great!"

"No, it's terrible!"

"It will mitigate climate change."

"No, it won't."

"Fracking cannot be made safe, even through proper regulation."

116. *See* John R. Nolon & Steven E. Gavin, *Hydrofracking: State Preemption, Local Power, and Cooperative Governance*, 63 Case W. Res. L. Rev. 995 (2013); John R. Nolon & Victoria Polidoro, *Hydrofracking: Disturbances Both Geological and Political: Who Decides?*, 44 Urb. Law. 507 (2012). John R. Nolon, *Pace/Yale Land Use Collaborative launches beta version of online fracking governance tool for local governments*, Land Use Prof Blog, http://lawprofessors.typepad.com/land_use/2016/01/pace-yale-land-use-collaborative-launches-beta-version-of-online-fracking-governance-tool-for-local-html (last updated Jan. 25, 2016).

"Yes, it can."

"Even if it can be done safely, don't go there, because it will take our focus away from promoting renewables."

To quote Kurt Vonnegut: "So it goes."[117]

Meanwhile, fracking is happening, and local governments are subjected to many of its associated risks. They either need to act or know—clearly and convincingly—why they should not. The federal government has stopped far short of comprehensive regulation of fracking; the states' regulations range from fair to poor, sometimes preempting local regulation but most often sharing regulatory authority over land use impacts.

The stakes couldn't be higher. "Think about it," as the fracking industry advertisement says; does the federal or state government, as part of their fracking regulations, control any of these local impacts?

- Pressures on housing supply and costs;
- Radical changes in community character;
- Loss of habitat and species;
- Deterrent effects on local growth;
- Impacts on recreational resources;
- Effects on agricultural land and operations;
- Causation of soil erosion and sedimentation;
- Creation of visual blight; or
- Increases in the cost of public health services.

The Land Use Law Center and its partners at the Yale School of the Environment have examined dozens of local fracking regulations and identified three dozen local impacts and risks found in the purposes section of their laws. With respect to a few of these impacts, federal or state regulations may require some level of mitigation, but these fall far short of controlling highly specific impacts felt in existing neighborhoods and on local environmental assets. Federal and state regulations are indifferent, as well, to the land use objectives of the comprehensive plan in any given community.

117. Kurt Vonnegut Jr., Slaughterhouse-Five or The Children's Crusade: A Duty-Dance With Death (Delacorte Press, 6th ed. 1969).

This indifference and the preemption of local control of fracking in some states are hard to understand. Why should this be more complicated than regulating any other intense industrial use? (Cement manufacturing comes to mind.) Why don't we allow it in industrial zones and subject it to a number of conditions as a specially permitted use? If imposing conditions can't fully protect local interests, why can't the fracking application be denied? Why should this one impactful land use be treated differently?

Consider that zoning is one of several responsibilities that local governments are delegated by their state legislatures. Think of these responsibilities as a three-legged stool. First, zoning determines how property is used and developed, and therefore dictates how valuable it will be. Second, localities have the power to impose property taxes on the assessed value of the land that they regulate. Third, municipalities are expected to use property tax revenues to fund municipal operations, provide capital infrastructure, and carry on the business of local government.

Given the complexity, comprehensiveness, and utility of these linked powers and duties, the judiciary is rightfully cautious about implying that state statutes that regulate fracking are intended by the legislature to inhibit local prerogatives. The importance of local land use regulation and the intertwined functions of local governments raise a *presumption against preemption*, in my view, that must be overcome to convince most state judges that their legislatures intended to preempt local zoning. Judges are inclined to say that if the state legislature passed statutes integrating zoning, taxation, and expenditure, why would they, in the case of fracking, remove one leg of the stool?

What has happened in Pennsylvania is instructive. Under previous state oil and gas law, the state courts had determined that local governments could regulate but not prevent fracking under local zoning. Following these judicial decisions, the state legislature adopted Act 13, which preempted local control.[118] The Act required local governments to include fracking as a permitted use in all zoning districts. This Act was invalidated by *Robinson Township v. Commonwealth*, which held that it failed to protect neighboring property owners from harm and created irrational land use classifications.[119] The power of municipalities to adopt comprehensive plans, to separate land uses through zoning, and the derivative rights of land owners, in the *Robinson* court's view, trumped state oil and gas legislation that on its face preempted local regulation.[120]

118. *See* 58 P.A. Cons. Stat. Ann. §3303 (West Supp. 2013).
119. 52 A.3d 463, 484-85 (Pa. Commw. Ct. 2012).
120. *Id.* at 480-94.

The court explained that zoning power was but "an extension of the concept of public nuisance which protects owners from activities that interfere with use and enjoyment of their property," citing the seminal *Euclid* case.[121] Essentially, the Act required municipalities to create zoning incompatible with their comprehensive plans; if mining and gas operations were to be included in all zones, as the Act required, zoning ordinances would inherently not comport with their comprehensive plans.[122] Thus, the court found, the state's interest in regulating fracking processes sits in direct conflict with local zoning interests.

B. *Water Scarcity and Land Use Planning*[123]

Another major zoning issue that has come up recently is water scarcity and how to deal with it in land use planning. When zoning was created, the availability of cheap and plentiful water was an unquestioned assumption In zoning's blueprint, there are few designs for water supply planning. This is the case even though land use planning determines water demand; the number and type of buildings allowed under zoning determine the per capita water use in a given community. Water supply planning was traditionally the province of the municipal water district, a separate water and sanitation district, or similar entity. Most of these were organized under state statutes that were originally—and remain today—legally disconnected from the zoning and land use planning enabling acts. Water demand and water supply planning have never been connected legally or institutionally.

This separation is a serious flaw in the legal system, particularly in those states with drought, limited snowmelt, and declining surface and groundwater supplies. Recent U.S. Drought Monitor reports state that 38 out of 50 states are abnormally dry.[124] It appears that 16 of them are in a moderate drought, 9 are in a severe drought, 2 are in extreme drought, and California is in an exceptional drought.

According to EPA, relief is not on the horizon: "Scientists project that climate change will make some of these extreme weather events more likely to occur and/or more likely to be severe."[125] Relatedly, according to the National

121. *Id.* at 481 (citing *Euclid*, 272 U.S. at 365).

122. *Id.* at 480-94.

123. *See* Elisabeth Haub School of Law at Pace University Land Use Law Center, Integrating Water Efficiency Into Land Use Planning in the Interior West: A Guidebook for Municipal Planners (Western Resources Advocates) (forthcoming).

124. *U.S. Drought Monitor Map Archive April 26, 2016*, U.S. DROUGHT MONITOR, https://droughtmonitor.unl.edu/maps/maparchive.aspx (last visited July 31, 2020)

125. *Understanding the Link Between Climate Change and Extreme Weather*, U.S. EPA, https://19january2017snapshot.epa.gov/climate-change-science/understanding-link-between-climate-

Aeronautics and Space Administration, "continued increases in human-produced greenhouse gas emissions drives up the risk of severe droughts in these regions."[126]

These predictions highlight the importance of connecting water supply and land use planning. Not only can land use planning reduce emissions but, as the Land Use Law Center's recent experience in the Interior West demonstrates, land use planning can also reduce per capita water use by up to 140 gallons per day.[127] With the populations of these states projected to increase—by as much as 100% in the near term in Colorado—reducing per capita consumption is the logical point at which to begin a comprehensive plan to balance supply and demand.

Zoning that permits large lots, low-density, and dispersed development increases water use per household. Compact, mixed-use development requires less water per household than single-family housing. The infrastructure requirements of both types of development are quite different.

In Utah, planners have determined that water demand drops from approximately 220 gallons per capita per day at a density of two units per acre, to about 110 gallons per acre at a density of five units per acre. More modestly, increasing residential density by 20% can yield a 10% per capita water savings. A study of household water use in Sacramento, California, showed 20-30% less water use in a new urban development than in the suburbs. Because of these significant effects, the link between land use patterns created by local zoning and water conservation needs to be clearly understood. Very few other water planning strategies can have a greater effect on limiting consumption.

Communities should begin by integrating water-efficient land use patterns and strategies into their comprehensive plans. Once this initial step is completed, this vision can be implemented through changes to the zoning code that permit water-efficient land uses in areas targeted for development, discourage development in areas targeted for conservation, and foster building types and landscapes that minimize the use of water.

Similarly, communities with limited room to grow can modify systems to accommodate higher densities and infill development. New forms of zoning, rather than those found in traditional residential zoning district provisions, can be adopted; ones that use new and varied ratios regarding setbacks, lot coverage, open space, livability space, and parking.

---

change-and-extreme-weather_.html (last updated Oct. 19, 2016).

126. *Megadroughts in U.S. West Projected to be Worst of the Millennium*, Nat'l Aeronautics & Space Admin. (Feb. 12, 2015), http://svs.gsfc.nasa.gov/cgi-bin/details.cgi?aid=4270.

127. Integrating Water Efficiency Into Land Use Planning, *supra* note 123.

Building and land use regulations can reduce water use in several other ways; for example, by mandating water-efficient interior and exterior fixtures and by requiring exterior landscaping practices and plants that reduce water use.

The Land Use Law Center's *Integrating Water Efficiency Into Land Use Planning in the Interior West: A Guidebook for Municipal Planners* discusses and illustrates several options for communities to consider in their efforts to foster water-conserving land use patterns, such as:

- Incorporate water-conserving land uses into as-of-right permitted uses;
- Foster water-efficient densities by permitting accessory dwelling units;
- Incorporate water-conserving land uses into conditionally permitted uses;
- Conditionally permit water-intensive uses upon water-conservation measures;
- Condition rezoning on water-conserving practices;
- Incentivize water conservation through bonus density zoning;
- Use planned unit development regulations to foster water conservation;
- Create a water conservation floating zone;
- Use overlay zoning to designate areas appropriate for conservation and those prioritized for growth; and
- Establish a TDRs program with sending districts to preserve green infrastructure and receiving districts to channel economic development.

Which of these options to choose depends on a number of factors, including the current land use configuration and types of buildings in the community. The pattern of development fostered and types of buildings allowed by zoning must respect the current architecture and land development of the community and build gradually from that base. The biggest factors to consider are density, the utilization of present infrastructure, and the cost of needed additional infrastructure.

C. Shaping and Attracting Economic Development[128]

Zoning historically assumed that the private market would inform developers what to build for maximum profit. Its job was to shape individual developments into appropriate human settlement patterns. The essential land use question, of course, is what type of a community is desirable and feasible to create. Changing demographics, financial markets, and environmental conditions require constant rethinking and restocking zoning's toolkit.

Today's ascendant demographic groups, such as millennials, immigrants, and senior households, prefer "walkups," that is, walkable urban places.[129] They have driven the real estate market toward urban centers and challenged urban planners to shape livable, sustainable, and lively neighborhoods. Fortunately, climate change mitigation also requires walkups, where buildings use less energy, water, and materials, and fewer vehicle trips are taken, resulting in fewer VMT. Zoning occupies a central position in creating the strategies needed to respond to these new market signals.

The Land Use Law Center's field laboratory is the Hudson Valley Region in New York. Ten years ago, our attention was captured by the changing demographics in the region and its apparent effect on the region's cities. To focus our energies, we organized a Mayors' Redevelopment Roundtable, a network of mayors, corporation counsels, and development commissioners representing the region's 12 largest urban communities. Our strategy was to work with the planning, legal, and development staff of the member communities on urban revitalization to identify common issues; conduct research; identify best land use practices; and provide assistance in implementation. In these places, zoning needs to attract economic development, rather than to simply shape it.

This is a report from the field; a quick summary of some of the issues selected for implementation and a few illustrations of best practices implemented. The highest priorities among the mayors were, not surprisingly, to increase tax ratables, keep expenditures in check, and improve their communities' aging infrastructure. They intended to accomplish these through five strategies: (1) job development; (2) sustainable development; (3) infill development; (4) scattered site projects; and (5) distressed property remediation. We found that zoning, land use regulations, and their associated strategies were effective tools to accomplish these objectives.

128. *See* John R. Nolon & Jessica A. Bacher, *The Role of Lawyers in Resolving Environmental Interest Disputes*, Real Est. L.J., Winter 2008.

129. Christopher B. Leinberger, *DC: The WalkUP Wake-Up Call*, Smart Growth America (2012), http://www.smartgrowthamerica.org/documents/Walkup-report.pdf.

Job Development: In this context, job development comprises new employment opportunities for millennials, immigrants, and low- and moderate-income residents. New development brings with it several opportunities to generate new employment prospects. Building and infrastructure development, including renewable energy projects, create construction jobs and jobs for those who serve construction projects. Many of these jobs require skilled, union labor, but a percentage of them can be filled by less skilled workers, including the young women and men who live in distressed neighborhoods. The city of Newburgh led the way among roundtable communities, insisting, during the land use review process, that all new and rehabilitation projects and municipal capital projects include local workers and provide them with the necessary training. This objective can be furthered by bonus density zoning to provide the funds developers need for training and supervision.

Sustainable Development: This topic aggregates TOD, promoting renewables, energy conservation in new and renovated buildings, affordable housing and balanced gentrification, designing for density, and green infrastructure, among others. The city of New Rochelle, through fast tracking the planning and rezoning of its downtown, offering density bonuses, and creating traffic improvements, stimulated a TOD project around its central transit station that is leveraging redevelopment of adjacent sites.[130] Yonkers created its own list of criteria for sustainable, or green, projects and requires compliance through its power pursuant to the State Environmental Quality Review Act to mitigate adverse environmental impacts by imposing mitigation conditions. Green buildings, for example, mitigate climate change (an adverse environmental impact). Peekskill is increasing zoning density and expanding land uses permitted in its waterfront TOD, as well as developing its parking lots there to create a sustainable neighborhood that will prime the pump for further downtown redevelopment.

Infill Development: Cities can accomplish many goals through infill development, which emphasizes the development of vacant lots, reuse of abandoned and underutilized buildings, and creative development of open spaces adjacent to corporate, medical, educational, and non-profit buildings. The city of Mount Vernon adopted numerous criteria from the U.S. Green Building Council's LEED-ND program to guide its rezoning of a transit station area in a developed neighborhood to shape the redevelopment of its remaining infill lots. White Plains is planning a significant TOD program concentrated on the coordinated development of infill sites in proximity to its

130. *Downtown's New Direction Will Smart Growth Get Us There?*, Westfar Communications and the Land Use Law Center at Pace Law School (Mar. 21, 2016).

commuter rail station. This plan begins with two projects comprising 561 rental apartments, retail space, and parking within a short walk of the city's transit center.

Scattered Site Projects: In some communities, development opportunities are scattered throughout their downtowns and adjacent urban neighborhoods. Prioritizing the development of a few such sites in order to leverage development nearby is a strategy of interest to the roundtable communities. The village of Brewster adopted an urban renewal plan that shaped its rezoning to encourage development of scattered sites throughout the neighborhoods within walking distance of its train station. The village of Port Chester selected five market-ready "hot spots" for redevelopment as the first step in warming up the market in adjacent neighborhoods.

Distressed Property Remediation: In order to revitalize downtowns, other neighborhoods, and infill sites, areas of concentrated distressed properties need to be addressed. Buildings and properties there provide an opportunity for affordable housing for existing residents, workforce housing for needed new employees, and sites for job development itself. The city of Poughkeepsie is planning a large-scale downtown-focused project that will use flexible zoning, coordinated transit, pedestrian and bikeways, development on underused parking lots, and a variety of funding sources to initiate pump-priming projects in the area. Newburgh created the first city-wide land bank in the state of New York, which is acquiring vacant lots and buildings, selectively demolishing some of them, promoting community gardening and security devices, and preparing sites for private market development, stimulated by new zoning techniques it recently adopted.

All of these projects and strategies create tensions among local interest groups and require the cooperation of multiple stakeholders, such as property owners, developers, equity advocates, city departments, taxpayers, and local resident leaders. They call for new approaches to project development and approval, including the use of consensus building techniques for community decision making. Lawyers who are trained in conflict resolution and settlement are particularly needed to advise their clients and local officials how to achieve economic development through strategies like those implemented through the Mayors' Redevelopment Roundtable. In these stories can be glimpsed the collaborative and creative work that needs to be done in zoning's second century.

D. Open Space Zoning Turns to Sequestration[131]

When the Land Use Law Center was asked in 1994 to report to President Bill Clinton's Council on Sustainable Development, we concluded that under present zoning, the amount of open space in the Hudson Valley Region would decline from 70% then to 30% by 2050. This estimate was calculated based on the rate at which large tracts of land were being subdivided into smaller, mostly residential parcels. At work were the mechanics of sprawl. Zoning maps adopted by the 256 municipalities in the region created a blueprint for future development, most of which would be residential subdivisions. Once zoned for single-family housing, local planning commissions approve subdivisions, applying standards in subdivision regulations that are adopted by local legislatures.

This erosion of open space, here and throughout the nation, gave rise to a movement. Land trusts came of age as open space concerns stimulated donations of land, development rights, or funds that could be used to acquire such land. Local voters began to approve bond resolutions or support real property tax increments to secure funds to purchase and set aside open space. State support for open space preservation manifested itself in a number of ways that involved direct appropriations, taxes, state bonds, tax exemptions, and local financing schemes. These land purchase and donation initiatives signaled a commitment to mitigate sprawl and its ill effects on the quality of life in developing communities, one parcel at a time.

In the aggregate, these funds allow the purchase of a small percentage of the land that needs to be preserved in order to change the ratio of open space to developed land that we projected in our report. This realization—here and elsewhere—led to an effort to prioritize purchases based on lands that matter most. In the eyes of some communities, this meant the purchase of lands that created a historic viewshed; for others, it meant acquiring land that provided needed ecosystem services. In still others, it meant creating a connected landscape that provided for the movement of critters, water, and people through nonfragmented natural areas.

A parallel—but too often disconnected—movement sprung up at the local level through changes in land use regulations and procedures. Some communities began to inventory their undeveloped parcels, prioritize their contributions to residents' quality of life and the environment, add open space components to their comprehensive plans, and adopt zoning and subdivision

131. *See* John R. Nolon, *Managing Climate Change Through Biological Sequestration: Open Space Law Redux*, 31 Stan. Envtl. L.J. 196 (2012).

regulations that preserved the natural resources associated with open space. Localities began to create a new blueprint, one that balanced open space preservation and development, through use of land exactions, mandatory clustering of development, deductions of constrained land from counting in developable lot calculations, and overlay zoning that added strict standards to development located in critical environmental areas. These efforts, when coordinated by a comprehensive plan, can achieve open space preservation—one community at a time.

Today, one-quarter of a century into this movement, attention is slowly focusing on sequestering lands: those that mitigate climate change by absorbing nearly one-fifth of the CO_2 emitted by vehicles, buildings, and enterprise. Biological sequestration of CO_2 emissions occurs within the vegetated environment: places like forests, pastures, meadows, and croplands. These landscapes naturally absorb and store carbon.

The local and state initiatives that have evolved to preserve and enhance open space provide a basis for a broader sequestration policy, one that builds on available legal technology and existing norms to respond to the looming global perturbation of climate change. The need, however, is to bring these local efforts to scale, particularly when the objective is to achieve a goal as ambitious as climate change mitigation.

With federal and state involvement, the efforts of land trusts and localities can transcend their one parcel and one community at-a-time impacts. Consider two recent examples.

In New Zealand, in heavily forested zones, the federal government identifies carbon accounting areas, uses geospatial mapping systems, establishes metrics, and measures increases in sequestration.[132] The owners of forested land are given accounts and issued certificates of tons sequestered; these credits are tradable, depending on the viability of carbon markets (a story for another day). Land trusts and local governments would benefit from such a scheme, especially from the monies it could bring to their preservation efforts while increasing the amount of CO_2 sequestered nationally.

A new law in California opened up opportunities to receive compensation for the carbon value of forests and a land trust in eastern Maine is leading the way. The California law requires polluters to reduce their carbon emissions over time but allows them to use approved "offset" projects to meet up to 8% of their emissions cap.[133] The first group of offset projects announced by

132. New Zealand Ministry of Agric. & Forestry, Introduction to Forestry in the Emissions Trading System (2011).
133. 17 Cal. Code of Regs. §95854.

the California Air Resources Board listed the Maine-based Downeast Lakes Land Trust preservation project as one of two forest offset projects selected.[134] Proceeds from the sale will allow the land trust to acquire and preserve an additional 55,000 acres of sequestering land.

E. *Land Use Law and Climate Change Management*[135]

The most salient zoning issue, as we celebrate the beginning of its second century, is how land use law can be used to mitigate climate change. When a New York City commission[136] (1916) and the Hoover Commission[137] (1922) created zoning, and the Court validated it[138] (1926), they had no idea that they were arming local governments to battle climate change. When the floating zone was first created in 1950, the village legislators in Tarrytown could not have known that this and other neo-Euclidean techniques could possibly evolve to address such an unfathomable menace.[139]

Over 100 years have passed, and we are now at work in coastal communities on Long Island helping local leaders adapt to sea-level rise and storm surges. They are digging through our database of strategies and thinking of creating a wholly new zone: an "expanding zone," one that grows as new data about climate change is received. They are trying to get ready to use the "R" word, "retreat," to explain the inevitable to their residents and business owners. They ask us whether they should create a retreat zone, an adaptation zone, and a safe zone to guide future development. They are utterly preoccupied by this ill-defined space between the mean high tide line and an elevation safe (at least for now) from inundation. They are handling and reshaping the tools that New York City, Hoover, the Supreme Court, and a century of local innovation gave them.

Can they adapt floating zoning, overlay zoning, TDRs, zoning, density bonus zoning, conservation easements, wetlands laws, and the land use system's other inventions to properly control development in these new zones? If they don't do something of that kind, will they eventually be held liable, legally or politically, for their failure after the next catastrophe occurs or gradual inundation destroys their sole-source drinking water aquifers? How

134. Carbon Program, Downeast Lakes Land Trust, https://www.downeastlakes.org/conservation/your-community-forests/forest-carbon-credits/ (last visited July 31, 2020).

135. John R. Nolon, *Climate Change and Sustainable Development: The Quest for Green Communities, Part I*, Plan. & Envtl. L., Oct. 2009, at 3; John R. Nolon, *Climate Change and Sustainable Development: The Quest for Green Communities, Part II*, Plan. & Envtl. L., Nov. 2009, at 3.

136. N.Y.C., N.Y. Building Zone Resolution (July 25, 1916).

137. A Standard State Zoning Enabling Act, *supra* note 12.

138. Village of Euclid v. Ambler Realty Co., 272 U.S. 365 (1926).

139. *See* Rodgers v. Village of Tarrytown, 96 N.E.2d 731 (N.Y. 1951).

do they account to their children and children's children for their time at zoning's helm?

Other local leaders are focused on mitigating climate change. Of course, this phenomenon is global, but urban communities are the principal sources of carbon emissions, which are the primary cause of climate change. The Land Use Law Center's Mayor's Redevelopment Roundtable serves the largest cities and urban villages in our region. These mayors want to know whether they can use zoning's inventions as well. The Presidential Climate Action Project says that "the greatest potential for reducing greenhouse gas emissions . . . is to reduce vehicle miles travelled (VMT)—the miles Americans drive each year."[140] Hundreds of local governments, including some in the roundtable, have adopted TOD zones and are rezoning for compact, mixed-use development to create walkable urban places. The new demographics—seniors emerging rapidly from their single-family cocoons, mobile millennials looking for lively urban neighborhoods, and immigrants seeking employment—are tipping the urban-suburban balance, and they are being zoned in through TOD and other zoning strategies. Our mayors are also interested in other tools such as energy code enhancements, design controls, green infrastructure, and other techniques to make their neighborhoods safe, lively, and livable places.

Zoning is adaptable to new challenges as it responds to changing conditions. We defenders of zoning are reminded, however, that zoning is parochial, extending only to municipal boundaries—far, far short of the reach it needs to effectively manage global climate change. We are also told that localities have limited assets and staff capacity to handle sophisticated problems. We point out that land use law is essential to mitigation. It regulates buildings, which consume 40% of the energy produced in the United States.[141] It is responsible for VMT, which contribute 28% of CO_2 as personal vehicles motor from origin to destination over a landscape created by zoning.[142] Further, the natural landscape, which sequesters 18% of CO_2, can be diminished or enhanced by zoning.

We are advised to pay attention to top-down, mostly federal solutions as our preferred path to a new era of effective climate control. This endless debate was sharpened in Paris at the Conference of the Parties (COP) in 2015.[143] Building on an insight of the U.N. Climate Change Conference in

140. Presidential Climate Action Project, *supra* note 112.
141. U.S. Energy Info. Admin., *supra* note 102.
142. *Sources of Greenhouse Gas Emissions*, U.S. EPA, https://www3.epa.gov/climatechange/ghgemissions/sources.html (last updated Apr. 11, 2020).
143. Paris Agreement to the United Nations Framework Convention on Climate Change, Dec. 12, 2015.

Warsaw in 2013, the Paris COP memorialized the nationally determined contributions (NDCs). The Paris Agreement turns climate policy upside down, changing the focus from nation-state dominated action to include on-the-ground solutions, guided, bolstered, and supported by state and national governments. This new approach operates from the bottom- up, engaging "sub-national" entities, cities, states, corporations, nongovernmental organizations, etc., to demonstrate how they can contribute to climate change mitigation. Whether the federal Administration fully withdraws from the Paris Accord, or not, these in NDCs that mitigate climate change and serve as models for other countries and their local and provincial governments.

This debate will continue. In March 2016, the United States submitted its NDC to the United Nations, relying primarily on stricter emissions standards for coal-fired energy generation plants and similar top-down contributions.[144] China, the world's leading emitter, took a different approach; its NDC includes emission reductions that rely on the construction of green buildings, renewable energy in buildings, low-carbon community operations, low-carbon transportation systems, and promoting pedestrian- and bicycle-oriented neighborhoods. By 2020, China says, 30% of travel will be by transit, and 50% of new buildings will be green.

China will have to allocate resources to the municipal level to implement its NDCs. The United States can follow suit. Funding, data, and technical assistance—conditioned on intermunicipal or regional cooperation—can remove the barriers to zoning's larger success. Such a program, funding actors in a system where all politics is local, can truly be a bipartisan effort, one that is much more likely to pass our curious Congress than most top-down solutions. This may be the path to zoning's new century.

144. *The Key Players in Climate Change*, N.Y. Times, Apr. 21, 2016, www.nytimes.com/interactive/2016/04/21/science/paris-agreement-carbon-dioxide-global-warming.html?_r=0.

Chapter Three
Low Carbon Land Use: Paris, Pittsburgh, and the IPCC

As noted in Chapter Two, during its first century, local land use law evolved into a flexible and powerful technique for achieving sustainable development at the local level. This chapter digs deeply into the authority and strategies that enable municipalities to lower their carbon footprint.[1] It describes and analyzes many methods, both traditional and innovative, to use the grass-roots power of local governments to reshape human settlements to mitigate climate change. The chapter demonstrates that land use regulation affects about 70% of the causes of carbon dioxide (CO_2) emissions and can be retooled to greatly reduce or capture urban carbon emissions. It also posits that mitigation efforts can lead to significant adaptation benefits, linking the two components of climate change management.[2]

I. Low-Carbon Land Use: A Natural Evolution of Local Practice

In 2014, the world caught up with local governments in the global race against climate change. That year, the Intergovernmental Panel on Climate Change (IPCC) embraced the critical role of municipal governments in mitigating the causes of climate change.[3] In 2015, the Paris Climate Agreement

1. Paris: the city hosted the Conference of the Parties (COP) that instigated a paradigm change in reacting to climate change; Pittsburgh: an exemplar of the bottom-up action heralded by the Paris Accord; Intergovernmental Panel on Climate Change (IPCC): its latest assessment report demonstrates the power of land use law to shape human settlements and to manage climate change at the local level. This chapter contains many statistics that when collected for this chapter in 2016, now seem outdated. Nevertheless, due to a lack of reports by the U.S. Environmental Protection Agency (EPA), such information cannot be adequately updated.
2. This chapter borrows heavily from: John R. Nolon, *Low Carbon Land Use: Paris, Pittsburgh, and the IPCC*, 40 U. Ark. Little Rock L. Rev. 661 (2018).
3. *See generally* Karen C. Seto & Shobhakar Dhakal, *Human Settlements, Infrastructure, and Spatial Planning*, *in* Climate Change 2014: Mitigation of Climate Change (O. Edenhofer et al. eds., 2014), https://archive.ipcc.ch/pdf/assessment-report/ar5/wg3/ipcc_wg3_ar5_chapter12.pdf.

adopted by the Conference of the Parties (COP) followed suit.[4] In 2019, the IPCC renewed its support for local mitigation as a key complement to global climate goals and initiatives.[5] For decades, the legal and practical ability of municipal governments to shape human settlements in ways that lower CO_2 emissions and enhance biological sequestration has been clear to land use practitioners. The recognition of a key role for the grass-roots level of government is consistent with an impressive body of theoretical work by scholars who focus on the relative competencies of various levels of government, the functioning of complex adaptive systems, institutional networks, and the dynamics of social change.

Notwithstanding this practical progress and these strong theoretical underpinnings, until recently the role of local governments in mitigating climate change was largely ignored internationally. Global leadership concentrated instead on top-down solutions, principally under the Kyoto Protocol adopted by the COP in 1997.[6] These annual COP meetings are organized under the United Nations Framework Convention on Climate Change (UNFCCC), an international environmental treaty adopted in 1992.[7] The framework it developed had little room for local climate change mitigation initiatives.

This was an unfortunate oversight. Not only do municipal governments have extensive legal authority to reduce CO_2 emissions, but their leaders are highly motivated to avoid the on-the-ground consequences of our changing climate.[8] The effects of climate change manifest themselves at the local

4. *See What Is the Paris Agreement?*, U.N. Climate Change, https://unfccc.int/process-and-meetings/the-paris-agreement/what-is-the-paris-agreement#:~:text=At%20COP%2021%20in%20Paris,a%20sustainable%20low%20carbon%20future.&text=As%20such%2C%20it%20charts%20a,in%20-the%20global%20climate%20effort (last visited Aug. 14, 2020).

5. Climate Change and Land, IPCC (2019), https://www.ipcc.ch/site/assets/uploads/2019/08/Fullreport-1.pdf.

6. Kyoto Protocol to the United Nations Framework Convention on Climate Change, Dec. 10, 1997, 2303 U.N.T.S. 162.

7. *Status of Ratification of the Convention,* UNFCCC, https://unfccc.int/process-and-meetings/the-convention/status-of-ratification/status-of-ratification-of-the-convention (last visited Aug. 14, 2020).

8. *See* U.S. Global Change Res. Program, Climate Science Special Report: Fourth National Climate Assessment, Vol. I, at 10, 12, 15 (D.J. Wuebbles et al. eds., 2017), https://science2017.globalchange.gov/downloads/CSSR2017_FullReport.pdf (The U.S. Global Change Research Program (USGCRP) released its "Climate Science Special Report: Fourth National Climate Assessment, Volume I" on the science of climate change in 2017. According to this report "it is *extremely likely* that human influence has been the dominant cause of the observed warming since the mid-20th century. For the warming over the last century, there is no convincing alternative explanation supported by the extent of the observational evidence."

> The last few years have also seen record-breaking, climate-related weather extremes, the three warmest years on record for the globe, and continued decline in arctic sea ice. These trends are expected to continue in the future over climate (multi-decadal) time-scales. . . . Global climate is projected to continue to change over this century and beyond. The magnitude of climate change beyond the next few decades will depend primarily on the amount of

level, where people are killed or injured, property is destroyed, businesses are shuttered, ecosystems are fouled, and where our democratic system is most vibrant.[9] The Land Use Law Center's on-the-ground experience demonstrates the proximity of government decision-makers to the practical problems caused by climate change. To illustrate, upon our discovery of the advent of local environmental law 20 years ago, we investigated why particular localities adopted these new laws. Through interviews with local leaders, we found they were profoundly perturbed by drinking water pollution, species disappearance, riverbank erosion, wetlands damage, and the loss of historic view sheds, to name a few. These influences motivated local leaders to create and implement grass-roots solutions, such as adopting local environmental laws.[10] Their reaction to the devastating effects of climate change is similar to each other's and explains why local governments have become involved. This progress is the natural evolution of a century-old legal system that has constantly innovated as new and profound changes in society have occurred.[11]

This chapter on low-carbon land use describes, organizes, and clarifies strategies that local governments are employing, using their state-delegated powers to plan community development and to regulate private building, determining in the process where and to what extent our natural landscapes are developed or conserved. In all 50 states, local governments have the legal power to shape human settlements and, in so doing, lower CO_2 emissions from buildings and vehicles, increase the sequestration of carbon by the natural environment, and promote distributed energy systems and renewable energy facilities that lower fossil fuel consumption.[12]

---

greenhouse (heat-trapping) gases emitted globally and on the remaining uncertainty in the sensitivity of Earth's climate to those emissions (*very high confidence*).

9. *See* David Brooks, *The Localist Revolution*, N.Y. Times, July 19, 2018: ("[U]nder localism, the crucial power center is at the tip of the shovel, where the actual work is being done. Expertise is not in the think tanks but among those who have local knowledge, those with a feel for how things work in a specific place and an awareness of who gets stuff done."). https://www.nytimes.com/2018/07/19/opinion/national-politics-localism-populism.html.

10. *See* John R. Nolon, *In Praise of Parochialism: The Advent of Local Environmental Law*, 26 Harv. Envtl. L. Rev. 365, 412 (2002).

11. *See* John R. Nolon, *Zoning's Centennial: A Complete Account of the Evolution of Zoning Into a Robust System of Land Use Law—1916-2016 (Part I)*, 39 Zoning & Plan. L. Rep. 1 (2016), http://digitalcommons.pace.edu/lawfaculty/1036/; John R. Nolon, *Zoning's Centennial: A Complete Account of the Evolution of Zoning Into a Robust System of Land Use Law—1916-2016 (Part II)*, 39 Zoning & Plan. L. Rep. 1 (2016), http://digitalcommons.pace.edu/lawfaculty/1037/; John R. Nolon, *Zoning's Centennial: A Complete Account of the Evolution of Zoning Into a Robust System of Land Use Law—1916-2016 (Part III)*, 39 Zoning & Plan. L. Rep. 1 (2016), http://digitalcommons.pace.edu/lawfaculty/1038/; John R. Nolon, *Zoning's Centennial: A Complete Account of the Evolution of Zoning Into a Robust System of Land Use Law—1916-2016 (Part IV)*, 40 Zoning & Plan. L. Rep. 1 (2017), http://digitalcommons.pace.edu/lawfaculty/1039/ [hereinafter Zoning's Centennial].

12. *See infra* Part IV.

The underlying theories supporting localism in this context are explored in part II. These include the successful workings of complex adaptive systems, including human communities and their governments: theories that help us understand the importance of grass-roots efforts to respond to contemporary challenges.[13] Part II refers to scholars of governmental policy who examine the importance of local communities drawing on concepts such as polycentricism, subsidiarity, and relative competencies. Sociologists, as students of social change, describe how innovations are adopted in human communities, observing that systemic change occurs primarily from the ground up, not from the top-down. None of these theories diminish the critical importance of higher levels of governments in addressing climate change, but they strongly urge that state, federal, and international governments effectively embrace the local role in creating their own regulatory and spending strategies.

Part III explores the recent movement at the international level to recognize the importance of local governmental strategies in mitigating climate change.[14] After discovering emerging literature on the practical successes of local governments in shaping human settlements in ways that lower emissions of CO_2, the IPCC added a chapter devoted to its importance in its Fifth Assessment Report on Climate Change, issued in 2014.[15] Notably, five years after this publication, the IPCC again stressed the value of multi-level mitigation in its Special Report on Climate Change and Land.[16] One year after the publication of the Fifth Assessment Report, the COP in Paris adopted a protocol that includes the role of local governments in contributing to mitigation through nationally determined contributions (NDCs).[17]

The details of how local land use law has been used to shape human settlements are discussed in part IV, which demonstrates how those efforts can lower the demand for energy generated by fossil fuels as a powerful antidote to climate change.[18] Local laws and their enforcement determine how many vehicle miles are driven, how much energy buildings consume, and how natural resources that capture CO_2 through biological sequestration can be preserved and enhanced.

Part V combines five strategies into a land use stabilization wedge.[19] These local strategies demonstrate how human settlements can be shaped in ways

13. *See infra* Part II.
14. *See infra* Part III.
15. *See* Seto & Dhakal, *supra* note 3.
16. *See* Climate Change and Land, *supra* note 5.
17. *What Is the Paris Agreement?*, *supra* note 4.
18. *See infra* Part IV.
19. *See infra* Part V. *See also* Chapter One.

that affect about 70% of CO_2 emissions or the means of recapturing them.[20] The components of this Wedge are buildings, transportation, sequestration, distributed energy, and renewable energy.[21] Local land use law in most states empowers municipalities to implement strategies with respect to all of these components.

Part VI describes the corollary adaptation benefits of these strategies, including creating resilient neighborhoods that both mitigate and adapt to climate change.[22] These adaptation benefits provide further evidence of the need to fully integrate the legal powers of local governments into the national framework of laws. Local governments, as it turns out, have the power to manage climate change by adopting both mitigative and adaptive policies, plans, and programs. This reality explains why localism is being endorsed by international policies such as the IPCC Assessment Report and the Paris Agreement. The chapter concludes in part VII, noting that if these strategies are encouraged and assisted by state and national governments, they can contribute significantly to global efforts to reach international climate change goals.[23]

II. A Theoretical Understanding of Grass-Roots Power

Scholars of many stripes endorse grass-roots strategies for confronting many of society's problems. This can surprise some, who are trained to think mostly about top-down efforts adopted by Congress and enforced by federal agencies. Yale law professor Robert C. Ellickson, for example, warns against the "Yale disease," which he calls the propensity of his students to look entirely to federal laws and federal courts for solutions, causing them to ignore or not understand state and local solutions.[24] He refers to the "principle of subsidiarity," "which holds that responsibility for dealing with a problem should be delegated to the most decentralized institution capable of handling that problem."[25] Professor Ellickson's notions are supported by Dr. Elinor Ostrom,

20. *See* U.S. EPA, Inventory of U.S. Greenhouse Gas Emissions and Sinks: 1990-2015, at ES-10, fig. ES-7, ES-11 (2017) (EPA 430-P-17-001) [hereinafter EPA Greenhouse Gas Inventory 2015]; U.S. EPA, Inventory of U.S. Greenhouse Gas Emissions and Sinks: 1990-2012, at ES-20 (2013) [hereinafter EPA Greenhouse Gas Inventory 2012]. *See also infra* text accompanying notes 104, 129, and 140.

21. *See infra* Part V.

22. *See infra* Part VI.

23. *See infra* Part VII.

24. Robert Ellickson, Losing Ground: A Nation on Edge, 275 (John R. Nolon & Daniel B. Rodriguez eds., 2007).

25. *Id.* at 274; *see also* Brooks, *supra* note 9 ("Localism is the belief that power should be wielded as much as possible at the neighborhood, city and state levels.").

a Nobel Laureate in economics, who advanced a polycentric approach to governance.[26] She warns against the "panacea trap,"[27] which is akin to the Yale disease. A panacea trap occurs where responsible actors believe there is a cure-all solution applicable to every environmental issue, regardless of the local circumstances. She too would assign key decision-making responsibility to those who are as close as possible to the scene of relevant events and to the actors involved.

Law professor I. Michael Heyman, with whom we met when we founded the Land Use Law Center 26 years ago, headed the Smithsonian Institution at the time and was known to us as a former Professor of Law and of City and Regional Planning at Berkeley and former Chancellor of the University of California. We had just completed a study of the sustainability of the Hudson Valley Region and were deeply concerned about the damage to natural resources caused by sprawl, a result of land use plans and zoning adopted by over 200 constituent local governments. He suggested that to foster sustainable human settlements, we build interconnected networks of local land use leaders, as he and others had done with the several communities that share land use jurisdiction in the San Francisco Bay area.

Nobel Laureate in physics, Dr. Murray Gell-Mann, attended our meeting with Professor Heyman. He had just been dubbed the "man who knows everything" by the *New York Times*.[28] Dr. Gell-Mann helped to establish the Santa Fe Institute,[29] was on the board of the MacArthur Foundation, and had just published his book on sustainability, *The Quark and the Jaguar*.[30] As a physicist, he based much of his thinking on the functions of "complex adaptive systems" in nature and human communities.[31] His writings

26. Elinor Ostrom et al., *Going Beyond Panaceas*, 104 PNAS 15176, 15176 (2007).
27. *Id.* at 15177.
28. David Berreby, *The Man Who Knows Everything; Murray Gell-Mann*, N.Y. Times, May 8, 1994, https://www.nytimes.com/1994/05/08/magazine/the-man-who-knows-everything-murray-gell-mann.html.
29. *See generally* Mitchell M. Waldrop, Complexity: The Emerging Science at the Edge of Order and Chaos 12 (1992) (providing details of the work conducted by the Santa Fe Institute on the science of complexity).
30. Murray Gell-Mann, The Quark and the Jaguar: Adventures in the Simple and Complex 17 (1994).
31. *Id.* at 17:

> A complex adaptive system acquires information about its environment and its own interaction with that environment, identifying regularities in that information, condensing those regularities into a kind of "schema" or model, and acting in the real world on the basis of that schema. In each case, there are various competing schemata, and the results of the action in the real world feedback to influence the competition among those schemata.

See also Thomas L. Friedman, *Where American Politics Can Still Work: From the Bottom Up*, N.Y. Times, July 3, 2018: ("Our country is actually a checkerboard of cities and communities—some that are forming what I call 'complex adaptive coalitions' and are thriving from the bottom up."). https://www.nytimes.com/2018/07/03/opinion/community-revitalization-lancaster.html.

focused on how ecological systems and human communities adapt to stress and crises. He discovered that healthy systems are divided into components that communicate regularly and rapidly to sense impending threats and to determine how to respond effectively.[32] In our meeting, both he and Professor Heyman pointed out that the land use boards within the typical local government are not communicating effectively and that their members need to be trained to do so. Similarly, they noticed that local governments which share regional challenges, such as sprawl, do not plan together and thus have difficulty perceiving the threats and developing strategies for responding.

All change related to land use manifests itself at the local level, and it is there that land use plans and regulations need to be changed to reorder human settlements. Change can be understood through multiple lenses, including the view of sociologists who study how change happens. One term for what they observe is the "diffusion of innovation," a term which was popularized by Dr. Everett Rogers.[33] Diffusion, he notes, includes the planned and spontaneous spread of new ideas, such as methods of containing sprawl, or implementing measures to mitigate climate change. We adopted his notions in establishing the Land Use Alliance Leadership Training Program and recruiting local "champions of change," as Dr. Rogers labels them,[34] to attend our training programs. We learned from Dr. Rogers that change happens when local champions reach out beyond their jurisdictions to peers and respected change agents to solve local problems, so we brought these resources into our training programs. By training these leaders and exposing them to potential adaptations, we taught them to connect locally and regionally, building on the connectivity principles urged upon us by Professor Heyman and Dr. Gell-Mann.

Urban planning scholars reference the behavior of complex adaptive systems and the field of diffusion of innovations to define how regional planning networks can work to rationalize land use planning and control. According to David E. Booher and Judith E. Innes:

> Network power emerges from communication and collaboration among individuals, agencies, and businesses in a society. Network power emerges as

32. Gell-Mann, *supra* note 30, at 17.
33. Everett M. Rogers, Diffusion of Innovation 6 (5th ed. 2003).
34. *Id.* at 414-15. (According to Rogers, "[a] champion is a charismatic individual who throws his or her weight behind an innovation, thus overcoming indifference or resistance that the new idea may provoke in an organization." Rogers writes that according to studies of organizational change, the "important qualities of champions were that they (1) occupied a key linking position in their organization, (2) possessed analytical and intuitive skills in understanding various individuals' aspirations, and (3) demonstrated well-honed interpersonal and negotiating skills in working with other people in their organization.").

> diverse participants in a network focus on a common task and develop shared meanings and common heuristics for action. It grows as these players identify and build on their interdependencies to create new potential. In the process, innovations and novel responses to environmental stresses can emerge. These innovations, in turn, make possible adaptive change and constructive action of the whole.[35]

When my Yale students explored why communities adopted exemplary local environmental laws, they found out that most resulted from the work of community leaders reacting to damage to the local environment. They named these "perturbations" and called this the "perturbation effect."[36] Scholars who study diffusion theory observe how change happens in social systems and document the processes by which successful change occurs.[37] Their focus is also on connectivity.[38] They observe that outside change agents are most successful when they place new tools in the hands of respected local leaders. When those leaders adopt an innovative solution, others pay attention. As a successful change occurs, the rest of the community catches on, a tipping point is reached, and the innovation becomes permanent. Successful change in these communities spread to nearby places confronting similar problems. In the study of urban planning, researchers describe how local and regional planning networks can be created to link local responses to address common, transboundary problems.

Local stakeholders represent the components of the municipal complex adaptive system. By being engaged in public processes, they can achieve consensus about how to respond to flooding, drought, mudslides, wildfires, sea-level rise, and storm surges—effects associated with climate change.[39] In response to these on-the-ground perturbations, they are motivated to learn how to mitigate the forces of climate change by reducing vehicle miles traveled (VMT), creating energy- efficient buildings, permitting and encouraging renewables and distributed energy generation facilities, and preserving

35. David E. Booher & Judith E. Innes, *Network Power in Collaborative Planning*, J. PLAN. EDUC. & RES. 221, 225 (2002) ("Like a complex adaptive system, [the planning network] as a whole is more capable of learning and adaptation in the face of fragmentation and rapid change than a set of disconnected agents.").
36. Students in the author's classes at the Yale School of Forestry and Environmental Studies conducted research on local environmental and smart growth laws adopted by municipalities in all 50 states, identifying well-crafted and exemplary laws and interviewing the local land use leaders involved in drafting and securing the adoption of these laws. *See* YALE SCHOOL OF FORESTRY & ENVIRONMENTAL STUDIES, REPORT NUMBER 2: GAINING GROUND INFORMATION DATABASE (John R. Nolon et al. eds., 2004) (describing the methodology and conclusions of this research).
37. *See, e.g.*, Booher & Innes, *supra* note 35.
38. *See* John R. Nolon, *Champions of Change: Reinventing Democracy Through Land Law Reform*, 30 HARV. ENVTL. L. REV. 1 (2006).
39. *See* id.

natural systems that sequester carbon. As the local evidence of climate change becomes more and more evident, opinions often change as local leaders engage in solving the problems that threaten their environment and economy. They become committed to effective action and react aggressively to opportunities and threats.

III. Emerging Global Support for Local Solutions

Low-carbon land use is a logical subject to be included in the periodic assessment reports of the IPCC. The IPCC was formed by the World Meteorological Organization and the United Nations Environment Programme in 1988.[40] It began issuing climate change assessment reports in 1990 and warning, from the outset, that business as usual will result in unprecedented warming of the planet.[41] The first three assessment reports ignored the potential of shaping human settlements to mitigate climate change.[42]

There was a tip of the hat to low-carbon land use in the IPCC's Fourth Assessment Report, issued in 2007.[43] While the report noted that climate change can be managed by controlling sprawl, promoting compact, mixed-use development, and modern land use planning, the IPCC was reluctant to go further and include a full chapter on the details because there was insufficient evidence in the literature documenting that strategy.

I attended an Expert Meeting on Human Settlement and Infrastructure organized by the IPCC in Calcutta in 2011. The correspondence that I received stated that "[o]ne motivation for this meeting is the significant percentage of global greenhouse gases attributable to human settlements and their infrastructure."[44] We knew then that land use patterns can be shaped by land use law to mitigate climate change. Our task was to demonstrate that there was ample research to support a chapter on human settlement in the next assessment report.

40. *History*, IPCC, https://www.ipcc.ch/about/history/ (last visited Aug. 14, 2020).
41. Climate Change: The IPCC 1990 and 1992 Assessments, IPCC (1992), https://archive.ipcc.ch/ipccreports/1992%20IPCC%20Supplement/IPCC_1990_and_1992_Assessments/English/ipcc_90_92_assessments_far_full_report.pdf.
42. *Id.*; IPCC Second Assessment: Climate Change 1995, IPCC (1995), https://archive.ipcc.ch/pdf/climate-changes-1995/ipcc-2nd-assessment/2nd-assessment-en.pdf; Climate Change 2001: Synthesis Report, IPCC (2001), http://www.grida.no/publications/267.
43. Climate Change 2007: Synthesis Report, IPCC (2007), https://archive.ipcc.ch/pdf/assessment-report/ar4/syr/ar4_syr_full_report.pdf.
44. Letter from Ottmar Edenhofer et al., Co-Chairs of IPCC Working Group III, to John R. Nolon, Distinguished Professor of Law, Elisabeth Haub School of Law (Feb. 2, 2010) (on file with author).

We prepared for this Expert Meeting by publishing a report on the literature that was published in 2011.[45] Our report demonstrated what many of the assembled experts knew: that the techniques mentioned in the Fourth Assessment Report, and many more like them, can be employed to reduce carbon emissions at the local level. The input of this group of experts was instrumental in convincing the IPCC to add a full chapter on the subject in its next report.[46]

Chapter Twelve of the IPCC's Fifth Assessment Report addresses the relationship between the shape of human settlements and climate change mitigation.[47] It focuses heavily on urban form, infrastructure, and land use mix. The chapter notes that mixed-use neighborhoods shape development so as to reduce the amount of CO_2 through the efficient use of energy and the reduction of vehicle trips and auto emissions.[48] This new chapter includes climate change mitigation strategies like use restrictions, density regulations, urban containment instruments, building codes, parking regulations, design regulations, and affordable housing mandates.[49] The chapter discusses land acquisition and management through the transfer of development rights and increasing green space and urban carbon sinks.[50]

As if to prove the IPPC right, local and state governments began to organize "sub-national" consortia to carry this message to Paris to influence the content of the agreement to be entered into by COP21. The "Under2 MOU," for example, was created in 2015 in order to influence policy at the convention.[51] It included a commitment by signatories (subnational governments) and endorsers (national governments) to reduce their GHG emissions 80–95% below 1990 levels by 2050.[52] It was signed by 222 jurisdictions representing countries on 6 continents, 1.3 billion people, and over 43% of

45. Margaret E. Byerly, *A Report to the IPCC on Research Connecting Human Settlements, Infrastructure, and Climate Change*, 28 Pace Envtl. L. Rev. 936 (2011), https://digitalcommons.pace.edu/pelr/vol28/iss3/8.
46. Seto & Dhakal, *supra* note 3, at 923.
47. *Id.* at 930.
48. *Id.* at 956.
49. *Id.* at 962-63.
50. *Id.* at 963-64.
51. The governments that have ratified the United Nations Framework Convention on Climate Change (UNFCC) are known as Parties to the Convention and meet annually at a Conference of the parties, or the COP. Currently, there are 197 Parties to the Convention. *See Climate: Get the Big Picture*, UNFCCC, http://bigpicture.unfccc.int/#content-the-paris-agreement (last visited Aug. 14, 2020).
52. *Frequently Asked Questions*, UNDER2 (Aug. 14, 2020), http://www.under2coalition.org/frequently-asked-questions.

the global economy.[53] Among the United States signatories were 12 cities, 11 states, and 2 counties.[54]

The Paris Agreement[55] on combating climate change and its effects was reached on December 12, 2015 at the UNFCCC COP21.[56] It endorsed the role of local governments in mitigating climate change and invited their participation in the international agreement by memorializing bottom-up strategies as nationally determined contributions (NDCs).[57] This approach broadened international climate policy by including state and local government actors and inviting them to demonstrate how they can contribute to climate change mitigation.

The United States signed the agreement on Earth Day and ratified it by acceptance on September 3, 2016.[58] The United States submitted its NDC to the United Nations (U.N.) in March 2016, relying primarily on stricter emissions standards for coal-fired energy generation plants and similar top-down contributions.[59] China, the world's leading emitter, took a different approach; its NDC includes emission reductions that rely on the construction of green buildings, renewable energy in buildings, low-carbon community operations, low-carbon transportation systems, and promoting pedestrian- and bicycle-oriented neighborhoods.[60] By 2020, China says, 30% of travel will be by transit and 50% of new buildings will be green.

The outpouring of support for state and local actions to manage climate change following adoption of the Paris Agreement demonstrates the sub-national commitment to climate change mitigation. One thousand two hundred non-party stakeholders, for example, signed the "Paris Pledge for

53. *Biggest Ever Gathering of Global States and Regions on Climate Action*, UNDER2 (Aug. 14, 2020), https://www.under2coalition.org/news/biggest-ever-gathering-global-states-and-regions-climate-action.
54. *States and Regions*, UNDER2 (Aug. 14, 2020), http://www.under2coalition.org/members.
55. Conference of the Parties' Twenty-First Session, U.N. Framework Convention on Climate Change, *Paris Agreement*, U.N. Doc. FCCC/CP/2015/L.9/Rev.1 (Dec. 12, 2015) [hereinafter *Paris Agreement*].
56. *What Is the Paris Agreement, supra* note 4. The Paris Agreement sought to limit the rise of global temperatures below 2 degrees Celsius and aid countries in adapting to the changes wrought by climate change. April 22, 2016, Earth Day, marked the day parties could sign the Agreement. *Climate: Get the Big Picture, supra* note 51. It entered into force on November 4, 2016, after the "double threshold," ratification by 55 countries representing 55% of emissions, was met. As of Aug. 14, 2020, 189 parties have ratified the agreement. *Paris Agreement—Status of Ratification*, UNFCCC, https://unfccc.int/process/the-paris-agreement/status-of-ratification (last visited Aug. 14, 2020).
57. *Paris Agreement—Status of Ratification, supra* note 56.
58. *Chapter XXVII: Environment*, United Nations Treaty Collection, https://treaties.un.org/Pages/ViewDetails.aspx?src=TREATY&mtdsg_no=XXVII-7-d&chapter=27&clang=_en (last visited Aug. 14, 2020).
59. *The Key Players in Climate Change*, N.Y. Times, Apr. 21, 2016, https://www.nytimes.com/interactive/2016/04/21/science/paris-agreement-carbon-dioxide-global-warming.html.
60. Embassy of the People's Republic of China in the Republic Of the Philippines, Enhanced Actions on Climate Change: China's Intended Nationally Determined Contributions 9-10 (unofficial translation July 3, 2015) https://www.fmprc.gov.cn/ce/ceph/eng/xwdt/t1278239.htm.

Action" to demonstrate their commitment to the agreement's goals.[61] It was not intended to copy the good work being done by local governments, but to demonstrate "the breadth of support and scale of momentum for a transition to a low-emission and climate resilient economy."[62]

This post-Paris contagion was not halted by President Donald Trump's announcement of his intention to withdraw from the Paris Agreement on June 1, 2017.[63] If anything, the subnational support has grown exponentially. The U.S. Climate Alliance (USCA) was created in direct response to the federal government's decision to withdraw from the Paris Agreement.[64] It is a bipartisan coalition of 24 states and 1 territory[65] that accounts for 55% of the U.S. population and $11.7 trillion of the U.S. economy.[66] These subnational actors are committed to reducing greenhouse gas (GHG) emissions in accordance with the U.S. target under the Paris Agreement[67] and building the USCA Clearinghouse, a website that will collect climate information and data for use by policymakers and the public.[68]

Initially released on June 5, 2017, the "We Are Still In" pledge to uphold the Paris Agreement comprises a coalition of more than 3,800 business, economic, government, and cultural leaders representing 155.0 million Americans and $9 trillion of the U.S. economy, spanning all 50 states.[69] "America's Pledge" is a separate initiative working in conjunction with "We Are Still In"

---

61. *Letter from Minister Segolene Royal and Christiana Figures*, Paris Pledge for Action (Apr. 21, 2016), http://www.parispledgeforaction.org/wp-content/uploads/2015/08/Paris-Pledge-for-Action-Communication.pdf.
62. *About*, Paris Pledge for Action, http://parispledgeforaction.org/about/ (last visited Aug. 14, 2020).
63. Michael D. Shear, *Trump Will Withdraw U.S. From Paris Climate Agreement*, N.Y. Times, June 1, 2017, https://www.nytimes.com/2017/06/01/climate/trump-paris-climate-agreement.html. On Aug. 4, 2017, the U.S. State Department officially informed the United Nations of its withdrawal. Valerie Volcovici, *U.S. Submits Formal Notice of Withdrawal From Paris Climate Pact*, Reuters, Aug. 4, 2017, https://www.reuters.com/article/us-un-climate-usa-paris/u-s-submits-formal-notice-of-withdrawal-from-paris-climate-pact-idUSKBN1AK2FM. In accordance with the withdrawal process, the earliest date for the United States to completely withdraw is Nov. 4, 2020, one day after the U.S. presidential election.
64. *About: Alliance Principles*, U.S. Climate Alliance, https://www.usclimatealliance.org/alliance-principles/ (last visited Aug. 14, 2020).
65. *About: Governors*, U.S. Climate Alliance, https://www.usclimatealliance.org/governors-1/ (last visited Aug. 14, 2020). (California, Colorado, Connecticut, Delaware, Hawaii, Illinois, Maine, Maryland, Massachusetts, Michigan, Minnesota, Montana, Nevada, New Jersey, New Mexico, New York, North Carolina, Oregon, Pennsylvania, Puerto Rico, Rhode Island, Vermont, Virginia, Washington, and Wisconsin).
66. *U.S. Climate Alliance 2019 Fact Sheet*, U.S. Climate Alliance, https://www.usclimatealliance.org/us-climate-alliance-fact-sheet (last visited Aug. 14, 2020).
67. *About: Alliance Principles*, *supra* note 64 (26-28% reduction in GHG emissions below 2005 levels by 2025).
68. U.S. Climate Alliance: U.S. Climate Alliance Clearinghouse, http://usclimateallianceclearinghouse.org (last visited Aug. 14, 2020).
69. *"We Are Still In" Declaration*, We Are Still In, https://www.wearestillin.com/about (last visited Aug. 14, 2020).

to collect and organize the various climate actions of local actors across the United States.[70] Its September 2019 report quantifies the action of nonfederal actors in support of the Paris Agreement and found that 25 states, 430 cities, and over 3,800 climate action groups like businesses and communities, representing nearly 70% of U.S. gross domestic product, are still committed to implementing its goals.[71]

As of August 2020, 461 U.S. Climate Mayors representing 72 million Americans have committed to upholding the goals of the Paris Agreement.[72] Their statement was clear: "We will increase our efforts to cut greenhouse gas emissions, create a clean energy economy, and stand for environmental justice."

In initiating the U.S. withdrawal from the Paris Agreement, the president noted that he represented the citizens of Pittsburgh, not Paris.[73] Shortly thereafter, Pittsburgh city leaders pledged to implement their own climate action plans, and Pittsburgh Mayor Bill Peduto committed his city to the agreement by issuing an executive order in June 2017, pledging to continue efforts to cut energy consumption in half and develop a fossil fuel-free fleet of city vehicles.[74] The following year, Pittsburgh effectuated its pledge through a revitalized Climate Action Plan with clear goals for 2030, like establishing a fossil fuel-free fleet of vehicles and relying solely on renewable energy sources.[75]

On June 7, 2017, the mayor of Paris, Anne Hidalgo, and Mayor Peduto penned an op-ed responding to Trump's comments.[76] The article explores the plight of Pittsburgh as its steel industry declined; the emergence of Pittsburgh as a revitalizing force; the reclaiming of Parisian roads from polluting vehicles for pedestrian use; and the involvement of both cities in the Global Covenant of Mayors for Climate and Energy and the "We Are Still

70. *About America's Pledge*, America's Pledge, https://www.americaspledgeonclimate.com/about/ (last visited Oct. 10, 2019).

71. *The Reality of U.S. Climate Action: Non-Federal Leadership Is Delivering Ambition and Action*, America's Pledge (Sept. 2019), https://www.bbhub.io/dotorg/sites/28/2019/09/The-Reality-of-U.S.-Climate-Action-Non-Federal-Leadership-is-Delivering-Ambition-and-Action.pdf.

72. *Paris Climate Agreement*, Climate Mayors, http://climatemayors.org/actions/paris-climate-agreement/ (last visited Aug. 14, 2020).

73. Kim Lyons et al., *A Revitalized Pittsburgh Says the President Used a Rusty Metaphor*, N.Y. Times, June 2, 2017, https://www.nytimes.com/2017/06/02/upshot/a-revitalized-pittsburgh-suggests-the-president-used-a-rusty-metaphor.html?_r=0.

74. *See* Erin Haines Whack & Dake Kang, *Pittsburgh to Trump: You Don't Speak for Us on Climate*, AP News (June 2, 2017), https://www.apnews.com/162d760229dd4b42a87a6b2759b07538.

75. Climate Action Plan 3.0, City of Pittsburgh (2018), https://apps.pittsburghpa.gov/redtail/images/7101_Pittsburgh_Climate_Action_Plan_3.0.pdf.

76. Anne Hidalgo & William Peduto, *The Mayors of Pittsburgh and Paris: We Have Our Own Climate Deal*, N.Y. Times, June 7, 2017, https://www.nytimes.com/2017/06/07/opinion/the-mayors-of-pittsburgh-and-paris-we-have-our-own-climate-deal.html.

In" Pledge. These mayors find themselves united by "a desire to do what is best for our citizens and our planet. That means putting aside parochial politics and embracing the global challenge of fighting climate change."

These mayors know what the IPCC learned: that the legal system we use to control development enables local governments to affect about 70% of the sources of CO_2 emissions or their means of capture.[77] This connection between land use law and carbon emissions is addressed in part IV, immediately below.

IV. Mitigating Climate Change: The Land Use Connection

Local land use law can permit McMansions: super-large homes that consume outsized quantities of fossil fuel for heating and cooling. The law that allows the resulting emissions can be changed. Larger houses can be required to be more fuel efficient and home sizes can be capped. In Marin County, California, for example, a land use regulation requires that the larger the house, the more energy efficient it must be.[78]

Local law can also encourage or require passive construction results in ultra-low energy consuming buildings that use little power for space heating or cooling. Passive homes are a relatively recent innovation that have evolved quickly. They include a 30-unit apartment building for senior citizens in Milton, Vermont, where the fuel bill for the entire complex is less than any one of the single-family homes that the seniors are selling so that they can move in.[79] What architects and engineers can do, the law can encourage or require. These modest examples focus on the critical fact that residential and commercial buildings contribute nearly 40% of national CO_2 emissions.[80]

Another approach to lowering energy consumption in houses is to make them smaller; smaller homes have less space to heat and cool which reduces their contribution to fossil fuel emissions. Decades ago, in Petaluma, California, where zoning initially favored single-family construction, the city rebalanced the future housing stock by adopting the "Petaluma Plan" to accommodate sudden growth pressures in the 1970s.[81] The plan—and the

---

77. *See supra* note 20. *See also infra* text accompanying notes 104, 129, and 140.
78. *See* County of Marin, Cal., Ordinance §19.04.140 (2019).
79. *See* Jeffrey Spivak, *Multiple Efficiencies for Multifamily*, Am. Plan. Ass'n Mag., Oct. 2017, http://eecoordinator.info/wp-content/uploads/2017/12/Planning-magazine-Passive-Housing.pdf.
80. *See* EPA Greenhouse Gas Inventory 2015, *supra* note 20. *See also infra* text accompanying note 104.
81. Construction Indus. Ass'n of Sonoma Cty. v. City of Petaluma, 522 F.2d 897, 900-01 (9th Cir. 1975).

zoning that implemented it—limited growth to 500 dwelling units per year.[82] Using an intricate point system, it rewarded builders who proposed projects that conformed to the plan and its environmental design standards. The land use regulations required that new housing produced be evenly divided between single-family and multi-family dwelling units, a consequence which caused less energy consumption and fewer emissions per capita.

The per capita result is critical. The population of the United States is growing, and that growth is significant. It matters where and how people live. In 2015, the average New York City dweller emitted 6.1 metric tons of CO_2 equivalent emissions annually.[83] Nationally, the per capita average emission metric is 19 tons.

Similarly, land use regulations can reduce VMT. The movement of personal vehicles through the built environment contributes more than 20% of CO_2 nationally.[84] Cars travel to convey their occupants from where they live to where they work, play, shop, and learn. The more distance between these destinations, the more miles travelled, and the more emissions generated. By creating mixed-use, higher density zones around transit stations, local governments can significantly lower CO_2 emissions. When density is increased for both residential and commercial uses, the distance between origin and destination is shorter, and walking, bicycling, and mass transit services are more feasible. Studies have shown that mixed-use zoning and increased population density decrease automobile ownership and the number of vehicle trips taken and VMT.[85]

Centering growth has a corollary benefit. It focuses needed development on urban places and moves it away from undeveloped open spaces. In those places, ecological services on which life and prosperity depend are preserved as a consequence. One of those services is the biological sequestration of CO_2.[86] Up to 18.2% of CO_2 emissions are sequestered by the natural environment.[87]

As sprawling development consumed increasing amounts of open lands during the last quarter of the 20th century and into the 21st, local land

82. *Id.* at 901.

83. Inventory Of New York City's Greenhouse Gas Emissions, City of New York 8 (2017), https://www.dec.ny.gov/docs/administration_pdf/nycghg.pdf.

84. *See* EPA Greenhouse Gas Inventory 2015, *supra* note 20, at ES-11.

85. *See* U.S. Dep't of Transp., Transportation's Role In Reducing U.S. Greenhouse Gas Emissions—Volume 1: Synthesis Report To Congress ES-7 (2010), http://www.reconnectingamerica.org/assets/Uploads/DOTClimateChangeReport-April2010-Volume1and2.pdf [hereinafter Transportation's Role].

86. *See infra* Part V.C.

87. *See* John R. Nolon, *Land Use for Energy Conservation and Sustainable Development: A New Path Toward Climate Mitigation*, 27 J. Land Use & Envtl. L. 296, 312 (2012) [hereinafter *A New Path*].

use law responded. Its toolbox is now full of sequestration-enhancing implements: clustering development; planned unit development ordinances; and neighborhood tree canopy enhancement standards, for example. Sustainable neighborhood design standards include green roofs, rain gardens, vegetated swales, xeriscaped lawns, biologically rich site design, and connected green landscapes. All of these land use laws protect and enhance the biologically sequestering environment and reduce the climate changing emissions from all sources.

The connections between land use law and emissions are demand-side strategies. They either reduce the demand for fossil fuels by lowering energy use in buildings and the emissions attributable to VMT, or they capture the resulting emissions through the natural environment. All told, these strategies address about 70% of the sources of CO_2 emissions or the means of capturing them.[88]

These strategies operate in a different policy sphere from more traditional GHG mitigation initiatives such as a carbon tax, cap-and-trade mechanisms, or clean power regulations affecting coal-fired generation. At the national level, these supply-centered strategies are mostly on hold for the duration of the current administration.[89] The opposite is true of strategies employing land use tools on the demand-side.[90] As demonstrated above, the Paris Agreement embraced these strategies as valued NDCs to climate change mitigation.[91]

The concept that municipal governments can physically shape their own development is not well understood. The uniform, single-use settlement pattern was originally created by zoning designed communities to accomplish discrete objectives such as protecting child health and safety, controlling traffic congestion, and providing housing and commercial space to meet market demands.[92] As time progressed, the environmental and economic harm caused by the resultant urban patterns led many local governments to reshape their settlements.

The 1972 Petaluma Plan discussed above rebalanced the future housing stock of the city through zoning reform that required an even mix of single-family and multi-family housing.[93] The local legislature changed its land use

88. *See supra* note 20. *See also infra* text accompanying notes 104, 129, and 140.
89. *See, e.g.*, Lisa Friedman & Brad Plumer, *EPA Announces Repeal of Major Obama-Era Carbon Emissions Rule*, N.Y. Times, Oct. 9, 2017, https://www.nytimes.com/2017/10/09/climate/clean-power-plan.html. *See also* John Schwartz, *Major Climate Change Rules the Trump Administration Is Reversing*, N.Y. Times, Aug. 29, 2019, https://www.nytimes.com/2019/08/29/climate-rule-trump-reversing.html.
90. *See infra* Part V.
91. *See supra* notes 55-60 and accompanying text.
92. *Zoning's Centennial*, *supra* note 11.
93. Construction Indus. Ass'n of Sonoma Cty. v. City of Petaluma, 522 F.2d 897, 901 (9th Cir. 1975).

law to achieve more environmentally friendly design, protect open space, create a greenbelt around the community, provide for a variety of housing choices, evenly distribute housing between the east and west sides of the city, and service growth efficiently.[94] Only in retrospect do we recognize these strategies as mitigation measures that reduce per capita energy consumption and protect the sequestering environment.

Petaluma's reforms were not novel, even in 1972. In 1937, for example, the local legislature in Bridgeport, Connecticut, amended its zoning ordinance to allow small commercial developments along major arterials in single-family neighborhoods in order to reduce downtown traffic congestion.[95] As the population increased in Bridgeport's single-family zones, more and more residents drove to the central business district to shop for goods and services. The commercial uses allowed in these new small districts included hardware, grocery, and drug stores, bake shops, and beauty parlors. Permitting these developments reduced downtown congestion, but also vehicle trips and VMT, one of the largest contributors to CO_2 emissions. This climate change mitigation effect was not on the minds of Bridgeport's legislators at the time, but the zoning technique they created can be used today to reduce carbon emissions from vehicle travel.

A decade after Bridgeport's innovation, the village of Tarrytown, New York, adopted a floating zone to provide affordable garden apartments to attract workers needed for employers whose businesses were essential to stabilizing the village's real property tax base.[96] The 1947 zoning ordinance created a floating garden apartment zone, but it did not specify where the dwelling units would be permitted. This was left to private-market developers who could petition the village legislature for a zoning map amendment, allowing them to build garden apartments. Significant landscaping was required to buffer the effect of multi-family housing in single-family neighborhoods where the new housing type was permitted.[97] By zoning for workforce housing close to jobs and requiring significant landscaping, the village created a mechanism that communities today can use to mitigate climate change.

In the 1980s, Omaha, Nebraska, reconfigured its urban form by adopting a planned unit development zoning ordinance.[98] This legislative reform permitted the developer to create a large, mixed-use neighborhood, while

94. *Id.* at 901-02.
95. Bartram v. Zoning Comm'n of City of Bridgeport, Conn., 68 A.2d 308, 310 (Conn. 1949).
96. Rodgers v. Village of Tarrytown, 96 N.E.2d 731, 732 (N.Y. 1951).
97. *Id.* at 732-33.
98. Giger v. City of Omaha, 232 Neb. 676, 679, 442 N.W.2d 182, 187 (1989).

preserving much of the rezoned acreage as open space.[99] The city entered into a multi-phase agreement with the developer that specified the many details of the development—techniques designed to allow the developer to meet new market needs for mixed-use development and protect the downstream riparian owners from flooding.[100] Indirectly, climate change was mitigated, and community resilience promoted the creation of a walkable neighborhood and the preservation of sequestering open space.

As discussed above, there are many who doubt that parochial local governments can respond in any significant way to the challenge of global climate change. There are, however, many local land use tools available to them that clearly reduce or sequester carbon emissions. The local climate change mitigation toolbox has been stocking up for decades. Techniques created for a different purpose are now being used by localities for a highly challenging purpose. As the first responders to climate-caused disasters and damage, local leaders are highly motivated to act. The wisdom of the IPCC in including shaping human settlements as a critical mitigation strategy in its Fifth Assessment Report and Special Report on Climate Change and Land is increasingly evident as local governments quicken the pace of adopting such tools to respond to the perturbations of climate change.[101]

V. Implementation: The Land Use Stabilization Wedge

In 2004, Princeton Profs. Stephen Pacala and Robert Socolow provided a framework for mitigating climate change through "stabilization wedges," each capable of preventing at least a billion metric tons of carbon emissions annually using existing technology.[102] This part presents a variation—the land use stabilization wedge.[103] Whether, in the aggregate, the existing land use techniques described below will prevent a billion or more metric tons of emissions each year depends on how many, and to what extent, local governments embrace them. This, in turn, may depend on how well their role in climate change mitigation is understood and supported by state and federal governments.

---

99. *Id.*, 442 N.W.3d at 187-88.
100. *Id.* at 698-99, 442 N.W.3d at 198.
101. Seto & Dhakal, *supra* note 3, at 930; Climate Change and Land, *supra* note 5.
102. Stephan Pacala & Robert Socolow, *Stabilization Wedges: Solving the Climate Problem for the Next 50 Years With Current Technologies*, 305 Science 968, 970 (2004), http://science.sciencemag.org/content/305/5686/968.
103. *See* John R. Nolon, *The Land Use Stabilization Wedge Strategy: Shifting Ground to Mitigate Climate Change*, 34 Wm. & Mary Envtl. L. & Pol'y Rev. 1 (2009) [hereinafter *Land Use Wedge Strategy*].

A. *Buildings Contribute 35% of CO_2 Emissions in the United States*

The first component of the land use stabilization wedge is buildings. The most recent U.S. Environmental Protection Agency (EPA) Greenhouse Gas Inventory estimates that residential and commercial buildings emit 35% of domestic CO_2 emissions.[104] The increased demand for new residential and commercial space is related directly to the consumption of fossil fuel and CO_2 emissions.[105] As a result, the legal authority to regulate building location and construction so as to reduce these emissions can be a critical component of climate change mitigation policy.

According to the U.S. Census Bureau, the U.S. population will increase by over 90 million people during the next 40 years.[106] Using today's domestic household size, there will be around 35 million new households.[107] This increase in population will expand market demand for new residential and commercial buildings and the rehabilitation or replacement of millions of structures that will age-out during the next four decades.[108]

The land use standards that dictate energy efficiency in new and substantially rehabilitated buildings are created by state and local governments.[109] The size and shape of buildings and their interior spaces, their thermal efficiency, and whether they are served by efficient energy sources are dictated and influenced by zoning and other local land use regulations.

Regarding building construction, state legislatures adopt energy conservation codes for buildings, which in many states are then adopted, enforced,

---

104. *See* EPA Greenhouse Gas Inventory 2015, *supra* note 20 (Total U.S. CO_2 emissions are 5,411.4 million metric tons of CO_2 equivalents (MMT CO_2 Eq.). After distributing electricity-related CO_2 emissions, the commercial and residential sectors make up 1,913.3 MMT CO_2 Eq. or 35% of total U.S. emissions.).
105. *See supra* Part IV.
106. Sandra L. Colby & Jennifer M. Ortman, Projections of the Size and Composition of the U.S. Population: 2014 to 2060, at 1 (2015), https://census.gov/content/dam/Census/library/publications/2015/demo/p25-1143.pdf ("Between 2014 and 2060, the U.S. population is projected to increase from 319 million to 417 million, reaching 400 million in 2051.").
107. U.S. Census Bureau, Households and Families: 2010, at 1 (Apr. 2012), https://www.census.gov/prod/cen2010/briefs/c2010br-14.pdf ("Of the total population in 2010, 300.8 million lived in 116.7 million households for an average of 2.58 people per household." Ninety-eight million additional people divided by 2.58 = 37.9 million additional households.).
108. *See A Look at the U.S. Commercial Building Stock: Results From EIA's 2012 Commercial Buildings Energy Consumption*, U.S. Energy Info. Admin. (Mar. 4, 2015), https://www.eia.gov/consumption/commercial/reports/2012/buildstock/ ("the commercial building stock is still fairly old, with about half of all buildings constructed before 1980; the median age of buildings in 2012 was 32 years"); Josh Miller, *The Aging Housing Stock*, Eye on Housing (Jan. 20, 2014), http://eyeonhousing.org/2014/01/the-aging-housing-stock/ ("41% of the owner occupied housing stock in the U.S. was built prior to 1969").
109. *See supra* text accompanying notes 88-102.

and enhanced by municipal governments.[110] Locally enforced energy codes ensure that all new and substantially rehabilitated buildings are constructed with energy conservation in mind. The International Codes Council (ICC) gradually strengthens these energy conserving code requirements and reissues new recommended standards every several years.[111] Most states have adopted the ICC's International Energy Conservation Code (IECC) as a baseline to conserve energy in new and substantially rehabilitated buildings.[112] State law in some states allows local governments to adopt enhancements to the state energy code that achieve even greater conservation. In New York, the state developed the NY Stretch Code—Energy 2020, suitable for adoption by local governments.[113] Once adopted by a local government, developers will be required to build residential structures to standards that are roughly 20% more efficient than the base energy code currently in effect. Commercial building will be roughly 7% more efficient.[114]

The novel idea of requiring large, energy-consumptive houses to be more energy efficient was demonstrated above by its incorporation into local law in Marin County, California.[115] The county requires large homes less than 4,000 square feet to either exceed energy conservation code requirements by 15%, by 20% if equipped with a photovoltaic system, or simply be all electric.[116] If the home is more than 4,000 square feet (sq. ft.), the standard is higher. If the energy sources are mixed, the home must exceed the state code in efficiency by 35% and generate as much energy as it is expected to use. If a home above 4,000 sq. ft. is all electric, it must exceed the state code by 20%. Alternatively, homeowners can opt to be compliant with Passive House Institute US (PHIUS) Standards. PHIUS provides guides for homeowners and developers to significantly decrease energy consumption and costs.[117]

Similarly, the town of Greenburgh, New York, amended its local code to require that "all new one- or two-family dwelling or multiple single-family

110. *See, e.g.*, *NYStretch Code-Energy 2020*, N.Y. State Energy Res. & Dev. Auth., https://www.nyserda.ny.gov/All-Programs/Programs/Energy-Code-Training/NYStretch-Energy-Code-2020.

111. *See* Jessica A. Bacher & Jennie C. Nolon, *Zoning and Land Use Planning: Energy Codes, Green Building Initiatives, and Beyond*, 38 Real Est. L.J. 231, 234 (2009).

112. *See, e.g.*, 2018 International Energy Conservation Code, ICC (Aug. 31, 2017), https://codes.iccsafe.org/public/document/iecc2018.

113. *NYStretch Code-Energy 2020*, *supra* note 110.

114. *Energy Codes: Training, Support Services, and Stretch Codes*, N.Y. State Energy Res. & Dev. Auth., https://www.nyserda.ny.gov/All%20Programs/Programs/Energy%20Code%20Training#:~:text=NY%2DStretch%20Energy%20Code%E2%80%932020,commercial%20provisions%20of%20ASHRAE%2090.1%2D (last visited Aug. 20, 2020).

115. *See* County of Marin, Cal., Ordinance §19.04.140 (2019).

116. *Id.* §19.04.100(E).

117. About PHIUS, Passive House Alliance, https://www.phius.org/about/mission-history (last visited Aug. 14, 2020).

dwelling (townhouse) of three stories or less . . . [b]e built to achieve a HERS [Home Energy Rating System] Index of 70 or less on the Residential Services Network (RESNET) Home Energy Rating System (HERS) . . . ."[118]

Also in New York, the town of Blooming Grove offers homebuilders a density bonus under its zoning code to encourage them to adopt Energy Star.[119] Energy Star is a voluntary set of standards, one of many that local governments may reference in their zoning and energy code requirements.[120] It governs appliances, heating and cooling systems, the thermal envelope, electrical, ventilation, and equipment efficiency. The town awards a 10% increase in the number of homes that can be constructed under local zoning in exchange for making them all Energy Star-compliant.[121]

Local land use boards can require developers and their design consultants to follow an integrated design process, where they collaborate during the early stages of the project review process to achieve the greatest possible energy conservation and cost reduction. It is at this stage that decisions can be made about building orientation, form, shading, energy-efficient exterior lighting, window size and location, rooflines and extensions, reflective roofing, height-to-floor ratios, and building features that relate to passive ventilation and cooling.

Using similar powers and administrative techniques, localities can promote the construction of passive homes, both single- and multi-family. Instead of mechanized systems providing heating or cooling, passive buildings rely on the construction materials and techniques to use significantly less energy.[122] Buildings in the United States which implement the latest passive house standards will only use 10 to 25% of the energy of similar-size, conventionally constructed residential structures.[123] Techniques used include thick insulation, exterior air sealing, fluid-applied silicone air barriers over plywood sheathing, triple-paned windows, and high-efficiency heat-recovery ventilators.

In Milton, Vermont, a nonprofit developer created multi-family senior apartments using passive building techniques.[124] The heating bill for these 30 senior households is expected to be 80% less than the cost of energy required by similar-size buildings, and even less than what the owners of many single-family homes in the community pay for heat. This technique holds great

118. *See* Town of Greenburgh, N.Y., Code §100-20 (2011).
119. *See* Blooming Grove, N.Y., Town Code §235-14.1(A)(3) (2011).
120. Bacher & Nolon, *supra* note 111, at 234.
121. Blooming Grove, N.Y., Town Code §235-14.1(A)(3).
122. Spivak, *supra* note 79, at 38.
123. *Id.* at 40.
124. *Id.* at 38.

promise as passive houses are continuing to draw support from around the country with certified Passive House construction doubling almost every year.[125]

B. *Transportation—Personal Vehicles Contribute 19% of CO_2 Emissions*

The second component of the land use stabilization wedge focuses on transportation, which is the largest source of CO_2 emissions from fossil fuel combustion in the United States.[126] In 2016, Americans drove more than 3.2 trillion miles,[127] 89.8% of which is attributable to light-duty motor vehicles, i.e., passenger vehicles and light-duty trucks such as minivans and sports utility vehicles.[128] Light-duty motor vehicles account for 59.4% of total transportation CO_2 emissions, which contributes 19.1% of national CO_2 emissions.[129]

The Fifth Assessment Report of the IPCC, Chapter Twelve, targets the shaping of human settlements as a key to climate change mitigation.[130] It focuses on "the patterns and spatial arrangement of land use, transportation systems, and urban design elements, including the physical urban extent, layout of streets and buildings, as well as the internal configuration of settlements."[131] Chapter Twelve also notes that "areas with a high mix of land uses encourage a mix of residential and retail activity and thus increase the area's vitality and the aesthetic interest of the neighbourhood."[132] Land use regulations can ensure attractive buildings, personal neighborhood scales, and amenable green infrastructure.

---

125. *Id.* at 38-39.
126. *See* EPA Greenhouse Gas Inventory 2015, *supra* note 20, at ES-11, fig. ES-7 (After distributing electricity-related emissions, transportation CO_2 emissions account for 34.5% of U.S. CO_2 emissions from burning fossil fuels).
127. *See* U.S. Dep't Transp., Traffic Volume Trends 2, Fed. Highway Admin. (2016), https://www.fhwa.dot.gov/policyinformation/travel_monitoring/16dectvt/16dectvt.pdf.
128. Table VM-1 FHWA Highway Statistics (FHWA 1996 through 2016), Fed. Highway Admin. (May 2018), https://www.fhwa.dot.gov/policyinformation/statistics/2016/vm1.cfm.
129. *See* EPA Greenhouse Gas Inventory 2015, *supra* note 20, at ES-11 (After distributing electricity-related emissions, the transportation sector contributes 1,740.1 MMT CO_2 Eq. or 32% of total U.S. CO_2 emissions. The largest sources of transportation emissions are passenger cars (42.3%); medium- and heavy-duty trucks (23.6%); and light-duty trucks, which include sport utility vehicles, pickup trucks, and minivans (17.1%). This article focuses on light-duty motor vehicles, i.e. passenger cars and light-duty trucks, which account for 1,3033.62 MMT CO_2 Eq. or 59.4% of U.S. transportation emissions and 19.1% of total U.S. emissions.).
130. Seto & Dhakal, *supra* note 3, at 930.
131. *Id.* at 942.
132. *Id.* at 956.

Like Chapter Twelve of the IPCC Fifth Assessment, a 2010 U.S. Department of Transportation report finds that GHG emissions can be decreased by using transportation strategies.[133] It calculates that these strategies, including land use law reform, could decrease GHG emissions from transportation by 6% to 21% by 2050.[134] Similarly, an Obama Administration report in 2016 identified a "pathway" to reduce GHG emissions involving smart growth patterns of development such as walkable, livable, mixed-use development.[135]

These fine points are critical. Promoting compact, mixed-use development by itself may not reduce driving much, particularly if walking and biking options are not part of the neighborhood design. There is a current debate raging in the urban planning literature on this point,[136] with recent statistical analyses suggesting less correlation between compact, mixed-use development and driving than previously posited.[137] On-the-ground experience and common sense, however, make it clear that this type of development, enhanced by livable design, conveniently located shops and amenities, safe passage, and supportive infrastructure, lures many drivers from their cars and lowers trips and miles traveled significantly.[138] Little can be done to reduce emissions from personal travel without this type of neighborhood development. What can be done to reduce emissions in compact, mixed-use neighborhoods is to provide a variety of mobility options including projects that enhance walking and biking, provide for safe and attractive pedestrian experiences, and create a human-scale sense of place.

The successful development of transit stations and rail and bus lines is dependent upon land use densities and mixed-use development. There must be a large enough number of commuters in a transit station area to provide a base level of ridership. In addition, ridership must be sufficiently diverse to ensure that people are traveling to work, to shop, to seek entertainment, and to go home at various times during the day, thereby increasing the cost efficiency of the transit system.

Even where communities are not served by transit systems, local leaders can create compact, mixed-use neighborhoods that reduce car trips and miles traveled. Zoning controls can limit the size of housing units and combine

133. Transportation's Role, *supra* note 85, at ES-7.

134. *Id.* at ES-6.

135. *See* The White House, United States Mid-Century Strategy for Deep Decarbonization 33, 56-57 (2016), https://obamawhitehouse.archives.gov/sites/default/files/docs/mid_century_strategy_report-final.pdf.

136. *News Release: Study Sparks Debate Over Relationship Between Compact Development and Driving*, Am. Plan. Ass'n (Feb. 27, 2017), https://www.planning.org/blog/blogpost/9120808/.

137. *See* Mark R. Stevens, *Does Compact Development Make People Drive Less?*, 83 J. Am. Plan. 7 (2017).

138. *See* Reid Ewing & Robert Cervero, *"Does Compact Development Make People Drive Less?" The Answer Is Yes*, 83 J. Am. Plan. 19, 23 (2017).

retail, office, and residential land uses, putting services, shops, and jobs in closer proximity to homes. Communities not yet served by transit can designate one or more priority growth districts and create overlay zones for them that allow greater densities and more land uses than permitted in the underlying zoning districts. By clustering development strategically, these growing localities position themselves for future service by commuter rail or bus rapid transit, thereby becoming "transit ready."

Suburban areas that adopt higher density, mixed-use zoning will find it easier politically to adopt strong environmental protection ordinances applicable to the land outside high-density zones. Where state law permits, density bonuses may be provided in denser suburban zones and cash contributions made by developers in exchange. This money can be used to purchase development rights from landowners in sensitive environmental areas outside the higher density zone, areas that mitigate climate change through biological sequestration. This balance between development and conservation can be accomplished within transit-served urban areas as well— highlighting again zoning's ability to create sustainable settlement patterns and to mitigate climate change.

C. *Sequestration—Captures 18% of Domestic CO_2 Emissions*

The green edge of the land use stabilization wedge is the biological sequestration of CO_2. It occurs within the natural environment: resources such as forests, pastures, meadows, croplands, urban trees, and green infrastructure.[139] These landscapes naturally absorb and store approximately 18.2% of domestic CO_2 emissions.[140] Perpetuating and expanding the sequestering environment is fundamentally a land use issue, one that is well within the capacity of land use law to address.

The discussion above on transportation described how shaping human settlements to promote walkable, livable communities directly mitigates climate change by reducing VMT and energy consumed in buildings. Compact, mixed-use and sustainable neighborhood development promoted by land use regulations are, therefore, essential strategies for lowering emissions. Fortunately, they also promote biological sequestration. Such development attracts population growth to urban places by creating healthy neighborhoods for living, working, and recreating, which preserves existing open space in outlying areas. One estimate calculates that doubling urban density

139. *See* EPA Greenhouse Gas Inventory 2015, *supra* note 20, at ES-8.
140. *See* EPA Greenhouse Gas Inventory 2012, *supra* note 20, at ES-20.

alone would accommodate the entire projected population increase by mid-century, thereby saving an area the size of Connecticut[141]—and all of its sequestering resources—from development.[142]

Strategies that create green infrastructure in developing and developed places, while adding marginally to sequestration, are necessary if urban communities are to attract additional residents and workers. They are essential adaptive techniques as well. In developed cities, for example, tree canopies can be increased; green infrastructure added; urban gardens promoted; and buildings oriented to cool living environments, lessen the heat island effect, make cities attractive places to live, and soften the effects of higher densities.

If urban places do not accommodate population growth, outlying lands become targets for residential and commercial development. In these places, land use law can be particularly effective in designating and protecting lands that sequester carbon.[143] As suburban subdivisions are developed, they can be better situated in the existing vegetated landscape through thoughtful land use regulations. Furthermore, local governments can shape suburban and ex-urban land development to reduce land coverage and impervious surfaces, limit flooding, retain and add vegetation, protect community character, and prevent ground and surface water pollution. Together, such strategies limit development densities and tend to push population growth back toward developed centers and corridors.

Municipal governments in suburban and exurban areas have a long history of concern for the loss of open space and ecosystem services to encroaching development.[144] Decades-old local open space preservation laws and programs yield a number of strategies that can now be employed as sequestration techniques. These include standards regarding environmentally sensitive area designation, erosion and sedimentation control, grading, filling, drainage, soil disturbance, removal of vegetation, floodplains control, natural resource management, watershed, groundwater, watercourse, and wetland protection, landscaping requirements, ridgeline, steep slope, scenic resources, shoreline

141. *Connecticut Population, Land Area, and Density by Location*, Conn. Dep't Econ. & Community Dev., http://www.ct.gov/ecd/cwp/view.asp?A=1106&Q=250664 (last visited Aug. 14, 2020) (The area of Connecticut is 4845.4 square miles.).

142. *Land Use Wedge Strategy*, *supra* note 103, at 14:

> At a density of 15, rather than 7.5 dwelling units per acre, 40 million new households will consume half as much land. At 7.5 units per acre, these households will occupy nearly 5.5 million acres for housing alone. Doubling the net density per acre reduces that figure to roughly 2.5 million acres, a savings of nearly three million acres, just under 5,000 square miles: an area about the size of the state of Connecticut.

143. *See* Bronson W. Griscom et al., *Natural Climate Solutions*, 114 PNAS 11645 (2017).

144. For more information documenting the statements in this paragraph, see John R. Nolon, *Managing Climate Change Through Biological Sequestration: Open Space Law Redux*, 31 Stan. Envtl. L.J. 195 (2012) [hereinafter *Open Space Law Redux*].

regulation, stormwater management, timber harvesting regulations, tree protection and canopy expansion, and the transfer of development rights from lands to be preserved to developable areas.

Most local environmental laws and natural resource protections of this type are enacted because of perturbations at the community level: the loss of a cherished viewshed, the gradual decline of visible open space, surface water or groundwater contamination, increased flooding, or the disappearance of treasured wildlife, among others. These disturbing influences motivate local stakeholders and their elected officials to act to address their causes. As a result, local governments are becoming increasingly reliable partners in the global effort to manage climate change.

This comes at a critical time. Local legal strategies that preserve and enhance the sequestering environment now have a place on the global stage due to the advent of NDCs in the Paris Agreement.[145] NDCs include contributions to climate change mitigation adopted by local governments that can be counted toward participating countries' efforts to achieve international climate mitigation goals.[146] Enhancing biological sequestration using local land use authority is such a contribution.

D. *Distributed Energy—Lost in Transmission*

When President Trump announced his decision to withdraw the United States from the Paris Agreement, he quipped that he was elected to represent the residents of Pittsburgh, not Paris.[147] His clever alliteration was hugely ironic.[148] Pittsburgh has long been a leader in mitigating climate change, using its local land use power and democratic processes to reduce energy consumption and fossil fuel emissions. The city's zoning code, in fact, aggressively facilitates one of the most promising mitigation measures, that of promoting distributed, or on-site, power generation.[149]

The most recent EPA Greenhouse Gas Inventory estimates that residential and commercial buildings emit 35% of domestic CO_2 emissions.[150] Shockingly, two-thirds of the fuel used to generate electrical power in the United States is lost as escaped heat at the point of generation and in transmission.[151]

145. *See Paris Agreement*, *supra* note 72.
146. *See supra* Part III.
147. *See* Shear, *supra* note 63.
148. *See* Lyons, *supra* note 73.
149. *See A New Path*, *supra* note 87.
150. *See* EPA Greenhouse Gas Inventory 2015, *supra* note 20, at ES-10, fig. ES-7.
151. E-mail from Tom Bourgeois, Deputy Director, Pace Energy and Climate Center, to John R. Nolon, Distinguished Professor of Law, Elisabeth Haub School of Law (Sept. 24, 2012, 12:31 pm) (on file with author).

Many of our electrical generation plants are located at sites far removed from where the power is needed: where people live and work and industry operates. Much of the energy lost to generate electricity for the conventional power grid can be saved by on-site or distributed energy generation.

Pittsburgh, apparently unbeknownst to President Trump, is a model smart city. In response to the U.S. Department of Transportation's Smart City challenge in 2015,[152] the city developed a plan to create innovative, interconnected infrastructure that responds efficiently and affordably to the transportation and energy needs of local residents.[153] The city called it SmartPGH: a plan to integrate multiple interconnected systems, including a network of micro-grids that generate electricity on-site, greatly reducing the energy lost in remote generation and transmission.

The U.S. Department of Energy's research and development program defines a micro-grid as "a group of interconnected loads and distributed energy resources within clearly defined electrical boundaries that act as a single controllable entity with respect to the grid. A micro-grid can connect and disconnect from the grid to enable it to operate in both grid-connected or island-mode."[154] Micro-grids can capture the heat used to generate power by converting it to the energy needed to cool and heat connected buildings. This is called combined heat and power (CHP).[155]

Micro-grids usually operate at the scale of multiple buildings, a city block, or a larger neighborhood and are, therefore, ideally subject to local planning and regulation.[156] They can be prevented or furthered by land use standards. At the local level, on-site generation and CHP facilities cannot be developed if not permitted by local zoning. Pittsburgh used its delegated power to adopt zoning and land use regulations to enable micro-grids to develop.[157] The City Council amended its municipal code to add a Performance Point System that

---

152. *Smart City Challenge*, U.S. Dep't of Transp., https://www.transportation.gov/smartcity (last updated June 29, 2017).

153. City of Pitt., Once More Into the Future Dear Friends, https://www.transportation.gov/sites/dot.gov/files/docs/Pittsburgh-SCC-Technical-Application.pdf (last visited Aug. 14, 2020).

154. U.S. Dep't of Energy, Summary Report: 2012 DOE Micro-Grid Workshop 1 (June 30, 2012) https://www.energy.gov/sites/prod/files/2012%20Microgrid%20Workshop%20Report%2009102012.pdf.

155. *See A New Path*, *supra* note 87, at 312.

156. *See* U.S. Dep't Of Energy, *supra* note 154.

157. *See* City of Pitt., P.A., Zoning Code art. VI, ch. 915, §915.07.B, https://library.municode.com/pa/pittsburgh/codes/code_of_ordinances?nodeId=PIZOCO_TITNINEZOCO_ARTVIDEST_CH915ENPEST_915.07PEPOSY. (This is a link to the Performance Point System within the Environmental Performance Standards, which are part of the Pittsburgh Zoning code. This point system incentivizes desired sustainable actions by rewarding developers with bonuses depending on how many points they accumulate by implementing the sustainable standards. Performance-based metrics are used to reward developers who do sustainable development, e.g. micro-grids.)

incentivizes sustainable development. It awards developers density bonuses for points that they accumulate by developing sustainably, including the development of distributed energy systems such as micro-grids.

For zoning to permit or promote a land use, it must define that use and specify where it may be located and how it is to be regulated or facilitated. In one of the first such definitions of its kind, the Pittsburgh Zoning Code says: "Distributed Energy Systems shall mean a range of smaller-scale technologies designed to provide electricity and thermal energy closer to consumers. These approaches include fossil and renewable energy technologies, micro-grids, on-site energy storage, and combined heat and power systems."[158]

Pittsburgh enacted into law what the United States Green Building Council encourages developers to do to qualify for certification under its Leadership in Energy and Environmental Design (LEED) for Neighborhood Development (LEED-ND) rating program.[159] The council notes that zoning can allow for district heating and cooling facilities, as well as solar and wind systems, to be installed in certain buildings or their sites; land use review protocols can be used to encourage owners to provide them, and density bonuses can be granted to provide a financial incentive for them.

As demonstrated here, many energy technologies and facilities cannot be built if they are not permitted at the local level by zoning. Localities, like Pittsburgh, have the ability to incentivize energy conserving development through density bonuses and partnerships involving funds from local capital budgets. Innovations in energy technology can be furthered and assimilated by an informed public that understands the seriousness of current problems and the feasibility of new solutions. Since zoning must conform to a comprehensive land use plan developed with robust citizen participation, land use planning provides a valuable opportunity to engage and inform the public.

E. *Renewable Energy—Community Power*

Community power is an emerging tool for implementing renewable energy technology. It is also a metaphor for the power of local governments to further or frustrate that resource. Historically, land use regulations were more of a hindrance than a help to the adoption of renewable energy facilities. In some communities, the soft costs of renewable energy facilities, including the expense of securing local approval for wind and solar energy systems,

158. *See id.* §915.07.C(7).
159. *Open Space Law Redux*, *supra* note 144, at 226-30.

remained high while the cost of the systems declined. In others, these facilities were simply zoned out. This is changing and the pace of change is rapid.

The Pittsburgh Zoning Code defines distributed energy systems to include "a range of smaller-scale technologies designed to provide electricity and thermal energy closer to consumers," including renewable energy facilities.[160] The source of power for micro-grids, which is incentivized by this zoning law, can be small-scale renewable energy systems, such as community solar systems and small- to mid-size individual or clustered wind turbines or on-site solar panels.

Communities, like Pittsburgh, using their land use power, are mitigating climate change by defining types of emerging sources of renewable power and permitting those sources in zoning districts, requiring property owners to accommodate these sources or creatively incentivizing them in a variety of ways. The facilities supported by local land use laws can be called community power systems. These systems are studied as part of land use planning, being called for in comprehensive plans, defined by zoning codes, and permitted in certain districts, either as-of-right, as accessory or secondary uses, or as special permitted uses. Larger, higher intensity systems can be permitted by zoning but are often subject to protective standards.

A few state legislatures have preempted local authority to regulate renewable energy systems, particularly large-scale projects that are subject to state agency regulation and licensing.[161] But most mid-size and smaller systems remain subject to local regulation under the plenary authority delegated to local government to control private development.[162] This is understandable; the risks and impacts of energy systems are experienced firsthand locally by the residents of these communities.

When, for example, wind power companies first approach a community with a proposal to develop towers over 200 feet high, with blades nearly as long as a football field, neighbors naturally oppose them until their risks are understood and mitigated by regulation.[163] Less dramatically, a proposal to cluster a few smaller towers to serve on-site needs or even a single wind turbine on a residential roof will meet opposition initially. Residents, par-

160. *See* City of Pitt., P.A., Zoning Code art. VI, ch. 915, §915.07.C(7).

161. *See, e.g.*, John R. Nolon & Jessica A. Bacher, *Wind Power: An Exploration of Regulations and Litigation*, N.Y. L.J., Feb. 20, 2008, https://digitalcommons.pace.edu/lawfaculty/667/; John R. Nolon, *Mitigating Climate Change by Zoning for Solar Energy Systems: Embracing Clean Energy Technology in Zoning's Centennial Year*, Zoning & Plan. L. Rep., Dec. 2015, at 5 n.17, https://digitalcommons.pace.edu/lawfaculty/997/ [hereinafter *Embracing Clean Energy Technology*].

162. *Embracing Clean Energy Technology*, *supra* note 161, at 4.

163. For more information documenting the statements in this paragraph, see Nolon & Bacher, *supra* note 161.

ticularly adjacent neighbors, are concerned about the noise, visual interruption, ice throws, the strobe effect, change of neighborhood character, and the consequent diminution of their property values.[164] Since land use laws are based on intense democratic participation by the public, these risks have to be examined and, where they are well founded, reduced or eliminated.

Local governments typically begin the process of regulating wind power by doing studies of wind generation systems, exploring both the risks and benefits, and memorializing their findings in a comprehensive land use plan amendment or adopting a land use policy.[165] They then define various types and sizes of wind energy systems and prohibit them in inappropriate locations and permit them in others, with needed safeguards. These laws create spacing and set back requirements, limit or buffer noises, require aesthetic controls, and impose regulations on noise levels, viewshed interruptions, heights, location, size, lighting, color, or design. Some laws require local licenses and even provide for decommissioning.

Zoning for solar energy facilities proceeds in the same way. When the Land Use Law Center was retained to help draft a model solar energy law for communities in New York, we started by working with industry representatives to understand the various types, shapes, intensities, and other characteristics of these facilities. We realized that building integrated solar systems are part of the structure itself and should be exempted from land use regulation. Small-scale roof-top and ground-mounted systems should be permitted as-of-right or as accessory uses, and larger scale systems were subject to special permits and site plan regulations.[166]

New York encourages local governments to expedite small-scale solar systems through its Unified Solar Permit (USP).[167] It applies to solar systems with a capacity of 12 kilowatts or less that are not subject to architectural or historical review board approval, do not require a zoning variance or a special use permit, and that are roof-mounted, compliant with building and related codes, and meet mounting and weight distribution requirements.

Without assured access to the rays of the sun, property owners may be discouraged from installing solar panels because the cost of the systems may not be recouped over time if sunlight is diminished by development on adjacent parcels. In most states, solar easements or nuisance actions for blocking the

---

164. *See, e.g.*, Burch v. Nedpower Mount Storm, Ltd. Liab. Co., 220 W. Va. 443, 449 (W. Va. 2007).
165. *See* Nolon & Bacher, *supra* note 161.
166. *See Open Space Law Redux*, *supra* note 144 (for solar power regulation).
167. *See Unified Solar Permit*, N.Y. State Energy Res. & Dev. Authority, https://www.nyserda.ny.gov/All-Programs/Programs/Clean-Energy-Communities/Clean-Energy-Communities-Program-High-Impact-Action-Toolkits/Unified-Solar-Permit (last visited Aug. 14, 2020)

sun's energy are not recognized by common law.[168] Nevertheless, they can be created by local government regulation. Typically, these regulations require written and recorded solar easements that define easement dimensions, how the easement will terminate, and compensation for easement maintenance or interference, among other provisions.[169] This is an especially viable technique when applied through subdivision regulations to new developments.

Some localities are requiring developers to install solar energy systems or, short of that, to make buildings solar ready.[170] Other communities incentivize, rather than require, these solar facilities, typically by providing density bonuses for solar panels, solar readiness, and solar access easements.[171]

VI. Resilience and Other Corollary Benefits of Localism

One of the first transit-oriented development projects that we worked on, after creating the Land Use Law Center, was the Hudson Park development in the city of Yonkers, New York. This was in the late 1990s when our focus was on sustainable development. That project eventually became a model of climate change mitigation featuring energy efficiency and reduced use of automobiles, greatly lowering per household fossil fuel consumption and CO_2 emissions of building residents.[172]

As a sustainable development, however, Hudson Park did much more than mitigate climate change. It was built at a density of 130 units per acre, adjacent to an express stop on the commuter railroad. Compared to sprawling subdivision developments, Hudson Park reduced average per household impervious coverage by 96%, lowered per capita water use by 60%, and avoided disrupting wetland and watercourse environments needed for adaptation to climate change and sequestration.[173] At 90% lot coverage, Hudson Park paved 36,000 sq. ft. per acre. At 130 dwelling units per acre, that amounts to 275 sq. ft. coverage per household. The average suburban single-family home on a half-acre, in contrast, creates 8,000 sq. ft. of impervious coverage per household. On a per household basis, Hudson Park greatly reduced flooding and storm water damage, reduced nonpoint source pollution of surface water, conserved potable water, and preserved natural resources and their ecological

168. *Embracing Clean Energy Technology*, *supra* note 161, at 24.
169. *Id.* at 25.
170. *Id.* at 27-28.
171. *Id.* at 29.
172. More information on Hudson Park is available in a case study prepared for the Urban Land Institute, Westchester/Fairfield Chapter in 2018. The report is on file with the author.
173. All calculations in this paragraph are the author's.

functions.[174] Its effect was to make development resilient, adapting to climate change, as much as it was to mitigate climate change.

The corollary benefits of compact, mixed-use developments like Hudson Park are many and impressive. In addition to mitigating climate change, as this chapter demonstrates, they also enable local governments to adapt to climate change. For instance, they avoid the use of prime agricultural soils, wetlands and species habitat: natural resources that create resilient open spaces.[175] Such developments reduce surface water pollution, because they create much less impervious coverage per household for buildings, paving, roads, and parking structures.[176] By leaving natural landscapes in place, they also allow nature to retain the capacity to filter precipitation, absorb and retain stormwater, and reduce the speed and devastation of flooding.[177]

Sustainable development projects, by reducing VMT per capita, also protect water quality by lowering tailpipe emissions and the hard metals and other toxic substances that drop off the undercarriage of vehicles onto impervious surfaces, such as driveways and parking lots, where they are washed into nearby rivers, streams, and other surface waters.[178]

To match the increasing focus of climate change adaptation to protect public health, sustainable development projects and sustainable neighborhoods can incorporate various strategies. For example, plans can maximize green infrastructure, promote walking and bicycling, provide active recreation areas, zone in public health services, and provide incentives to merchants to provide healthy foods.[179]

---

174. *Supra* note 172 and accompanying text.

175. *Open Space Law Redux*, *supra* note 144, at 327. Following the trend of making green buildings more sustainable, the U.S. Green Building Council's LEED system for rating and certifying projects, initially focused on building resource efficiency, has been supplemented with the LEED-ND system, which considers ranking factors such as the location of a project in a region to avoid building on wetlands, watercourses, and on prime agricultural land.

176. *See* Melissa G. Kramer, U.S. EPA, Our Built and Natural Environments: A Technical Review of the Interactions Among Land Use, Transportation, and Environmental Quality 94 (2d ed. 2013), https://www.epa.gov/sites/production/files/2014-03/documents/our-built-and-natural-environments.pdf.

177. *See* Christina M. Lyerly et al., New Insights: Science-Based Evidence of Water Quality Improvements, Challenges, and Opportunities in the Chesapeake 35 (2014), http://ian.umces.edu/pdfs/ian_report_438.pdf.

178. U.S. EPA, Protecting Water Resources With Smart Growth 30-31 (2004), https://www.epa.gov/sites/production/files/2014-04/documents/protecting-water-resources.pdf.

179. *See* Jennie Nolon Blanchard, *Legal Lessons: Zoning to Fight Obesity*, Am. Plan. Ass'n Mag., April 2018, https://www.planning.org/planning/2018/apr/legallessons/.

VII. Conclusion

Working at the local level on developments that mitigate climate change leverages additional environmental benefits, including many that are effective strategies for creating resilient developments and neighborhoods. These local initiatives help their communities adapt to climate change. In sum, they enable local governments to adopt and implement development plans that draw from the full spectrum of climate change management.[180]

Basing climate change management strategies on a sound local footing takes advantage of local government's significant legal authority and the powerful and demonstrated commitment of local citizens to solve on-the-ground environmental problems. A key lesson learned from observing change taking place locally is that state and federal governments must recalibrate their policies and programs to take full advantage of the partnership that grass-roots governments offer. Most transformative change in our country has started locally and then built into significant national movements.[181] So it should be with the growing imperative to manage climate change effectively.

---

180. *See* Fatima Denton et al., *Climate-Resilient Pathways: Adaptation, Mitigation, and Sustainable Development, in* Climate Change 2014: Impacts, Adaptation, and Vulnerability 1117 (C.B. Field et al. eds. 2014) ("Because both adaptation and mitigation are parts of climate-resilient pathways, and because each benefits from progress with the other . . . integrating the two kinds of climate change responses within the broader context of sustainable development has been suggested as an aspirational goal.").

181. *See* James Fallows, *The Reinvention of America*, Atlantic , May 2018:

> The more we traveled, the more parallels and resonances we saw. . . . Every place had its local features, but together these efforts formed a pattern whose sweep and power can be hard to discern from any single instance. . . . And the evidence of past waves of reform, from the labor-rights and women's suffrage movements of the early 1900s through the civil-rights and environmental movements of mid-century, suggests that national transformations must start from local roots.

https://www.theatlantic.com/magazine/archive/2018/05/reinventing-america/556856/.

Chapter Four
Waiting for SCOTUS: Negotiating in Transition

The 1992 U.S. Supreme Court total takings case, *Lucas v. South Carolina Coastal Council,*[1] seriously discourages municipalities from designating no-build zones to prevent property and personal damage from anticipated sea-level rise and storm surges. *Lucas* was decided just as the United Nations was beginning its exploration of the consequences of climate change. We knew that the climate was warming and that greenhouse gases (GHGs) were the culprit, and there was a growing consensus that humankind was largely responsible. But we had much to learn about this frightening phenomenon. Two years later, Justice John Paul Stevens, dissenting in *Dolan v. City of Tigard* wrote: "In our changing world one thing is certain: uncertainty will characterize predictions about the impact of new urban developments on the risks of floods, earthquakes, traffic congestion, or environmental harms."[2] A quarter of a century later, climate change science is all the more certain, the consequences are clearer and more frightening, and it is obvious that human behavior is the cause. Still, however, we do not know precisely where and by how much sea level will rise, where coastal storms will occur, or how fierce they will be. Regarding any given coastal community, there is doubt as to these things. This chapter starts with a look at this uncertainty, then discusses the difficulty of preventing development in particularly vulnerable areas using traditional regulatory techniques in light of the *Lucas* holding. It continues by exploring how, through negotiation, reference to sea-level rise projections, and the sensitive use of existing local land use procedures, lawyers can propose and advocate for effective alternative strategies. It concludes by explaining how we can embrace the challenges of these rapidly changing times by reorienting legal education and the practice of law so that lawyers can create needed new legal institutions, procedures, and strategies.

1. 505 U.S. 1003 (1992).
2. 512 U.S. 374, 411 (1994) (Stevens, J., dissenting)

I. *Tempora Mutantur*[3]

These are challenging times. Scientists and objective observers now are certain that the climate is changing and that human behavior is its cause.[4] The 2018 report of the U.S. Global Change Research Program details the many readily observable impacts of climate change.[5] Rampant and repeated flooding in the Northeast and fires of unprecedented intensity and frequency in the drought-plagued Southwest are only the most recent evidence of deteriorating environmental conditions.[6] This research report also forecasts likely future changes that include more intense hurricanes with related increases in wind, rain, and storm surges[7]; sea-level rise in coastal areas[8]; and even drier conditions in some already drought-ridden regions.[9] These changes, it reports, will affect human life and health as well as water supply, agriculture, coastal areas, and many other aspects of the natural environment.[10]

The U.S. Supreme Court agrees. In *Massachusetts v. U.S. Environmental Protection Agency*, the Court wrote:

> The harms associated with climate change are serious and well recognized. Indeed, the [National Research Council] Report itself—which EPA regards

3. "*Tempora mutantur, et nos mutamur in illis.*" *See* Livingston's dissent in *Pierson v. Post*: "If anything, therefore, in the digests or pandects shall appear to militate against the . . . foxhunter, we have only to say tempora mutantur; and if men themselves change with the times, why should not laws also undergo an alteration?" 3 Cai. 175 (N.Y. Sup. Ct. 1805).
4. *See* Kevin Trenberth, *Check With Climate Scientists for Views on Climate*, Wall St. J., Feb. 1, 2012, https://www.wsj.com/articles/SB10001424052970204740904577193270727472662 ("Research shows that more than 97% of scientists actively publishing in the field agree that climate change is real and human caused. It would be an act of recklessness for any political leader to disregard the weight of evidence and ignore the enormous risks that climate change clearly poses.").
5. U.S. Global Change Research Program, Fourth Nat'l Climate Assessment (2018) [hereinafter Fourth Nat'l Climate Assessment]. The U.S. Global Change Research Program was charged with the responsibility of preparing this report by the Federal Advisory Committee Act. *See also* Chapter One.
6. Hurricane Sandy caused 132 deaths in the United States, damaged 377,000 buildings in New York and New Jersey, cost $71 billion in damages in the two states, and resulted in up to $22 billion in insurance payouts. Andy Newman, *Comparing Hurricanes: Katrina vs. Sandy*, N.Y. Times, Nov. 28, 2012, at A28.
7. *See* Ning Lin et al., *Physically Based Assessment of Hurricane Surge Threat Under Climate Change*, 2 Nature Climate Change 462-67 (June 2012).
8.

> Climate change-driven sea-level rise occurs for two main reasons. First, water expands as it increases in temperature, and rising global air temperatures have been causing corresponding increases in ocean temperatures. Second, hotter atmospheric temperatures are also causing ice caps and glaciers all over the world to melt, providing influxes of fresh water to the oceans and increasing the total volume of water that they hold.

Robin Kundis Craig, *A Public Health Perspective on Sea-Level Rise: Starting Points for Climate Change Adaptation*, 15 Widener L. Rev. 521, 526 (2010).

9. Melissa Gaskill, *Climate Change Threatens to Create a Second Dust Bowl*, Sci. Am., Nov. 27, 2012, http://www.scientificamerican.com/article.cfm?id=climate-change-threatens-second-dust-bowl.
10. Craig, *supra* note 8, at 521.

> as an objective and independent assessment of the relevant science, . . . identifies a number of environmental changes that have already inflicted significant harms, including the global retreat of mountain glaciers, reduction in snow-cover extent, the earlier spring melting of ice on rivers and lakes, [and] the accelerated rate of rise of sea levels during the 20th century relative to the past few thousand years.[11]

Climate change is caused by the accumulation of GHGs in the atmosphere. The accumulated GHGs admit solar radiation but block the escape of heat.[12] This chemical process, known as the greenhouse effect, causes the planet to warm and weather conditions to change, which in turn exacerbates the frequency and ferocity of storms and flooding.[13] Carbon dioxide (CO_2) makes up approximately 81% of total U.S. GHG emissions and is primarily emitted by electricity-generation plants, buildings of every type, and automobile tailpipes.[14] The amount of CO_2 in the atmosphere has increased from a pre-industrial rate of 280 parts per million (ppm) to 414 ppm today.[15] Scientific opinion has concluded that 350 ppm is the tipping point beyond which climate change becomes particularly dangerous to society, especially with regard to sea-level rise caused by the warming of the seas and the melting of polar ice caps, arctic ice, glaciers, and formerly permanent mountain snow caps.[16]

The absence of effective national and international GHG emission-reduction mechanisms raises a serious concern that government inaction will permit an alarming increase in accumulation of these gases in the atmosphere.[17]

11. 549 U.S. 497, 521 (2007) (internal quotation marks omitted); *see generally* Coalition for Responsible Regulation v. EPA, 684 F.3d 102, 114 (D.C. Cir. 2012) (affirming EPA's endangerment finding that CO_2 and other GHG emissions constitute a danger to public health and can be regulated under the Clean Air Act). The Court found that EPA's finding was based on good science and careful research.
12. Our Built and Natural Environments: A Technical Review of the Interactions Between Land Use, Transportation, and Environmental Quality 65-66 (June 2013), https://www.epa.gov/sites/production/files/2014-03/documents/our-built-and-natural-environments.pdf.
13. *Id.* at 68-70.
14. *About the Emissions Inventory*, U.S. EPA, https://www.epa.gov/ghgemissions/inventory-us-greenhouse-gas-emissions-and-sinks (last updated Apr. 13, 2020) (reporting that in 2018, CO_2 accounted for 81% of all U.S. GHG emissions and that the main sources are electricity generation, transportation, and industrial operations.).
15. *Carbon Dioxide*, National Aeronautics & Space Admin. (NASA), https://climate.nasa.gov/vital-signs/carbon-dioxide/ (last updated June 2020); Rebecca Lindsey, *Climate Change: Atmospheric Carbon Dioxide*, Climate.Gov (Aug. 14, 2020), https://www.climate.gov/news-features/understanding-climate/climate-change-atmospheric-carbon-dioxide.; Robert E. Lang et al., *American Demographics—Circa 2109*, Planning, May 2009, at 10.
16. James Hansen et al., *Target Atmospheric CO_2: Where Should Humanity Aim?*, 2 Open Atmos. Sci. J. 217, 217, 226 (2008) (paleoclimate evidence suggests that 350 parts per million (ppm) of CO_2 will keep global temperatures to within 2 degrees Celsius of their current levels).
17. *See* Commission on America's Climate Choices, Nat'l Acad. of Sci., America's Climate Choices 21 (2011) (showing projections ranging from 450 ppm to over 950 ppm by 2100); *see also* Trenberth, *supra* note 4:

Strategies that reduce or capture carbon emissions are needed to respond to this phenomenon. One such strategy is to preserve and enhance forests.[18] Trees and the vegetated environment naturally absorb and store more than 15% of total U.S. carbon emissions.[19] Most biological sequestration results from carbon uptake and storage by forests.[20]

At early common law, however, trees were regarded as a nuisance to farming, a critical economic enterprise during the period of westward expansion. Clearcutting was not only allowed; it was encouraged. In a 1911 case, *Pardee v. Camden Lumber*, a West Virginia court wrote: "In early days, [forests were] regarded as an encumbrance and burden upon lands. Having nothing but forests, the chief object or purpose of land owners everywhere was to get rid of the forests, and prepare their lands for agriculture."[21] After examining cases holding that forests constitute nuisances, the court refused to apply those precedents to the controversy at hand. Times had changed. A century before *Pardee*, forests were a nuisance; at the turn of the 20th century, the West Virginia court deemed them an economic asset. Today, over 100 years later, they may well be invaluable. The mitigation of climate change through organic sequestration underscores the importance of forests and other vegetated landscapes to the survival of society.

Change in society causes adjustments to statutes as well as the common law. Reliance on nuisance law to control the use of private property proved inadequate to protect property investments and the quality of community life in post-industrial America.[22] Threatened by the march of skyscrapers up Fifth Avenue and industrial development along rail lines paralleling Euclid Avenue, the city of New York and the village of Euclid, Ohio, respectively

---

The National Academy of Sciences of the U.S. (set up by President Abraham Lincoln to advise on scientific issues), as well as major national academies of science around the world and every other authoritative body of scientists active in climate research have stated that the science is clear: The world is heating up and humans are primarily responsible. Impacts are already apparent and will increase. Reducing future impacts will require significant reductions in emissions of heat-trapping gases.

18. John R. Nolon, *Managing Climate Change Through Biological Sequestration: Open Space Redux*, 31 Stan. Envtl. L.J. 195, 196-97 (2012).

19. U.S. EPA, Inventory of U.S. Greenhouse Gas Emissions and Sinks: 1990-2009, Executive Summary ES-7 (2011), https://www.epa.gov/sites/production/files/2015-12/documents/us-ghg-inventory-2011-executive-summary.pdf [hereinafter EPA Greenhouse Gas Inventory Exec. Summary].

20. *Id.* (863.1 teragrams (Tg) of CO_2 equivalent (eq.) attributed to forest land out of a total of 1,015.1 Tg CO_2 eq. sequestered by all U.S. carbon sinks). Given the statistics presented in this report, the following strategies are important to the current U.S. biological sequestration portfolio: forest land remaining forest land; cropland remaining cropland; grassland remaining grassland; and converting land to grassland.

21. 73 S.E. 82, 85 (W. Va. 1911).

22. *See* Newman F. Baker, Legal Aspects of Zoning 33-39 (1927); Seymour I. Toll, Zoned American (1969).

adopted innovative and comprehensive zoning ordinances that drastically limited the ways in which private property could be used.[23]

In finding such regulations constitutional, the Supreme Court in *Village of Euclid v. Ambler Realty Co.* noted that "while the meaning of constitutional guaranties never varies, the scope of their application must expand or contract to meet the new and different conditions which are constantly coming within the field of their operation. In a changing world, it is impossible that it should be otherwise."[24] Within a half century following the *Euclid* decision, local governments were using their delegated police and zoning power in a novel way: to adopt a wide range of innovative environmental laws, responding to perturbations in the local environment, and further restricting the use of private land.[25] Today, sea-level rise requires a new paradigm for controlling the development of coastal lands that sit in harm's way, calling for significant adjustments in the law and legal practice.

This chapter looks closely at climate change and sea-level rise, as well as the challenges they pose to the legal system, practice of law, and legal education. Part I explains that the law, both in its interpretation and application, periodically changes to address the needs of a changing society. Part II explains the process and rate by which the physical environment is changing because of climate change and also describes some responsive changes that are already observable in legal institutions, strategies, and statutes. This part also reflects on how the lack of certainty regarding the pace of sea-level rise shapes these evolving legal strategies. Further, it refers to path dependency theory to suggest that certain prospects of sea-level rise present a unique opportunity for fundamental legal change, such as banning or heavily regulating the construction of new buildings in threatened areas. Part III explores how the total-takings barrier of the *Lucas v. South Carolina Coastal Council*[26] decision confounds attempts to prevent building in vulnerable coastal communities. Although *Lucas* contains interpretative threads that infuse some flexibility in its application to these new conditions, its core principle combines with other practical and political difficulties to militate against severe development restrictions in coastal areas. Part IV illustrates how, through negotiation and the sensitive use of existing local land use procedures, lawyers can propose and advocate for effective alternatives to the traditional regulatory approach. Part V concludes by explaining how we can embrace the

23. *See generally* TOLL, *supra* note 22.
24. 272 U.S. 365, 387 (1936).
25. *See* John Nolon, *In Praise of Parochialism: The Advent of Local Environmental Law*, 26 HARV. ENVTL. L. REV. 365, 365-77 (2002).
26. 505 U.S. at 1003.

challenges of these rapidly changing times by reorienting legal education and the practice of law so that lawyers can create needed new legal institutions, procedures, and strategies.

II. Changing Climate, Institutions, and Strategies

In order for the law to adapt to climate change, it must measure and react to the extent and nature of that change. The less certain we are about the particulars, the more challenging it is to develop needed changes to legal regimes and practices. We know that climate change is occurring, but we do not know, for example, how fast sea levels will rise, precisely where along coastal waters inundation will occur, or where and how ferociously storm surges will strike. Additionally, the more quickly and efficiently society addresses the causes of climate change, the less impact it will have. This lack of certainty is particularly apparent if one focuses on the land use dimensions of climate change.

Climate change is caused in significant part by the generation of electricity needed to heat and cool buildings[27] and by the combustion of fossil fuels in day-to-day travel in and around the built environment. Human activity that removes vegetation from the natural landscape, such as residential subdivision development, further exacerbates the problem, given that vegetation sequesters a significant percentage of annual carbon emissions.[28] In short, how buildings are built, where they are located, how many vehicle miles Americans travel from place to place, and how much vegetated land will be consumed by land development all matter a great deal.[29]

Sprawl development causes numerous environmental problems as a result of its emphasis on large-lot, single-family housing and the rigid separation of building uses among districts.[30] Local land use regulations have permitted and promoted sprawl development over the past several decades, resulting in an unsustainable rate of energy consumption and CO_2 emissions.[31]

27. The U.S. Department of Energy (DOE) projects that by 2035, residential and commercial buildings will use 76.5% of the total electricity in the United States. *See* U.S. DOE, *U.S. Residential and Commercial Buildings Total Primary Energy Consumption, in* BUILDINGS ENERGY DATA BOOK tbl.1.1.1: U.S. Residential and Commercial Buildings Total Primary Energy Consumption, http://web.archive.org/web/20130214212625/http://buildingsdatabook.eren.doe.gov/docs/DataBooks/2010_BEDB.pdf TableView.aspx?table=1.1.1 [hereinafter BUILDINGS ENERGY DATA BOOK].
28. *See* EPA GREENHOUSE GAS INVENTORY EXEC. SUMMARY, *supra* note 19, at ES-1 to ES-7.
29. For a complete explanation of this assertion, see generally John R. Nolon, *The Land Use Stabilization Wedge Strategy: Shifting Ground to Mitigate Climate Change*, 34 WM. & MARY ENVTL. L. & POL'Y REV. 1 (2009).
30. *See, e.g.*, Michael Lewyn, *Sprawl in Canada and the United States*, 44 URB. LAW. 85, 86-87 (2012).
31. Nolon, *supra* note 29, at 11.

Emerging policies in some states promote an alternative human settlement pattern: compact, mixed-use development concentrated in and around existing urbanized areas.[32] States are entering into compacts to create new and promising institutions tasked with climate change mitigation, and innovative strategies include efforts to unite stakeholders in voluntary approaches to mitigate the effects of climate change.[33] We are nonetheless guided by estimates, not certainty, with respect to these matters, despite encouraging evidence that these more sustainable development policies and initiatives will succeed in reducing the consequences of climate change. Although the trends are clear, the pace of their development is not. In this section, we examine these important climate change influences and the types of institutions and strategies that are evolving to better mitigate and adapt to climate change.

A. *Uncertain Forces Affecting the Rate of Climate Change and Sea-Level Rise*

The generation of electricity to heat and cool buildings is responsible for over one-third of total CO_2 emissions.[34] Recent population growth has increased demand for development. The United States population in 1990 was 248,709,873[35]; as of 2010, it was 308,745,538.[36] There were 102.2 million housing units in 1990,[37] compared with 2010.[38] In 1990, the residential

32. *See* Smart Growth Public Infrastructure Policy Act, N.Y. Envtl. Conserv. Law §6-0105 (McKinney 2010). It states:

> It is the purpose of this article to augment the state's environmental policy by declaring a fiscally prudent state policy of maximizing the social, economic and environmental benefits from public infrastructure development through minimizing unnecessary costs of sprawl development including environmental degradation, disinvestment in urban and suburban communities and loss of open space induced by sprawl facilitated by the funding or development of new or expanded transportation, sewer and waste water treatment, water, education, housing and other publicly supported infrastructure inconsistent with smart growth public infrastructure criteria.

33. *See infra* Parts II.B & C.
34. John R. Nolon, *Land Use for Energy Conservation and Sustainable Development: A New Path Toward Climate Change Mitigation*, 27 J. Land Use & Envtl. L. 295, 299 (2012).
35. *1990 Census*, U.S. Census Bureau, https://www2.census.gov/library/publications/decennial/1990/cp-1/cp-1-1.pdf?# (last visited Aug. 17, 2020).
36. 2010 Census Data, U.S. Census Bureau, https://www.census.gov/programs-surveys/decennial-census/decade.2010.html (last visited Aug. 17, 2020).
37. U.S. Census Bureau, 1990 Census of Population and Housing: 1990 Population and Housing Unit Counts, https://www.census.gov/prod/cen1990/cph2/cph-2-1-1.pdf (last visited Aug. 17, 2020).
38. Christopher Mazur & Ellen Wilson, U.S. Census Bureau, Housing Characteristics: 2010, C2010BR-07, at 2 (2011), https://www.census.gov/prod/cen2010/briefs/c2010br-07.pdf. Note that of these 131.7 million, only 116.7 million were occupied.

sector consumed 10.45 quadrillion British thermal units (BTUs),[39] while that figure increased to 15.56 quadrillion in 2010. The commercial sector consumed 9.48 quadrillion BTUs in 1990 and 14.42 quadrillion BTU in 2010.[40]

Nationally, the U.S. Environmental Protection Agency (EPA) found that "[t]ransportation activities . . . accounted for 33 percent of CO_2 emissions from fossil fuel combustion in 2009 . . . . Nearly 65 percent of [these] emissions resulted from gasoline consumption for personal vehicle use."[41] A count of the total vehicle miles traveled (VMT) by Americans presents a useful measure of transportation levels. Annual VMT rose from 2.1 trillion in 1990 to 2.9 trillion in 2010.[42] VMT have increased three times faster than the population since 1980.[43] This increase appears to have resulted largely from personal auto use, as "[VMT] by light-duty motor vehicles (passenger cars and light-duty trucks) increased 39 percent from 1990 to 2009."[44] In fact, "[VMT] may exceed seven trillion . . . miles by 2055."[45]

According to projections, the U.S. population will continue to grow, calling for more building and electricity, and causing more energy consumption and driving.[46] These projections hold that by the year 2039, the U.S. population will have increased by nearly one-third to over 400 million people.[47]

---

39. "One Btu is the heat required to raise the temperature of one pound of water by one-degree Fahrenheit." *How We Meter*, University of Va., https://energytracker.fm.virginia.edu/meter.html (last updated July 26, 2018); Buildings Energy Data Book, *supra* note 27, at tbl.2.1.1.
40. *Id.* at tbl.3.1.1.
41. EPA Greenhouse Gas Inventory Exec. Summary, *supra* note 19, at ES-9.
42. *Id.* at ES-6.
43. Keith Bartholomew & Reid Ewing, *Land Use-Transportation Scenario Planning in an Era of Global Climate Change* 4 (Nov. 5, 2007), https://pdfs.semanticscholar.org/a050/5d9246ba381719f2e6074 1e9db0aad250d65.pdf.
44. U.S. EPA, Inventory of U.S. Greenhouse Gas Emissions and Sinks: 1990-2009, Complete Report 2-21, https://www.epa.gov/sites/production/files/2015-12/documents/us-ghg-inventory-2011-complete_report.pdf.
45. American Ass'n of State Highway and Transp. Officials, Future Needs of the U.S. Surface Transportation System 18 (2007).
46. *U.S. Population Projections, Table 1: Projections and Components of Change for the United States: 2010 to 2050*, U.S. Census Bureau (Aug. 14, 2008), https://www2.census.gov/programs-surveys/popproj/tables/2008/2008-summary-tables/np2008-t1.csv. The United States population in 2006 was 299.4 million people. *Statistical Abstract of the U.S., Population*, U.S. Census Bureau, https://www.census.gov/prod/2007pubs/08abstract/pop.pdf. Population projections are estimates only. They depend on fertility, immigration, and aging trends that are difficult to project. That said, most credible evidence indicates that the U.S. population will increase significantly throughout the next century. ("[I]t is very likely that the U.S. population will be at 400 million by midcentury." Lang et al., *supra* note 15.) Calculations used in this article assume generally that within three or four decades there will be 100 million more Americans and that the average household size will be 2.5 persons per household, resulting in a net increase of 40 million households. The official projection for the next 100 years conducted by the U.S. Census Bureau, using a medium scenario for growth, projects a doubling of the 2000 population by the year 2100, a total of 571 million people.
47. Lang et al., *supra* note 15, at 10.

Between 2010 and 2030, it is projected that the private sector will add 37 million new homes and 76 billion square feet of nonresidential construction to accommodate this growth and to replace obsolete buildings.[48] The addition of 100 million people translates into 40 million new households whose members will live, work, and shop in these buildings, traveling largely by car.

To the extent that these population and settlement increases occur, the accumulation of CO_2 in the atmosphere will continue to escalate. The Intergovernmental Panel on Climate Change (IPCC)[49] reported an atmospheric CO_2 concentration of 353 ppm in 1990[50] and 379 ppm in 2005.[51] As of August 2019, the National Oceanic and Atmospheric Administration reported that the global atmospheric CO_2 concentration was approximately 407.75 ppm.[52] With additional households, continued building, and more driving, these accumulations will only increase further.

That these changes will cause additional sea-level rise is clear. The greenhouse effect causes polar ice and glaciers to melt, reduces the reflection of the sun's rays, and warms seawater through intensified absorption of solar radiation.[53] Warmer seawater increases both the wind speed of coastal storms

---

48. *See* Arthur C. Nelson, Reshaping Metropolitan America: Development Trends and Opportunities To 2030, at 80-82 (2013).

49. Intergovernmental Panel On Climate Change, Climate Change 2007: Synthesis Report (2007), https://www.ipcc.ch/site/assets/uploads/2018/02/ar4_syr_full_report.pdf.[hereinafter IPCC Synthesis Report] (The Intergovernmental Panel on Climate Change was formed in 1988 as a scientific body that reviews and assesses the most recent scientific, technical, and socio-economic information relevant to climate change. More than 150 countries participate in working groups of the IPCC. The Fourth Assessment Report was released in 2007.). *See generally* John R. Nolon & Patricia E. Salkin, Climate Change and Sustainable Development Law in a Nutshell 22-23 (2011) (indicating the sufficiency of the reports on which the IPCC report was based by stating that

    [o]ver 40 writing teams and 450 lead authors—selected as lead authors because of their expertise—contributed to the Fourth Assessment Report. The report contains over 18,000 citations to scientific reports, the majority of which were published in peer- reviewed journals. The lead authors were assisted by over 800 scientists and analysts who participated as contributing authors on specific topics. These authors contributed their time and were assisted by four Technical Support Units with paid staff.

50. R.T. Watson et al., *Greenhouse Gases and Aerosols, in* Climate Change: The IPCC Scientific Assessment 5 (J.T. Houghton et al., eds., 1990), https://www.ipcc.ch/site/assets/uploads/2018/03/ipcc_far_wg_I_full_report.pdf.

51. IPCC Synthesis Report, *supra* note 49, at 37.

52. *Trends in Atmospheric Carbon Dioxide*, NOAA Earth Sys. Res. Lab., http://www.esrl.noaa.gov/gmd/ccgg/trends/global.html (last visited Aug. 17, 2020) (under Recent Global CO_2 heading); *see also* J.D. Harrington et al., *Study Finds Ancient Warming Greened Antarctica*, NASA (June 17, 2012), http://www.nasa.gov/home/hqnews/2012/jun/HQ_12-202_Antarctica_Greener_Warmer.html.

53. Global warming results from the accumulation of man-made gases, released into the atmosphere from such activities as the burning of fossil fuels, deforestation, and the production of chlorofluorocarbons, which trap solar heat in the atmosphere and raise temperatures worldwide. Global warming could result in significant global sea-level rise by 2050 resulting from ocean expansion, the melting of snow and ice, and the gradual melting of the polar ice cap. Sea-level rise will result in the loss of natural resources such as beaches, dunes, estuaries, and wetlands and will contribute to the salinization of drinking water supplies. Sea-level rise will also result in damage to properties, infrastructures, and

and the moisture they release. Increased water temperature also melts sea ice, ultimately contributing to sea-level rise.[54] The U.S. Climate Change Science Program (CCSP) found that "[e]xtrapolating the recent acceleration of ice discharges from the polar ice sheets would imply an additional contribution up to 0.20 [meter (m) to the IPCC estimates]. If melting of these ice caps increases, larger values of sea-level rise cannot be excluded."[55] Therefore, "thoughtful precaution suggests that a global sea-level rise of 1 [meter] to the year 2100 should be considered for future planning and policy discussions."[56] Indeed, studies more recent than the CCSP's report indicate that "[e]ven for the lowest emission scenario [generated by previous estimates], sea-level rise is then likely to be ~1 m; for the highest, it may even come closer to 2 m [over 1990 levels]."[57]

"Thoughtful precaution" is an appropriate term. Despite the overwhelming consensus that sea levels will rise as carbon emissions and global temperature increase, experts do not know precisely when or where that rise will occur, or by how much.[58] This makes it difficult to control coastal development in the near term, for example, through prescriptive regulation. Do we know for sure that buildings constructed today will be affected by inun-

---

public works. There is a growing need to plan for sea-level rise. Coastal Zone Act Reauthorization Amendments of 1990, Pub. L. No. 101-508, 104 Stat. 1388-299, 6203(a)(3) & 16 U.S.C. §1451(l) (codified as amended at 16 U.S.C. §§1451-1455).

54. Fourth Nat'l Climate Assessment, *supra* note 5, at 1495 ("Global sea level is rising, primarily in response to two factors: 1) thermal expansion of ocean waters and 2) melting of land-based ice, both due to climate change. Thermal expansion refers to the physical expansion (or increase in volume) of water as it warms.")); *see also* Vincenzo Artale et al., *Observations: Oceanic Climate Change and Sea Level*, *in* Climate Change 2007: The Physical Science Basis 408 (2007), https://www.ipcc.ch/site/assets/uploads/2018/02/ar4-wg1-chapter5-1.pdf ("[G]lobal mean sea level change results from two major processes[:] . . . i) thermal expansion, and ii) the exchange of water between oceans and other reservoirs (glaciers and ice caps, ice sheets, other land water reservoirs . . .)."); *see generally* *Water—Thermal Properties*, Engineering Toolbox, https://www.engineeringtoolbox.com/water-thermal-properties-d_162.html (last visited Aug. 17, 2020) (showing that water expands when heated).

55. *See* U.S. Climate Change Sci. Program, Coastal Sensitivity to Sea-Level Rise: A Focus on the Mid-Atlantic Region 13, 15 (2009), https://training.fws.gov/courses/csp/csp3112/resources/Climate_Change/Coastal_Sensitivity_to_Sea_Level_Rise.pdf [hereinafter CCSP Coastal Sensitivity].

56. *Id.* at 20; *see also* James G. Titus, *Greenhouse Effect, Sea-Level Rise and Land Use*, 7 Land Use Pol'y 138, 141, 144 (1990). "In many states the total shoreline retreat from a [one meter] rise would be much greater than suggested by the amount of land below the [one meter] contour on a map because shores would also erode."

57. Martin Vermeer & Stefan Rahmstorf, *Global Sea Level Linked to Global Temperature*, 106 Proc. Nat'l Acad. Sci. U.S. 21527, 21531 (2009), http://www.pnas.org/content/106/51/21527.full.pdf; *see also, generally*, Asbury H. Sallenger Jr. et al., *Hotspot of Accelerated Sea-Level Rise on the Atlantic Coast of North America*, Nature Climate Change (June 24, 2012), https://www.nature.com/articles/nclimate1597.

58. Sallenger et al., *supra* note 57, at 1:

> Climate warming does not force sea-level rise (SLR) at the same rate everywhere. Rather, there are spatial variations of SLR superimposed on a global average rise. . . . Here, we present evidence of recently accelerated SLR in a unique 1,000-km-long hotspot on the highly populated North American Atlantic coast . . . .

dation or storm surges during their useful lives? This lack of certainty has inhibited coastal regulation, but it has not checked the growth of new legal institutions and the emergence of new coping strategies.

The certainty of sea-level rise itself, however, is precipitating changes in law, policy, and institutions during a crisis of unknown proportions. We are seeking new solutions. Path dependence theory explains these changes to an extent. The theory posits that "an outcome or decision is shaped in specific and systematic ways by the historical path leading to it."[59] It refers to the causal relationship between stages in a sequence.[60] In other words, path dependence suggests that "what happened at an earlier point in time will affect the possible outcomes of a sequence of events occurring at a later point in time."[61]

When path dependence theory is applied to the law, it suggests that early decisions—whether court cases, agency rules, or institutional policies—can lock in future judicial doctrine, regulatory policy, and administrative action.[62] Theorists who study path dependency believe that "the opportunities for significant legal change in a common law system are brief and intermittent, occurring during critical junctures when new legal issues arise or higher courts or legislatures intercede."[63] These junctures, or punctuations, offer opportunities to shape and reform decision making and policies.

Climate change and the growing evidence of its harmful consequences have, most certainly, brought us to such a juncture in American law. The question here is how our recent understanding of, and adjustment to, climate change has caused path-altering changes in institutional arrangements and

---

59. Oona A. Hathaway, *Path Dependence in the Law: The Course and Pattern of Legal Change in a Common Law System*, 86 Iowa L. Rev. 601, 604 (2001).

60. Holmes said:

> [I]f we want to know why a rule of law has taken its particular shape, and more or less if we want to know why it exists at all, we go to tradition. We follow it into the Year Books, and perhaps beyond them to the customs of the Salian Franks, and somewhere in the past, in the German forests, in the needs of Norman kings, in the assumptions of a dominant class, in the absence of generalized ideas, we find out the practical motive for what now best is justified by the mere fact of its acceptance and that men are accustomed to it. The rational study of law is still to a large extent the study of history. History must be a part of the study, because without it we cannot know the precise scope of rules which it is our business to know. It is a part of the rational study, because it is the first step toward an enlightened scepticism, that is, toward a deliberate reconsideration of the worth of those rules.

Oliver Wendell Holmes Jr., *The Path of Law*, 10 Harv. L. Rev. 457, 469 (1897).

61. Hathaway, *supra* note 59, at 604 (quoting William H. Sewell, Jr., *Three Temporalities: Toward an Eventful Sociology*, *in* The Historic Turn in the Human Sciences 226-63 (Terrance J. McDonald ed., 1996)).

62. J.B. Ruhl & James Salzman, *Mozart and the Red Queen: The Problem of Regulatory Accretion in the Administrative State*, 91 Geo. L.J. 757, 818 (2003).

63. Hathaway, *supra* note 59, at 605.

led policymakers and professionals to implement impressive new institutions and strategies.

B. *Changes in Institutions*

Concern over the consequences of climate change and the lack of effective action at the national and international levels has led state governments to create new institutions to manage climate change. In this section, we examine the workings of the Regional Greenhouse Gas Initiative (RGGI), the Transportation Climate Initiative (TCI), and the California Air Resources Board (CARB). All three chart new paths for managing climate change and have the potential to alter the rate at which the causes of climate change occur. The coincidence of these state and interstate initiatives—and the failures at the international and national levels—presents a powerful opportunity for progress at the local, state, and regional level.

The United Nations Framework Convention on Climate Change (UNFCCC) was signed at the Earth Summit in Rio de Janeiro in 1992.[64] The Convention created a Conference of the Parties (COP) and charged it with meeting regularly to develop mechanisms to implement the UNFCCC's commitment to GHG reductions.[65] The third meeting of the COP was held in 1997 in Kyoto, Japan, resulting in an agreement that committed developed countries to limit the tons of CO_2 they may emit.[66] This cap was to be implemented in two ways: (1) through the purchase of emission reduction units (ERUs) from other developed countries; and (2) through the clean development mechanism, which allows developed countries to earn ERUs by implementing emissions-reductions projects in developing countries.[67]

The Kyoto Protocol, which expired in 2012 and was extended through 2020 pursuant to the Doha Amendment,[68] was reviewed in December 2009 at the 15th meeting of the COP in Copenhagen.[69] The parties failed to agree on whether the Protocol would continue, but they did endorse achieving economy-wide emission targets by 2020 in an effort to cap global temperature increases at 2 degrees Celsius—or 3.6 degrees Fahrenheit—a temperature identified as the tipping point for global warming.[70] Developed countries

64. Kyle W. Danish, *The International Regime, in* Global Climate Change and U.S. Law 31, 33 (Michael B. Gerrard ed., 2008).
65. *Id.* at 35.
66. *Id.* at 36.
67. *Id.* at 42-44.
68. U.N. Framework Convention on Climate Change, *Kyoto Protocol,* UNFCCC, http://unfccc.int/kyoto_protocol/items/2830.php (last visited Aug. 17, 2020).
69. Nolon & Salkin, *supra* note 49, at 6.
70. *Id.* at 7.

that signed the Copenhagen Accord, including the United States, agreed to report biennially on the progress they make in reducing emissions.

In June 2009, the Waxman-Markey Bill—known as the American Clean Energy and Security Act of 2009—passed the U.S. House of Representatives, setting the stage for a highly effective cap and trade program in the United States.[71] The bill would have curbed GHGs by setting a limit on overall national emissions while allowing utilities, manufacturers, and other emitters to trade pollution permits or allowances among themselves. But the comparable bill in the U.S. Senate failed to emerge from committee,[72] and by the time the Copenhagen Accord was signed, it was highly doubtful that initiatives at the national level in the United States would be successful. This set the stage for effective state and interstate action as one method of fulfilling the country's Copenhagen obligations.

1. Regional Greenhouse Gas Initiative

In 2005, the governors of the 10 states that were parties to the RGGI in the Northeast[73] signed a Memorandum of Understanding (MOA) establishing emissions caps and a trading system to implement them.[74] Participating states currently include: Connecticut; Delaware; Maine; Maryland; Massachusetts; New Hampshire; New Jersey; New York; Rhode Island; and Vermont. The cap-and-trade program has not only secured the support of critical stakeholders—like power plant owners and environmental leaders—but has also proven to have a workable collaborative governing structure, which has begun to show effective results.[75]

The governors of the member states negotiated and signed an MOA in 2005, promulgated regulations based on a model rule, and created an implementing agency to administer the program, naming the member states' environmental and energy commissioners to serve as directors.[76] The regulations apply to fossil fuel-fired power plants with a capacity of 25 megawatts (MWs)

71. H.R. 2454, 111th Cong. (2009)
72. The Clean Energy Jobs and American Power Act, S. 1733, 111th Cong. (2010).
73. *See* Regional Greenhouse Gas Initiative, http://www.rggi.org (last visited Aug. 17, 2020). The body that administers RGGI is RGGI Inc.
74. *Memorandum of Understanding*, Regional Greenhouse Gas Initiative, http://www.rggi.org/design/history/mou (last visited Aug. 17, 2020).
75. N. Jonathan Peress, *RGGI After One Year: Evaluation and Lessons*, 41 Aba Trends 12-13 (May/June 2010).
76. *Model Rule and MOU Versions*, Regional Greenhouse Gas Initiative, https://www.rggi.org/program-overview-and-design/design-archive/mou-model-rule (last visited Aug. 17, 2020).

or more.[77] RGGI capped CO_2 emissions at 96.2 million tons through 2020.[78] This cap is scheduled to fall by 28.9% to 67.3 million tons by 2030. States distribute CO_2 allowances in quarterly auctions, and regulated power plants purchase the number of allowances they need to equal their projected emissions. The revenue generated by these auctions is divided among member states for investment in clean-energy technology and energy-efficiency development programs.[79] Each state may direct RGGI proceeds to encourage a clean-energy economy within its borders or put them to other uses.[80]

Over the first 32 auctions, auction revenue from allowance proceeds totaled more than $2.5 billion.[81] From 2008-2013, states invested 67% of that revenue into energy programs designed to improve energy efficiency, promote the deployment of renewable energy technologies, and provide energy bill payment assistance. Additionally, the revenue provides for some GHG reduction programs aimed at abating carbon emissions, reducing VMT, and encouraging carbon sequestration.[82] RGGI reports that evaluations of these state programs show benefits of $3 to $4 for each dollar invested.[83]

An independent study published in November 2011 reported that the initiative had saved electricity consumers almost $1.1 billion and created 16,000 new jobs in the first three years of its existence.[84] The study found that while the program had led to a less-than-one-percent increase in electricity rates, the energy-efficiency measures that auction proceeds funded—including retrofitting homes and buildings—had reduced demand and thereby lowered energy bills.[85] Savings averaged $25 for residential consumers, $181 for com-

77. Peress, *supra* note 75, at 12; *see also Fact Sheet: The Regional Greenhouse Gas Initiative (RGGI)*, Regional Greenhouse Gas Initiative, https://www.home-performance.org/news/documents/RGGI_Fact_Sheet.pdf (last visited Aug. 17, 2020).
78. Regional Greenhouse Gas Initiative, Annual Report on the Market for RGGI CO_2 Allowances: 2019 5 (May 2020), https://www.rggi.org/sites/default/files/Uploads/Market-Monitor/Annual-Reports/MM_2019_Annual_Report.pdf.
79. *See Investments of Proceeds*, Regional Greenhouse Gas Initiative, https://www.rggi.org/investments/proceeds-investments (last visited Aug. 17, 2020) [hereinafter RGGI Investments]; *see also* discussion of the Cleaner, Greener Communities Program in New York, *infra* notes 122-125 and accompanying text.
80. *See RGGI Investments*, *supra* note 79.
81. *The Regional Greenhouse Gas Initiative: A Fact Sheet*, Regional Greenhouse Gas Initiative 2, https://www.ceres.org/sites/default/files/Fact%20Sheets%20or%20misc%20files/RGGI%20Fact%20Sheet.pdf (last visited Aug. 17, 2020).
82. *The Investment of RGGI Proceeds in 2018*, Regional Greenhouse Gas Initiative 41 (2020), https://www.rggi.org/sites/default/files/Uploads/Proceeds/RGGI_Proceeds_Report_2018.pdf
83. *About RGGI*, The Regional Greenhouse Gas Initiative Project Series, https://www.rggiprojectseries.org/about-rggi (last visited Aug. 17, 2020).
84. Paul J. Hibbard et al., The Economic Impacts of the Regional Greenhouse Gas Initiative on Ten Northeast and Mid-Atlantic States 4-7 (2011), https://www.mass.gov/files/2017-07/economic_impact_rggi_report.pdf.
85. *Id.* at 30.

mercial consumers, and $2,493 for industrial consumers.[86] Furthermore, one of the study's authors stated that CO_2 emissions in the region were "6 percent lower than they would have been without the program."[87]

The program completed its second comprehensive review in 2017.[88] Cumulatively, about 11% of unsold CO_2 allowances have been retired.[89] Unsold retired allowances are not "offered for sale at future auctions . . . effectively reducing the emissions cap."[90] Although the program has proven successful, the oversupply of allowances has limited its impact.[91]

2. Transportation and Climate Initiative: Building Sustainable Communities[92]

Another promising new institution that is addressing the causes of climate change is the TCI. RGGI, described immediately above, is not guided by the involvement of state transportation agencies. But because the transportation sector contributes nearly 30% of GHG emissions in the Northeast and Mid-Atlantic region, an obvious need exists to incorporate transportation strategies as part of these efforts to mitigate climate change in the Northeast.[93] In June 2010, transportation, energy, and environment officials from

86. *Id.* at 4.
87. Mireya Navarro, *Regional Cap-and-Trade Effort Seeks Greater Impact by Cutting Carbon Allowances*, N.Y. Times, Jan. 26, 2012, at A22, https://www.nytimes.com/2012/01/27/nyregion/in-greenhouse-gas-initiative-many-unsold-allowances.html.
88. *Program Review*, Regional Greenhouse Gas Initiative, https://www.rggi.org/program-overview-and-design/program-review (last visited Aug. 17, 2020).
89. *Allowance Distribution,* Regional Greenhouse Gas Initiative, https://www.rggi.org/allowance-tracking/allowance-distribution (last visited Aug. 24, 2020).
90. Cong. Research Serv., R41836, The Regional Greenhouse Gas Initiative: Background, Impacts, and Selected Issues 8 (July 16, 2019), https://fas.org/sgp/crs/misc/R41836.pdf. *See also* Shama Gamhkar & J. Mitch Pickerill, *The State of American Federalism 2011-2012: A Fend for Yourself and Activist Form of Bottom-Up Federalism*, 42 Publius: J. Federalism 357, 370 n.6 (2012), http://publius.oxfordjournals.org/content/42/3/357.full.pdf+html?sid=0a4d06ff-7004-4783-bb89-24d6a1a7aa63 ("On January 17, New York, Connecticut, Delaware, Massachusetts, Rhode Island, and Vermont announced that they were permanently eliminating 72 percent of the unsold carbon allowances, or a total of sixty-seven million. (Each allowance amounts to one ton of carbon dioxide emissions.)").
91. Bloomberg reported that the value of global carbon markets fell over 20% in the first quarter of 2012. Although the value of the carbon market is down, the trading has increased by 17% from 2011-2012. *See Bloomberg: World's Carbon Markets Down 20 Per Cent in 2012,* BusinessGreen (Apr. 5, 2012), https://www.businessgreen.com/news/2166311/bloomberg-worlds-carbon-markets-cent-2012.
92. "It is very difficult to get consensus where officials are working together within a state. But across state lines, tension goes away and consensus comes together." Telephone Conversation with Jeanne Herb, Research Program Coordinator, Nat'l Ctr. for Neighborhood & Brownfields Redevelopment (Apr. 13, 2012).
93. *See Northeast and Mid-Atlantic States Launch Major Climate and Transportation Initiative*, Transp.& Climate Initiative of the Ne. & Mid-Atl. States, https://www.transportationandclimate.org/content/northeast-and-mid-atlantic-states-launch-major-climate-and-transportation-initiative (last visited Aug. 17, 2020).

12 Northeast and Mid-Atlantic jurisdictions launched the TCI.[94] The TCI's chief goals are to reduce GHG emissions, "minimize the transportation [sector's] reliance on high-carbon fuels," reduce VMT, and promote sustainable development and a clean-energy economy.[95]

The TCI's Declaration of Intent specifies that the regional collaboration is expected to:

- Reduce traffic congestion;
- Encourage job growth and accommodate the flow of goods and services . . . ;
- [Establish] state and local land use strategies that . . . increase[] commercial and residential housing density and encourage transit-friendly design;
- Improve the performance of existing highway, transit, and other transportation modes while enhancing neighborhoods and urban centers; and
- Promote mixed-use development that supports viable alternatives to driving.[96]

To achieve these goals, the TCI has identified four main areas to address: (1) clean vehicles and fuels; (2) sustainable community development; (3) communication and information technology; and (4) freight transportation efficiency.[97] For the purposes of this chapter, the principal focus is on TCI's efforts to shape human settlements through land use strategies, the enhancement of urban centers, and the promotion of mixed-use development. TCI's member agencies have pledged to partner with housing and land use agencies at the local, regional, and federal levels to expand transportation options, enhance natural resource protection, and minimize adverse environmental

94. Participating jurisdictions include Connecticut, Delaware, Maine, Maryland, Massachusetts, New Hampshire, New Jersey, New York, Pennsylvania, Rhode Island, Vermont, and Virginia. *See About Us*, Transp.& Climate Initiative of the Ne. & Mid-Atl. States, https://www.transportationandclimate.org/content/about-us (last visited Aug. 17, 2020).

95. *See Northeast and Mid-Atlantic States Launch Major Climate and Transportation Initiative*, *supra* note 93.

96. Jared Snyder, *The Transportation and Climate Initiative of the Northeast and Mid-Atlantic States: An Agenda for Progress*, *in* Clean Air: Law, Policy, & Practice 194 (ALI-ABA Course of Study, SS023 ALI-ABA, Dec. 2-3, 2010).

97. *Transportation and Climate Initiative Kicks Off Work in Four Areas*, Transp.& Climate Initiative of the Ne. and Mid-Atl. States, https://www.transportationandclimate.org/content/transportation-and-climate-initiative-kicks-work-four-areas (last visited Aug. 17, 2020).

impacts.[98] The TCI's initial efforts in this area have been to develop state-level smart growth planning policies that promote transit-oriented development (TOD) and decrease travel demand.[99] It is also working toward bridging federal support and local action for sustainable development policies by "leveraging state resources." For example, the TCI seeks to "incorporat[e] climate change . . . [considerations] in state infrastructure investment; develop[] metrics [that] reflect climate [change] impacts in state-level policies; [encourage] partnering [between] regional and local entities to promote consistent practices . . . [in building] sustainable communities; develop[] best practices and model . . . policies . . . ; [and] . . . enhance...state climate action planning." These initiatives have "the potential to greatly reduce the region's climate impact, up to triple the reductions from RGGI," according to 2019 modeling.[100] As a consortium of state agencies, TCI can influence a remarkable range of resources and policy decisions at a large enough scale to favorably impact climate change.

3. California Air Resources Board

On the West Coast, a new strategy undertaken by the CARB shows real promise for mitigating climate change by reducing GHG emissions through land use and transportation planning. California's State Legislature enacted AB 32, the California Global Warming Solutions Act, in 2006.[101] The statute requires the state to reduce GHG emissions by 25% to 1990 levels by the year 2020.[102] A decade after this Act's passage, "California extended and strengthened the limit on greenhouse gas emissions with the passage of SB 32 in 2016. The state raised its goal for greenhouse gas emissions to 40 percent below 1990 levels by 2030."[103] CARB, the agency responsible for implementing the statute, is currently implementing this GHG cap-and-trade program. The rules establish an emission cap that covers nearly 85% of the state's GHG emissions. The proceeds going to California for the cap-and-trade program

98. *TCI Sustainable Communities Agreement,* Georgetown Climate Ctr. (June 8, 2011), http://www.georgetownclimate.org/tci-sustainable-communities-agreement.

99. Transp. & Climate Initiative of Ne. & Mid-Atl. States (TCI) 10, http://climatechange.transportation.org/pdf/markstout_trclimateinit.pdf (last visited Aug. 17, 2020).

100. Ethan Goffman, *The Transportation Climate Initiative, Explained,* Greater Wash. (May 21, 2020), https://ggwash.org/view/77721/the-transportation-climate-initiative-explained#:~:text=Indeed%2C%20TCI%20projections%20suggest%20between,been%20linked%20to%20air%20pollution.

101. Cal. Health & Safety Code Ann. § 38550 (West Supp. 2012).

102. David R. Wooley & Elizabeth M. Morss, Clean Air Act Handbook §10:18 (21st ed. 2011).

103. *California Leads Fight to Curb Climate Change,* Envtl. Def. Fund, https://www.edf.org/climate/california-leads-fight-curb-climate-change (last visited Aug. 24, 2020).

currently total $13.172 trillion.[104] These proceeds, like RGGI's, can be dedicated to renewable energy, TOD, and forest restoration projects.[105]

Recognizing transportation's enormous impact on the state's GHG emissions and the necessity of discouraging sprawl, California took a further step in 2008 by enacting SB 375, the Sustainable Communities and Climate Protection Act[106] to "help implement AB 32 by aligning planning for housing, land use, transportation, and greenhouse gas emissions."[107] SB 375 seeks to advance these goals in a number of ways. It requires regional transportation plans to include strategies to reduce GHG emission, connects zoning and housing development plans to regional transportation plans, and incentivizes certain types of development.[108] Under SB 375, CARB develops regional GHG emission "targets for 2020 and 2035 for [the] automobile[] and light-truck [sectors]."[109]

California's 18 metropolitan planning organizations (MPOs)[110]—which are transportation planning agencies that dictate the expenditure of federal transportation funds—must then prepare a sustainable communities strategy

104. CARB, Cal. Cap-and-Trade Program: Summary of Proceeds to Cal. and Consigning Entities (June 2020), https://ww2.arb.ca.gov/sites/default/files/classic//cc/capandtrade/auction/proceeds_summary.pdf.

105. Paul Rogers, *Windfall of Cash Could Hit State Treasury From Global Warming Program*, MERCURYNEWS.COM (Apr. 7, 2012), http://www.mercurynews.com/ science/ci_20348096/windfall-cash-could-hit-state-treasury-from-global.

106. Sarah Mawhorter, et al., *California's SB 375 and the Pursuit of Sustainable and Affordable Development*, Terner Center 3 (July 2018), http://ternercenter.berkeley.edu/uploads/SB375_July_2018_Final.pdf.

107. Senate Transp. & Hous. Comm., SB 375 Bill Analysis (Aug. 22, 2008), http://www.leginfo.ca.gov/pub/07-08/bill/sen/sb_0351-0400/sb_375_cfa_20080903_100317_sen_comm.html.

108. Elisa Barbour & Elizabeth A. Deakin, Smart Growth Planning for Climate Protection, 78 J. Am. Plan. Ass'n 70, 71 (2012).

109. *Id.* at 73.

110. Metropolitan Planning Organizations, Wis. Dep't of Transp., https://wisconsindot.gov/Pages/doing-bus/local-gov/plning-orgs/mpo.aspx (last visited Aug. 17, 2020).

> A metropolitan planning organization is an organization of primarily local elected officials who provide a forum for local decision-making on transportation issues of a regional nature. The federal government requires that an MPO be designated for each urbanized area with a population greater than 50,000.
>
> This designation must be agreed on by the governor and the units of general purpose local governments that together represent at least 75 percent of the affected population (including the central city or cities as defined by the Bureau of the Census).
>
> Each MPO has a policy board that is generally comprised of chief elected officials who represent different parts of the region served by the MPO. This board is advised by a technical committee (typically referred to as a Technical Advisory Committee, or TAC) that consists of planning and engineering staff from jurisdictions within each region.
>
> The TAC develops high quality technical tools and analysis for the region and advises the MPO policy board on technical and administrative issues related to regional transportation planning. Some MPOs also utilize a citizen advisory committee and other specialized committees to advise the policy board.

within their regional transportation plans with the goal of reducing VMT in order to reach the region's GHG emissions target. If the target cannot be met, SB 375 requires the MPOs to adopt an alternative planning and settlement strategy to achieve the emission-reduction target.

C. Changes in Strategies

These institutional changes enable and encourage stakeholders to create innovative strategies to manage climate change. For example, TCI could create a certification system for cities that adopt land use plans and regulations promoting compact, mixed-use developments, and those cities could be eligible for RGGI funding in the nine participating states in order to implement those plans and regulations. Apart from such institutional strategies, lawyers and other professionals can adopt a variety of nonregulatory approaches to climate change problem-solving. Their abilities in this regard are evident in the following examples.

1. Negotiated Dispute Resolution and Rulemaking

Two years before California enacted the Global Warming Solutions Act, CARB promulgated vehicle emissions standards for GHGs for vehicle model years 2009-2016. The standards become increasingly stringent over time, with an estimated 30% reduction in GHG emissions by 2016. Before the regulations could take effect, however, California had to overcome several obstacles to justify and assert its authority to regulate. For one, states were able to issue emissions standards only upon EPA's waiver of federal preemption under the Clean Air Act (CAA), which California sought in 2005.[111] If a waiver was granted, this would result in separate and more stringent standards in California and several other states that joined in the waiver request. Although the request was initially denied in 2008 under the outgoing Bush

Funding for MPO transportation planning is provided through a combination of federal, state and local funds.

111. Letter from Catherine Witherspoon, Exec. Officer, Cal. EPA, to Stephen L. Johnson, Adm'r, U.S. EPA (Dec. 21, 2005), http://www.regulations.gov/#!documentDetail;D=EPA-HQ-OAR-2006-0173-0017; *see also California Greenhouse Gas Waiver Request*, U.S. EPA, https://www.epa.gov/regulations-emissions-vehicles-and-engines/california-greenhouse-gas-waiver-request (last updated Aug. 19, 2019); 42 U.S.C.A. §7543(a)-(b) (West 2012).

Administration,[112] President Barack Obama issued a directive for his administration to reconsider California's application.[113]

Additionally, the auto industry had also challenged California's regulations in court, arguing that they were preempted by the Energy Policy and Conservation Act (EPCA). Under the EPCA, the National Highway and Traffic Safety Administration (NHTSA) was required to set corporate average fuel economy (CAFE) standards, but CARB had set more stringent emission targets than the federal CAFE standards. At the same time, EPA was also studying federal options for regulating GHG emissions under the CAA. Upon issuing a determination that new vehicle emissions would endanger public health, EPA was required under the CAA to set emissions standards for new vehicles. As a result, while California had to struggle to assert its legal authority over vehicle emissions, the auto industry faced the prospect of three regulators—the state of California, the NHTSA, and EPA—each possessing flexibility under their respective enabling statutes to create compliance programs for new automobiles.

In this volatile situation, the parties turned to a nonregulatory process—beyond the traditional administrative and judicial system—to create a voluntary agreement.[114] As a result of this process, the auto industry and state and federal agencies agreed to a negotiated set of standards, which would be implemented and enforced through novel legal devices such as good-faith letters of commitment and nonbinding memoranda of understanding. One of the lead participants in this process, Prof. Jody Freeman, described the strategy in this way:

> Finally, the new policy relied on a number of creative procedural innovations beyond joint rulemaking. The "letters of commitment" signed by the stakeholders, although not legally binding, resemble legal documents. They envision a detailed step-by-step process of implementation, which requires reciprocal demonstrations of good faith by regulators and industry: the auto companies would stay the lawsuits upon issuance of the NOI; EPA would make a final decision on California's preemption waiver; EPA and NHTSA would propose the new rule; California would formally amend its regulations to implement the new agreement; the auto industry would dismiss its preemp-

112. Notice of Decision Denying a Waiver of Clean Air Act Preemption for California's 2009 and Subsequent Model Year Greenhouse Gas Emission Standards for New Motor Vehicles, 73 Fed. Reg. 12156 (Mar. 6, 2008), https://www.govinfo.gov/content/pkg/FR-2008-03-06/pdf/E8-4350.pdf.

113. The information regarding this negotiation is taken from Jody Freeman, *The Obama Administration's National Auto Policy: Lessons from the "Car Deal,"* 35 Harv. Envtl. L. Rev. 343, 349-59 (2011). During the negotiations described, Ms. Freeman served as energy and climate counsel to the White House.

114. *Id.* at 369.

tion lawsuits; and so on. All of this was done, not under a consent decree and with the imprimatur of the court in the context of litigation, but voluntarily. Thus the parties entered an agreement that is best described as a "trust, but verify" regime.

Professor Freeman believes that these kinds of innovations that improve and supplement the regulatory process can be duplicated using

> joint rulemaking or similar uniformity-promoting mechanisms, along with extralegal tools like commitment letters that can memorialize agreements and specify implementation plans. Indeed, one of the most lasting legacies of the car deal may be its example of how agencies might use such regulatory and dispute resolution techniques to simplify and harmonize regulation.[115]

2. Incentives for Sustainable Development to Mitigate Climate Change

There are no federal or state standards for certifying a city as one that promotes sustainable development. There are, however, climate action plans and a few initiatives working in that direction. The International Council for Local Environmental Initiatives (ICLEI) runs a national climate campaign for local governments.[116] ICLEI developed a STAR Community Index that gives guidance to localities regarding indicators they can follow in order to qualify as a sustainable city.[117] Communities in New York can take a pledge to serve as a climate smart community by setting goals to reduce GHG emissions and adapt to predicted climate change.[118] One of the 10 steps in the Climate Smart Communities (CSC) program includes the promotion of climate protection through community land use tools.[119] Communities are instructed to "update land use policies, building codes and community plans in ways that reduce sprawl, minimize development in floodplains and protect forests."

Sustainable Jersey is a completed rating system that municipalities can follow to become "Sustainable Jersey Certified" at one of two levels by earn-

115. *Id.* at 374.

116. *See* International Council for Local Envtl. Initiatives, http://www.icleiusa.org/ (last visited Aug. 17, 2020).

117. *See STAR Community Index*, International Council for Local Envtl. Initiatives, http://www.starcommunities.org/wp-content/uploads/2014/05/Original-STAR-Sustainability-Goals-2010.pdf (last visited Aug. 17, 2020).

118. *See Climate Smart Communities Program*, N.Y. State Dep't Envtl. Conservation, https://www.dec.ny.gov/energy/76483.html (last visited Aug. 17, 2020).

119. *New York Communities: Get Climate Smart*, N.Y. State Dep't Envtl. Conservation, http://www.cameronengineering.com/climatesmart/pdf/Resources%20-%20Fact%20Sheet%20-%20Climate%20Smart%20Communities.pdf (last visited Aug. 17, 2020).

ing points under the categories of "Prosperity," "Planet," and "People."[120] There are 18 subcategories with more than 100 items for which credits can be earned.[121] These items are as diverse as setting up a buy-local program, hosting green fairs, creating safe routes to school, and offering green-building training. One of the subcategories is "Land Use and Transportation," which has 14 items within it.

The current convention for certification allows cities to earn points in a broad range of categories, giving them many options for obtaining favorable ratings.[122] None of these systems yet provide a sufficient emphasis on the tremendous potential for the emissions reductions that come from compact, mixed-use development and transit orientation.

The Cleaner, Greener Communities Program in New York could potentially lead to the creation of such a system. Funded with some of the state's RGGI proceeds,[123] the program began with the development of a regional sustainability plan in 10 regions of the state that already have economic development councils (EDC) and economic development strategies. In 2011, New York launched this economic development initiative and used nearly $1 billion in state funds to support job-producing projects that conform to the regional economic development strategies. In 2012, the state initiated the Cleaner, Greener Communities Program, formed sustainable planning groups in each region, and charged them with the development of sustainability plans by the end of the calendar year.[124] In 2013, the EDCs began administering these regional sustainability plans as part of the regions' articulated economic development strategies.[125] Compliance with the sustain-

---

120. *See* Sustainable Jersey, https://www.sustainablejersey.com/fileadmin/media/Grants_and_Resources/Green_Team_Resources/Program_Overview/Sustainable_Jersey_Overview_Brochure.pdf (last visited Aug. 17, 2020).

121. *See Sustainable Jersey Actions*, Sustainable Jersey, http://www.sustainablejersey.com/actions-certification/actions/ (last visited Aug. 17, 2020).

122. Land Use Law Ctr., Pace Law Sch., Preliminary Report on Certifying Sustainable Cities 13-15 (Winter 2012) (unpublished manuscript) (on file with author).

123. N.Y. State Energy Research & Dev. Auth., Cleaner, Greener Communities Program (June 2014), www.nyserda.ny.gov/-/media/Files/Publications/PPSER/Program-Evaluation/2014ContractorReports/2014-Cleaner-Greener-PLM.pdf [hereinafter Cleaner, Greener Communities Program].

124. *See* Mid-Hudson Planning Consortium, Zoning and Planning for a Sustainable Region: Certifying Sustainable Communities (Nov. 2012), https://law.pace.edu/sites/default/files/LULC/Conference_2012/Zoning%20and%20Planning%20for%20a%20Sustainable%20Region.pdf.

125. N.Y. State Energy Research & Dev. Auth., N.Y's Regional Greenhouse Gas Initiative Inv. Plan (Oct. 16, 2013) https://www.nyserda.ny.gov/-/media/Files/EE/RGGI/2013-RGGI-operating-plan.pdf.

ability plan will be necessary for communities to qualify for $90 million in additional program funds also taken from RGGI proceeds.[126]

These regional plans can provide model language for localities to use in creating mixed-use, compact development zones; TOD; sustainable neighborhood development; district energy zones where new development is served by combined heat and power and on-site energy generation; and similar strategies that lower the emissions attributable to new development by a significant degree. The program could require communities to adopt an appropriate number of these model initiatives in order to receive funding from the EDCs. The state can then use these models to determine which localities to certify as sustainable—a rather different approach from the current sustainable communities certification programs. This approach, if adopted in New York, could serve as a model for the nation or, at the least, for the 12-state TCI consortium.

3. Negotiated Settlements in Lieu of Regulation

In another example of compromise and collaboration, a new natural gas drilling project in Utah has been approved by the U.S. Bureau of Land Management. Anadarko Petroleum Corporation plans to drill 3,675 new wells over 10 years, requiring "594 miles of new roads, 1100 miles of buried and surface gas and water pipelines, and seven miles of . . . power lines."[127] The drilling project would probably "not have been allowed to move forward without lengthy challenges if the company had not been willing to compromise." The Uintah Basin has experienced deteriorating air quality as a result of wintertime ozone—a "relatively rare phenomenon"—and some experts say that the ozone precursor pollutants come from the thousands of gas wells and equipment in the basin.

Anadarko officials have committed to pollution reduction strategies to curb the project's impact to regional air quality; more specifically, the company has agreed to implement technology like electric-powered compressor engines and a closed-loop pipeline to capture and/or reduce fugitive emissions of natural gas and other pollutants. Additionally, the company met with the Southern Utah Wilderness Alliance and committed to limit the number of wells to be drilled in wilderness-quality lands along the White

126. *See* Cleaner, Greener Communities Program, *supra* note 123; *see also* N.Y. State Energy Research & Dev. Auth., N.Y's RGGI-Funded Programs: Status Report, Year Ending December 31, 2010 2-2 (2011) ("New York State enacted numerous deficit reduction measures that included the transfer of $90 million in RGGI auction proceeds to the General Fund.").

127. Scott Streater, *Utah Drilling Project Earns Praise From Enviros*, Energywire (Apr. 9, 2012), http://www.eenews.net/energywire/2012/04/09/4.

River. Anadarko's general manager of regulatory affairs commented that the agreement provides "a common-sense solution that satisfies the environmentalists' concerns while boosting badly needed domestic energy production."

Hydraulic fracturing (colloquially known as hydrofracking) represents another context in which the current regulatory paradigm is inadequate. Until recently, the federal government has been relatively absent from the regulatory conversation, while state and local governments have struggled with the issue of whether states should preempt local land use control—with results differing from state to state.[128] Horizontal hydrofracking is a recently evolved well stimulation technique—designed for areas underlain by large shale formations—in which millions of gallons of water containing large amounts of proprietary chemicals are pumped down the wells under high pressure to create fractures in the hydrocarbon-bearing shale.[129] This causes the release of the natural gas contained in the shale and allows it to be pumped to the surface.

Hydrofracking is directly related to climate change mitigation, since gas-powered electric-generating plants emit less GHG than do coal-fired operations. But the science of hydrofracking is uncertain; there is much debate about the life-cycle effect of gas production on climate change, for example, and the technology may generate a host of other environmental and economic consequences.[130] This gives rise, first, to settlement-based solutions in lieu of regulation, such as those demonstrated in the Uintah Basin example discussed above. Second, it encourages government agencies to assume new roles and embrace innovative strategies that operate independently of the regulatory function or as its complement.[131]

4. Statutes That Embody Stakeholder Negotiations

These negotiated settlements can be induced, to a degree, by state regulation itself. In 2011, for example, the New York State Legislature adopted a statutory utility siting system that furnishes much of the power to the state, without excluding local governments and stakeholders from influencing the official permit outcome.[132] This law reauthorized and revised Article X of

128. *See generally* John R. Nolon & Victoria Polidoro, *Hydrofracking: Disturbances Both Geological and Political: Who Decides?*, 44 Urb. Law. 507 (2012).
129. *See* Enviro. N.J. Research & Pol'y Ctr., The Costs of Fracking: The Price Tag of Dirty Drilling's Environmental Damage 7-9 (2012), http://www.environmentnewjersey.org/sites/environment/files/reports/The%20Costs%20of%20Fracking%20vNJ.pdf.
130. *See* Nolon & Polidoro, *supra* note 128, at 509.
131. *Id.* at 526-30.
132. *See generally* N.Y. Pub. Serv. Law §§160-173 (2011).

the Public Service Law, allowing an electric-generation siting board—which includes two residents of the affected community serving as ad hoc members—to review and approve the siting of electric utility generators of 25 MWs or greater.[133] This board is empowered to override local land use laws that it deems "unreasonably burdensome."[134]

Following the expiration of a previous version of Article X but prior to the adoption of this law, localities regulated this land use and often opposed or significantly delayed the approval of generation plants that were vitally needed by the state's power grid. In establishing a state-controlled siting system, the New York State Legislature required input from the affected locality and local stakeholders.[135] In addition to requiring local residents to sit on the siting board, the revised Article X requires applicants to set up a fund that will enable affected local governments, environmental groups, and the community at large to hire experts, lawyers, and other consultants to participate in the process of creating a scope of review for the proposed utility.[136]

The revised version of Article X encourages applicants to enter into agreements with these parties regarding the scope of review and requires the appointment of a hearing examiner to resolve any disputes that arise over the scoping.[137] While it does not impose a collaborative decision-making process on affected agencies, governments, and private actors, this legislative approach sets the table and provides significant resources to develop such a process.

The previous four examples of new institutions, processes, and statutes evolving in response to climate change provide an important context for evaluating legal strategies that will be effective in practice. These examples illustrate how lawyers and lawmakers are exploring and creating options to regulate and prevent the negative effects of climate change. The traditional approach to determining where to develop land is a regulatory one, and lawyers and legal educators tend to default to regulations as a solution to such problems. In the next section, we address the difficulties involved in severely limiting or banning development in coastal areas sensitive to inundation and severe storms; this sets the stage for employing nonregulatory devices and methods.

133. *Id.* §162.
134. *Id.* §168(3)(e).
135. *Id.* §166(j), (k).
136. *Id.* §163(4)(a).
137. *Id.* §163(5)

III. Sea-Level Rise Confronts the Legacy of *Lucas*

Climate change experts agree that sea levels will rise and that coastal storms will become stronger as temperatures increase. Since these conditions will damage or destroy properties built in vulnerable areas, strict regulations should be enacted to prevent new development in carefully crafted no-build zones—in particular, areas that are likely to be inundated, and areas that are subject to the highest winds and most severe flooding.[138] In *Lucas*, however, the Court held that regulations preventing all economic use of the land are compensable takings, unless the landowner's use of the land constituted a nuisance or was otherwise inconsistent with preexisting background principles of state law.[139] This is an unfortunate catch-22 situation for land use regulators: caution suggests that they must proscribe development in dangerous areas, yet they must also be careful not to effect a compensable taking. It is possible, however, that *Lucas'* prescriptive language and seemingly narrow exceptions provide courts leeway to interpret the case using background principles of state law to uphold severe restrictions in threatened areas, demonstrating the tendency of the law to change with the times.

A. *Sea-Level Rise*

Sea-level rise presents one of the most pressing challenges of the 21st century, expected to expose over four million properties worth an estimated $710 billion to storm surges and flooding.[140] As of the date of its Fourth Assessment Report, the IPCC predicted a global average sea-level rise of 0.18 meters to 0.59 meters by the end of the century.[141] A more recent report by the CCSP, however, found that "the recent acceleration of ice discharges from the polar ice sheets would imply an additional contribution up to 0.20 m [to the IPCC estimates],"[142] which suggests "that a global sea-level rise of 1 [meter] to the year 2100 should be considered for future planning and policy discussions."[143] Indeed, studies more recent than the CCSP's report indicate

138. One option for preventing development in the most threatened coastal areas is to amend zoning and building codes to require that new development be protected from flooding (through elevating the land, building on platforms, anchoring buildings to concrete slabs, etc.) and fortified against hurricane force winds (by requiring better materials and construction techniques). There is a point, however, beyond which building technology is simply not up to the task of protecting buildings and their occupants from severe damage. It is in these places that, inevitably, the issue of banning development will be raised and discussed, presenting the questions and issues addressed in this part.

139. 505 U.S. at 1030.

140. Howard Botts et al., 2012 Corelogic Storm Surge Report 8 (2013).

141. IPCC Synthesis Report, *supra* note 49, at 45.

142. CCSP Coastal Sensitivity, *supra* note 55, at 15.

143. *Id.* at 20.

that "[e]ven for the lowest emission scenario [generated by the IPCC], sea-level rise is then likely to be ≈1 m; for the highest, it may even come closer to 2 m [over 1990 levels]."[144]

Since 1990, policymakers have done little to advance effective responses to sea-level rise.[145] Generally speaking, there are three main policies toward sea-level rise: (1) retreat; (2) accommodation; and (3) protection.[146] Retreat policies aim to minimize the hazards of sea-level rise by restricting, prohibiting, or removing development from vulnerable areas. Examples of "[r]etreat strategies include rolling easements, [government] land purchases, and setback requirements." Accommodation strategies attempt to minimize damage to structures from flooding and storm surges. Options include "minimum floor elevations and . . . structural bracing" to protect against "surging water and high winds."[147] Protective measures essentially defend against the threats of sea-level rise—such as "flooding, . . . [damage to] infrastructure, shore erosion, salinity intrusion[,] and the loss of natural resources"—and are typically implemented on a smaller scale, for example, by individual buildings or sites rather than entire neighborhoods. Defensive solutions may be split into "hard and soft structural [options]."[148] Hard options include dikes, levees, floodwalls, seawalls, revetments, bulkheads, groins, detached breakwaters, tidal barriers, and salt water intrusion barriers.[149] Soft options include beach renourishment, dune building, and constructed wetlands, reefs, or barrier islands.[150]

Consider, for example, the erosive effect of sea-level rise on the West Coast of the United States. Erosion along San Francisco's Ocean Beach coastline—a 3.5-mile stretch of beach—threatens significant San Francisco Bay area infrastructure, including "the Great Highway, a $220 million wastewater treatment plant, and a[n] . . . . underground pipe" that carries sewage-tainted storm water.[151] With California officials estimating that the sea level could

144. Vermeer & Rahmstorf, *supra* note 56, at 21531.

145. *C.f.*, J. Dronkers et al., Intergovernmental Panel on Climate Change, Report of the Coastal Mgmt. Subgroup, Strategies for Adaptation to Sea-Level Rise 6-8 (1990), http://www.papers.risingsea.net/federal_reports/IPCC-1990-adaptation-to-sea-level-rise.pdf [hereinafter IPCC Sea Level Rise] (noting possible responses to sea-level rise); City of New York, Vision 2020: New York City Comprehensive Waterfront Plan 109-10 (2011), https://www1.nyc.gov/site/planning/plans/vision-2020-cwp/vision-2020-cwp.page [hereinafter NYC Waterfront Plan] (same).

146. *See* NYC Waterfront Plan, *supra* note 145, at 109.

147. IPCC Sea-Level Rise, *supra* note 145, at 7.

148. *Id.* (internal quotation marks omitted).

149. *Id.* at 8.

150. *Id.*; NYC Waterfront Plan, *supra* note 145, at 110.

151. Felicity Barringer, *Both Coasts Watch Closely as San Francisco Faces Erosion*, N.Y. Times, Mar. 24, 2012, at A18, http://www.nytimes.com/2012/03/25/science/earth/san-francisco-fights-erosion-as-coastal-cities-watch-closely.html?_r=1.

rise by 14 inches by 2050, local, state, and federal officials are considering whether "herculean efforts [should] be made to preserve the beach, the pipe and the plant, or [whether the community] should . . . simply bow to nature[.]" One study said that sea-level rise could impose more than $650 million in infrastructure repair costs by the end of the century, a large proportion of which stem from the wastewater treatment plant.

Officials are struggling to determine the most effective option for their respective localities. Indeed, these decisions require difficult judgments. Shoreline armoring protects infrastructure, but it interferes with the public's beach access and is destructive to vegetation and bird habitats. Beach nourishment replenishes lost sand and allows reconstruction of dunes and animal habitats, but sand infusions are often cost-prohibitive.[152] Moreover, just one fierce storm can undo all nourishment efforts. Retreat allows the shoreline to move naturally inland, but it necessitates the removal of roads and loss of other infrastructure, putting homes and other structures at risk.[153]

Notwithstanding these complexities, officials in San Francisco developed a Sea-Level Rise Action Plan in 2016.[154] The plan "include[s] narrowing the Great Highway . . . eventually rerouting it away from the coast . . . ." The Ocean Beach Master Plan developed by the San Francisco Bay Area Planning and Urban Research Association, "recommends eventual retreat for portions of the Great Highway and rerouting of the Highway . . . ." It also recommends accommodating sea-level rise "by improving natural infrastructure, dunes and vegetation, and replacing roads and parking lots with open space, bicycle, and pedestrian paths."

South Carolina's State Legislature has moved toward a policy of retreat and accommodation. It declared that the dynamic beach-dune system along its coast remains "extremely important" because it "generates approximately two-thirds of [the state's] annual tourism industry revenue" and functions as "a storm barrier," a "habitat for numerous species," and a "natural healthy environment for the citizens" of the state.[155] Recognizing that "development . . . has been [unwisely] sited too close to the system," the legislature deemed it in "both the public and private interests to protect the system

152. National Oceanic & Atmospheric Admin., State, Territory, and Commonwealth Beach Renourishment Programs: A National Overview 3 (2000), https://coast.noaa.gov/data/czm/media/finalbeach.pdf.

153. *Id.* at 11.

154. City and Cty. of S.F., S.F. Sea-Level Rise Action Plan (Mar. 2016), https://default.sfplanning.org/plans-and-programs/planning-for-the-city/sea-level-rise/sea-level-rise-action-plan-final-draft-full.pdf.

155. S.C. Code Ann. §48-39-250(1)(a)-(d) (2008).

from this unwise development."[156] Because armoring provides a "false sense of security,"[157] South Carolina chose to "severely restrict the use of hard erosion-control devices to armor the beach-dune system and to encourage the replacement of hard erosion-control devices with soft technologies."[158] The state prohibits most erosion-control structures seaward of a setback line based on the crest of the dune system.[159]

State policies dealing with the issues of whether and how state programs should protect the coasts leave unexplored the issue of whether local governments, under their land use plans and regulations, should restrict development along the coasts. What happens, for instance, if a state like South Carolina adopts a policy of retreat and ceases all efforts to build protective structures but local governments continue to allow development in areas that will be inundated as state-planned retreat happens? Conversely, what happens if the state government adopts a policy of armoring coastal communities and a local government wishes to prevent development in an area that it knows is particularly vulnerable to inundation and coastal storms? The authority to regulate land use has been delegated to local governments to protect the public interest.[160] At a minimum, state and local coastal development policies must be coordinated, and local land use regulations that permit the construction of homes and other buildings in areas mapped for inundation should be reconsidered. Where zoning allows such construction, it permits development in high-risk coastal zones to the detriment of homebuyers, tenants, equity investors, mortgagees, and the taxpayers who finance supportive infrastructure in such areas.

Where local governments severely regulate coastal development, whether by their own initiative or in accordance with state policy, they face a formidable obstacle in the total-taking doctrine of the *Lucas* case, decided over two decades ago when much less was known about sea-level rise and the effect of higher global temperatures on coastal storms. This case must be understood and evaluated for interpretive paths that can align its holding with present realities.

---

156. *Id.* §48-39-250(4).
157. *Id.* §48-39-250(5).
158. *Id.* §48-39-260(3).
159. *See id.* §§48-39-220(A)-(D), -290(B)(2)(a)-(b) (explaining the prohibition of erosion control structures based on the crest of the dune system).
160. John R. Nolon, *Historical Overview of the American Land Use Law System: A Diagnostic Approach to Evaluating Governmental Land Use Control, in* Comparative Land Use Law and Global Sustainable Development 581, 587-88 (Cambridge Univ. Press 2006).

B. *The Legacy of* Lucas

State and local regulations that prohibit building on coastal lands raise complicated Fifth Amendment issues. Do they not, on their face, destroy all economic value, thereby constituting a total taking under *Lucas*?[161] *Lucas* involved a state regulation that prevented shoreline development on the Isle of Palms, South Carolina, a barrier-island community.[162] The South Carolina Coastal Council prevented David Lucas from building homes on two lots because of their proximity to ecologically sensitive dunes. The Court held that a regulation that destroys all "economically viable use"[163] of a claimant's property constitutes a taking unless, under the "background principles of the [s]tate's law,"[164] the property use the regulation prohibits is "not part of his title to begin with."[165] For example, if the state's nuisance law would permit surrounding property owners to enjoin an owner's use of land for unhealthy enterprises like brick-making, a regulation prohibiting that use is not a taking.[166] On remand, the state court found that nuisance law constituted no bar to the development proposed by Mr. Lucas.[167] Accordingly, it awarded him compensation for the taking of his property by the state regulation.

Notably, in an effort to emphasize the importance of state law in regulatory takings jurisprudence, the majority cited the Court's "traditional resort to 'existing rules or understandings that stem from an independent source such as state law' to define the range of interests that qualify for protection as 'property' under the Fifth and Fourteenth Amendments."[168] The Court further noted that although "[i]t seems unlikely that common-law principles would have prevented the erection of any habitable or productive improvements on [Lucas]'s land[,] . . . [t]he question . . . is one of state law to be dealt with on remand."[169] It has been over 20 years since the *Lucas* decision, and we have accumulated most of our knowledge about sea-level rise during that time. Nevertheless, the language of the *Lucas* decision itself, in light of its enumerated exceptions, the seriousness of climate change, and the coastal damage it portends, may provide courts the leeway they need to

161. 505 U.S. at 1030.
162. *Id.* at 1006-07.
163. *Id.* at 1016 (internal quotation marks omitted).
164. *Id.* at 1029.
165. *Id.* at 1027.
166. *See generally* Hadacheck v. Sebastian, 239 U.S. 394, 413 (1915) (holding that despite the preexisting use of the land as a brickyard, the changing character of the surrounding area rendered the use a hazard to public health).
167. Lucas v. South Carolina Coastal Council, 424 S.E.2d 484, 486 (S.C. 1992).
168. *Lucas*, 505 U.S. at 1030 (quoting Board of Regents of State Colls. v. Roth, 408 U.S. 564, 577 (1972)).
169. *Id.* at 1031.

support no-build zones and highly prescriptive regulations regarding coastal development.

C. *Reinterpreting the Legacy of* Lucas *in a Changing Environment*

This quote from the *Lucas* decision underscores the ambivalence of the common law with respect to changing conditions: "The fact that a particular use has long been engaged in by similarly situated owners ordinarily imports a lack of any common-law prohibition (though changed circumstances or new knowledge may make what was previously permissible no longer so)."[170] Is sea-level rise a "changed circumstance"? Are recent scientific reports and maps "new knowledge"? Further, how will South Carolina's adoption of a state policy against coastal armoring—threatening the disappearance of coastal land due to sea-level rise—change the legal landscape?[171] Is it possible that new knowledge about the harm to the coastal environment and our new-found appreciation of ecosystem services[172] would now sustain a nuisance claim against coastal development in some locations?[173]

Several defenses are available to local governments when their no-build zones are attacked as total takings under *Lucas*. And courts may be receptive to these defenses, even where they are novel. In 1924, the Oregon Supreme Court encouraged progressive interpretation of common-law principles with this language:

> The very essence of the common law is flexibility and adaptability. . . . If the common law should become . . . crystallized . . . , it would cease to be the common law of history, and would be an inelastic and arbitrary code. It is one of the established principles of the common law, which has been carried along with its growth that precedents must yield to the reason of different or modified conditions.[174]

---

170. *Lucas*, 505 U.S. at 1031 (citing Restatement (Second) of Torts §827 (1965)).

171. *See supra* notes 155-59 and accompanying text.

172. "'[E]cosystem services,' refers to 'a wide range of conditions and processes through which natural ecosystems, and the species that are part of them, help sustain and fulfill human life.'" Keith H. Hirokawa, *Sustaining Ecosystem Services Through Local Environmental Law*, 28 Pace Envtl. L. Rev. 760, 760 (2011) (quoting Gretchen Daily et al., Ecosystem Services: *Benefits Supplied to Human Societies by Natural Ecosystems*, 2 Issues in Ecology 1, 2 (1997)).

173. *See* J.B. Ruhl, *The "Background Principles" of Natural Capital and Ecosystem Services—Did* Lucas *Open Pandora's Box?*, 22 J. Land Use & Envtl. L. 525, 540 (2007):

> [W]hen [damage to] the environment can be linked to utilitarian costs and benefits, which is precisely what the burgeoning research on natural capital and ecosystem services is revealing about ecological resources, the common law is more likely to pay attention. The cases are not numerous by any means, but there is evidence that this theme is being picked up in the law of public nuisance and of the public trust doctrine.

174. In re Hood River, 227 P. 1065, 1086-87 (Or. 1924).

For instance, the law of nuisance is one of the oldest and most contextual doctrines of common law, and courts may expand it to support regulations that prevent coastal development. Nuisance is but one of many "background principles of state law"[175] that can be relied upon to show that beachfront development is not part of the landowner's title.[176]

1. Public Trust and the Doctrine of Waste

A classic formulation of the public trust doctrine was articulated by the Supreme Court in *Shively v. Bowlby:*

> By the common law, both the title and the dominion of the sea, and of rivers and arms of the sea, where the tide ebbs and flows, and of all the lands below high- water mark, within the jurisdiction of the crown of England, are in the king. Such water and the lands which they cover, either at all times, or at least when the tide is in, are incapable of ordinary and private occupation, cultivation, and improvement; and their natural and primary uses are public in their nature . . . .[177]

Is it possible, in South Carolina for example, where the state has adopted a policy against armoring the beach and interrupting the rise of the sea, that the public enjoys a future interest in coastal properties and that current owners, by analogy to the law of life estates, have an obligation not to waste the inheritance of the remaindermen? Perhaps more consistent with the ownership of a fee simple, is the present interest of littoral owners subject to a condition subsequent, with the public owning a future interest similar to the reversionary interest known as either a possibility of reverter or a right of entry?[178] In either case, the current right to use the land might be properly

---

175. Michael C. Blumm & Lucus Ritchie, Lucas's *Unlikely Legacy: The Rise of Background Principles as Categorical Takings Defenses*, 29 HARV. ENVTL. L. REV. 321, 333 (2005) ("[T]he *Lucas* defense is not limited to harm-preventing nuisance restrictions. Instead, the background principles defense potentially applies to any use-limiting regulation.").

176. *See* Glenn P. Sugamelli, Lucas v. South Carolina Coastal Council*: The Categorical and Other "Exceptions" to Liability for Fifth Amendment Takings of Private Property Far Outweigh the "Rule,"* 29 ENVTL. L. 939, 959 (1999). "In the years since *Lucas* was decided, the Supreme Court has consistently allowed state (and federal) courts leeway to define general or state-specific background principles, rejecting every petition for certiorari that has attempted to challenge decisions that denied takings claims based on background principles."

177. Shively v. Bowlby, 152 U.S. 1, 11 (1894).

178. If the transfer of title at the dynamic property boundary of the shore is a contingent future interest, then the littoral owner could be seen as holding a fee simple defeasible subject to the future condition of sea-level rise. A fee simple defeasible is a type of property interest in which the fee holder's title is subject to the performance (or non-performance) of a condition specified by the grantor. Once that condition occurs, however, the fee owner immediately loses title to the property and it passes to the third party who held the contingent future interest. Margaret E. Peloso & Margaret R. Caldwell,

regulated to prevent waste of the public's future interest.[179] Does this mean that a regulation requiring removal of buildings after they are inundated by sea-level rise would be sustained under this background principle?[180] If so, could a locality require a developer to impose a deed restriction requiring the building to be removed in the future if inundation occurs?

2. Natural Use Doctrine

A rough analogy to a local no-build zone can be found in a 1963 New Jersey opinion that invalidated as a regulatory taking the creation of a Meadow Development Zone that prevented residential development in a 1,500-acre swamp to preserve open space and prevent flooding.[181] The land use regulation limited development to a variety of agricultural, outdoor recreational, conservation, and public uses, which the court found left no economically viable use of the land. Nearly 30 years later, the New Jersey courts, based on their more evolved understanding of swamps as valuable wetlands, disregarded the holding in the earlier case. In *Gardner v. New Jersey Pinelands Commission*, the court upheld a development restriction that prohibited the residential development of farmland because the restriction permitted only agricultural uses with limited possibilities for other economic development of the land.[182]

The *Gardner* court rejected the landowner's takings claim, finding a lack of investment-backed expectations, and in the course of its opinion, the court disapproved of much of the language in the 1963 case.[183] The court relied on *American Dredging Co. v. State Department of Environmental Protection*,[184] which noted:

> Where the effect of the governmental prohibition against use is not in furtherance of a governmental activity, such as flood control or preservation of land for a park or recreational area, but rather to preserve the land for ecological

Dynamic Property Rights: The Public Trust Doctrine and Takings in a Changing Climate 30 Stan. Envtl. L.J. 51, 87 (2011).

179. Because the state will take title to coastal lands submerged by sea-level rise, "it appears the state could maintain an action in waste, and the logical extension is that the state may also use the prevention of waste as a justification to deny development. Waste is a common law property doctrine and as such qualifies as a *Lucas* background principle." *Id.* at 85.

180. *See* discussion *infra* Part IV.

181. Morris Cnty. Land Imp. Co. v. Parsippany-Troy Hills Twp., 193 A.2d 232, 234, 241-42 (N.J. 1963).

182. 593 A.2d 251, 257 (N.J. 1991).

183. *Id.* at 261-62.

184. *See generally* American Dredging Co. v. State Dep't of Envtl. Prot., 391 A.2d 1265 (N.J. Super. Ct. Ch. Div. 1978), *aff'd*, 404 A.2d 42 (N.J. Super. App. Div. 1979).

> reasons in its natural environment without change, the consideration of the reasonableness of the exercise of the police power must be redetermined.[185]

It was during the 30-year period between *Gardner* and *Morris County* that land use patterns rapidly sprawled beyond urban boundaries, and the resulting ecological damage became manifest. By the date of *Gardner*, a discernible environmental ethic had entered land use legislation and jurisprudence.

3. Permitting Minimal Use of a Parcel

Case law suggests that allowing some economic use of the land will save a regulation from a total takings claim. In *Lucas*, the state regulation prevented all development of Mr. Lucas' two residential lots. In *Gardner*, however, the regulation allowed some but, in the eyes of the owner, minimal economic use of the land. Where developers propose significant projects near the beach, is it a total taking if a small portion of the land is allowed to be developed, such as the portion of the parcel least likely to be inundated? Where some development value remains, a takings claim will be decided using the multi-factor balancing test of *Penn Central Transportation Co. v. City of New York*.[186] One of the factors includes "the extent to which the regulation has interfered with distinct investment backed expectations." If it is now known that sea-level rise endangers development, does a landowner have legitimate expectations to fully develop the parcel?[187]

---

185. *Id.* at 1268. A number of other cases in New Jersey failed to follow or distinguished the *Morris County* case. *See, e.g.*, Matter of Loveladies Harbor Inc., 422 A.2d 107, 111 (N.J. App. Div. 1980); Usdin v. State Dep't of Envtl. Prot. of Water Res., 414 A.2d 280, 285-86 (N.J. Super. Ct. Law. Div. 1980); N.J. Bldg. Ass'n v. Department of Envtl. Prot., 404 A.2d 320, 330 (N.J. App. Div. 1979); Toms River Affiliates v. Department of Envtl. Prot., 355 A.2d 679 (N.J. App. Div. 1976); Sands Point Harbor, Inc. v. Sullivan, 346 A.2d 612, 614 (N.J. App. Div. 1975).
186. 438 U.S. 104, 124 (1978). In *Palazzolo v. Rhode Island*, 533 U.S. 606, 632 (2001), almost all of the plaintiff's land was designated as coastal wetlands, leaving only a fraction of the land eligible for development. The Court, in referring to the state court's holding regarding the plaintiff's regulatory taking claim, stated:

    > The court did not err in finding that petitioner failed to establish a deprivation of all economic value, for it is undisputed that the parcel retains significant worth for the construction of a residence. The claims under the *Penn Central* analysis were not examined, and for this purpose the case should be remanded.

187. *See* S.D. Dep't of Legislative Audit, Accounting Manual, Sec. IV—Accounting Records illus. 23: Useful Life Table (Apr. 2002), https://legislativeaudit.sd.gov/resources/counties/County_Section_4/County_Section%204_Useful_Life_Table.pdf [hereinafter S.D. Useful Life Table]; *see also, e.g.*, *Palazzolo*, 533 U.S. at 617 (explaining the holding of Penn Central):

    > Where a regulation places limitations on land that fall short of eliminating all economically beneficial use, a taking nonetheless may have occurred, depending on a complex of factors including the regulation's economic effect on the landowner, the extent to which the regulation interferes with *reasonable investment-backed expectations*, and the character of the government action. (Emphasis added.)

4. Changes in the Regulatory Environment

In *Colorado Department of Health v. The Mill*, mill owners brought a takings action challenging the Department of Health's regulations imposing use restrictions on the uranium mill operation.[188] The Colorado Supreme Court held that The Mill should have known that "the right to make any use of the property that would create a hazard to public health by spreading radioactive contamination was excluded from The Mill's title at the onset."[189] The court, in referring to the "regulatory environment" governing radioactive materials, held that the restrictions fell under the "background principles" exception to the *Lucas* total taking doctrine.[190] This included Colorado common-law nuisance, state nuisance statutes, the department's regulations, and federal standards contained in the Uranium Mill Tailings Radiation Control Act.[191]

Is the danger to life and property inherent in building on coastal properties vulnerable to inundation and storm surges analogous to the dangers of radioactive contamination? Are recent international, national, and state scientific studies and maps sufficiently well understood to qualify as changed circumstances under the language of *Lucas* and the Restatement of Torts?[192] Do these create an environment in which severe regulations are to be expected, following the logic of *The Mill* case?

IV. Easing the Transition: Above Regulations

The prospect of enacting regulations to control coastal development is frustrated not only by the *Lucas* doctrine but also by the uncertainty of how much the sea level will rise in any given location,[193] the relatively long-term nature of the dangers involved, and the practical considerations of imposing severe limitations on local property owners. Local officials in particular understand that local property owners acquired their properties knowing that they were zoned for housing development or other economically viable uses. They also

188. State Dep't of Health v. Will, 887 P.2d 993, 997 (Colo. 1995).
189. *Id.* at 1002.
190. *Id.* at 1001-02.
191. *Id.* at 1002-03.
192. *See* 505 U.S. at 1031.
193.

> [S]ea-level rise poses two challenges for leaders trying to formulate adaptation plans. First, sea-level rise is slow, measured in millimeters per year, and the full extent of climate change-driven sea-level rise is expected to take centuries to manifest. This is a planning horizon outside the political ken of most governmental bodies; indeed, planning horizons longer than a few decades are extremely rare. Second, scientists are still uncertain as to the extent of the problem. Specifically, how high will the oceans rise?

Craig, *supra* note 8, at 521.

understand that these owners have been paying local property taxes on their parcels, assessed at their market value as zoned. They further understand that property owners vote, have local political influence, and belong to industry groups that lobby state officials. For all of these reasons, officials may be reluctant to legislate a no-build zone based on the uncertainty of sea-level rise and its potential impact on their coast during the short- and mid-term future. As a result, they might ask their municipal attorneys if there are any nonregulatory options available to limit development in vulnerable coastal areas. Although fraught with consequences of their own, there are readily available alternatives to onerous coastal regulation.

A. *Comprehensive Planning*

A reasonable starting point toward a nonregulatory approach would be to adopt a component of the local comprehensive plan that both embodies the most recent scientific findings and projections regarding sea-level rise and cautions prospective purchasers regarding development on vulnerable coastal properties.[194] A chapter on sea-level rise in the comprehensive plan of the city of Bainbridge Island, Washington, entitled the Environmental Element,[195] is directly on point in this regard. Flooding and erosion are principal concerns for the city, and its objectives are to minimize, reduce, or eliminate their impact.[196] This code component mandates no net loss of the city's aquatic resources, maintenance of its vegetated buffers between proposed development and aquatic resources, and preservation of stream courses and riparian habitat.[197] It also calls for the transfer and purchase of development rights.[198] To mitigate damage due to frequent floods, the plan limits future development and alteration of natural floodplains, mandates the preservation of stream channels and natural protective barriers, revises the Flood Insurance Rate Map to reflect the natural migration of frequently flooded areas, and requires the implementation of nonstructural protective methods

194. In some states, this may be problematic given pronouncements by the state legislature, governor, or state agencies that flatly prevent public action to be taken based on climate change. For example, despite the North Carolina Coastal Resource Commissions Report recommending that the state plan for approximately 39 inches of sea-level rise, the North Carolina Senate passed legislation that prevents state and local agencies from developing regulations related to sea-level rise. Instead, the state's coastal management will have to rely on historic data about sea-level rise, not data accounting for climate change. Rob Young, *Shoot the Messenger: Carolina's Costly Mistake on Sea Level Rise*, Yale Env't 360 (2012), https://e360.yale.edu/features/north_carolina_costly_mistake_on_climate_change.

195. City of Bainbridge Island, 2016 Comprehensive Plan: Environmental Element (Feb. 28, 2017), https://www.bainbridgewa.gov/DocumentCenter/View/7800/5-ENVIRONMENTAL?bidId=.

196. *Id.* at 8.

197. *Id.* at 5-6.

198. *Id.* at 4.

such as setbacks and natural vegetation.[199] These requirements are imposed by the National Flood Insurance Program, which limits the availability of flood insurance to property owners who build in accordance with local zoning prescriptions that regulate development in Special Flood Hazard Areas designated by the Federal Emergency Management Agency (FEMA) Flood Insurance Rate Maps.[200] When applied to areas subject to coastal flooding due to storm surges, this program provides an effective method of putting property purchasers on notice of worsening conditions along the coasts since the FEMA maps are regularly updated to reflect current conditions.

Several components of the comprehensive plan in Collier County, Florida, create a planning framework for coastal development.[201] One of its objectives calls for "mechanisms or projects which limit the effects of development and which help in the restoration of the natural functions of coastal barriers and affected beaches and dunes."[202] Another declares that "[d]evelopment and redevelopment proposals shall consider the implications of potential rise in sea level."[203] More specifically, the plan states that where an "[environmental impact statement] is required, an analysis shall demonstrate that the project will remain fully functional for its intended use after a six-inch rise in sea level."[204] Given current sea-level rise projections, this six-inch metric dovetails roughly with the useful life of newly constructed buildings, ensuring that investors and occupants of such buildings will not be deprived of the benefit of the new building over time.[205]

Comprehensive plans are not regulatory documents.[206] They establish a vision for future development, and they contain goals, objectives, and recommended strategies, such as those contained in the Collier County and Bainbridge examples. Future zoning, in most states, must be in conformance with the comprehensive plan, and the plan can guide local boards that approve development projects in discharging their duties.[207] The development-review and approval process may adopt informal protocols that further the objec-

---

199. *Id.* at 6-7.

200. *See* Floor Disaster Protection Act of 1973, 42 U.S.C. §§4001-4130 (documenting how NFIP works).

201. Collier Cnty. Planning Servs. Dep't, County Growth Management Plan: Conservation and Coastal Management Element 46-50 (2011), http://www.colliergov.net/Modules/ShowDocument.aspx?documentid=41172.

202. *Id.* at 46.

203. *Id.* at 48.

204. *Id.* at 50.

205. *See* Fannie Mae, Estimated Useful Life Tables (Aug. 2019), https://multifamily.fanniemae.com/sites/g/files/koqyhd161/files/2019-08/4099f.pdf.

206. *See* Barry Cullingworth & Roger W. Caves, Planning in the USA: Policies, Issues, and Processes 126 (3d ed. 2009).

207. *Id.* at 131-32.

tives of the comprehensive plan.[208] Where a comprehensive plan refers to and incorporates by reference future sea-level rise projection data (including maps and documents indicating the probable effect of sea-level rise on coastal development), it can provide a predicate for a non-regulatory approach to project review and approval.

B. *The Project Application Process*

Planners who advise local land use boards can use the information contained in a sea-level rise component of the comprehensive plan to revise the application requirements governing local administrative review of project submissions. They can require, for example, that the developer submit site drawings that identify any portion of the parcel likely to be inundated by sea-level rise during the useful life of the building.[209] They can further require—through conditions imposed on subdivision and site plan approvals—that the developer place any buildings and infrastructure in a location that guarantees the safety of occupants and the stability of the building during its useful life. Applicants can be provided with sea-level rise maps issued from a variety of sources, including state agencies,[210] legislative committees, governor's task forces,[211] university institutes,[212] or other respected and objective nonprofit organizations. Depending on the source, these maps may be given judicial recognition, support a court's finding of rationality for actions taken to condition or deny the application, and be used to defend substantive due process attacks on such decisions.

In addition, the developer can be required to document the sources of financing secured for the project, including equity investors and construction and permanent lenders. Where sea-level rise projection maps are contained in an official document like the comprehensive plan or issued by responsible agencies or organizations, investors and lenders will likely be on notice of

208. *Id.* at 134-35.

209. *See* S.D. Useful Life Table, *supra* note 186.

210. *See, e.g.,* Assessment Report of Regional Differences Within Fla., S. Fla. Regional Council (July 2016), https://floridadep.gov/sites/default/files/CRI_Assessment_Report_of_Regional_Differences_within_Florida.pdf.

211. *See, e.g.,* Adaptation Subcomm., Governor's Steering Comm. on Climate Change, The Impacts of Climate Change on Connecticut Agriculture, Infrastructure, Natural Resources and Public Health 105 (2010), https://www.adaptationclearinghouse.org/resources/the-impacts-of-climate-change-on-connecticut-agriculture-infrastructure-natural-resources-and-public-health.html..

212. *See, e.g.,* Klaus H. Jacob et al., Lamont-Doherty Earth Observatory of Columbia Univ., Risk Increase to Infrastructure Due to Sea-Level Rise 16 (2000), http://geodesy.unr.edu/hanspeterplag/library/documents/2000_jacob_etal_ny_infrastructure.pdf.; *Model of Sea Level Rise, Coastal Erosion, and Wave Overtopping in Waimanalo*, Univ. of Hawaii: Sea Level Rise Website (2008), http://www.soest.hawaii.edu/coasts/sealevel/Runup_animation.html.

them and will only be willing to invest if they believe the project is economically viable. If investors conclude that the project is not economically feasible, then it will sink under its own weight and fail to proceed any further in the local review and approval process. Any claim that the local process resulted in the taking of value of the proposed project can be countered by showing that investors and lenders made their decision based on knowledge they gained about the long-term viability of the proposed investment through the exercise of due diligence. Under the *Lucas* doctrine, it is not the regulation that prevents the development in this instance but rather the private market risks.[213] To substantiate any *Lucas* claim, the owner would also have to show that all economic value of the property was taken.[214] Proposals that envision less construction on the land in order to avoid development on potential inundation areas would likely be approved under this process, precluding availability of the total taking argument.

C. Environmental Impact Review

Development projects in some states are subject to review under "little NEPAs," which require an assessment of the project's impact on the environment.[215] Environmental impact reviews routinely consider the effect of conditions and circumstances around a proposed development site. Federal and state environmental review statutes mandate review of the potential impact of sea-level rise during the lifetime of a proposed building on public health and safety, on the structural integrity of proposed buildings and infrastructure, and on the environment.[216]

The Council on Environmental Quality issued a draft National Environmental Policy Act (NEPA) guidance document suggesting that an environmental impact statement should consider "[t]he relationship of climate change effects to a proposed action . . . including the relationship to proposal design, environmental impacts, mitigation, and adaptation measures."[217] In New York, the State Department of Environmental Conservation (DEC) has been directed "to incorporate climate change adaptation strategies into DEC programs, actions and activities, as appropriate . . . ," including in environ-

213. *See* 505 U.S. at 1034-35.
214. *Id.* at 1015.
215. *See, e.g.*, N.Y. Dep't of Envtl. Conservation, *Environmental Impact Assessment in N.Y. State*, http://www.dec.ny.gov/permits/357.html (last visited Aug. 17, 2020).
216. *See* Patrick Woolsey, *Sea-Level Rise Addressed in Environmental Impact Statements*, L. Blog (Dec. 12, 2011), http://blogs.law.columbia.edu/climatechange/2011/12/12/sea-level-rise-addressed-in-environmental-impact-statements/.
217. Memorandum from Nancy H. Sutley, Chair, Council on Envtl. Quality, to Heads of Federal Departments and Agencies (Feb. 18, 2010); 40 C.F.R. §1502.15 (1978).

mental impact statements prepared under the State Environmental Quality Impact Review Act (SEQRA).[218] Such analyses should "[i]dentify potential adverse impacts from climate change," and

> [i]n analyses and decision-making, use best available scientific information of environmental conditions resulting from the impacts of climate change (e.g., . . . sea-level rise and increased coastal flooding); [i]ncorporate adaptive management into program planning and actions, which uses scientifically based and measurable evaluation, testing of alternative management approaches, and readjustment as new information becomes available[.]

Even where state law does not require a discrete environmental impact review, state and local site-plan review requirements may require a review of certain environmental impacts where they have a close nexus with the proposed project.[219] Local governments have the expressed or implied power in most states to adopt reasonable site-plan and subdivision regulations and, where supported by expert reports and reliable maps, such regulations can be amended to include standards that protect property and people from dangers and "menaces" such as storm surges or inundation.[220]

D. *Project Approval Conditions*

Once a project is submitted for the review of a local planning board to approve the subdivision or site plan, the reviewing agency can place reasonable conditions on the approval of the proposed development for the protection of the public health, safety, or welfare. These conditions can be negotiated with the applicant. For example, a board could decide to approve the project only on the condition that the developer agrees to remove any buildings that are destroyed by storms or that are inundated by sea-level rise.[221] Under the pub-

218. N.Y. Dep't of Envtl. Conservation, *Commissioner's Policy—Climate Change and DEC Action*, http://www.dec.ny.gov/regulations/65034.html (last visited Aug. 17, 2020).

219. *See, e.g.*, Town of Wawayanda, N.Y. Zoning Code, art. VII, §195-68(N) (2013) (requiring applicants for site-plan approval to demonstrate conformance with stormwater pollution prevention plan), http://ecode360.com/12930522; N.Y. Vill. Law §7-725-a (McKinney 2011); N.Y. Gen. City Law §27-a(4) (McKinney 2003); N.Y. Town Law § 274-a(4) (McKinney 2004) (all stating that "the authorized board shall have the authority to impose such reasonable conditions and restrictions as are directly related to an incidental to the proposed site plan").

220. *See, e.g.*, Town of Carlisle, N.Y., Site Plan Regulations 56 (2013):

> The purpose of these regulations is to protect the health, welfare, and safety of the inhabitants of the Town of Carlisle by enforcement of the Carlisle Site Plan Review Regulations so that land to be subdivided may be free from the peril of flood, fire, health endangerment, or other *menace* prior to the erection of buildings." (Emphasis added.)

https://www4.schohariecounty-ny.gov/PdfFiles/TCAR/CarlisleSitePlan.pdf. *See also* John R. Nolon, Open Ground: Effective Local Strategies for Protecting Natural Resources 12-13 (2003).

221. *See* Nathanial Gronewold, *N.Y. State Begins Planning for Sea-Level Rise*, Sci. Am., Nov. 19, 2010, https://www.scientificamerican.com/article/new-york-state-begins-planning/ (the N.Y. State Sea-Level

lic trust doctrine in most states, littoral property that is gradually inundated by sea-level rise belongs to the state and is no longer private property.[222]

This condition can be strengthened in a variety of ways. The developer could be required to indemnify the municipality should it have to bear any future costs resulting from the damage to or destruction of infrastructure or the property itself. The developer could agree to insure against its own future liabilities by posting a bond, providing a letter of credit, or purchasing liability insurance. If the developer cannot secure these guarantees at an affordable price and the planning board does not approve the project, the locality is insulated from a total takings claim because the private market's risk assessment—rather than local regulation—has prevented the development.[223] In property-law terms, caveat emptor. A prospective purchaser of property is charged with due diligence, including knowledge of sea-level rise projections, maps that support them, and the risks and costs of developing in areas vulnerable to inundation and storm surges.

Alternatively, or additionally, the developer could be required to impose deed restrictions, such as conservation easements, that require the developer to remove or relocate buildings and restore ecosystem services where the property is inundated or suffers severe damage. Normally such restrictions protect the environment from the adverse impacts of proposed development in the present, but there is no reason that they could not be used to protect the environment, including the public, in the future.

E. *Contingency Bargaining*

This type of negotiated project review may prove essential for the future development of coastal properties vulnerable to near-term sea-level rise. Developers normally have short-term financial objectives, measured by the time it takes them to secure approvals, build, obtain a certificate of occupancy, and sell the buildings. Even where they retain title, their objectives are almost always shorter term than the useful lives of their buildings or the time it will take for sea-level rise to inundate their projects. To be sure, they will argue that their properties will not be damaged by sea-level rise, and they may be able to back up their assertions with data produced by scientists who doubt mainstream projections, have different maps of their own, or believe that

Rise Task Force argues that "[g]overnments can make development in coastal areas less attractive by requiring development projects to internalize the risks of sea level rise and storms in coastal development planning and decision making").

222. *See* discussion *supra* Part III.B.

223. *See* Lucas v. South Carolina Coastal Council, 505 U.S. 1003, 1034-35 (1992) (Kennedy, J., concurring in judgment).

climate change is a passing phenomenon.[224] These possibilities demonstrate the problem with regulating at a time when the scientific understanding of risks continues to evolve and estimates of the dates when risks will materialize remain uncertain.

Contingency bargaining can prove useful in these situations. In business dealings, contingency contracts allow parties to accommodate disagreements about future events, such as sea-level rise (in our context) or the number of likely viewers of a proposed television series (in a more familiar context).[225] In the television example, a deal may be based on an estimate of viewers, but the network may receive a rebate or draw from an escrow fund if the viewers are fewer than projected. Alternatively, the parties could stipulate to a surcharge to the benefit of the scriptwriter if the viewers exceed the projected number. In a similar fashion, a developer and a local land use board could agree that if a project becomes inundated or damaged by storm surges within an agreed-upon period, the local board may draw funds from an escrow account to cover its remediation costs, or it could secure developer's contingent liabilities with a bond, insurance policy, or underlying indemnity agreement.[226]

Practical difficulties limit the ability to achieve this type of accommodation in a zoning regulation, particularly a no-build zone, which has an all-or-nothing consequence. The regulator says: "Because the sea level is expected to inundate your property within X period, we are prohibiting all development and your property now has no value." The developer says: "But those projections are contested, and there is doubt that sea-level rise will affect this particular area of the coastline very much." If the regulator proceeds, the developer can bring a *Lucas*-style total takings case or a substantive due process action alleging that the regulation is arbitrary and capricious, leaving the matter in the hands of judges.

Not only is the negotiated, nonregulatory approach less likely to be litigated—or won by the developer if it is taken to court—but it is consistent with evolving norms in the land use review and approval process in a growing number of states. Developers are accustomed to providing indemnities, bonds, insurance, lines of credit, and escrow accounts. They are familiar with

224. *See* Young, *supra* note 194.

225. "[G]enuinely held disagreements about the future present an important opportunity for negotiators to discover an attractive exchange. The vehicle for capturing this potential is the contingent agreement." Michael L. Moffitt, *Contingency Agreements*, THE NEGOTIATOR'S FIELDBOOK 455 (2006).

226. Moffitt counsels that "[o]ne challenge in crafting a contingent agreement is identifying the boundaries of future possible conditions with sufficient clarity to know what obligations attach." *Id.* at 457; *see also* DAVID A. LAX & JAMES K. SEBENIUS, THE MANAGER AS NEGOTIATOR: BARGAINING FOR COOPERATION AND COMPETITIVE GAIN 97 (1986) ("Even when negotiators have discovered a difference in forecasts, however, considerable ingenuity may be required to find an appropriate uncertain event that all sides can observe and that no one can manipulate.").

local governments that impose protective deed restrictions on their land for environmental purposes. Their current experience with these mechanisms resides in a much lower risk context, to be sure, but the extreme risks that threaten coastal development call for appropriate responses. If regulation cannot, as a practical matter, serve as one of these responses, negotiated settlements of disputes over coastal construction can. The situation necessitates scaling up the use of familiar processes and techniques such as those described above.

V. Conclusion: The Role of Lawyers and Legal Education

In considering the regulation of coastal development and many other aspects of climate-change management, we have entered a transitional era. Profound conflicts of opinion and the absence of scientific certainty make it difficult for existing institutions to solve problems through traditional litigation, regulation, and decision-making processes. The practice of law, the administrative decision-making model, and the law school curriculum are path dependent,[227] directed by more than thirty years of traditional approaches to solving problems. In this pivotal moment, these paths will change; lawyers are challenged to rethink their practices, agencies to rethink their strategies, and law professors to rethink what they teach.

This chapter documents a sea change both in the environment and in approaches to problem-solving in the context of sea-level rise and coastal land development. It reports on the innovative institutions and strategies created by agency officials, industry representatives, and their attorneys.[228] Their achievements should inform legal practice, administrative procedures, and legal education. In light of the constant appeals for law schools to reorient their teaching toward the experiences of lawyers in practice, particularly those practicing at the cutting edge, law schools should be ready to heed the call.

Twenty-eight years ago, the American Bar Association's Task Force on Law Schools and the Profession: Narrowing the Gap, issued its report entitled, *Legal Education and Professional Development—An Educational Continuum*.[229] A key finding of the report was that law schools were not adequately instilling the types of professional skills and values necessary to the practice

227. *See supra* notes 59-63 and accompanying text.
228. *See supra* Part II.B.
229. American Bar Ass'n, Legal Education and Professional Development—An Educational Continuum (MacCrate Report) (1992).

of law in their students.[230] Thirteen years ago, two additional reports stepped up and sharpened this criticism of legal education: the Carnegie Foundation's, *Educating Lawyers*, in 2007,[231] and the Clinical Legal Education Association's report entitled, *Best Practices for Legal Education*.[232]

These critiques urge law schools to change their teaching goals and methods to ensure that law school graduates are ready for practice in the modern era. This chapter describes contemporary challenges that lawyers face, but these challenges differ markedly from the litigate-and-regulate approach to environmental protection that characterized practice in the first three decades of the federal environmental law era. They differ from the advocate-and-decide approach to influencing land use decision making, as well. There, lawyers practice and professors teach vigorous adjudication in administrative tribunals, such as planning boards and zoning boards of appeal, with litigation as the ever-present default.

A key principle of legal education found in *Best Practices* is that law schools should commit to preparing students to practice law "effectively and responsibly in the contexts they are likely to encounter as new lawyers."[233] Because sea-level rise may be the cutting edge of climate change, it is a worthy context for exposing law students to the challenges of practice—particularly as the consequences of climate change worsen. For today's students to be prepared, they need to know that the law is not a code of rigid rules. Instead the law is an organic body that changes with the times, particularly in modern times, when existing rules and practices seem inapplicable to emerging disputes and circumstances.[234]

Students need to understand when legal rules work and when they must be revised. Major changes in the legal rules occurred in *Pardee v. Camden*

---

230. *Id.* at 266:

> If professional competence is the goal, the fact is troubling that so many young lawyers are seen as lacking the required skills and values at the time the lawyer assumes full responsibilities for handling a client's legal affairs. Much remains to be done to improve the preparation of new lawyers for practice, both in law school and after law school, in bridge-the-gap and other skills- oriented CLE programs.

231. *See* William M. Sullivan et al., Educating Lawyers: Preparation for the Profession of Law 12-13 (2007).

232. Roy Stuckey et al., Best Practices for Legal Education: A Vision and a Road Map 8-27 (2007). The Clinical Legal Education Association was incorporated in 1992 with a mission of developing and supporting clinical education as a means of preparing law students and lawyers for more effective legal practice. *See Mission*, CLEA, http://cleaweb.org/mission (last visited Aug. 17, 2020).

233. *See* Stuckey et al., *supra* note 232, at 39.

234. *See* Hathaway, *supra* note 59, at 641 (arguing that

> [u]nlike biological evolution, legal evolution is not always constrained to draw on the existing stock of material during periods of rapid change. A higher court may create a new legal rule that departs significantly from the past rule, though it will remain constrained to some extent by its own precedents and by the decisions of any higher court.

Lumber Co.,[235] *Village of Euclid v. Ambler Realty Co.*,[236] and *Massachusetts v. U.S. Environmental Protection Agency.*[237] What was happening in society at each of these junctures that led the law to strike out on a new path? What role did lawyers play in gathering the facts, identifying the issues, and advocating a new paradigm? Why did the courts abide their pleadings?

What are the appropriate roles for the private sector and each level of government in solving problems during times of crisis? When progress stalled at the Conference of the Parties to the United Nations Framework Convention on Climate Change at Copenhagen, what could the U.S. government do to effectively lower carbon emissions?[238] What then occurred after the promise of Waxman-Markey deflated with the collapse of a congressional solution in Kerry-Boxer?[239] How did stakeholders avoid the uncertainty of regulations in the Uintah Basin[240] and with respect to setting corporate average fuel economy standards?[241]

What teaching lessons emerge from the creation and potential impact of the Regional Greenhouse Gas Initiative (RGGI) and the Transportation and Climate Initiative (TCI)—interstate institutions operating largely outside the ambit of federal influence?[242] The states that created them seemed reinvigorated by inept approaches at higher levels of government and have created entirely new agencies with access to impressive resources. These resources in turn can be used to incentivize local governments to adopt and implement land use plans that greatly reduce energy consumption and carbon emissions. Can government policy at the interstate level work with market forces to shape human settlement patterns so as to drastically reduce per capita carbon emissions? RGGI and TCI are worthy experiments that merit study and support. What are the advantages and disadvantages of this more devolved approach to action needed to solve such critical problems?

As states move toward a posture of accommodation and retreat from sea-level rise, how can the legacy of *Lucas'* total takings doctrine be reinterpreted?[243] Common-law doctrines of nuisance, waste, and public trust[244] can be seen in new light as hard-headed practices of due diligence, real property estates, and judicial precedents combine to shape our understanding of the background

235. *See* 73 S.E. 82, 83, 85-86 (W. Va. 1911).
236. *See* 272 U.S. 365, 386-88 (1926).
237. *See* 549 U.S. 497, 498-99 (2007).
238. *See* Danish, *supra* note 64, at 29-33.
239. *See generally* H.R. 2454 111th Cong. (2009).
240. *See* Streater, *supra* note 127.
241. *See* Freeman, *supra* note 113, at 344-46.
242. *See generally* Regional Greenhouse Gas Initiative, *supra* note 73.
243. *See* Lucas v. South Carolina Coastal Council, 505 U.S. 1003, 1004 (1992).
244. *See* discussion *supra* Parts III.B & C.

principles of state law[245] and legitimate investment-backed expectations.[246] Traditional processes used by administrative boards can be tweaked and supplemented to employ and memorialize the deals that rely on contingency bargaining—deals that accommodate uncertainty in ways that regulation cannot.[247]

These questions and observations merit exploration in the law school curriculum. The intersections of the common law, statutory principles, administrative regimes, regulatory takings jurisprudence, transactional practice, administrative adjudication, and intergovernmental policy can teach law students the intricate interconnectedness of the law and legal institutions. With this framework in mind, they will graduate from law school ready for the challenges their profession faces. The progress described in this chapter has created a new "regulatory environment"[248]: one in which lawyers are learning to operate above regulations and beyond the confines of current practices, using new tools and techniques appropriate to a rapidly changing world.

245. *See* discussion *supra* Parts III.B & C.
246. *See* discussion *supra* Parts III.B & C.
247. *See* discussion *supra* Part IV & notes 226-27.
248. *See* Colorado Dep't of Health v. The Mill, 887 P.2d 993, 1001 (Colo. 1994).

Chapter Five
Extreme Adaptation: Disaster Planning and Mitigation

Chapter Four carried the sobering message that the U.S. Supreme Court's regulatory takings jurisprudence creates a formidable barrier to preventing development in vulnerable areas, such as low-lying coastal zones or floodplains. This chapter adds additional negative information about the increasing frequency and ferocity of natural disasters that significantly expands vulnerable areas throughout the country. It then explores disaster planning and mitigation efforts at the grass-roots level where the impact of disasters is first felt, where first responders toil, and where help is needed in response. It describes state and federal hazard mitigation planning and then demonstrates the positive trend toward integrating local land use planning into the state and federal regime. In so doing, the chapter describes the creation and operation of a reflexive and resilient legal system that better leverages the resources of all levels of government.

I. Disaster Planning

The field of disaster planning is crowded and complex. The players are many and the disasters diverse. It is a challenging multidisciplinary subject. We experience a variety of disaster events: hurricanes and coastal flooding, sea-level rise and storm surges, severe rainstorms and inland flooding, landslides and severe erosion, heat waves, droughts, wildfires, tornadoes, and earthquakes.

The frequency of these events is quickening. The United States has endured 265 climate and weather disasters since 1980 each of which did more than $1 billion in damage, resulting in a total cost exceeding $1.77 trillion.[1] In 2019 alone, there were 14 weather and climate disaster events with losses exceeding $1 billion each across the United States. These included three flooding events, eight severe storm events, two tropical cyclones, and one raging wildfire. The 1980-2019 annual average is 6.5 events, compared to the annual average for

1. *Billion-Dollar Weather and Climate Disasters: Overview*, NOAA Nat'l Ctrs. for Envtl. Info., https://www.ncdc.noaa.gov/billions/ (last visited May 21, 2020).

the most recent five years of 13.8 events. 2019 was the fifth consecutive year (2015-2019) in which 10 or more billion-dollar weather and climate disaster events occurred in the United States.

These diverse disasters, in turn, have spawned a litany of terms found in the literature of disaster planning: a challenge to its researchers. Consider, for example, disaster resilience, disaster prevention, disaster recovery, disaster risk reduction, disaster mitigation, hazard mitigation planning, hazard resilience, catastrophe management engineering, catastrophic risk management planning, adaptive management, management of natural hazards, climate resilience, climate change adaptation, and infrastructure resilience, to name a few. Each term has its authors and actors.

Take, as an example, *hazard mitigation planning*. "The purpose of hazard mitigation is to reduce potential losses from future disasters. The intent of mitigation planning, therefore, is to maintain a process that leads to hazard mitigation actions. Mitigation plans identify the natural hazards that impact communities, identify actions to reduce losses from those hazards, and establish a coordinated process to implement the plan."[2] The practitioners of hazard mitigation planning are elected and appointed officials at all levels of government, engineers, urban planners, land use and real estate lawyers, architects, geographers, statisticians, sociologists, environmentalists, climate scientists, hydrologists, geologists, biologists, and soil scientists, among others.

The worsening impacts of climate change heighten the challenge these actors face. They are becoming aware of the connection between planning to mitigate the damage from individual disasters and the larger phenomenon of global warming. Part IV below makes this point; it describes the work of several municipalities to intersect land use, climate, and hazard planning. Santa Cruz, California, for example, adopted a climate adaptation plan as an amendment to its hazard mitigation plan, which contains strategies to deal with flooding, sea-level rise, severe weather events, coastal erosion, and wildfires.[3] "Plan Manitou" is an integrated comprehensive (land use) plan and hazard mitigation plan adopted in 2017 by Manitou Springs, Colorado. The integrated approach is designed to ensure natural hazard planning considerations were incorporated throughout the long-range planning process. The plan is the city's road map to guide future growth, support economic,

2. FEMA, Local Mitigation Plan Review Guide 5 (Oct. 2011); 44 C.F.R. §201.1(b) (2019).
3. *See infra* Part IV(B).

environmental, and social sustainability, and assure that the city remains resilient in the fact of future challenges.[4]

The term "hazard mitigation planning" reflects on another complexity: disaster law itself. The term is adopted from the Stafford Act, as amended by the Disaster Mitigation Act (DMA).[5] The DMA provides pre-disaster and post-disaster recovery funding and technical assistance to states and local governments. Eligibility for much of this federal assistance requires that states establish hazard mitigation agencies, adopt hazard mitigation plans, and provide help to local governments to adopt hazard mitigation plans. Local hazard planning engages traditional land use mechanisms such as comprehensive planning, zoning, and site plan approval. In some communities, it calls out innovations like transfer or purchase of development rights and overlay zoning. At the local level, areas vulnerable to disasters are identified and land use and building construction standards enforced to adapt to disasters and mitigate the damage they cause. Legal practitioners must understand all of the relevant statutes and regulations of all three levels of government to advise their client municipalities and developers.

In all of this, there is one irreducible minimum: the effect of natural disasters is local. They engage municipal officials and the professionals who advise them. They are not spectators, but the first affected and first to respond. It is at the local level that property is destroyed, lives are lost, public health is threatened, infrastructure damaged, and that the phone rings first. Local leaders must know the legal power they have and the strategies that they can design to deal effectively with this growing list of natural disasters. They also need a clear-eyed understanding of what help they can expect from state and federal officials, how much and when. This chapter is written for them.

This chapter concerns human settlements, how resilient they are to natural disasters, and whether and how to rebuild in their wake. To this end, it explores the governmental role in permitting property development and redevelopment, which in our federal legal system is predominately the jurisdiction of local governments. Locally, hazard mitigation planning links with a host of governmental functions, including land use planning and regulation. Here, too, one encounters a thicket of terms: the entire field of land use

4. *See infra* Part. IV(N).

5. Pub. L. No. 106-390, 114 Stat. 1552 (2000). The most recent federal statute is the Disaster Recovery Reform Act of 2018, Division D of Pub. L. No. 115-254, which was enacted on Oct. 5, 2018. Previously Congress adopted the Sandy Recovery Improvement Act of 2013 (SRIA, Division B of Pub. L. No. 113-2) and the Post-Katrina Emergency Management Reform Act of 2006 (PKEMRA, Pub. L. No. 109-295). These statutes amend the Robert T. Stafford Disaster Relief and Emergency Assistance Act, Pub. L. No. 93-288, 88 Stat. 143 (1974) (codified at 42 U.S.C. §§5121-5207).

law must be mastered to integrate local power into the devolved requirements of state and federal hazard mitigation planning.

Local governments have the legal power to adopt comprehensive plans, zoning, subdivision and site plan regulations, and standards to protect natural resources, such as floodplains, coastal ecosystems, inland wetlands, and forests: all assets threatened by disaster events. Local governments enforce a variety of codes that affect the design and specifications of buildings themselves, including building, plumbing, fire protection, electrical, and energy codes. Municipal legislatures also adopt administrative procedures and create administrative agencies, such as planning and zoning boards, for the review and approval of development projects.

Development and redevelopment projects must navigate these local boards before they can begin construction. At the end of the land use approval process, the locality issues the developer a Certificate of Occupancy, certifying compliance with all of its land use standards and that the building is safe for human occupation. Dramatically put, much of the weight of the inverse pyramid of federal disaster planning law rests on the individual project Certificate of Occupancy issued by the local building department. In the review process preceding its issuance, local administrative staff and land use boards can control development and redevelopment in disaster-vulnerable neighborhoods to protect property, persons, and infrastructure. This assumes, of course, that the process embodies effective hazard mitigation planning.[6]

---

6. *See* Gavin Smith, *Involving Land Use Planners in Pre-Event Planning for Post-Disaster Recovery*, 80 J. Am. Plan. Ass'n 306, 306 (2014) (failure to plan can hinder a community's ability to create a more resilient and sustainable vision of the future.); Patricia E. Salkin, *Sustainability at the Edge: The Opportunity and Responsibility of Local Governments to Most Effectively Plan for Natural Disaster Mitigation*, 38 ELR 10158, 10162 Jan. 2008) (local land use regulations protect and preserve human life and property from natural disasters); Phillip Berke et al., *Evaluation of Networks of Plans and Vulnerability to Hazards and Climate Change: A Resilience Scorecard*, 81 J. Am. Plan. Ass'n 287, 288, 299 (2015) (integration of community-based hazard mitigation strategies into local plans reduces the risk of disaster caused by natural hazards.); Philip R. Berke & Thomas J. Campanella, *Planning for Post-Disaster Resiliency*, 604 ANNALS Am. Acad. Pol. & Soc. Sci. 192, 202-03 (2006) (mandating pre-disaster planning in local comprehensive plans for new urban planning increases resiliency and reduces dependency on recovery aid); Yue "Gurt" Ge & Michael K. Lindell, *Plan County Planners' Perceptions of Land Use Planning Tools for Environmental Hazard Mitigation: A Survey in the U.S. Pacific States*, 43 Env't & Plan. B: Plan. & Design 716, 733 (2016) (planners can use a broad range of land use tools to tailor resiliency planning to meet community needs).

II. First Affected and First to Respond: Local Disaster Planning

A. *Understanding the Scope of Local Land Use Control*

In the United States, state legislatures have delegated extensive legal authority to local governments to determine what type of development can be built within their jurisdictions, including disaster-prone areas and vulnerable neighborhoods. State constitutions give state legislatures the authority to protect the public health, safety, welfare, and morals and to grant this power to municipalities. This inherent state authority is called the police power. The Constitution of the United States, in turn, reserves to the states the powers that are not specifically delegated to the national government.[7] The police power and other powers reserved to the states are not powers conferred upon the states, but ones that have always resided within their dominion.[8] Historically, the police power has been equated with the general governmental objective of securing the public welfare through regulatory means.[9] The Supreme Court has held that the police power inherently lies within the authority of the states, and it is extremely broad, in that it encompasses a host of factors under the general term "public welfare."[10]

7. *See* U.S. Const. amend. X ("The powers not delegated to the United States by the Constitution, nor prohibited by it to the States, are reserved to the States respectively, or to the people."). *See also* James Madison, Federalist No. 45, 292-93 (C. Rossiter ed. 1961) ("The powers delegated by the proposed Constitution to the federal government are few and defined. Those which are to remain in the State governments are numerous and indefinite.... The powers reserved to the several States will extend to all the objects which, in the ordinary course of affairs, concern the lives, liberties, and properties of the people, and the internal order, improvement, and prosperity of the State.").

8. *See* Brian W. Ohm, *Some Modern Day Musings on the Police Power*, 47 Urb. Law. 625, 626 (2015) ("The police power is *not*, as often cited, a power that is 'conferred . . . by the Tenth Amendment, U.S. Const., upon the individual states.' The Tenth Amendment did not confer anything on the states. Rather, in the United States, sovereignty resides with the people." (footnotes omitted)); *see also* John R. Nolon, *Historical Overview of the American Land Use System: A Diagnostic Approach to Evaluating Governmental Land Use Control*, 23 Pace Envtl. L. Rev. 821, 825 (2006) ("[The U.S. Constitution] created a federal government that has the power to legislate only within the parameters of the specific powers delegated to it in the Constitution. Notably, the full police powers of the states were not delegated to the federal government.").

9. *See* 4 William Blackstone, Commentaries on the Laws of England: Public Wrongs 162 (photo. reprint 1979) (1765–69) (defining police power as "the due regulation and domestic order of the kingdom, whereby the inhabitants of a State, like members of a well-governed family, are bound to conform their general behaviour to the rules of propriety, good neighbourhood and good manners, and to be decent, industrious and inoffensive in their respective stations.").

10. Berman v. Parker, 348 U.S. 26, 32-33 (1954):

> Public safety, public health, morality, peace and quiet, law and order—these are some of the more conspicuous examples of the traditional application of the police power to municipal affairs. Yet they merely illustrate the scope of the power and do not delimit it . . . . The concept of the public welfare is broad and inclusive . . . . The values it represents are spiritual as well as physical, aesthetic as well as monetary. It is within the power of the legislature to

Local governments are delegated authority over land use planning and the development of buildings and infrastructure through state legislation such as planning enabling acts, zoning enabling acts, and home-rule authority; these and other statutes combine to give localities the power to shape human settlements to further economic development while protecting the environment and preventing hazards to human health. By controlling the built environment, localities are able to protect the public safety, welfare, and morals. It is no surprise that these delegated powers include the ability to promote the obvious benefits of disaster-resilient neighborhoods.

The principle of subsidiarity is based on the notion that problem-solving responsibility should be the job of the most decentralized level of government with authority to deal with that problem.[11] There is a single actor implication in this phrasing, and it begs a question regarding the capacity of the decentralized institution. Complex land use issues like resilience and disaster planning always engage local people and their governments, since that is where the problems manifest themselves.

Nearly all local governments have been delegated significant legal authority from their state legislatures to adopt the types of strategies illuminated by the case studies discussed later in this chapter. Even with ample legal authority and many model strategies to choose from, local governments regularly form partnerships with one or more regional, state, or federal agencies to supplement their ability to deal with the problem. This is particularly true with respect to disaster planning and recovery, where their technical capacity and financial resources are dwarfed by the realities of natural disasters. In such instance, municipalities reject the single actor implication of the principle and instinctively collaborate with other agencies to leverage their parochial capacity. In so doing, they embrace a principle of collaborative subsidiarity.[12] This principle describes well the partnership required to succeed at hazard mitigation planning.

B. *The Federal Role in Disaster Planning and Mitigation*

Much of the discussion about natural disasters focuses on the role of governors and the president, that is, the power, responsibilities, and actions of the federal and state governments. As the coronavirus pandemic exploded,

determine that the community should be beautiful as well as healthy, spacious as well as clean, well-balanced as well as carefully patrolled. (Citations omitted.)

11. *See infra* note 12 and accompanying text.
12. For a complete discussion of this principle, *see* John R. Nolon, *Calming Troubled Waters: Local Solutions*, 44 Vt. L. Rev. 1, 54-66 (2019).

governors of some states ordered residents to shelter in place and allowed only essential businesses to remain open. Local mayors have emergency powers, as well, and some acted before their governors, but ultimately state power trumps that of localities. In controlling land use, the same formula exists: states delegate their police power to localities, which is significant, but it can always limit or withdraw that authority. Together, state and local governments reign supreme in controlling land use and the built environment in order to promote the public welfare, exercising the police power reserved to them in our federal system.

In the arena of disaster planning, however, Congress plays a critical role and writes the rules of engagement under the DMA. The DMA establishes national legislative objectives that provide an opportunity to enhance local land use planning to promote disaster mitigation initiatives. The Act provides that in order to qualify for federal hazard mitigation grants, state and local governments must "develop and submit for approval to the President a mitigation plan that outlines processes for identifying the natural hazards, risks, and vulnerabilities of the area under the jurisdiction of the government."[13]

The Federal Emergency Management Agency (FEMA) defines the responsibilities of local governments as follows:

> (1) Prepare and adopt a jurisdiction wide natural hazard mitigation plan as a condition of receiving project grant funds under the [Hazard Mitigation Grant Program] . . . . [and] (2) At a minimum, review and update the local mitigation plan every 5 years from date of plan approval . . . to continue program eligibility.[14]

FEMA explains its basic approach in this way:

> For a community to succeed in reducing risks in the long term, the information and recommendations of the mitigation plan should be integrated throughout government operations. Through the planning process, partnerships are formed, and sustained action can increase the community's resilience to disasters. Many other local plans, such as comprehensive, stormwater management, sustainability, economic development, and area plans present opportunities to address hazard mitigation in a way that can support multiple community objectives. Mitigation plans must describe the community's process to integrate the data, analysis, and mitigation goals and actions into other planning mechanisms. First, the plan must identify the existing planning mechanisms where hazard mitigation information and actions may be

13. Disaster Mitigation Act of 2000, Pub. L. No. 106-390, 114 Stat. 1558-59, §322 (2000) (codified at 42 U.S.C. §5165 (2006)).
14. 44 C.F.R. §201.3(d) (2019).

incorporated. In this context, planning mechanisms mean governance structures used to manage local land use development and community decision making.[15]

The proper role of state governments, according to FEMA, includes coordinating "all State and local activities relating to hazard evaluation and mitigation" and providing "technical assistance and training to local governments to assist them in applying for HMGP planning grants, and in developing local mitigation plans."[16] Under DMA regulations, state governments are to submit to FEMA either "standard"[17] or "enhanced"[18] plans. FEMA has approved multi-hazard mitigation plans for all 50 states.

Local hazard mitigation plans are intended to, among other things, "serve as the basis for the State to provide technical assistance and to prioritize project funding."[19] FEMA states that "[a]n open public involvement process is essential to the development of an effective plan."[20] Local plans must be submitted to the state hazard mitigation officer for "initial review and coordination."[21] The state then forwards the plan to FEMA for "formal review and approval." A total of 25,300 local governments have current (FEMA-approved or approvable-pending-adoption) local mitigation plans, and an additional 241 Native American governments have FEMA-approved tribal mitigation plans.[22]

These regulations describe a coordinated intergovernmental system of mitigation planning and implementation. In adopting the DMA in 2000, Congress took stock of the nation's disaster response, recovery, and mitigation efforts and created a more coordinated approach to planning at all levels of government, one that assigns roles to each. Under the DMA, a framework

15. FEMA, Local Mitigation Planning Handbook 6-9 (Mar. 2013), https://www.fema.gov/media-library-data/20130726-1910-25045-9160/fema_local_mitigation_handbook.pdf (emphasis added); *see also* 44 C.F.R. §201.6(c)(4)(ii) (the plan must include a process by which local governments incorporate the requirements of the mitigation plan into other planning mechanisms such as comprehensive or capital improvements, when appropriate).
16. 44 C.F.R. §201.3(c).
17. *Id.* §201.4.
18. *Id.* §201.5.
19. *Id.* §201.6.
20. *Id.* §201.6(b).
21. *Id.* §201.6(d)(1).
22. *Hazard Mitigation Plan Status*, FEMA, https://www.fema.gov/hazard-mitigation-plan-status# (last updated Feb. 26, 2020). As of April 8, 2020, 15 states earned FEMA approval for their enhanced state mitigation plan. These states are now eligible to receive more funds under the Hazard Mitigation Grant Program following a disaster declaration. To receive approval of an enhanced plan, a state must show that it has developed a comprehensive mitigation program and is capable of managing increased funding for its mitigation goals. States with enhanced mitigation plans include California, Colorado, Florida, Georgia, Iowa, Kentucky, Missouri, Nevada, North Carolina, North Dakota, Ohio, Oregon, South Dakota, Washington, and Wisconsin.

of federal, state, and local cooperation is evident that could be a blueprint for an integrated federalist approach to a host of land use and environmental problems. FEMA affirms this in its *Local Mitigation Plan Review Guide*, where it states that "FEMA supports, coordinates and reviews local plans as a means to: [f]oster federal, state, and local partnerships for hazard mitigation; [p]romote more resilient and sustainable communities; and [r]educe the costs associated with disaster response and recovery . . . ."[23]

III. State and Local Partnerships

Like the Coastal Zone Management Act (CZMA), adopted by Congress in 1972,[24] the DMA deals squarely with the limitations of federal authority and the reserved powers of state governments. These statutes envision partnerships with states through which links are created with their local governments. The CZMA affects 35 states and territories.[25] In adopting the CZMA, Congress expressed its understanding of the proper role of state and local governments by recommending that coastal management implementation take place at a local rather than the national level.

Prior to the enactment of the CZMA, the *Stratton Report* noted:

> The States are subject to intense pressures from the county and municipal levels, because coastal management directly affects local responsibilities and interests. Local knowledge frequently is necessary to reach rational management decisions at the State level, and it is necessary to reflect the interests of local governments in accommodating competitive needs . . . . [T]he States must be the focus for responsibility and action in the coastal zone. The State is the central link joining the many participants, but in most cases, the States now lack adequate machinery for [the] task. An agency of the State is needed with sufficient planning and regulatory authority to manage coastal areas effectively and to resolve problems of competing uses. Such agencies should be strong enough to deal with the host of overlapping and often competing jurisdictions of the various Federal agencies. Finally, strong State organization is essential to surmount special local interests, to assist local agencies in solving common problems, and to effect strong interstate cooperation.[26]

The CZMA established a process for the development of individual state coastal zone management programs. Using incentives, rather than pen-

23. Local Mitigation Plan Review Guide, *supra* note 2, at 1.
24. 16 U.S.C. §§1451-1465 (2019).
25. *See id.* §1453(4).
26. Commission on Marine Science, Engineering and Resources, Our Nation and the Sea: A Plan for National Action 56-57 (1969).

alties, the Act urges but does not require state implementation.[27] It offers states unobstructed power to regulate their coastal areas, without federal agency interference, if they adopt policies consistent with the standards of the CZMA, and it provides for grants to states to prepare coastal plans and to establish administrative agencies and mechanisms to implement them.[28] States in turn are encouraged to fund local coastal plans and empower local governments to be responsible for issuing permits for building in coastal areas.

The DMA goes further in this direction. In requiring state and local hazard mitigation plans, its goal is to encourage comprehensive, integrated plans that are coordinated through appropriate state, local, and regional agencies. Local mitigation plans serve as the basis for technical assistance and funding from the state; local plans must be submitted to the State Hazard Mitigation Officer for review and coordination. The state then forwards the plan to FEMA for formal review and approval.

In addition to state-local partnerships spawned by the CZMA and the DMA, there are numerous examples of state-local partnerships independently occurring to protect natural resources. A few examples follow:

In Georgia, for example, the delegation of comprehensive planning authority to local governments is tied to the state's interest in protecting and preserving natural resources, the environment, and the vital areas of the state.[29] Under the rules of the Department of Community Affairs, Office of Planning, and Quality Growth, local land use planning is to strike a balance between the protection and preservation of vulnerable natural and historic resources and respect for individual property rights.[30] Under separate state legislation, local governments in Georgia are required to identify existing river corridors and adopt river corridor protection plans as part of their planning process.[31] They also have the authority to regulate shore land developments.

Connecticut statutes give local zoning commissions flexibility to design individual programs in order to meet their municipal development and conservation needs and to take into account unique conditions. The Connecticut State Legislature has provided towns and cities with the authority to protect the environment, to acquire open space lands from private owners, and to establish conservation commissions.[32] State statutes establish a detailed

27. *See* 16 U.S.C. §1452.
28. *See id.* §§1452, 1455.
29. Ga. Code Ann. §§36-70-1, 50-8-3.
30. Ga. Comp. R. & Reg. §110-3-2.04(f).
31. Ga. Code Ann. §12-2-8.
32. Conn. Gen. Stat. §§7-148(c)(8), 7-131(b), 7-131(a).

system for the creation of an inland wetlands and watercourse protection regime that allows local wetland agencies to have significant control over development affecting wetlands and watercourses.[33] Development applications must contain a soil erosion and sediment control plan, and local zoning and subdivision regulations must make proper provisions for soil erosion and sediment control.

In North Carolina, the state legislature has adopted a legislative rule of broad construction of powers delegated to local governments.[34] A city of Raleigh rule that required that a developer create open space in a subdivision and convey title to it to a private homeowners' association was upheld using this legislative rule of construction. The reach of this rule is evident in *Homebuilders Ass'n of Charlotte v. City of Charlotte*, which upheld the power to impose user fees on applicants for rezoning, special use permits, plat approvals, and building inspections, despite the absence of expressly delegated authority.[35] Legal experts in North Carolina explain that the state's zoning enabling statute, which allows localities to regulate the percentage of lots that may be occupied, the size of yards, courts, and other open space, "provides authority to require buffers along waterways, to protect important natural areas, and to set requirements that authorize or even mandate clustered development schemes."[36] All of these techniques can be used to create more disaster-resilient communities. In addition, North Carolina's Coastal Areas Management Act (CAMA) of 1974 aims to encourage cooperative land use planning between state and local governments.[37] All coastal communities must adopt land use plans in conformance with CAMA. It is the policy of the state that "adequate plans for post-disaster reconstruction should be prepared by and coordinated between all levels of government prior to the advent of a disaster."[38]

In New Hampshire, state law requires that if local governments adopt zoning regulations they must adopt master plans, which may contain various elements including natural resource and natural hazard protection.[39] Under these provisions, municipalities are authorized to develop coastal protection ordinances to carry out master plan policies regarding the protection of

33. *Id.* §22A-36.
34. N.C. Gen. Stat. Ann. §160A-4.
35. 442 S.E.2d 45 (1994).
36. David W. Owens, *Local Government Authority to Implement Smart Growth Programs: Dillon's Rule, Legislative Reform, and the Current State of Affairs in North Carolina*, 35 Wake Forest L. Rev. 671, 701 (2000).
37. N.C. Gen. Stat. Ann. §113A-115.1(b)(3) (2014).
38. North Carolina General Policy Guidelines for the Coastal Area, 5A N.C. Admin. Code 07M.0501 (2014).
39. N.H. Rev. Stat. Ann. §§674:2, 674:16, 674:18.

natural resources and natural hazard areas. New Hampshire municipalities are empowered to use a variety of innovative land use mechanisms to phase growth in an orderly way and to conserve open space and natural resources by clustering permitted development on discrete portions of land parcels.

Linking All Levels of Government in Coastal Regulation

A local law in New Hampshire, adopted by the city of Dover, illustrates how state laws, linked to federal statutes and international conventions, can result in compatible changes in local law and a fully integrated system of law. Dover responded to the state Comprehensive Shorelands Protection Act by adopting an Overriding Districts Ordinance.[a] Its authority to take action is found in the state land use enabling act.[b] The state of New Hampshire adopted the Shorelands Protection Act to conform to the policies of the federal CZMA, linking state and federal initiatives. The Dover ordinance provides a further linkage by protecting local wetlands, watercourses, and steep slopes in the state-designated shoreland areas within its jurisdiction. With the maintenance of high water quality as its objective,[c] this local ordinance aims directly at the objectives of an international compact: the U.N. Convention on the Law of the Sea, which states that land-based activities should not contribute to the pollution of adjacent coastal waters.[d]

a. Dover, N.H., Zoning Code, art. VII.
b. N.H. Rev. Stat. Ann. §674.16.
c. Dover, N.H., Zoning Code §170-27(A).
d. U.N. Convention on the Law of the Sea, arts. 197 & 207, 21 I.L.M. 1262, Dec. 10, 1982 (entered into force Nov. 16, 1994), *available at* http://www.un.org/Depts/los/index.htm.

Maine has incorporated sea-level rise into its planning and regulations. The state's Natural Resources Protection Act acknowledges the fragile and dynamic nature of dune systems and the uncertainty of the extent of future change in sea level.[40] The Act requires a permit for activities in a coastal sand dune system. The Maine Department of Environmental Protection, in its corresponding Coastal Sand Dune Rules, "anticipates that sea level will rise approximately two feet in the next 100 years," and concludes that "[u]nder any scenario of increasing sea level, the extensive development of sand dune areas and the construction of structures increase the risk of harm, to both the coastal sand dune system and the structures themselves."[41] Standards for all projects require that a project may not be permitted if "it is likely to be severely damaged" by the two-foot rise in sea level over 100 years.[42]

40. Maine Natural Resources Protection Act, Me. Rev. Stat. Ann. tit. 38, §480-A (2007).
41. Maine Dep't of Envtl. Prot., Rules for the Department of Environmental Protection §355(1), http://www.maine.gov/sos/cec/rules/06/chaps06.htm.
42. *Id §355(5)(C).*

Since 2000, the Maryland Department of Natural Resources (DNR) has pursued policies for responding to a rise in sea level of two to three feet in this century. In 2007, the governor established the state Commission on Climate Change, which included an adaptation and response working group. In August 2008, the commission released its climate action plan that contains an Adaptation and Response Toolbox designed to "give state and local governments the right tools to anticipate and plan for sea-level rise and climate change."[43] Maryland's focus includes "agriculture, water resources, bay & aquatic ecosystems, forest & terrestrial ecosystems, human health, and growth & land use."[44] Maryland's Living Shorelines program presents management options that "allow for natural coastal processes to remain through the strategic placement of plants, stone, sand fill, and other structural and organic materials."[45] DNR assists localities to assess their ability to address sea-level rise and provides guidance on various means to incorporate adaptation strategies into local planning frameworks and regulations, and has held training and workshops throughout the state.

Following several serious storms, the state of New York initiated the New York Rising Reconstruction Program, funded primarily by federal recovery dollars.[46] It focuses on empowering communities that suffered serious storm damage to establish and carry out strategies to rebuild and prepare for extreme weather events in the future. Over 100 local governments participated in this effort, each interested in developing local resiliency strategies appropriate for its circumstances. They are eligible for grants of $3 to 25 million depending on FEMA estimates of local storm damage.

One of the state's contributions to these localities is a report on community resiliency techniques, which gathers and briefly describes approaches used by communities to increase their resilience.[47] This report contains a land use section and recommends techniques from other communities, mostly in other states, that restrict development in floodplains; define growth boundaries; insinuate resiliency in comprehensive plans; adopt regulations to pro-

43. Maryland Comm'n on Climate Change, *Chapter 5: Comprehensive Strategy for Reducing Maryland's Vulnerability to Climate Change*, *in* Climate Action Plan 1, 25 (2008) [hereinafter Md. Climate Action Plan], https://mde.maryland.gov/programs/Air/ClimateChange/MCCC/Publications/2008ClimateActionPlan.pdf.

44. Maryland Comm'n on Climate Change, Update To Governor & General Assembly 9 (2010), http://www.mde.maryland.gov/programs/Air/ClimateChange/Documents/2010%20November%20Report.PDF.

45. *See* Maryland Climate Action Plan, *supra* note 43, at 22.

46. *N.Y. Rising Community Reconstruction Program*, N.Y. State, http://stormrecovery.ny.gov/community-reconstruction-program (last visited May 22, 2020).

47. New York Dep't of State, Resilience Implementation and Strategic Enhancements (RISE): Local Assessment Tool (Jan. 2020), https://www.dos.ny.gov/opd/programs/resilience/Community_Resilience_C-RISE.pdf.

tect sensitive resources facing development pressures; create overlay zoning to protect natural resource areas or high-hazard areas; prevent nonconforming uses from being rebuilt after storms; create buffers around coastal wetlands; establish surface water setbacks; and regulate development to protect wetlands, floodplains, woodlands, and steep slopes, and to preserve trees.

South Carolina's Office of Ocean and Coastal Resource Management (OCRM) declared in a statement of policy:

> It has been clearly demonstrated that erosion problems of this State are caused by a persistent rise in sea level, a lack of comprehensive beach management planning, and poorly planned oceanfront development, including construction of hard erosion control structures, which encroach upon the beach/dune system. Sea-level rise in this century is a scientifically documented fact. Our shoreline is suffering from its effects today. It must be accepted that regardless of attempts to forestall the process, the Atlantic Ocean, as a result of sea-level rise and periodic storms, is ultimately going to force those who have built too near the beachfront to retreat.[48]

OCRM concluded:

> The long-range public good is the same as the long-range private good. If the dry sand beaches of this State disappear because of the failure of its people and governmental natural resource managers to protect the beach/dune system, future generations will never have the opportunity to use and enjoy this valuable resource.[49]

The state's CZMA adopts retreat and re-nourishment as basic state policies for beach preservation and restoration.[50]

IV. Local Planning for Resilient Neighborhoods

A. *Traditional Land Use Techniques and Disaster Planning*

Localities can use their traditional land use authority to create disaster-resilient communities as a key objective of a community's land use regime. Much of the recent activity at the local level in disaster planning is a response to conditions imposed on hazard mitigation funding described above. Importantly, local land use power enables municipalities to adopt compliant hazard mitigation plans, but it also allows them to exceed federal- and state-imposed requirements, responsive to unique local conditions.

48. S.C. Code Ann. Regs. §30-1(C)(4) (2014).
49. *Id.* §30-1(C)(7).
50. *Id.* §30-1(C)(6).

The local land use authority described in Part II above comes from a variety of state statutes, most of which pre-date and are independent of hazard mitigation initiatives. Under the Zoning Enabling Act promulgated by the U.S. Department of Commerce decades ago for adoption by the states, localities can adopt land use controls to encourage "the most appropriate use of land throughout the municipality."[51] Most local zoning laws are adopted to "protect the public, health, safety, and welfare." Laws that lessen the prospect of damage from natural disasters certainly encourage the most appropriate use of land and protect these public interests. Further, state statutes that delegate authority to localities to adopt subdivision and site plan regulations make it clear that standards may be included in such regulations that prevent and control menaces or hazards, such as the impacts of storms and other calamities.

Local governments, through their land use powers, can retreat, accommodate, or protect in reaction to disasters. Using a variety of techniques, localities can promote development in non-vulnerable areas; require better building techniques, including elevations, set-back development from dangers; and require builders to locate their development on the least hazardous portions of their sites. In these ways, localities can adapt to hazards and protect the development that will occur in areas that will be damaged. Ultimately, as the effects of climate change continue, retreat from some disaster events will be their strategy of choice.

Retreat, if it means adopting a no-build zone is unlikely to become local policy in the short term. Local officials understand that there are practical, political, legal, and equitable reasons to resist a total ban on development. They understand that local property owners acquired their properties knowing that they were zoned for discrete economical uses. They also understand that these owners have been paying local property taxes on their parcels, assessed at their market value as zoned. Their attorneys know that creating no-build zones risks challenge as a total taking under the Fifth and Fourteenth Amendments.[52] They further understand that property owners vote, have local political influence, and belong to industry groups that lobby state officials. Accordingly, officials may be reluctant to legislate a no-build zone, particularly in light of the uncertainty regarding how much disasters will impact specific locations in the short- and mid-term future.

As a result, they might ask their municipal attorneys if there are any non-regulatory options to limiting development in vulnerable areas. Although

51. *See* U.S. Dep't of Commerce, A Standard State Zoning Enabling Act §3 (1926).
52. *See* Lucas v. South Carolina Coastal Council, 505 U.S. 1003 (1992).

fraught with consequences of their own, there are readily available alternatives to complete bans on building. A number of land use strategies may be considered either alone or in combination, as the following material demonstrates.

B. Land Use Tools Applied

1. Comprehensive Planning

The ideal starting point toward a robust resiliency strategy is to adopt a component of the local comprehensive plan that embodies both the most recent scientific findings and projections regarding disaster events. On point is a sea-level rise chapter in the comprehensive plan of the city of Bainbridge Island, Washington, entitled the Environmental Element.[53] Flooding and erosion are principal concerns, and the city's objectives are to minimize, reduce, or eliminate their impacts. This plan component mandates no net loss of the city's aquatic resources, maintenance of its vegetated buffers between proposed development and aquatic resources, and preservation of stream courses and riparian habitat, and it calls for the transfer and purchase of development rights. To mitigate damage due to frequent floods, the plan limits future development and alteration of natural floodplains, mandates the preservation of stream channels and natural protective barriers, revises the flood insurance rate map to reflect the natural migration of frequently flooded areas, and requires the implementation of nonstructural protective methods such as setbacks and natural vegetation.

Several components of the comprehensive plan in Collier County, Florida, create a planning framework for coastal development. One of its objectives calls for "mechanisms or projects which limit the effects of development and restore the natural functions of coastal barriers, including beaches and dunes."[54] Another declares that "[d]evelopment and redevelopment proposals shall consider the implications of potential rise in sea level."[55] More specifically, the plan states that "owners of shoreline development projects that require an [environmental impact statement] shall provide an analysis that demonstrates the project will remain fully functional for its intended use

53. *See* Bainbridge Island, Wash., Comprehensive Plan: Environmental Element (2016), https://www.bainbridgewa.gov/DocumentCenter/View/7800/5-ENVIRONMENTAL?bidId= [hereinafter Bainbridge Comp. Plan]. *See infra* Part IV(L).

54. Collier County Planning Servs. Dep't, County Growth management Plan: Conservation & Coastal management Element 46 (2017), https://www.colliercountyfl.gov/home/showdocument?id=74267.

55. *Id.* at 48.

after a six-inch rise in sea level."[56] Given current sea-level rise projections, this six-inch metric dovetails roughly with the useful life of newly constructed buildings, ensuring that investors and occupants of such buildings will not be deprived of the benefit of the new building over time.

Comprehensive plans are not regulatory documents. They establish a vision for future development, and contain goals, objectives, and recommended strategies, such as those contained in the Collier County and Bainbridge examples. Future zoning, in most states, must be in conformance with the comprehensive plan and the plan can guide local boards that approve development projects in discharging their duties. Informal protocols in the development review and approval process may be adopted that further the objectives of the comprehensive plan. Where a comprehensive plan refers to and incorporates by reference future disaster projections, data, maps, and documents the probable effect of disaster events to the development of vulnerable areas, it supports regulatory changes to achieve resilience and strengthen the hand of local staff in reviewing specific development proposals.

Miami-Dade County Climate Change Task Force Findings

Developed Miami-Dade County as we know it will significantly change with a three- to four-foot sea-level rise. Spring high tides would be at about six to seven feet; freshwater resources would be gone; the Everglades would be inundated on the west side of Miami-Dade County; the barrier islands would be largely inundated; storm surges would be devastating; and landfill sites would be exposed to erosion contaminating marine and coastal environments.[a]

a. Science & Tech. Comm., Miami-Dade County Climate Change Task Force, *Statement on Sea Level in the Coming Century, in* Second Report & Initial Recommendations 3-4 (2008), www.miamidade.gov/environment/library/brochures/08-10-04-ccatf-recommendations.pdf.

2. Project Application Process

Based on information contained in a resilience component of the comprehensive plan, local staff members can revise the requirements for submitting projects for administrative review and approval by planning boards. They can require, for example, that the developer submit site drawings that identify any portion of the parcel likely to be affected by a disaster during the useful life of the building. They can further specify that the developer place buildings and infrastructure in locations that guarantees the safety of occupants and the stability of the building during its useful life or strengthen the

56. *Id.* at 50.

building to withstand disasters' effects. Applicants can be given data from a variety of sources such as state agencies, legislative committees, governor's task forces, university institutes, or other respected and objective nonprofit organizations. Depending on the source, these maps and data may be given judicial recognition, support the rationality of actions taken to condition or even deny the application, and be used to defend substantive due process attacks on such decisions.

In addition, the developer can be required to document the sources of financing lined up for the project, including equity investors and construction and permanent lenders. Where reliable data and maps are contained in an official document like the comprehensive plan or are issued by responsible agencies, investors and lenders will likely be on notice of them and only be willing to invest if they believe that the project is economically viable. If investors conclude that the project is not economically feasible, then it may sink of its own weight and not proceed further in the local review and approval process. The locality can counter any claim that the local process resulted in the taking of value of the proposed project with the statement that the investors and lenders made their decision based on their due diligence and what they learned from independent and reliable sources about the long-term viability of the proposed investment.

3. Environmental Impact Review

Development projects in some states are subject to review under "little National Environmental Protect Act (NEPA)," which require an assessment of the impact of the project on the environment.[57] The effect of conditions and circumstances raised by a proposed development is routinely considered in environmental impact reviews. The potential impact of disaster damage during the lifetime of a proposed building on public health and safety, on the structural integrity of proposed buildings and infrastructure, and on the environment is subject to review under federal and state environmental review statutes.

The Council on Environmental Quality issued a draft NEPA guidance document suggesting that an environmental impact statement should consider the relationship of climate change effects to a proposed action, including the relationship to proposal design, environmental impacts, and mitigation measures.[58] In New York, the State Department of Environmen-

57. National Environmental Policy Act, 42 U.S.C. §4321-4370 (2019).
58. Memorandum from Nancy H. Sutley, Council on Environmental Quality (Feb. 18, 2010); *see* 40 C.F.R. §1502.15 (2019).

tal Conservation (DEC) has been directed "to incorporate climate change adaptation strategies into DEC programs, actions and activities, as appropriate . . .[,]" including in environmental impact statements prepared under the State Environmental Quality Impact Review Act (SEQRA).[59] Such analyses should "[i]dentify potential adverse impacts from climate change" and

> [i]n analyses and decision-making, use best available scientific information of environmental conditions resulting from the impacts of climate change (e.g., increased air and water temperatures, decreased air quality, sea-level rise and increased coastal flooding); [i]ncorporate adaptive management into program planning and actions, which uses scientifically based and measurable evaluation, testing of alternative management approaches, and readjustment as new information becomes available.

County Requires Sea-Level Rise Impact Analysis

The Resource Protection chapter of Collier County's Land Development Code requires a mandatory sea-level rise impact analysis for shoreline development.[a] The analysis must show that the development will remain fully functional for its intended use after a six-inch rise in sea level.[b]

a. Collier County, Fla., Land Dev. Code, §3.03.05 (2008).
b. *See supra* notes 58-60 and accompanying text for discussion on Collier County comprehensive planning.

Even where state law does not require a discrete environmental impact review, state and local site plan review requirements may require a review of certain environmental impacts where they have a close nexus with the proposed project.[60] Local governments have the expressed or implied power in most states to adopt reasonable site plan and subdivision regulations and, where supported by expert reports and reliable maps, such regulations can be amended to include standards that protect property and people from dangers and "menaces" such as storm surges, inundation, wildfires, or earthquakes.

4. Project Approval Conditions

Once a project is submitted for the review and approval of a local planning board for subdivision or site plan approval, the reviewing agency can place reasonable conditions on its approval of the proposed development to protect

59. *Commissioner's Policy—Climate Change and DEC Action*, New York Dep't of Envtl. Conservation, www.dec.ny.gov/regulations/65034.html (last visited May 25, 2020).
60. *See* N.Y. Village Law §7-725-a, N.Y. Gen. City Law §27-a, and N.Y. Town Law §274-a.

the public health, safety, or welfare. These conditions can be negotiated with the applicant. One such condition would be to approve the project subject to the condition that the developer agrees to remove any buildings that are damaged or destroyed by disaster events.[61]

This condition can be strengthened in a variety of ways. The developer could be required to indemnify the municipality should it have to bear any future costs regarding the damage or destruction of infrastructure or the property itself. The developer could be asked to insure against its own future liabilities by posting a bond, providing a letter of credit, or purchasing liability insurance. If the developer cannot secure these guarantees at an affordable price and the planning board does not approve the project, the locality is insulated from a total takings claim because it is the private market's risk assessment that has prevented the development, rather than local regulation. In property law terms, *caveat emptor*. A prospective purchaser of property is charged with due diligence, including knowledge of disaster projections, data and maps that support them, and the risks and costs of developing in vulnerable areas.

Alternatively, or additionally, the developer could be required to impose deed restrictions, such as conservation easements, that require the developer to remove or relocate buildings and restore ecosystem services where the property suffers severe damage. Normally such restrictions protect the environment from the adverse impacts of the proposed development in the present, but there is no reason that they could not be used to protect the environment, including the public, in the future.

Wetlands Regulations to Protect Coastal Lands

The town of Falmouth, Massachusetts, explicitly addresses the impacts of accelerated sea-level rise through extensive wetlands regulations.[a] The wetland ordinance and regulations identify specific resource areas for protection, including coastal wetlands, beaches, dunes, and marshes; land subject to tidal action, flooding, inundation, or coastal storm flowage; and any land within 100 feet of the protected resource areas. The regulations require special protection for coastal floodplains immediately landward of salt marshes, coastal beaches, dunes, banks, and barrier beaches. Any buildings in these areas should be designed to incorporate a relative sea-level rise of at least one foot per 100 years in FEMA-designated A-zones and at least two feet per 100 years in FEMA-designated V-zones.

a. Falmouth, Mass. Code §235 (wetland protection); Falmouth, Mass. Code §240-77-79 (wetland regulations). Falmouth Wetlands Regulations, F.W.R. §10.00.

61. *See* New York State Sea-Level Rise Task Force, Draft Report to the Legislature 14 (Dec. 2010), https://www.dec.ny.gov/docs/administration_pdf/slrtffinalrep.pdf.

5. Contingency Bargaining

Perhaps developing properties in designated disaster-vulnerable areas should be handled in many communities through negotiated project review, or contingency bargaining. Developers normally have short-term financial objectives, measured by the time it takes them to secure approvals, build, obtain a certificate of occupancy, and sell the buildings. Even where they retain title, their objectives are almost always shorter term than the useful lives of their buildings or the time that it may take for a disaster to strike. They, to be sure, will argue that their properties will not be damaged, and they may be able to back up their assertions with data produced by scientists who doubt mainstream projections and have different data and maps of their own.

Contingency bargaining can be used in such situations. In business dealings, contingency contracts allow parties to accommodate disagreements about future events, such as sea-level rise in our context or the number of likely viewers of a proposed television series in a more familiar context. A deal is struck in the television example based on an estimate of viewers, but the network gets a rebate or draws from an escrow fund if the viewers are fewer than projected. Alternatively, if the viewers exceed the projected number, a surcharge is stipulated to the benefit of the scriptwriter. In a similar fashion, negotiation between a developer and a local land use board can arrive at an agreement that the project may not be damaged by a storm event within an agreed period, with the local board taking the position that, if it is, there should be consequences, such as drawing funds to cover its remediation costs from an escrow account or using a bond, insurance policy, and underlying indemnity agreement to secure the developers' contingent liabilities.

This type of accommodation is difficult to achieve in adopting a zoning regulation, particularly a no-build zone, which has an all-or-nothing consequence. The regulator says: "because a disaster is expected to damage your property within X period, we are prohibiting all development and your property now has no value." The developer says: "but those projections are contested, and there is doubt that a disaster will affect this particular area or cause substantial damage." If the regulator proceeds, the developer can bring a total takings case or a substantive due process action alleging that the regulation is arbitrary and capricious, leaving the matter in the hands of judges.

Not only is the negotiated, nonregulatory approach less likely to be litigated, or won by the developer if it is taken to court, but it is consistent with evolving norms in the land use review and approval process in a growing number of states. Developers are accustomed to providing indemnities, bonds, insurance, lines of credit, and escrow accounts. They also have experience with having protective deed restrictions imposed on their land for environmental and risk prevention purposes. Their current experience with these mechanisms is in a much lower risk context, to be sure, but the extreme risks that threaten development in vulnerable areas call for appropriate responses. Consider for example a requirement that developers must include consumer risk disclosure statements in the deed of title.[62] If appropriate risk regulation is politically infeasible, negotiated settlements of disputes over construction in disaster-vulnerable areas can be. The situation necessitates scaling up the use of familiar processes and techniques, such as those described above.

V. Disaster Planning and Implementation Local Case Studies

As a means of supporting and guiding municipalities in mitigating hazards, FEMA has showcased numerous examples of local governments using innovative hazard mitigation strategies. In 2013, FEMA published a comprehensive report providing tools for local officials to integrate hazard mitigation into local planning.[63] This report illustrates how local governments can integrate hazard mitigation into "the full range of community planning activities."[64] These illustrations were instrumental in preparing the case studies for Kings County and the city of Berkeley, California, below. The FEMA report also noted the planning activities conducted by the city of Talent, Oregon.[65] Further research revealed that the city of Talent lies in a county that has prepared a comprehensive multi-jurisdictional hazard mitigation plan.[66] This plan provided the information for the Jackson County and city of Ashland, Oregon, case studies below.

Another FEMA document that has been instrumental in preparing the case studies below is entitled *Climate Smart Hazard Planning*.[67] This document provides a list of links to a variety of local hazard mitigation and cli-

62. *See infra* Part IV(J).
63. FEMA, Integrating Hazard Mitigation Into Local Planning: Case Studies and Tools for Community Officials (Mar. 2013), https://www.fema.gov/media-library-data/20130726-1908-25045-0016/integrating_hazmit.pdf.
64. *Id.* at 1-1.
65. *Id.* at 5-6.
66. *See* Jackson Cty, Or., Jackson County Multi-Jurisdictional Natural Hazard Mitigation Plan (Mar. 2018), https://jacksoncountyor.org/emergency/DesktopModules/Bring2mind/DMX/API/Entries/Download?EntryId=46424&Command=Core_Download&language=en-US&PortalId=13&TabId=1569.
67. FEMA, Climate Smart Hazard Planning, http://www.ecoadapt.org/data/documents/ClimateHazardPlanning_Resources.pdf (last visited May 28, 2020).

mate adaptation plans. While some have since become outdated, the most recent hazard mitigation plans for the jurisdictions listed are available on their respective government webpages. The following case studies for the city of Lewes, Santa Cruz, and Delaware City were prepared with reference to these mitigation plans.

While FEMA-approved local hazard mitigation plans often address wildfire hazards, many communities have also adopted wildfire mitigation strategies. The report *Wildfire Planning Guide for Idaho Communities* illustrates the wide range of strategies used by communities.[68] . This report provided the information for the Boise and Kootenai County, Idaho, case studies below.

A. *City of Lewes, Delaware*

Bordered by tidal wetlands, tributaries, and beaches, the city of Lewes, Delaware, is uniquely vulnerable to coastal hazards.[69] The nearby coast is affected by a tropical storm system an average of once every two years,[70] and currently, over one-third of all city parcels lie within the FEMA 100-year floodplain.[71] Due to its vulnerability, the city has developed an innovative approach to coastal hazard mitigation. Drawing off frameworks provided by FEMA and the ICLEI—Local Governments for Sustainability, the city created a unified plan "to proactively mitigate natural hazards and adapt to climate change."[72] The plan recognizes the overlap between natural hazards and climate change and calls for the integration of these concerns into the city's comprehensive plan and zoning codes.[73]

Actions listed in the city's comprehensive plan include the adoption of "wetlands, wellhead and recharge protections, open space preservation, open space, and wetlands buffers and clustering to encourage environmentally sensitive development."[74] The city's hazard mitigation and climate adaptation action plan proposes enhancing its comprehensive plan by including flood-risk maps and natural hazards data that highlight explicitly "the future flood threat to the community."[75] The plan aims to enhance the city's zoning code

68. Stephen R. Miller, et al., *Wildfire Planning Guide for Idaho Communities* (Jan. 2020), *available at* https://ssrn.com/abstract=3556531.
69. City of Lewes, Del., The City of Lewes Hazard Mitigation and Climate Adaptation Plan 1, 1126 (June 2011), https://www.ci.lewes.de.us/DocumentCenter/View/1849/Lewes_Hazard_Mitigation_and_CLimate_Adaptation_Action_Plan_FinalDraft_8-2011?bidId=.
70. *Id.* at 14.
71. *Id.* at 16.
72. *Id.* at 7, 9.
73. *Id.* at 53.
74. *Id.* at 53.
75. *Id.* at 54.

by calling for the use of a "specific development prohibition in floodplain areas," as well as "land development criteria and low-density zoning to reduce the damage potential within the floodplain."[76] Additional recommendations include creating a floodplain setback and a "freeboard standard" (a height requirement for homes in the floodplain).[77]

B. City of Santa Cruz, California

The city of Santa Cruz is a beachfront and bluff-top community situated on the northern edge of California's Monterey Bay.[78] This location exposes the city to a wide range of natural hazards, including erosion, flooding, landslides, drought, wildfires, earthquakes, and tsunamis.[79] Recognizing that many of these hazards are exacerbated by climate change, the state adopted Senate Bill 379, which requires local hazard mitigation plans to "address climate adaptation and resiliency strategies applicable to that city or county."[80] Accordingly, the city of Santa Cruz prepared a climate adaptation plan update in 2018 as an appendix to its local hazard mitigation plan.[81] While these documents stand alone as separate plans, they are intended to work in unison to adapt to and mitigate natural hazards.[82]

Santa Cruz's climate adaptation plan proposes numerous adaptation strategies that mitigate the city's vulnerability to these hazards. One of the highest priority strategies listed is the identification of areas where the City can manage retreat from the coast's rising seas.[83] Other approaches focus on coastal erosion, flooding, wildfire, and drought.[84] One strategy aimed at mitigating coastal erosion is the development of "setbacks adjacent to cliffs." Another approach is to allow construction that alters natural shoreline processes only when required for specific purposes. Qualifying purposes include the service of coastal-dependent uses, the protection of existing beaches or structures from erosion, the creation of wildlife habitat, and the elimination or mitigation of adverse impacts on the local shoreline sand supply. Strategies

76. *Id.* at 55.
77. *Id.* at 55, 57.
78. City of Santa Cruz, Climate Adaptation Plan Update: 2018-2023 11-12 (2018), http://www.cityofsantacruz.com/home/showdocument?id=73396 [hereinafter Santa Cruz Climate Adaptation Plan].
79. *Id.* at 12.
80. S. B. 379, 2015-2016 Reg. Sess. (Cal. 2015) (codified at Cal. Gov't Code §65302 (West 2020)).
81. City of Santa Cruz, Local Hazard Mitigation Plan: Five-Year Update: 2018-2023 ii (2018), http://www.cityofsantacruz.com/home/showdocument?id=73416.
82. Santa Cruz Climate Adaptation Plan, *supra* note 78, at 10.
83. *Id.* at 74.
84. *Id.* at app. G.

aimed at reducing flood-related hazards include the maintenance of floodplain and floodway regulations and mitigation of development in these areas. Approaches to mitigate wildfire impacts include requiring "new development in areas susceptible to wildfires to be responsible for fire prevention activities (use of fire-resistant and fire-retardant building and landscape materials) and to also provide a defensible zone to inhibit the spread of wildfires." The plan also calls for increased vegetation management efforts (such as creating and mowing fuel breaks, clearing underbrush, and protecting perimeters of parks, green belts, and open spaces) to prevent wildfires. The plan addresses drought-related hazards through strategies to "protect and preserve tree canopy and other native coastal vegetation."

C. Delaware City, Delaware

Delaware City is a community "framed by water."[85] It borders the Delaware River, C&D Canal, and Dragon Run Creek, and contains numerous wetlands on its landward side.[86] In addition, the city rests on land less than 50 feet in elevation, under which clay and swampy soil allow relatively little water to percolate downward.[87] These conditions create an environment ripe for flooding. Almost half of the city is within a 100-year floodplain, and the severity and frequency of floods will only increase with the changing climate.[88] Recognizing this reality, Delaware City promulgated a hazard mitigation and climate adaptation action plan to mitigate future losses.

Included in this plan are strategies to increase community resilience and mitigate flood-related damage.[89] Such measures include the construction of flood barriers, improvements to drainage systems, and enhancement of the surrounding wetlands. The plan contains a variety of land use tools capable of mitigating hazards in flood-prone environments such as Delaware City.[90] Among these are the incorporation of "hazard and climate concerns into local comprehensive plans"; the use of zoning and floodplain overlays, setbacks, and buffer zones; and the conversion of "vulnerable land to protected natural system uses."

85. Delaware City, Delaware City Hazard Mitigation and Climate Adaptation Action Plan 15 (Jan. 2014), https://delawarecity.delaware.gov/files/2014/12/Delaware-City-Hazard-Climate-Action-Plan_no-appendices_January-20141.pdf.

86. *Id.* at 1-5 to 1-6.

87. *Id.* at 1-6.

88. *Id.* at 1-6, 1-19.

89. *Id.* at 6-1 to 6-2.

90. *Id.* at 6-2 to 6-4.

The city presented these and other tools to a group of Delaware City residents, who selected the most urgent and valuable tools from among these options.[91] These tools were then formulated into a "framework for the future of climate adaptation and hazard mitigation in Delaware City."[92] Short-term strategies include "encourage[ing] the use of porous pavement, vegetative buffers, and islands in large parking areas," as well as "promoting on-site water retention and management on individual properties."[93] Mid-term strategies include "identify[ing] sites for green infrastructure/places to implement ecosystem tools," and "encourage[ing[the use of Low Impact Development techniques."[94] Long-term strategies include the "[p]urchase of land in select vulnerable locations (to potentially be turned into a park)."[95]

D. Kings County, California

Kings County, located in California's San Joaquin Valley, is a predominately rural, agricultural-based county.[96] Its arid environment and proximity to the San Andreas Fault expose it to a variety of natural hazards, including earthquakes, floods, droughts, wildfires, and extreme heat.[97] In 2007, the county adopted a multi-hazard mitigation plan to reduce potential losses resulting from these natural hazards.[98] The county then incorporated policy recommendations from this hazard mitigation plan into the Health and Safety Element of the 2035 Kings County General Plan as "guiding policies in dealing with natural disasters."[99]

Many of these policies use land use strategies to mitigate risk, particularly risks posed by earthquakes, flooding, and wildfire. For example, policies that mitigate earthquake hazards include "prohibit[ing] new construction along known fault zones," and "require[ing] agriculture or open space land uses" to serve as buffers.[100] In addition, the county "require[s] large minimum parcel sizes in agricultural and natural resource conservation zones" to "lower

91. *Id.* at 6-4 to 6-7.
92. *Id.* at 6-7.
93. *Id.* at 6-11.
94. *Id.* at 6-9, 6-11.
95. *Id.* at 6-12.
96. Kings Cty., Cal., 2035 General Plan: Introduction 1-3, 1-7 (2010), https://www.countyofkings.com/home/showdocument?id=3108.
97. Kings Cty,, Cal., 2035 General Plan: Health and Safety Element HS-5 to HS-21 (2010), https://www.countyofkings.com/home/showdocument?id=13515 [hereinafter Kings County Health and Safety Element].
98. *Id.* at HS-2.
99. *Id.* at HS-3.
100. *Id.* at HS-42 to HS-43.

development density in seismic-intensive zones."[101] The Element also recommends that "[c]consideration of future development proposals in areas of potential liquefaction [areas where the supporting capacity of soil is reduced] should place primary emphasis upon communicating to developers" such liquefaction potential.[102]

The Element's policies relating to flood and fire mitigation also emphasize land use strategies. One of the Element's objectives is to "[d]irect new growth away from designated flood hazard risk areas and regulate new development to reduce the risk of flood damage to an acceptable level."[103] To accomplish this, the Element proposes policies of "reserve[ing] FEMA designated flood hazard areas for agricultural and natural resource conservation uses," and "direct[ing] new urban growth to existing cities and community districts, or away from New Community Discouragement Areas." The Element's fire hazard mitigation policies include "review[ing] development proposals . . . to determine whether a site is located within a Very High Fire Hazard Severity Zone."[104] These zones are "subject to Wildland-Urban Interface Fire Areas Building Standards and defensible space requirements."

E. City of Berkeley, California

The hilly and seismically active environment of the San Francisco Bay area creates unique fire and seismic hazards for the city of Berkeley.[105] Situated on a parallel fault system, the chance of a 6.7 magnitude or higher earthquake occurring here in the next 30 years is approximately 70%. Hazards accompanying earthquakes can include not only ground failure and structural collapse, but fire. Earthquakes are likely to trigger "numerous simultaneous ignitions, broken mains, and demands on fire personnel." The city's surrounding fuel-rich hillsides and forests exacerbate these fire hazards.

The city has addressed such risks by promulgating a local hazard mitigation plan and incorporating mitigation policies and actions directly into its General Plan. Many of these mitigation actions utilize land use strategies. For example, the Housing Element of the plan calls for the identification of

101. *Id.* at HS-8.
102. *Id.* at HS-11.
103. *Id.* at HS-44.
104. *Id.* at HS-49.
105. *See* Department of Planning & Dev., *General Plan: Disaster Preparedness and Safety Element*, City of Berkeley (2001), https://www.cityofberkeley.info/Planning_and_Development/Home/General_Plan_-_Disaster_Preparedness_and_Safety_Element.aspx [hereinafter *Berkeley Disaster Preparedness and Safety Element*].

"zoning districts where emergency shelters shall be allowed as of right."[106] The Disaster Preparedness and Safety Element of the plan calls for utilization of the environmental review process when appropriate to mitigate hazards.[107] A policy listed in the Environmental Management Element is to "[e]ncourage drought-resistant . . . and fire-resistant plants."[108] This reduces fire danger by minimizing water use.

Other actions included in the Disaster Preparedness and Safety Element include restraints on development in hazard-prone areas. For instance, actions include "requir[ing] soil investigation and/or geotechnical reports" for development in areas with "soil-related constraints" (such as liquefaction).[109] The placement of "structural design conditions on new development" is also called for "to ensure that recommendations of the geotechnical/soils investigations are implemented." The element also calls for consideration of "zoning amendments to prevent future development, including the prohibition of new second units" in vulnerable areas.

F. *City of Boise, Idaho*

While wildfire is a risk for nearly all Idaho communities, the city of Boise is especially fire-prone.[110] Between 2000 and 2015, the city experienced 32 wildfires within two miles of its borders. The city's risk is exacerbated by wildland urban interface (WUI) development patterns, characterized by the expansion of remote development into wildlands.[111] Expanding development into the surrounding wildland of the foothills increases the risk of personal and property damage from wildfires.

The city uses its comprehensive plan to mitigate this risk.[112] The plan's principal objective is to protect life and property from natural hazards."[113] The plan outlines goals and policies "intended to minimize the potential for harm to people and property."[114] One such goal is to "minimize the degree

106. Department of Planning & Dev., *General Plan: Housing Element*, City of Berkley (2010), https://www.cityofberkeley.info/Planning_and_Development/Home/General_Plan_-_Housing_Element.aspx.

107. *Berkeley Disaster Preparedness and Safety Element*, *supra* note 105.

108. Department of Planning & Dev., *General Plan: Environmental Management Element*, City of Berkley (2001), https://www.cityofberkeley.info/Planning_and_Development/Home/General_Plan_-_Environmental_Management_Element(2).aspx.

109. *Berkeley Disaster Preparedness and Safety Element*, *supra* note 105.

110. Miller, *supra* note 68, at 9.

111. *Id.* at 1011.

112. *Id.* at 36.

113. Boise City, Idaho, Blueprint Boise: Boise's Comprehensive Plan 2-75 (2018), https://www.cityofboise.org/media/3021/blueprintboise_all.pdf.

114. *Id.* at 2-76.

of risk to life and property from wildfire." This goal is supported by policies such as the implementation of development standards, "strict controls over the use of water during wildland fires," and the maintenance of wildfire response plans.

The Boise plan further states that "[w]here Foothills developments are adjacent to undeveloped areas, wildfire hazards shall be assessed and minimized through subdivision design, street layout, building design, and landscape and building materials restrictions."[115] Among these restrictions is the requirement that the Foothills Planning Area "be developed at densities of one unit per forty acres," and that development must "conform to the WUI fire prevention regulations." Under the city's Development Code, conditional use permit decisions must include a finding that "the proposed use is in compliance with the Comprehensive Plan."[116]

G. *Kootenai County, Idaho*

Most of Kootenai County, situated in the mountainous terrain of northwestern Idaho, is in a moderate to moderate-high risk fire zone.[117] Those who reside in or near the county's WUI face the highest risk. The WUI in Kootenai County "includes virtually all of the county except cities' downtown cores." The county's Community Wildfire Protection Plan projects that "wildfire will likely continue to present a risk as the WUI becomes more developed and populated."[118]

The county has taken numerous steps to mitigate risks posed by increased development. For example, it requires planned unit developments in timbered areas to submit a "wildfire mitigation plan, prepared by a professional forester, approved by the fire district, the director, or Idaho department of lands."[119] The county also clusters development by offering "a bonus density for conservation-oriented subdivision[s], which must preserve at least twenty percent of property within the subdivision."[120] Subdivision proposals must provide "plans for eliminating dangerous vegetative and fuel conditions in and around proposed building sites."[121] Canopy cover in these sites must "be

115. *Id.* at FH-17.
116. Boise, Idaho, Dev. Code §11-03-04 (6)(v) (2013).
117. Kootenai Cty Office of Emergency Mgmt., 2020 Kootenai County Multi-Jurisdictional All Hazard Mitigation Plan: Volume I, Draft Version E-10, E-35 (2020), https://www.kcsheriff.com/DocumentCenter/View/530/2020-Kootenai-County-Hazard-Mitigation-Plan---Vol-1---PUBLIC-DRAFT-pdf.
118. *Id.* at E-11.
119. Miller, *supra* note 68, at 84-85.
120. *Id.* at 39.
121. *Id.* at 39-40.

less than 50%, with lower branches pruned." The ground must be "relatively free of debris," and "ladder fuels and dead and dying trees" must be removed, among other requirements. In addition, site development proposals "must verify that power lines will be installed underground."

H. Wilbarger County, Texas

Located in the rolling plains of northern Texas, Wilbarger County is uniquely prone to extreme weather patterns.[122] Its position in the Zone IV wind zone subjects the entire county to winds "as high as 250 mph."[123] These winds can form tornadoes strong enough to rip "strong frame houses" off their foundations, sending "automobile sized missiles flying through the air in excess of 330 yards."[124] From 1954 to 2019, there were 48 tornado events in the county, causing $97.302 million in property damage.[125] The county is also highly susceptible to drought, having a probability of one event occurring every two to three years.[126] While droughts can vary in duration and intensity, they have resulted in immeasurable damage. Between 2011 and 2015, "[e]xtreme and severe drought persisted in western north Texas through over forty-five months," which resulted in significant loss of crops.[127]

Due to the risks posed by drought and strong wind and tornados, the county has proposed numerous actions in its hazard mitigation plan that can be used to prepare for and mitigate these hazards. For strong winds and tornados, the plan proposes implementing development requirements such as safe rooms in new schools and care facilities, tie-downs for mobile homes and propane tanks, "the use of steel connectors in new and existing construction," and the burial of utility lines.[128] The plan also calls for the implementation of "a routine tree trimming program that clears tree limbs near power lines."[129] For drought mitigation, the plan proposes "implement[ing] a 'green infrastructure' program," smart growth initiatives, and landscape ordinances.[130] For all hazards, including both drought and tornadoes, the plan calls for the

122. Wilbarger Cty., Wilbarger County Hazard Mitigation Plan 2020 Draft (2019), http://www.co.wilbarger.tx.us/upload/page/4147/docs/nrpcwilbargercountyhmappublic.pdf.
123. *Id.* at 10-2.
124. *Id.* at 10-4.
125. *Id.* at 10-7.
126. *Id.* at 5-10.
127. *Id.* at 5-9.
128. *Id.* at 17-25, 17-27 to 17-30, 17-34.
129. *Id.* at 17-10.
130. *Id.* at 17-18 to 17-19, 17-33.

"[i]ncorporation of a formal hazard mitigation plan in long-term community development planning activities."[131]

I. *Louisville Metro, Kentucky*

Louisville Metro is a "merged city-county government" lying along the Ohio River in northern Kentucky.[132] Like Wilbarger County to the south, Louisville Metro is located in a severe wind zone, making it vulnerable to some of the most devastating tornadoes in the country.[133] The state's humid, subtropical climate presents a further hazard during the summer months: extreme heat.[134] This hazard is exacerbated by climate change[135] and the Louisville Metro's growing heat island effect (where human activities in urban areas increase those areas' temperatures).[136] In some parts of Louisville, this effect can result in a 10-degree temperature increase, which can put its population at extreme risk. According to the National Weather Services' statistical data, "heat causes more fatalities per year than floods, lightning, tornadoes, and hurricanes combined."[137]

In its hazard mitigation plan, Louisville Metro proposes mitigating extreme heat and tornado hazards risks through several innovative approaches. For tornado hazard mitigation, the plan proposes using a property tax incentive to encourage the construction of safety rooms in houses.[138] The plan further proposes "require[ing] all new manufactured home parks to build a safe room." For combatting extreme heat, the plan proposes "adopt[ing] policies incentivizing or requiring minimum albedo levels at the time of routine roof, street, and parking lot resurfacing and for all new development."[139] Materials with higher albedo levels (levels of solar reflectance) absorb less heat and can thereby mitigate the urban heat island effect.[140] The plan also calls for using vegetation management to mitigate extreme heat. Specific activities proposed to do so include "set[ting] tree planning and green roof goals by

131. *Id.* at 17-18.
132. Louisville Metro, 2016 Louisville Metro Hazard Mitigation Plan 89 (2016), https://louisvilleky.gov/sites/default/files/emergency_services/pdf_files/lm_hmp_2016_final.pdf [hereinafter Louisville Metro Hazard Mitigation Plan].
133. *Id.* at 45.
134. *Id.* at 11014.
135. *See id.* at 10.
136. *The Urban Heat Island Project*, Louisville Open Data, https://data.louisvilleky.gov/story/urban-heat-island-project (last visited May 28, 2020).
137. Louisville Metro Hazard Mitigation Plan, *supra* note 132, at 108.
138. *Id.* at 220.
139. *Id.* at 225.
140. *Heat Islands: Using Cool Roofs to Reduce Heat Islands*, U.S. EPA, https://www.epa.gov/heat-islands/using-cool-roofs-reduce-heat-islands (last updated Aug. 12, 2016).

district, enhanc[ing] tree cover through a public tree planting program, and protec[ting] existing canopy through the adoption of a comprehensive tree protection ordinance."[141]

J. Clarke County, Virginia

Approximately 50% of U.S. land "east of the Mississippi River is underlain by soluble and potentially karstic bedrock."[142] While such bedrock is regionally unique, a common characteristic is its potential to dissolve.[143] In Kentucky, around half of the state has "karst or potential for karst," which creates risks for sinkholes, flooding, and groundwater contamination.[144] Clarke County, Virginia, has "experienced a major example of groundwater contamination first-hand in 1981" when a town was "forced to abandon its public well system due to contamination from nitrates, phenols, and herbicides—none of which could be traced to a single source."[145] Due to this, and other experiences with karst-related hazards, the county adopted "a comprehensive set of land use planning tools to guide development in karst areas."[146]

In its comprehensive plan, the county has a policy of "prohibit[ing] land uses that have significant adverse environmental impacts, recognizing especially the interrelationships among natural resources, especially between ground and surface waters in Karst topography and steep slopes."[147] Another policy is to "recognize that karst terrain underlies the majority" of certain areas, and to take steps "whenever possible" to prevent groundwater contamination.[148] The plan's policy "[f]or new development and re-development projects that require a land use change," is to "ensure use of the onsite sewage treatment method that provides the maximum protection to surface/groundwater resources and karst terrane."

In its zoning ordinance, the county mandates numerous requirements for site development that mitigate karst-related hazards. For example, the code prohibits construction and land disturbances "within a minimum buffer dis-

141. Louisville Metro Hazard Mitigation Plan, *supra* note 132, at 225.
142. Kentucky Division Emergency Mgmt., 2018 Kentucky Hazard Mitigation Plan: Karst and Sinkhole Hazards KGS37 (2018), https://kyem.ky.gov/recovery/Documents/CK-EHMP%202018,%20S3-S6,%20Risk%20Assessment,%20Hazard%20Identification,%208,%20Karst,%20Original%20Submittal.pdf.
143. *Id.* at KGS36.
144. *Id.* at KGS36 to 38.
145. Clarke Cty. Planning Dep't, 2013 Clarke County Comprehensive Plan 114 (Mar. 2014), https://www.clarkecounty.gov/home/showdocument?id=1888.
146. Bradley P. Belo, *Natural Hazard Mitigation Planning for Kast Terrains in Virginia* 14 (May 2003), https://vtechworks.lib.vt.edu/bitstream/handle/10919/37115/etd.pdf?sequence=1&isAllowed=y.
147. 2013 Clarke County Comprehensive Plan, *supra* note 145, at II6.
148. *Id.* at II8.

tance of 25 feet from the discernable edge of a sinkhole or other karst feature. Vegetation in the buffer area shall not be altered from predevelopment conditions."[149] Further, "[u]nderground utilities located within 100 feet of karst features shall be laid out so that they do not intersect those features." Before a building permit can be issued, a "[g]eotechnical stud[y] shall be conducted at each proposed structure site," and remediation must be done if the study finds karst features. The code also requires a Consumer Disclosure Statement to be included in the Deed of Dedication that states:

> This property is located in an area identified as having karst features. Karst features are created by groundwater dissolving sedimentary rock such as limestone. Features include sinkholes, fissures enlarged by dissolution, and caves. Geologic tests were conducted and one or more of these features were identified on this property. Karst features are unstable and collapse may occur. Measures have been taken to ensure structural stability in this area; however, karst areas are dynamic and geologic changes may cause future structural instability. Fertilizers, herbicides, and pesticides shall not be applied within designated buffer areas.

K. *Hawaii County, Hawaii*

Hawaii County (coterminous with the "Big Island" of Hawaii) lies on perhaps some of the country's most distinctive geography.[150] Formed by five volcanos, three of which are currently active, "[t]he island extends from craggy ocean cliffs and beaches of black, green and golden sand to mountain peaks that are snow-covered in winter."[151] These features, coupled with its tropical climate, make the island a prominent tourism destination. They also create, however, a wide range of natural hazards. Presidential disaster declarations have been issued in this county for volcanos, hurricanes, earthquakes, heavy rains, flooding, wildfires, mudslides, and tsunami waves, among other events.[152]

In its multi-hazard mitigation plan public review draft for 2020, the county addresses this diverse array of hazards. In areas particularly hazard prone, the plan proposes updating and overlaying hazard zones and "develop[ing] conditions for land use and design" within them.[153] In addition, the plan calls

149. Clarke County Ky., Zoning Ordinance ch. 188, art. 6, §H-15-e (2020).
150. Hawaii Cty, Haw., County of Hawai'i Multi-Hazard Mitigation Plan 41, 44 (May 2020), http://records.co.hawaii.hi.us/Weblink/1/edoc/104769/2020-05-18_HawaiiCountyHMP_PublicReviewDraft.pdf.
151. *Id.* at 44.
152. *Id.* at 43.
153. *Id.* at 237.

for integrating hazard mitigation "into other plans, ordinances and programs that dictate land use decisions in the community, including capital improvement programs, the general plan, recovery plans and strategic plans."[154] The hazard mitigation plan also lists various hazard-specific strategies. Actions to mitigate flooding include enforcement of a flood damage prevention ordinance.[155] Volcanic hazard mitigation actions include the institution of "a home buyout program that targets eligible properties impacted by lava flows." Coastal erosion mitigation actions include "update[ing] county shoreline setback policies."[156] Wildfire mitigation actions include the use of "fire breaks around communities and along roadways." In addition, the plan lists a catalog of best mitigation practices for each natural hazard that poses a risk to the county.[157] Due to a variety of factors, not all initiatives in the catalog were included in the county's action plan.[158] The catalog itself, however, serves as a comprehensive resource in guiding local hazard mitigation.

L. *City of Bainbridge Island, Washington*

The city of Bainbridge Island has explicitly addressed the potential for sea-level rise in the Environment Element of its comprehensive plan. Adopted in 2017, the plan recognizes that Bainbridge Island is potentially subject to sea level-related impacts including flooding and erosion. The overall goal of the element is to avoid adverse impacts where possible; to minimize, reduce, or eliminate impacts over time; and to compensate for unavoidable impacts.[159] The plan outlines protections for critical areas including transfer of and purchase of development rights; provides for the use of the city's Shoreline Management Master Program to address and protect marine fish and marine shoreline habitat; mandates no net loss of the city's remaining regulated aquatic resources; requires the maintenance of vegetated buffers between proposed development and aquatic resources; calls for the preservation of stream courses; and the protection or restoration of natural functions of riparian habitat.

The frequently flooded areas component of the element specifically recommends mitigating measures that include a limitation on development and the alteration of natural floodplains; preservation of stream channels and natural protective barriers; revision of the flood insurance rate map to reflect

154. *Id.* at 237.
155. *Id.* at 235.
156. *Id.* at 237.
157. *Id.* at 22-1 to 22-10.
158. *Id.* at 22-1.
159. *See* Bainbridge Comp. Plan, *supra* note 53, at EN-2.

the natural migration of frequently flooded areas; and implementation of nonstructural protective methods such as setbacks and the use of natural vegetation.[160]

Bainbridge Island, Washington: Sea-Level Rise

Sea-level rise may happen as the result of natural or human activity such as geologic subduction or climate change. Here in the Puget Sound we experience the effects of both the geologic and climatological forces. Cumulative sea-level rise has serious implications for the shorelines and lowland areas of the island such as beach and bluff erosion and loss of intertidal zones. These areas serve such purposes as nursery habitat, feeding grounds for fish and fowl, stormwater collection, and water filtration.[a]

a. BAINBRIDGE ISLAND, WASH., COMPREHENSIVE PLAN: ENVIRONMENTAL ELEMENT EN-7 (2016).

M. Town of Duck, North Carolina

North Carolina's Coastal Areas Management Act of 1974 encourages cooperative land use planning between state and local governments[161] and it is the state's policy that "adequate plans for post-disaster reconstruction should be prepared by and coordinated between all levels of government prior to the advent of a disaster."[162] The *State Design and Construction Guidelines* for local hazard mitigation plans further provide that coastal communities should "outline a post-disaster permitting process that facilitates repairs but remains steadfast to the need to mitigate against future disasters."[163]

The town of Duck, on North Carolina's Outer Banks, is a coastal community that has adopted local regulations implementing these state coastal policies.[164] The code chapter on Rebuilding and Reconstruction sets out procedures for assessing damage, declaring a building moratorium, and defining types of moratoriums that may be declared in the aftermath of a damaging storm.[165] The ordinance is intended to ensure that rebuilding occurs "in an orderly manner," and with the opportunity to identify "appropriate areas for post-storm change and innovation."[166]

160. *Id.* at EN-6.
161. N.C. GEN STAT. §§1131-100 to 1134.3 (2014).
162. 15A N.C. ADMIN. CODE 07M.0501 (2020).
163. NORTH CAROLINA DIVISION EMERGENCY MGMT., TOOLS & TECHNIQUES: PUTTING A HAZARD MITIGATION PLAN TO WORK 4 (1998), https://p2infohouse.org/ref/51/50524.pdf.
164. *See* DUCK, N.C., CAMA CORE LAND USE PLAN (2005).
165. DUCK, N.C., CODE §152 (2019).
166. DUCK, N.C., CODE §§152.01, 152.04 (2019).

N. *Manitou Springs, Colorado*

Adopted April 2017, "Plan Manitou" is the city's integrated comprehensive plan and hazard mitigation plan.[167] The Plan is the city's roadmap to guide future growth, support economic, environmental, and social sustainability, and assure that the city remains resilient in the face of future challenges. The Plan emerged from the need to create a comprehensive plan as well as address natural hazards and risks present in the community. The integrated approach was designed to ensure natural hazards planning considerations were incorporated throughout the long-range planning process. The Plan was spurred, in part, by a series of major flood events that heavily impacted the community in 2013, and again in 2015, as well as the community's proximity to the 18,247-acre Waldo Canyon Fire in 2012. The collective impact of these recent events was significant—damage to infrastructure and property, high recovery costs, and lasting impacts on local businesses and tourism created a sense of vulnerability and underscored the need to plan for long-term risk reduction and resiliency.

One of the primary goals of this Plan is to "minimize risks to property, infrastructure and lives from natural hazards and disasters."[168] The Plan includes strategies for addressing specific hazards and at-risk areas. For high hazard areas (including those identified as flood, wildfire, steep slope, and geologic hazard areas), one policy is to "[g]uide new development away from and discourage density increases." The use of incentives, where feasible, is suggested as a means of doing so. For flood hazard areas, policies include "[e]ncourag[ing] flood mitigation measures for existing structures," and "[d]iscourag[ing] additional development . . . in mapped floodplain areas, to the extent feasible, through the use of incentives, clustering, and other techniques."[169] For steep slopes and geologic hazards, the policy is to "[a]void development on slopes with grades steeper than 30 percent to the maximum extent practicable." Wildland-Urban Interface areas are particularly prone to wildfires. The policy for mitigating risks to development in these areas is to "[a]dopt and implement best practices for 'Firewise' development and landscaping techniques that help protect property, homes, and lives from

167. City of Manitou Springs, Colo., City of Manitou Springs Community Master Plan & Hazard Mitigation Plan (2017), https://planmanitou.com/wp-content/uploads/2017/05/Plan-Manitou_Adopted_May2017.pdf.

168. *Id.* at 67.

169. *Id.* at 69.

wildfires within the WUI," and to "[a]void increasing residential densities" in these areas.[170]

O. Jackson County and the City of Ashland, Oregon

Jackson County lies in southwestern Oregon, surrounded by the Cascade and Klamath Mountain ranges.[171] These ranges contain steep slopes, with topsoil uniquely "susceptible to landslides, torrential flooding, and sheet erosion." The county's multi-jurisdictional natural hazard mitigation plan addresses these hazards by proposing mitigation actions. For flooding, measures include "encourage[ing] private property owners to restore natural systems within the floodplain, and to manage riparian areas and wetlands for flood abatement."[172] For landslides, the plan proposes utilizing maps that identify hazard areas "and propose comprehensive plan and land use policies accordingly." In addition, the plan urges cities to implement the proposed actions through comprehensive land use plans and zoning ordinances.[173]

In an addendum to this plan, various cities within Jackson County have listed separate mitigation action items. The city of Ashland proposes using numerous land use strategies to mitigate flood risk, such as "restor[ing] wetlands and us[ing] techniques like floodplain benching . . . to increase floodwater storage capacity."[174] The city also proposes using green infrastructure and low impact development BMPs in development codes such as "bioswales in city-owned rights-of-way to minimize local and downstream flooding."[175]

Ashland incorporates hazard mitigation strategies into its municipal code.[176] The city uses a Physical and Environmental Constraints overlay district to regulate areas with a high natural hazard risk.[177] Regulations on land use, new development, and activities such as alteration of land and tree removal apply in certain areas. Areas exposed to flooding are classified as Flood Plain Corridor Lands. The code requires development to be located outside designated flood plains "to the maximum extent feasible." Land that

---

170. *Id. See* Miller, *supra* note 68, at 143-44 (discussing "Firewise" program as a nonregulatory wildfire prevention tool); *see also Firewise Communities USA*, Nat'l Fire Protection Ass'n, https://www.nfpa.org/Public-Education/Fire-causes-and-risks/Wildfire/Firewise-USA.
171. Jackson County Multi-Jurisdictional Natural Hazard Mitigation Plan, *supra* note 66, at 2-1.
172. *Id.* at 4-10.
173. *Id.* at 5-1.
174. *Id.* at AA-8.
175. Jackson County Multi-Jurisdictional Natural Hazard Mitigation Plan, *supra* note 66, at AA-8.
176. *Id.* at 43.
177. *Id.* at 44.

is "within the floodway channels" or that has a "slope greater than 35 percent" is classified as Severe Constraint Land.[178] Development in these areas is allowed only upon the completion of a geologic engineering study.[179]

Areas at risk for landslides are classified as Hillside Land.[180] These lands are subject to provisions controlling erosion and slope failure, "such as re-vegetation requirements, surface and groundwater drainage, and tree conservation, protection, and removal standards."[181] Subdivisions in these areas must also "conduct a geotechnical survey." Land within the city is also classified based on its wildfire risk. Developments proposed within the wildfire lands overlay must submit a fire prevention and control plan which requires mapping and analyzing the fire hazards that could affect the property.[182] While the code classifies some land as unbuildable based on its natural hazard risk, it also provides that "density may be transferred out of unbuildable areas to buildable areas of a lot provided that certain standards are met."[183]

VI. Conclusion: Linking Levels of Governance

Legal frameworks, such as those evident in the CZMA and DMA, can provide society effective mechanisms for analyzing risks and reorganizing to abate them. The challenge in creating resilient communities to adapt to climate change is to create a resilient decision-making process equal to the task. The United Nations International Strategy for Disaster Reduction defines "resilience" as:

> The capacity of a system, community or society potentially exposed to hazards to adapt by resisting or changing in order to reach and maintain an acceptable level of functioning and structure. This is determined by the degree to which the social system is capable of organizing itself to increase its capacity for learning from past disasters for better future protection and to improve risk reduction measures.[184]

Resilience, then, is more than the physical accommodation of disaster events in the natural and built environment; it is also a process of improv-

178. Ashland, Or., Code §18.3.10.060.
179. *Id.* §18.3.10.110.
180. *Id.* §18.3.10.090.
181. Jackson County Multi-Jurisdictional Natural Hazard Mitigation Plan, *supra* note 66, at 44.
182. *Id.* at 45.
183. Ashland, Or., Code §18.3.10.120.
184. *Terminology: Basic Terms of Disaster Risk Reduction*, Int'l Strategy for Disaster Reduction, https://www.eird.org/eng/terminologia-eng.htm (last visited May 25, 2020).

ing decision making in response to external threats.[185] This understanding is embodied in what legal scholars call "reflexive law."[186] Reflexive law draws its name from the basic notion that law can encourage "self-critical reflection" among actors about their performance.[187] This theory promotes the design of legal procedures, such as the intergovernmental process of creating a local hazard mitigation plan, that cause stakeholders to share information, interact, and reflect on what they propose to do.

At the local level, reflexive law theory is at work in procedures that cause local land use agencies, regulated developers, and citizens to identify and mitigate the impact of anticipated disasters on vulnerable neighborhoods. The emphasis of reflexive law is on creating norm-consistent procedures that cause public officials to consider matters of public importance, assess the situation, and react at the grass-roots level; this instead of a top-down federal system that requires locals to simply apply standard-based regulations that trigger comply-or-defy responses.[188] The relevant norms discussed in this chapter are adapting a community's comprehensive plan to include hazard mitigation planning, implementing that plan through traditional land use techniques and processes, and responding innovatively to state and federal requirements that come with incentives such as technical assistance and funding.

185. Susan Cutter et al., *A Place-Based Model for Understanding Community Resilience to Natural Disasters*, 18 Global Envtl. Change 589, 600 (2008).

186. *See* John R. Nolon, *Katrina's Lament: Reconstructing Federalism*, 23 Pace Envtl. L. Rev. 987, 1000-04 (2006).

187. See Eric W. Orts, *Reflexive Environmental Law*, 89 Nw. U. L. Rev. 1227, 1255 (1995). The term "reflexive law" appeared as early as 1983 in an article by German sociologist Gunther Teubner that examined the evolution of legal systems. He saw a reflexive legal system as a valuable means of mediating the complex nature of contemporary society and as an improvement over earlier concepts of law that primarily set rules governing the interactions of autonomous private actors or directed private and public actions to accomplish legally-established outcomes. *See* Gunther Teubner, *Substantive and Reflexive Elements in Modern Law*, 17 L. & Soc'y Rev. 239 (1983).

188. *See* Tim Iglesias, *Housing Impact Assessments: Opening New Doors for State Housing Regulation While Localism Persists*, 82 Or. L. Rev. 433, 496-510 (2003). Iglesias suggests the intriguing idea of requiring local governments to conduct periodic housing impact analyses as a method of causing local officials, in their established role as guardian of local residents' interests, to reexamine their land use laws to determine whether they meet existing housing needs. The procedures would require localities themselves to generate information regarding housing needs, evaluate the impacts of current zoning standards on housing affordability, and consider the adoption of workable methods of facilitating the provision of needed housing. Without disturbing the local officials' understanding of their traditional role in such matters, the legal requirement introduces new norms into the local conversation: the importance of meeting local housing needs and the ability of local regulation to influence the provision of affordable housing. "Enforcement" of the norm of meeting housing needs is influenced and directed by the participants in the impact analysis itself: residential developers, senior citizen groups, housing advocates, employers in need of work force housing, etc. Local officials are more likely to yield to these influences than to top-down directed inclusionary zoning mandates simply because they arise within a legal system that conforms to and respects their normative understanding of their role and the proper process of decision making.

This chapter explores how federal and state laws can be linked, vertically and horizontally. The CZMA includes among its policies the mitigation of disaster damage. The DMA is a federal law that encourages state and local governments to conduct disaster mitigation planning by rewarding them if they do so. These laws enjoy horizontal consistency at the federal level; they both promote economic development that is compatible with environmental protection. They operate vertically as well, relying on state and local authority to adopt coastal protection and hazard mitigation plans consistent with federal policies and encourage grass-roots implementation with federal and state funding and technical assistance. Using their police power authority, the states have created comprehensive regimes for land use control relying mostly on local land use planning and regulation, completing the vertical dimension. This local authority is guided by the input of local citizens, nongovernmental organizations, and businesses and, in turn, by state policies enacted in response to federal law.

Land use law evolves. It is a flexible and expansive vessel into which new content is poured and from which the old is drained. Consider a local comprehensive plan and its hazard mitigation component. Today it contains the vision of yesterday's leaders of their community's future and the measures they selected to achieve their vision. As things change, the plan can be amended to respond to tomorrow's challenges and opportunities.[189]

---

189. *See* Gunther Teubner, Law as an Autopoietic System 67 (1993):

> [S]ubstantive legal norms remain indispensable. It is only that the process of their production and justification has to give way to a "socially adequate" proceduralization. . . . The question is whether we are dealing with command and control regulation through state economic policy or with regulation through decentralized mechanisms of self-regulation. In the latter case, the law of the state regulates only the contextual conditions.

Chapter Six
Troubled Waters and the Problems With Federalism

This chapter views the nature of the federal legal system through the lens of water law. At the federal level, the legal system is ill-equipped to protect water supply and quality from the ravages of overdevelopment and climate change. Federal legislation mainly regulates point source pollution of navigable surface waters. It does not permit federal agencies to protect surface water from nonpoint source pollution, or to protect groundwater and ephemeral wetlands. Meanwhile, state and local governments are empowered to fill in the gaps; anecdotal evidence indicates that they have been doing so more frequently as source water pollution has worsened. This chapter explains the devolution of significant power to municipalities to control water pollution from private land development, describes dozens of local gap-filling water protection techniques, and traces the evolution of intergovernmental collaborations that hold some promise of piecing together the fragmented pieces of our water law system. It ends with a description of the Principle of Collaborative Subsidiarity as a foundation for climate change management. Issues of climate change management and adaptation to COVID-19 raise related concerns about the fragmented federal legal system and call for a firm embrace of the same principle.

I. Introduction

A. *A Watershed Moment*

The event was a local land use leadership training program in the upstate New York Sawkill Watershed on controlling the alarming risks of water pollution. Local land use board members and elected officials gathered to learn how to prevent public health and ecosystem harms caused by the effects of land use and development on local water quality.[1] After we covered the local

1. The Land Use Law Center at Pace Law School regularly conducts multi-day Land Use Leadership Training Programs for local officials from the 250 municipalities in the Hudson River Valley. Students

land use strategies suitable to the task, we asked for questions. Margaret, a local planning board chair, whose family member had been diagnosed with cancer attributed to drinking contaminated water, raised her hand. She asked us to explain this country's water law system and why, despite federal and state environmental laws, she and her fellow local leaders had to use their municipal land use authority to prevent water pollution. This seemingly simple question, which we were unable to answer to her satisfaction, led to the Land Use Law Center's two-year water law project and was the impetus for this chapter.[2]

Margaret's question cuts through all of the nuanced jurisprudential and ideological rhetoric and analysis that characterizes so many law school water law colloquia and legal scholarship. It goes directly to the heart of the issue. If we can't explain clearly how the legal system actually works and how to solve present problems, then we lose credibility in discussions in city halls, courtrooms, and the classroom. Instead of expressing an opinion about a pending federal rule change or a U.S. Supreme Court decision regarding some nuance of federal water law, Margaret's question requires that we explain water law so she can decide what to do to address her community's water problem. Should she lobby Congress, the U.S. Environmental Protection Agency (EPA), the state legislature, one or more state agencies, or her city council or town board? If the legal system is not logical, we need to explain why and offer some solutions that can be employed now for Margaret, her family, and her watershed.

B. The "Occult" Origins of Water Law

In 1861, the Ohio Supreme Court decided *Frazier v. Brown* in which it adopted the Absolute Use Rule of groundwater use.[3] The doctrine stood until 1984, when, in *Cline v. American Aggregates*, the court reversed course and

from the Elisabeth Haub School of Law at Pace University conduct research on the land use issues that the leaders raise in these training initiatives.

2. This chapter was developed by the author in conjunction with delivering the 15th Annual Distinguished Norman Williams Lecture at Vermont Law School in the spring of 2019. Among many of his accomplishments, Professor Williams maintained a two-volume casebook on American land planning law. The final sentence of his introduction to the casebook reads as follows:

> If experience in this field teaches anything, it suggests that not all wisdom is derived from reported appellate opinions. Life in the real world is quite different, and those facets which are really important in understanding the actual problem often do not filter through the legal process. In a word, read, mark, and inwardly ponder these materials—but don't believe a word of it.

This chapter was originally published in substantial part by the *Vermont Law Review*: John R. Nolon, *Calming Troubled Waters: Local Solutions*, 44 Vt. L. Rev. 1 (2019).

3. Frazier v. Brown, 12 Ohio St. 294 (1861).

adopted the Restatement's Reasonable Use Rule.[4] The *Frazier* court held that "[t]he law recognizes no correlative rights in respect to underground waters percolating, oozing or filtrating through the earth . . . . Because the existence, origin, movement and course of such waters, and the causes which govern and direct their movement are so secret, occult and concealed, any attempt to administer a set of legal rules in respect to them would be involved in hopeless uncertainty, and would be, therefore, practically impossible."[5] This rendered neighbors who share the use of a groundwater aquifer nearly impotent; the unreasonable use of their shared resource was *damnum sine injuria:* a wrong without a remedy.

In *Cline*, the court reversed course, noting that

> [a] primary goal of water law should be that the legal system conforms to hydrologic fact. Scientific knowledge in the field of hydrology has advanced in the past decade to the point that water tables and sources are more readily discoverable. With notable exceptions, it is now possible for land use professionals to trace the impact of pumping groundwater to serve one parcel on the quality and quality of groundwater underlying neighboring properties. Thus, liability can now be fairly adjudicated with these advances which were solely lacking when this court decided *Frazier* more than a century ago.[6]

What science now reveals is the extraordinary close relationship between land use and development and the quality of water and health of watersheds. Part II of this chapter explores the advance of scientific knowledge related to water pollution and, based on that knowledge, describes the clear relationship between land use and water pollution. Land development increases impervious surface area, compacts soil, removes vegetation, and alters the flow of water above and below ground. If not carefully engineered, development can severely diminish the quality of water. Uncontrolled development increases the volume and rapidity of stormwater runoff, decreases infiltration, exacerbates flooding, and causes soil erosion and sedimentation. Runoff moving across developed surfaces picks up pollutants and sediments and carries them, unfiltered, into surface waters. We call this nonpoint source pollution, defined as "runoff, precipitation, atmospheric deposition, drainage, seepage, or hydrologic modification."[7] It comes from many diffuse sources

4. Cline v. American Aggregates Corp., 474 N.E.2d 324 (Ohio 1984).
5. *Frazier*, 12 Ohio St. at 311; *See also* Chatfield v. Wilson, 28 Vt. 49, 53 (Vt. 1855), where the court held that it is best to allow groundwater to be "enjoyed absolutely by the owner of the land," recognized no correlative right to groundwater between adjoining proprietors of land and refused to regulate it due to practical uncertainties.
6. *Cline*, 474 N.E.2d at 328.
7. *Basic Information About Nonpoint Source (NPS) Pollution*, U.S. EPA (2018), https://www.epa.gov/nps/basic-information-about-nonpoint-source-nps-pollution (last visited Aug. 4, 2020).

and is considered the leading source of domestic water quality problems. State governments report that 40% of all their impaired waters are contaminated solely by nonpoint source pollution.[8]

C. Fragmentation of Water Law: Troubled Waters

Part III reveals the unfortunate fact that federal law, despite these advances in scientific knowledge, does not conform to hydrologic fact but remains "occult," that is, mysterious and of limited help to local officials searching for practical solutions for their water problems. It goes on to sketch the plenary powers of state governments to use their reserved police powers to protect natural resources, such as watersheds, and the delegation of that power to local governments through the authority to adopt land use plans, zoning laws, and land use regulations.

The drinking water serving most homes in Margaret's community comes from groundwater wells, and much of the surface water pollution in her community is due to nonpoint source pollution, caused by surrounding development and land uses. She was surprised to learn that the Clean Water Act (CWA) effectively regulates neither of these. It is limited in its reach. Nonnavigable waters,[9] groundwater,[10] and nonpoint sources[11] all fall outside the statute's regulatory scope. Federal authority can, therefore, only go so far, leaving many gaps to be filled by the states and the municipalities to which they delegate power to regulate land use. State and local regulations can go

8. *Introduction to the Clean Water Act*, U.S. EPA Watershed Acad. Web. https://cfpub.epa.gov/watertrain/moduleFrame.cfm?parent_object_id=2788 (last visited Aug. 4, 2020).

9. 33 U.S.C. §1311(a) (2012) (prohibiting "the discharge of any pollutant by any person"); *id.* §1362(12) (defining discharge as "any addition of any pollutant to navigable waters from any point source").

10. *See* 40 C.F.R. pt. 230.3(o)(2) (2015) (exempting groundwater from the definition of waters of the United States); Army Corps of Eng'rs & EPA, Revised Definition of "Waters of the United States, Revised Definition of "Waters of the United States" 215 (Dec. 11, 2018) (EPA-HQ-OW-2018-0149), https://www.epa.gov/sites/production/files/2018-12/documents/wotus_2040-af75_nprm_frn_2018-12-11_prepublication2_1.pdf [hereinafter Revised Definition of "Waters of the United States"] (exempting groundwater from the pre-proposal redefinition of waters of the United States); *see also* Washington Wilderness Coal. v. Hecla Min. Co., 870 F. Supp. 983, 990 (E.D. Wash. 1994) (finding that courts generally agree that the CWA "do[es] not included 'isolated/nontributary groundwater'" but that courts are split on "whether tributary groundwater . . . is subject to CWA regulation").

11. 33 U.S.C. §1311(a) (prohibiting "the discharge of any pollutant by any person"); *id.* §1362(12) (defining discharge as "any addition of any pollutant to navigable waters from any point source").

beyond the limits of the CWA,[12] reaching isolated wetlands and intrastate waters,[13] groundwater, and the sources of nonpoint source pollution.[14]

Because of statutory, regulatory, and constitutional disconnections, the waters of the United States are troubled. Calming them, and answering Margaret's question, may depend on where one stands and where one observes the water law system. An apt metaphor is provided by Benjamin Franklin who described what happened when he dropped a cruet of oil on the rough waters of Clapham Pond. He reported that he watched

> it spread itself with surprising swiftness upon the surface; but the effect of smoothing the waves was not produced; for I had applied it first on the leeward side of the pond, where the waves were largest, and the wind drove my oil back upon the shore. I then went to the windward side where they [the waves] began to form; and the oil, though not more than a teaspoonful, produced an instant calm over a space of several yards square, which spread amazingly and extended itself gradually till it reached the lee side, making all that quarter of the pond, perhaps half an acre, as smooth as a looking glass.[15]

This chapter stands on the windward side of the waters, where the troubles begin. That is to say, it observes the problems where they first occur, on the lands around the local ponds, lakes, streams, wetlands, and rivers, and above groundwater aquifers. Water pollution is a local phenomenon; it affects local people and engages, as if by instinct, local legal powers. It is critical that we understand the authority that resides in this windward space and to learn how to use it collaboratively to fill the significant gaps in state and federal water law.

D. *Local Solutions*

In part IV, the chapter describes a host of local government gap-filling strategies that protect water quality and promote water conservation. These include aquifer and watershed overlay zoning, open space provisions in land use plans, urban growth boundaries, designated priority areas for growth, designated water conservation areas, creation of rain gardens and sedimentation

12. *See* Hess v. Port Auth. Trans-Hudson Corp., 513 U.S. 30, 44 (1994) ("[R]egulation of land use [is] a function traditionally performed by local governments.").
13. *See* Paul Edward Svensson, *The Supreme Court's New Federalism: The Authority of the U.S. Army Corps of Engineers Does Not Extend Over Isolated Intrastate Wetlands Under the Migratory Bird Rule*, 19 Pace Envtl. L. Rev. 165, 194 (2001) ("[O]nly a state possesses the authority to regulate land and water use in isolated, intrastate wetlands.").
14. 33 U.S.C. §1329 (2012).
15. Charles Tanford, Ben Franklin Stilled the Waves: An Informal History of Pouring Oil on Water With Reflections on the Ups and Downs of Scientific Life in General 71 (1989).

ponds, cluster development requirements to avoid development in vulnerable watershed areas, sedimentation controls of surface mining operations, special limitations on water use in subdivisions that exceed recharge levels, density bonuses for water conserving features in residences, aquifer protection districts, required wetland creation, use of pervious cover and detention ponds, adoption of EcoDistricts with provisions that lower per capita water consumption, use of a green building checklist including water conservation measures, adoption of tree preservation ordinances and Urban Tree Canopy goals, mandatory well testing provisions, stormwater management fees with incentives to reduce impervious coverage, local water conservation and permitting laws, and public nuisance laws.

These laws are adopted by local governments to fit the unique circumstances of each one, demonstrating the difficulty that a remote state or federal legislature might have in legislating to protect water quality and other public values. Many of the local solutions described in Part IV are not within the regulatory authority of the federal government and beyond the reach of the power that state legislatures have given their state water, health, and environmental conservation agencies.

E. *Collaborative Subsidiarity*

Critics of delegating land use authority to towns, villages, and cities cite several deficiencies in relying on such a parochial system of law. They push back against the principle of subsidiarity, the notion "which holds that responsibility for dealing with a problem should be delegated to the most decentralized institution capable of handling that problem."[16] The list of concerns includes the limited geographical jurisdiction of municipal governments,[17] their lack of technical capacity, inadequate financial resources, and resistance

16. Robert Ellickson, Losing Ground: A Nation on Edge 275 (John R. Nolon & Daniel B. Rodriguez eds., 2007); *see also* Graham R. Marshall, *Nesting, Subsidiarity, and Community-Based Environmental Governance Beyond the Local Level*, 2 Int'l J. of the Commons 75, 80 (2008):

> Although various definitions of this principle exist, they generally share in common the implication that any particular task should be decentralized to the lowest level of governance with the capacity to conduct it satisfactorily . . . . This conviction implied that a higher level of organization should refrain from undertaking tasks that could be performed just as well by a grouping closer to the individual.

17. *See* Golden v. Planning Bd. of the Town of Ramapo. 285 N.E.2d 291 (N.Y. 1972). The state's highest court stated that New York's "current zoning enabling legislation is burdened by the largely antiquated notion which deigns that the regulation of land use and development is uniquely a function of local government." *Id.* at 299. The court referenced criticisms of community autonomy finding that local land use control suffers from "pronounced insularism" and produces "distortions in metropolitan growth patterns." *Id.* It also noted that local control "crippl[es] efforts toward regional and State-wide problem solving, be it pollution, decent housing, or public transportation." *Id.*

to mandates from state and federal agencies.[18] Anti-localist scholars point to numerous additional reasons why untethered local control of land use is a bad idea. They cite a "race-to-the-bottom" mentality, not in my backyardism, inadequate information, and insufficient funding.[19]

Part V identifies and discusses several approaches to addressing these local deficiencies and how states, often, and federal agencies, less frequently, act to help overcome local barriers to effective action.[20] They include the provision of technical assistance, data, and model laws; state-mandated environmental impact review; authority to collaborate with neighboring municipalities; intergovernmental watershed planning; integration of small water providers and wastewater systems; and the creation of flexible regional networks.

In part VI, the chapter concludes with an analysis of the many theorists who support grass-roots efforts to solve land use problems.[21] The literature is filled with theories such as the subsidiarity principle, complex adaptive systems, diffusion of innovation, and flexible regional networks, among others. That section continues with a second look at, and further analysis of, the articles that are critical of reliance on local governments. The critics concede that local governments need to be involved in governmental systems to protect natural resources, even if such structures are to be assisted, initiated, or controlled by regional, state, or federal actors. There is disagreement among them as to which higher level of government should be the relevant actor. Some suggest state initiatives under a subfederal approach, others discuss federal-local structures with local officials acting as federal agents, some point to voluntary compacts with neighboring communities, and still others propose strong regional bodies.

The conclusion finds that there is general agreement among many scholars that local governments must play a key role in land use regulation, but that municipal governments need assistance and that collaborative structures should be created where interjurisdictional issues are involved. The chapter ends by proposing that the precise partnership needed depends on the problem being addressed, the circumstances of the situation, and the prevailing political culture. To accommodate the diversity of situations and the need for flexibility in approach, it constructs, explains, and recommends that strategists embrace the Principle of Collaborative Subsidiarity.

---

18. *See* Rena I. Steinzor, *Unfunded Environmental Mandates and the "New Federalism": Devolution, Revolution, orReform?*, 81 Minn. L. Rev. 97, 174-75 (1996) (arguing that local regulations will often keep only their local interest in mind when federal regulation does not exist or apply).
19. *See infra* notes 248-56 and accompanying text.
20. *See infra* Part V, for citations to the mechanisms mentioned in this paragraph.
21. *See infra* Part VI for citations to these theories.

II. Understanding the Land Use Impacts on the Water System[22]

Science has filled in many of the gaps that stymied judicial protection of groundwater in the *Frazier* case and obstructed a clear understanding by regulators of the connectivity of surface waters, wetlands, and groundwater. The failure of courts and legislatures to adequately protect drinking water is no longer caused by the lack of knowledge about how the hydrological system works. Science, as well, provides us with a clear understanding of how land use and development can adversely affect surface and groundwater and the other components of the natural water system. It is now the law that must catch up with impressive advances in science.

A. *Connectivity of the Waters of the United States*[23]

Starting with the fundamentals, scientists divide the water cycle into two compartments: (1) the atmospheric; and (2) the terrestrial.[24] In its atmospheric form, water vapor rises into the sky after evaporating from the surface of the land.[25] Evaporation occurs when surface waters (rivers, streams, and oceans) are heated and transform from a liquid to a gaseous state. Evapotranspiration contributes to atmospheric water when it transpires into the air by plant respiration. Sublimation, which is the transformation of solid snow and ice directly into water vapor, also adds moisture to the atmosphere.

Groundwater, wetlands, and surface water are the water cycle's terrestrial forms. Once water vapor rises into the atmosphere, cooler temperatures cause condensation of water molecules to form clouds. Clouds create pockets of air saturated with water. As the evaporation rate slows to less than the rate of condensation, droplets can grow into full rain droplets.[26] Condensation then takes the form of precipitation (rain, snow, sleet, and hail). Once precipita-

22. The author gratefully acknowledges the contributions to this part made by the two members of the research team who are joint degree students at Yale in the School of Forestry and Environmental Studies: Anthony Mazza, from Elisabeth Haub School of Law at Pace University and Christopher Denny, from Vermont Law School.
23. The reference here is to the interconnectedness of the water, in all of its forms, within the geographical boundaries of the United States, not "waters of the United States" as defined by the Clean Water Rule, which concededly fragments the natural water system. This fragmentation is explained in Part III.
24. Howard Perlman, *The Water Cycle*, USGS Water Sci. Sch. (2017), https://water.usgs.gov/edu/watercycle.html.
25. Howard Perlman, *Summary of the Water Cycle*, USGS Water Sci. Sch. (2016), https://water.usgs.gov/edu/watercyclesummary.html.
26. *Condensation and the Water Cycle*, USGS Water Sci. Sch. (2016), https://water.usgs.gov/edu/watercyclecondensation.html.

tion reaches the ground, it takes on its terrestrial form, becoming groundwater, wetlands, and surface water.

Surface waters are visible riparian bodies, such as lakes, rivers, and streams, as well as the water that travels through the upper layers of unsaturated soil, just above the water table.[27] Infiltration refers to the precipitation that percolates downward into the soil and into the water table and deeper groundwater aquifers. The subsurface flow of groundwater moves through the soil, drawn by gravity and capillary action.[28] Subsurface flow can reenter surface waters or can enter the water table, which is the section of porous materials (sand, silt, and clay) that is permanently saturated by water.[29] This is the area from which many water utilities, homeowners associations, industries, and farms access water by constructing wells.[30] Water may continue to flow below the water table and into aquifers, which are deep pockets of groundwater below bedrock that may be stored for centuries or millennia.

Vegetation plays a major role in the water cycle. Terrestrial water can evaporate directly from the soil and other porous surfaces or by plant respiration.[31] Plants release water vapor from the tiny openings in their leaves. Some groundwater is absorbed by plants and trees through their roots. The evapotranspiration of water from the leaves creates an upward pressure that enables the tree to draw water from the roots and up into branches like a straw, which hydrates the tree and regulates its temperature. A single, large tree can capture and filter over 35,000 gallons of water per year.[32] The positive contribution to the water supply of vegetative evapotranspiration is tremendous.

The confluence of these water features forms watersheds. The U.S. Geological Survey explains that "[a] watershed is an area of land that drains all the streams and rainfall to a single outlet such as the outflow of a reservoir, mouth of a bay, or any point along a stream channel."[33] Because reservoirs and streams are an appropriate reference, they often create the local or regional context for discussing strategies to protect the quality and quantity of drinking water sources. Viewed more broadly, these "local" watersheds are

---

27. Perlman, *supra* note 25.
28. *Id.* (Unsaturated cavities draw water into them the way that a towel absorbs water.)
29. *Groundwater*, N.Y. State Dep't of Envtl. Conservation (DEC), https://www.dec.ny.gov/lands/36064.html (last visited Aug. 4, 2020).
30. *The Hydrologic Cycle*, Idaho State Univ., https://digitalatlas.cose.isu.edu/hydr/basics/main/wtrcycl.htm (last visited Aug. 4, 2020).
31. Howard Perlman, *Evapotranspiration and the Water Cycle*, USGS Water Sci. Sch. (2016), https://water.usgs.gov/edu/watercycleevapotranspiration.html.
32. *Land for Clean Water*, Open Space Inst., https://www.openspaceinstitute.org/what/land-for-clean-water (last visited Aug. 4, 2020).
33. *Id.*

often part of larger jurisdictions; the interconnectivity of all water means that conflicts can arise from seemingly distant and unrelated actions.[34]

B. *Land Use and Development—Impacts on Water Quality*

This elementary description of the water cycle should guide the formulation of land use strategies and water quality policy by governmental agencies. It makes clear that the protection of groundwater and surface waters calls upon municipalities with the authority to regulate private development to adopt land use regulations that protect water quality in local watersheds, in concert with neighboring communities, regional bodies, and state and federal agencies that govern and can affect the larger, interconnected watersheds. The effect of land use and development on water quality is examined below in three categories: the impact on surface waters, sedimentation and eutrophication, and environmental impact on soils.

1. Surface Water Impacts From Poor Development Practices

Urban development changes the characteristics of surface waters, leading to what some water resource managers call the "urban stream syndrome—the complex but consistent pattern of degradation of urban streams relative to their undeveloped counterparts."[35] Pavement, rooftops, and compacted soils play the most important role in the urban stream degradation because these surfaces prevent water from naturally percolating into the ground. Residential developments and commercial land uses, common in urban development, effectively result in the construction of impervious surfaces of 44 to 72% of the urban landscape.[36] Worrisome stream degradation begins after more than 10% of a watershed is covered with these impervious surfaces.

Impervious surfaces also change runoff patterns, which affect stream hydrology.[37] Urban streams are adversely affected by increased flood-level flows from storm events. As more flooding occurs, the more the stream bed and bank are deepened and eroded. Bank erosion is particularly problematic in that it leads to increased sediment loading in the stream. Runoff travelling across impervious surfaces collects trash, oils, sediments, fertilizers, bacteria, and road treatment products. This polluted runoff flows directly into streams unless collected and treated by storm and sanitary sewer systems.

34. *The Hydrologic Cycle*, *supra* note 30.
35. Shimon C. Anisfeld, Water Resources 154 (2010).
36. *Id.* at 155.
37. *Id.* at 156.

2. Sediment Pollution and Cultural Eutrophication

Domestically, sediment pollution is the greatest threat to water quality.[38] It occurs when soil erodes, that is, when particles become detached from the ground and flow into streams.[39] Many factors affect soil erosion, including its texture, type, and structure; the vegetative cover; topographical features, particularly slope; climatic factors such as wind, temperature, and rainfall; and the velocity of water runoff. Land development practices and land use change directly impact the amount of sediment runoff because they alter the cover, grade, and structure of soils.[40] EPA estimates that human activities cause 70% of sediment pollution.[41]

Understanding the negative impacts of high sediment pollution due to land development highlights why land use regulations are needed to mitigate erosion and increase water quality. Filling a stream with dirt can cause numerous problems. These problems can range from covering up the bottom organisms' homes to depriving water plants of needed nutrients. Sediment pollution leads to physical, biological, and chemical impacts. Physical impacts include making surface waters shallower, impacting navigation, storage capacity, and water temperature.[42] Turbid water clogs the filtering function of water plants, increasing the cost of providing drinking water.[43] Biological impacts include burying organisms and plants, clogging fish gills, and increasing algae growth. Chemical impacts include reducing light energy and nutrient transport.[44]

Nutrients attach to the soil particles and wash into the surface waters.[45] Sediment particles carry the nutrients, such as nitrogen and phosphorus, needed to grow plants. Eutrophication is the process by which water becomes overly saturated with these nutrients.[46] Cultural eutrophication is when human activity increases the rate of this process. The result is intense plant growth such as algal blooms. When these plants die, decomposer organisms use oxygen as they consume dead plant matter. Because excess nutrients

38. *Protecting Water Quality From Agricultural Runoff*, U.S. EPA (March 2015), https://www.epa.gov/sites/production/files/2015-09/documents/ag_runoff_fact_sheet.pdf.
39. *2002 Connecticut Guidelines for Soil Erosion and Sediment Control*, Dep't of Energy & the Env't. 2-4 (2002), https://www.ct.gov/deep/lib/deep/water_inland/sesc/secs_chapter_1_5.pdf.
40. *Id.* at 2-7.
41. *What Is Sediment Pollution?* Mid-America Regional Council, https://cfpub.epa.gov/npstbx/files/ksmo_sediment.pdf (last visited Aug. 4, 2020).
42. *2002 Connecticut Guidelines for Soil Erosion and Sediment Control, supra* note 39 at 2-4, *Id.* at 2-7.
43. *Protecting Water Quality from Agricultural Runoff, supra* note 38.
44. *2002 Connecticut Guidelines for Soil Erosion and Sediment Control, supra* note 39, at 2-4. *Id.* at 2-7.
45. J. David Allan & Maria M. Castillo, Stream Ecology 255 (2d ed. 2007).
46. S.R. Carpenter et al., Nonpoint Pollution of Surface Waters With Phosphorus and Nitrogen 561 (1998).

enable more plant growth, there is more food for the decomposers. More food leads to more consumption as more oxygen is consumed. As the decomposers use up the available dissolved oxygen, the larger organisms, such as fish, essentially suffocate. Dead fish provides more food for the decomposers. This creates hypoxic or dead zones, which can greatly reduce biodiversity.

In some cases, the algal blooms can also include dangerous cyanobacteria.[47] Cyanobacteria, which is also known as blue-green algae, is harmful to humans and can be lethal to some animals, including dogs. "[T]he toxins in blue-green algae can cause severe neurological symptoms in canines that can lead to death within a couple of hours."[48] Toxic blooms seem to be on the rise and without proper management pose a significant health risk.

3. Environmental Impacts to Soil Structures Due to Construction

Construction changes a normal soil system resulting in different alkalinity or acidity, high compaction, and removal of the soil's mineral layer.[49] Removal of organic layers changes the potential or power of hydrogen—pH—of the soil, which creates an unnaturally high or low pH soil depending on the construction-induced mixing. The movement of large equipment during construction compresses the soil, which "crushes soil structure, impeding air, water, and root movement." Machinery flattens pore spaces between the soil particles. Compacted soils are, essentially, impervious surfaces that reduce recharge to groundwater aquifers. Compaction also closes organic pore spaces in soils, which builds up root-generated carbon dioxide (CO_2), slowing root respiration and plant growth. Grading of soils during construction also removes organic layers, leaving only the lower soil horizons, which tend to be more clay-like, impervious, and lower in nutrients.[50]

47. Lisa W. Foderaro, *Beware the Blooms: Toxic Algae Found in Some City Ponds*, N.Y. Times, July 7, 2017, https://www.nytimes.com/2017/07/07/nyregion/beware-the-blooms-toxic-algae-found-in-some-city-ponds.html.
48. *Id.*
49. William Elmendorf, Understanding Tree Planting in Construction-Damaged Soil (Pennsylvania State Univ. 2008), https://extension.psu.edu/understanding-tree-planting-in-construction-damaged-soils.
50. *Id.* at 488.

III. Waters of the United States—Gaps in Governmental Jurisdiction

The legal definition of "waters of the United States" under the CWA is quite different from the scientific definition of the water system discussed above. The sources of drinking water in the Sawkill Watershed, where Margaret's community is located, are both groundwater aquifers and surface waters. Both are fed and protected by wetlands of a variety of sizes and types. Rain and snow contribute volume to each water source: stormwater and melting snow can either percolate into the aquifers or run into surface waters. That precipitation is fed, in turn, by the evaporation of water from the surface. The connections here are obvious and the workings of these waters are well understood by scientists.

It is now 128 years since the Ohio court in the *Frazer* decision criticized the occult nature of water science. During that time, science has clarified the movements of water and sharpened the focus of courts and legislatures intent on protecting them. We have fallen far short, however, of the task of aligning law with hydrologic fact. The fundamental scientific fact of hydrology is the connectivity among types and sources of water. Regulation of water pollution, however, is a patchwork of mostly unconnected regimes. At the federal level, the law is particularly fragmented.[51] Under the CWA, for example, the federal government has authority over "navigable waters," while the states govern all other waters.[52]

A. Waters of the United States

Congress enacted the CWA pursuant to its authority to regulate interstate commerce under the Commerce Clause of the U.S. Constitution.[53] Congress has the authority "[t]o regulate Commerce with foreign Nations, and among the several States, and with the Indian Tribes."[54] This includes authority over channels of interstate commerce, including "navigable rivers, lakes, and

51. In this section, fragmentation at the federal level is demonstrated by reference to the CWA and does not discuss the role of ensuring clean water of the Safe Drinking Water Act, the Resource Conservation and Recovery Act, or the Comprehensive Environmental Response, Compensation, and Liability Act.

52. 33 U.S.C. §1311(a) (2012) (prohibiting the discharge of pollutants except in compliance with sections of the CWA); *id.* §1362(12) (defining "discharge" as "any addition of any pollutant to navigable waters from any point source"); *see also* Solid Waste Agency of N. Cook Cty. v. Army Corps of Eng'rs, 531 U.S. 159, 174 (2001) (noting that the states have "traditional and primary power over land and water use").

53. United States v. Deaton, 332 F.3d 698, 706 (4th Cir. 2003).

54. U.S. Const. art. I, §8, cl. 3.

canals of the United States."[55] "Traditionally navigable waters" are those that "are used, or are susceptible of being used, in their ordinary condition, as highways for commerce," as well as those "subject to the ebb and flow of the tide."[56] Included here, of course, are the "navigable rivers, lakes, and canals of the United States."[57] The Commerce Clause gives federal agencies power over activities substantially related to interstate commerce.[58] For example, Congress has the power to regulate non-navigable tributaries of navigable waters in order to protect downstream quality. Furthermore, activities that are entirely intrastate can have aggregate impacts on interstate commerce that bring them within Commerce Clause jurisdiction.[59]

The limits on Congress' authority under the Commerce Clause constrain CWA jurisdiction; the Act can only go as far as the Constitution allows.[60] As the Supreme Court explained, the reach of Commerce Clause authority "must be considered in the light of our dual system of government" and cannot swallow the line between what is federal and what is truly local.[61] In this way, authority over waters is fragmented and in many contexts, states have the sole power to implement protective regulations directly or by delegating that authority to their local governments.

This federalism structure is a hallmark characteristic of the CWA.[62] It is meant to respect states' traditional jurisdiction over their property.[63] The Act states that "[i]t is the policy of the Congress to recognize, preserve, and protect the primary responsibilities and rights of States . . . ." The federal government therefore has limited jurisdiction over water pollution, and leaves much regulation to the states and their municipalities.[64] If the interconnected groundwater, wetlands, and surface waters in watersheds are to be properly protected, state and local governments must implement their own laws addressing water pollution.[65]

55. *Gibbs*, 214 F.3d at 490 (quoting United States v. Miles, 122 F.3d 235, 245 (5th Cir. 1997) (DeMoss, J., concurring)).
56. The Daniel Ball, 77 U.S. 557, 563 (1870).
57. *Gibbs*, 214 F.3d at 490
58. United States v. Ashland Oil & Transp. Co., 504 F.2d 1317, 1328 (6th Cir. 1974).
59. Wickard v. Filburn, 317 U.S. 111, 129 (1942).
60. United States v. Holland, 373 F. Supp. 665, 671 (M.D. FlA. 1974).
61. National Labor Relations Bd. v. Jones & Laughlin Steel Corp., 301 U.S. 1, 37 (1937).
62. *See* Department of Energy v. Ohio, 503 U.S. 607, 633 (1992) ("[T]he [CWA] establishes a distinctive variety of cooperative federalism.").
63. 33 U.S.C. §1251(b).
64. *See, e.g., Solid Waste Agency of N. Cook Cty.*, 531 U.S. at 172-73 (holding that the CWA does not reach "non-navigable, isolated, intrastate waters" because such extensive jurisdiction would "encroach[] upon a traditional state power").
65. *See* 33 U.S.C. §1251 (recognizing that states have "the primary responsibilities and rights" over water resources).

1. Surface Water

The CWA does not clearly define what surface waters are subject to federal jurisdiction—so-called jurisdictional waters.[66] The Act simply states that the federal government regulates "navigable waters," which are statutorily defined as "waters of the United States." Congress did not define this term further but rather left its meaning to EPA and the U.S. Army Corps of Engineers.[67] EPA and the Corps have attempted to provide clarity by promulgating definitions of waters of the United States. The first regulatory definition appeared in 1977 and created four categories of jurisdictional waters: (1) "[c]oastal and inland waters, lakes, rivers, and streams that are navigable waters of the United States, including adjacent wetlands"; (2) "[t]ributaries to navigable waters"; (3) "[i]nterstate waters and their tributaries"; and (4) "[a]ll other waters of the United States . . . the degradation or destruction of which could affect interstate commerce."[68] Three years later in 1980, a new, similar definition was written that included traditionally navigable waters, interstate waters, the territorial seas, waters that could affect interstate or foreign commerce, impoundments of waters of the United States, tributaries of waters of the United States, and wetlands adjacent to waters of the United States.[69] This rule defined the definition of waters of the United States for the next several decades.[70] The rule was amended modestly thereafter, but versions promulgated 1986 and 1988 were largely the same,[71] and remained in place until 2015.[72]

In 2015, the Obama Administration promulgated a new definition of waters of the United States. This rule, known as the Clean Water Rule, differed from the long-standing provision in two key ways: (1) it no longer

66. *See id.* §1362(7) (defining "navigable waters" as "waters of the United States," but failing to define "waters of the United States").
67. *See id.* (failing to define "waters of the United States").
68. Regulatory Programs of the Corps of Engineers, 42 Fed. Reg. 37122, 37127 (July 19, 1977).
69. Consolidated Permit Regulations: RCRA Hazardous Waste; SDWA Underground Injection Control; CWA National Pollutant Discharge Elimination System; CWA Section 404 Dredge or Fill Programs; and CAA Prevention of Significant Deterioration, 45 Fed. Reg. 33290, 33424 (May 19, 1980) [hereinafter Consolidated Permit Regulations].
70. Stephen P. Mulligan, *Evolution of the Meaning of "Waters of the United States" in the Clean Water Act*, Congressional Research Service (2016), https://fas.org/sgp/crs/misc/R44585.pdf ("The two agencies continued to use [the 1980] definition (with modifications) until the Clean Water Rule was published in 2015.").
71. *Compare Consolidated Permit Regulations*, 45 Fed. Reg. at 33424, *with* Final Rule for Regulatory Programs of the Corps of Engineers, 51 Fed. Reg. 41206, 41217 (Nov. 13, 1986); Final Rule: Clean Water Act Section 404 Program Definitions and Permit Exemptions, 53 Fed. Reg. 20764, 20765 (June 6, 1988).
72. *See* Clean Water Rule: Definition of "Waters of the United States," 80 Fed. Reg. 37054, 37104 (June 29, 2015) (redefining waters of the United States).

included waters that could affect interstate commerce; and (2) it expanded jurisdiction to include waters with a significant nexus to other jurisdictional waters.[73] Thus, the 2015 Clean Water Rule both narrowed and broadened federal jurisdiction over water. Much of this jurisdictional expansion encompassed wetlands. Previously, wetlands were only covered if adjacent to a jurisdictional water.[74] Under the Obama formulation, wetlands were covered if they had a significant nexus to a jurisdictional water.[75] Therefore, wetlands no longer needed to touch jurisdictional waters. Furthermore, wetlands within a watershed could be aggregated to reach the required significance. This broadening of the Act's jurisdiction led to significant controversy.[76]

In 2017, Pres. Donald Trump signed an executive order requiring EPA and the Corps of Engineers to review the Clean Water Rule.[77] The agencies proposed to rescind the Rule[78] and to replace it with a rule that narrows CWA jurisdiction.[79] At the end of 2018, the agencies issued a pre-proposal version of a rule redefining waters of the United States.[80] The new definition includes traditionally navigable waters, their tributaries, and adjacent wetlands.[81] Furthermore, it states that wetlands are only considered "adjacent" if they abut a traditionally navigable water or have a "direct hydrologic surface connection with a navigable water."[82] This change will substantially reduce the jurisdiction of the CWA.

Under the new rule, waters of the United States will not include "[e]phemeral features,"[83] which "means surface water flowing or pooling only in direct response to precipitation (e.g., rain or snow fall)."[84] This exclusion will narrow CWA jurisdiction, especially in the West where many waters are impermanent.[85] For example, more than 90% of Arizona's surface waters are ephemeral or intermittent. Furthermore, an EPA letter from 2006 estimated that 40% of point source discharges regulated under the CWA (excluding

73. *Compare* 40 C.F.R. pt. 230.3(o) (2015) *with* 40 C.F.R. pt. 230.3(s) (1986).
74. *Id.* pt. 230.3(s) (1986).
75. *Id.* pt. §230.3(o)(vii) (2015).
76. *See* National Ass'n of Mfrs. v. Department of Def., 138 S. Ct. 617, 623 (2018) ("The [Clean Water] Rule prompted several parties . . . to challenge the regulation in federal court.").
77. Exec. Order No. 13778, 82 Fed. Reg. 12497, 12497 (Feb. 28, 2017).
78. Definition of "Waters of the United States"—Recodification of Pre-Existing Rules, 82 Fed. Reg. 34899, 34900 (July 27, 2017).
79. *See* Exec. Order No. 13778, 82 Fed. Reg. 12497, 12497 (Feb. 28, 2017); REVISED DEFINITION OF "WATERS OF THE UNITED STATES" *supra* note 10.
80. REVISED DEFINITION OF "WATERS OF THE UNITED STATES" *supra* note 10.
81. *Id.* at 214.
82. *Id.* at 216.
83. *Id.* at 220-21.
84. *Id.* at 222.
85. Darren Springer, *How States Can Help to Resolve the* Rapanos/Carabell *Dilemma*, 21 TUL. ENVTL. L.J. 83, 86 (2007).

storm water permits and non-storm water general permits) come from intermittent, ephemeral, or very small perennial streams . . . ."[86] While some intermittent waters appear to be covered by the new rule, there is persuasive evidence that CWA jurisdiction will be significantly narrower under the new definition of "waters of the United States."[87]

2. Groundwater

Groundwater is specifically excluded from waters that are subject to federal jurisdiction.[88] The legislative history of the CWA indicates that Congress left groundwater regulation to the states because "the jurisdiction regarding groundwaters is so complex and varied from State to State."[89] Congress "did not intend to interfere with or displace the 'complex and varied' state jurisdictions over groundwaters."[90]

Some federal jurisdiction over discharges to groundwater may nevertheless exist. In 2018, the U.S. Court of Appeals for the Fourth and Ninth Circuits held that the scope of the CWA encompasses point source discharges directly into groundwater if it is hydrologically connected to federal jurisdictional surface waters.[91] The U.S. Court of Appeals for the Sixth Circuit disagreed, holding that all discharges to groundwater are subject only to state jurisdic-

86. *Id.* at 91 (citing Letter from Benjamin Grumbles, EPA Assistant Administrator for Water, to Jeannie Christie, Executive Director, Association of State Wetlands Managers (Jan. 9, 2006)).
87. *See* Revised Definition of "Waters of the United States," *supra* note 10, at 222 ("The term *tributary* means a river, stream, or similar naturally occurring surface water channel that contributes perennial or intermittent flow to a [water of the United States]."). Another example of waters that will lose protection is the Delmarva bays. *Report Details Impact on the Chesapeake Bay of Trump's Proposed Rollback of Wetlands Regulations*, Envtl. Integrity Project (Dec. 12, 2018) [hereinafter *Impact on the Chesapeake Bay*], https://www.environmentalintegrity.org/news/report-details-impact-on-the-chesapeake-bay-of-trumps-proposed-rollback-of-wetlands-regulations/. Under the 2015 Rule, these wetlands could qualify for CWA jurisdiction if they passed the significant nexus test. 40 C.F.R. §230.3(o)(vii)(B). Under the new rule, however, at least 34,000 acres (about 54 square miles) of wetlands on the Delmarva peninsula in the Chesapeake Bay region will lose federal protection. According to the Environmental Integrity Project, another 38,000 miles of the region's intermittent and ephemeral streams (over half of the region's waterway mileage) will also fall outside CWA jurisdiction.
88. *See* 40 C.F.R. pt. 230.3(o)(2) (2015) (exempting groundwater from the definition of waters of the United States); Revised Definition of "Waters of the United States, *supra* note 10, at 215 (exempting groundwater from the pre-proposal redefinition of waters of the United States); *see also* Washington Wilderness Coal. v. Hecla Min. Co., 870 F. Supp. 983, 990 (E.D. Wash. 1994) (finding that courts generally agree that the CWA "do[es] not included 'isolated/nontributary groundwater'" but that courts are split on "whether tributary groundwater . . . is subject to CWA regulation").
89. S. Rep. No. 414, 92d Cong., 1st Sess. 73 (1971), 1972 U.S. Code Cong. & Admin. News 3668, 3749.
90. Exxon Corp. v. Train, 554 F.2d 1310, 1326 (5th Cir. 1977) (explaining that the CWA "leave[s] control of groundwater pollution exclusively to the states" and quoting S. Rep. No. 414, at 52-53, 2 Leg. Hist. 1470-71, 1972 U.S. Code Cong. & Admin. News 3718).
91. Hawaii Wildlife Fund v. County of Maui, 886 F.3d 737, 749 (9th Cir. 2018); Upstate Forever v. Kinder Morgan Energy Partners, Ltd. Partnership, 887 F.3d 637, 651 (4th Cir. 2018).

tion.[92] The Supreme Court has accepted a petition for certiorari filed in the Fourth and Ninth Circuit cases.[93] Furthermore, in 2018, EPA issued a notice seeking comment on whether it has the authority to regulate discharges to tributary groundwater, and if so, whether the CWA is the appropriate statute by which to regulate them.[94] Accordingly, it is possible that EPA or the Supreme Court could resolve this split and provide clarity on the scope of CWA jurisdiction in this developing area of the law. Nevertheless, for the foreseeable future, there is no clear answer on this issue, and the regulation of discharges to tributary groundwater remains ambiguous.

3. Nonpoint Source Pollution

In addition to omitting groundwater, the CWA does not regulate the largest contributor to water quality degradation: nonpoint source pollution.[95] The Act only regulates discharges that stem from a "point source," which is defined as "any discernible, confined and discrete conveyance."[96] The Act leaves nonpoint sources undefined, but the term is generally understood to occur "when rainfall or snowmelt, moving over and through the ground, picks up and carries natural and human-made pollutants, depositing them into lakes, rivers, wetlands, coastal waters and ground waters."[97] Some things held to be non-point sources include coal ash pits,[98] human activity,[99] and livestock.[100]

Congress elected not to focus federal regulation on nonpoint sources "in part because [they] were far more numerous and more technologically difficult to regulate."[101] Instead, the CWA leaves regulation of these diffuse discharges to the states and their local governments. While the CWA has largely

92. Kentucky Waterways All. v. Kentucky Utilities Co., 905 F.3d 925, 938 (6th Cir. 2018).
93. Petition for Writ of Certiorari, Haw. Wildlife Fund v. Cty. of Maui, No. 18-260 (Aug. 27, 2018); Petition for Writ of Certiorari, Upstate Forever v. Kinder Morgan Energy Partners, No. 18-268 (Aug. 28, 2018). The Supreme Court approved the petition in February 2019.
94. Clean Water Act Coverage of "Discharges of Pollutants" via a Direct Hydrologic Connection to Surface Water, 83 Fed. Reg. 7126 (Feb. 20, 2018) (to be codified at 40 C.F.R. pt. 122). In April 2019, EPA issued an interpretation of the CWA that it does not cover indirect discharges through groundwater: https://www.eenews.net/stories/1060169889.
95. *Polluted Runoff: Nonpoint Source (NPS) Pollution: Basic Information About Nonpoint Source (NPS) Pollution*, U.S. EPA (Aug. 10, 2018), https://www.epa.gov/nps/basic-information-about-nonpoint-source-nps-pollution.
96. 33 U.S.C. §1362(14) (2012).
97. *Polluted Runoff: Nonpoint Source (NPS) Pollution*, U.S. EPA (Dec. 17, 2018), https://www.epa.gov/nps; *see also* United States v. Earth Sci., Inc., 599 F.2d 368, 373 (10th Cir. 1979).
98. Sierra Club v. Virginia Elec. & Power Co., 903 F.3d 403, 410 (4th Cir. 2018).
99. United States v. Plaza Health Labs., Inc., 3 F.3d 643, 650 (2d Cir. 1993).
100. Oregon Nat. Desert Ass'n v. Forest Serv., 550 F.3d 778, 785 (9th Cir. 2008).
101. *Id.* at 780 (citing S. Rep. No. 92-414, at 39 (1972); 118 Cong. Rec. 10611, 10765 (1972)).

been successful in addressing point source pollution, the problem with nonpoint source pollution has become prominent.[102] According to EPA, the states have attested that degraded water quality now primarily stems from nonpoint sources.[103]

The CWA's difficulty in addressing nonpoint source pollution is illustrated by a statutory tool called the total maximum daily load (TMDL). When a water body is designated as impaired and cannot support its state-designated uses, e.g., drinking, fishing, recreational,[104] the CWA authorizes states to establish a TMDL for its designated impaired waters. A TMDL sets a target for the total amount of various pollutants that can be discharged into a water body. Then, it divides this total between point and nonpoint sources (setting "wasteload allocations" and "load allocations," respectively).[105] In practice, TMDLs can reduce pollution in a waterbody, but are seldom effective.[106] TMDLs "function primarily as planning devices and are not self-executing."[107] TMDLs can be incorporated into federally or state-required permits for point sources.[108] They cannot, however, be enforced against the originating sources of nonpoint degradation.[109] Therefore, although a TMDL initiative at the state level may set a limit on discharges for nonpoint sources, it may not lead to significant pollution reduction.[110]

In summary, citizens like Margaret, who expect federal environmental laws, regulations, and agencies to protect them and their communities from

---

102. *Introduction to the Clean Water Act*, U.S. EPA Watershed Acad. Web 4, https://cfpub.epa.gov/watertrain/pdf/modules/introtocwa.pdf.
103. *Polluted Runoff: Nonpoint Source (NPS) Pollution: Basic Information About Nonpoint Source (NPS) Pollution, supra* note 96.
104. *Introduction to the Clean Water Act, supra* note 103, at 9.
105. 40 C.F.R. §130.2; *id.* §130.7(c).
106. *See 2010 Assessment of Improvement and Recovered Waters With Total Maximum Daily Loads (TMDLs)*, U.S. EPA (March 2011), https://www.epa.gov/sites/production/files/2015-10/documents/tmdl-waters-improved.pdf (showing that from 2002 to 2010, 216 water bodies were "improved to the point that one or more of the original causes of impairment had been removed" due to TMDLs or TMDL alternatives).
107. City of Arcadia v. EPA, 265 F. Supp. 2d 1142, 1144 (N.D. Cal. 2003).
108. 40 C.F.R. §122.44(d)(1)(vii)(B).
109. *See* 33 U.S.C. §1311 (prohibiting the discharge of pollutants); *id.* §1362 (defining the "discharge of a pollutant" as "any addition of any pollutant to navigable waters from any point source); *see also* City of Arcadia v. Environmental Prot. Agency, 265 F. Supp. 2d 1142, 1145 (N.D. Cal. 2003):

    For nonpoint sources, limitations on loadings are not subject to a federal nonpoint source permitting program, and therefore any nonpoint source reductions can be enforced against those responsible for the pollution only to the extent that a state institutes such reductions as regulatory requirements pursuant to state authority.

110. *See Introduction to the Clean Water Act, supra* note 103, at 34 ("It is likely. . . that the CWA tools alone might not be sufficient to achieve needed reductions, especially in situations where non-point sources dominate loadings."). Although a separate and independent federal action, the EPA-directed Stormwater Management Program is effective in engaging local governments operating separate stormwater sewer systems to control non-point source pollution. *See infra* footnotes 212-17 and accompanying text.

water pollution, need to understand the CWA's considerable limitations. The amount of surface water protected from point source pollution is being reduced. Groundwater pollution is essentially unregulated by applicable CWA regulations. The largest source of water pollution—nonpoint source pollution—is outside its reach. Regulating these sources of water pollution is left to the states and their local governments. For this reason, local land use officials need to learn about the plenary power that state and their own legislatures have to prevent and mitigate water pollution and protect public health.

B. State and Local Jurisdiction: Filling the Gaps

Historically, states have delegated their authority to regulate and mitigate the effects of land use to local governments. Along with that power, states give local governments the authority to tax land development and the responsibility to use their tax revenues to pay the cost of municipal services. Those three powers are intertwined and create a state-wide system of law that permits and controls land development in the public interest, primarily through local lawmaking and administrative procedures.[111]

States give local governments broad and comprehensive control of urban development, human settlements, and land use projects. Local governments adopt comprehensive land use plans, zoning laws, subdivision and site plan regulations, and other land use laws.[112] The judiciary's traditional view that state-delegated local authority is to be narrowly construed under the so-called Dillion's Rule has been overruled in most states, with respect to local land use authority, and replaced with a broader interpretation.[113] A recent

111. John R. Nolon, *Historical Overview of the American Land Use System: A Diagnostic Approach to Evaluating Governmental Land Use Control*, 23 Pace Envtl. L. Rev. 821 (2006).

112. *Id.*

113. With respect to delegated local land use control, many states courts have largely abandoned Dillon's Rule in favor of a broad interpretation of local power. See for example: North Carolina:

> It is the policy of the General Assembly that the cities of this State should have adequate authority to execute the powers, duties, privileges, and immunities conferred upon them by law. To this end, the provisions of this Chapter and of city charters shall be broadly construed and grants of power shall be construed to include any additional and supplementary powers that are reasonably necessary or expedient to carry them into execution and effect.

Homebuilders Ass'n v. City of Charlotte, 442 S.E.2d 45, 49 (N.C. 1994). New York: "[T]he court recognizes that the power of local governments to zone and control land use is undoubtedly broad and its proper exercise is an essential aspect of achieving a satisfactory quality of life in both urban and rural communities . . . ." (N.Y. 1995); Delaware: "The permissive nature of the statute makes it clear that the state statute sets a floor and not a ceiling for the City to honor." City of Lewes v. Nepa, No. S17A-06-003, 2019 LEXIS 293, 3 (Del. 2019); Idaho: "In enacting the Local Planning Act of 1975, the legislature obviously intended to give local governing boards, such as the Kootenai County Commissioners, broad powers in the area of planning and zoning." Worley Highway Dist. v. Kootenai County, 663 P.2d 1135, 1137 (Idaho Ct. App. 1983); Pennsylvania: "Municipalities have trend of some state legislatures to preempt local authority has generally not touched on local power to protect natural resources.[114]

Part of Margaret's disappointment over the limitations of state agency authority was assuaged after she learned that this legal system prevails in all 50 states and principally relies on local governments and democratic processes to control land uses in order to protect the public health and ecosystems, including watersheds. The delegation of that power explains why state legislatures have not vested their state agencies with land use control so as not to compete with or hinder this traditional local jurisdiction. It also demonstrates why the opportunity—or responsibility—rests with local governments to fill the significant gaps in federal and state authority to regulate water quality. As we will see in Parts V and VI below, locals need and receive much assistance from state and federal agencies in this gap-filling role, but local power remains the foundation of the enterprise.

The dual U.S. system of federalism reserves to the states the powers that are not specifically delegated to the federal government by the Constitution.[115] The Tenth Amendment acknowledges the Constitution's reservation of powers.[116] The police power and other powers reserved to the states are not

broad authority to regulate land use in general and mineral extraction in particular." Southdown, Inc. v. Jackson Twp. Zoning Hearing Bd., 809 A.2d 1059, 1065 (Pa. Commw. Ct. 2002); Texas: "The power of local governments to zone and control land use is undoubtedly broad and its proper exercise is an essential aspect of achieving a satisfactory quality of life in both urban and rural communities." Barr v. City of Sinton, 295 S.W.3d 287, 297 (Tex. 2009). In addition to these judicial interpretations, some state legislatures have explicitly repealed the applicability of Dillon's Rule via statute. (See e.g. Guidebook for Municipal Officials of Mayor/ Council Cities 5 (2015). https://static.ark.org/eeuploads/arml/MayorCouncil_Guidebook_2015_WEB.pdf); some states have incorporated self-executing provisions related to home rule authority in their state constitutions. See Hon. John D. Russell & Aaron Bostrom, *Federalism, Dillon Rule, and Home Rule,* American City County Exchange White Paper 6 (Jan. 2016).

114. Some states have adopted laws that preempt municipal ability to pass any regulation related to entire areas of policy. With the exception of local control over fracking in a few states, these areas do not include those related to land use and natural resource protection. *See* Richard C. Schragger, *Federalism, Metropolitanism, and the Problem of States,* 105 Va. L. Rev. 1, 29 (2019).

115. "The powers not delegated to the United States by the Constitution, nor prohibited by it to the States, are reserved to the States respectively, or to the people." U.S. Const. Amend. X. *See also* James Madison, The Federalist No. 39, at 186 (Terence Ball ed., 2003) (Federal authority "extends to certain enumerated objects only, and leaves to the several States a residuary and inviolable sovereignty over all other objects."); James Madison, Federalist No. 45, 292-293 (C. Rossiter ed. 1961):

> The powers delegated by the proposed Constitution to the federal government are few and defined. Those which are to remain in the State governments are numerous and indefinite . . . . The powers reserved to the several States will extend to all the objects which, in the ordinary course of affairs, concern the lives, liberties, and properties of the people, and the internal order, improvement, and prosperity of the State.

116. U.S. Const. Amend. X ("The powers not delegated to the United States by the Constitution, nor prohibited by it to the States, are reserved to the States respectively, or to the people.") *See also* Santiago Legarre, *The Historical Background of the Police Power,* 9 U. Pa. J. Const. L. 745, 778 (2007) ("the [Tenth] Amendment functions as a principal constitutional basis of state police power") (citations omitted).

powers conferred upon the states, but ones that have always resided within their dominion.[117] So, to the extent that the Commerce Clause limits federal power to control water pollution, that jurisdiction remains with the states under their sovereign police power.

Although difficulties in defining the police power have plagued both courts and scholars,[118] the term has come to be understood as the power to protect the health, safety, and welfare of the public.[119] Historically, the police power has been equated with the general governmental objective of securing the public welfare through regulatory means.[120] The Supreme Court has held that the police power inherently lies within the authority of the states,[121] and it is extremely broad, in that it encompasses a host of factors under the general term "public welfare."[122] State supreme courts have likewise broadly

---

117. *See* Brian W. Ohm, *Some Modern Day Musings on the Police Power*, 47 Urb. Law. 625, 626 (2015) ("The police power is *not*, as often cited, a power that is 'conferred . . . by the Tenth Amendment, U.S. Const., upon the individual states.' The Tenth Amendment did not confer anything on the states. Rather, in the United States, sovereignty resides with the people.") (citations omitted) (emphasis in original). *See also* Nolon, *supra* note 112, at 825 ("The U.S. Constitution . . . created a federal government that has the power to legislate only within the parameters of the specific powers delegated to it in the Constitution. Notably, the full police powers of the states were not delegated to the federal government.").

118. Walter Wheeler Cook, *What Is the Police Power?* 7 Colum. L. Rev. 322, 322 (1907) ("No phrase is more frequently used and at the same time less understood than the police power."); Collins Denny Jr., *The Growth and Development of the Police Power of the State*, 20 Mich. L. Rev. 173, 173 (1921) ("The police power of the state is one of the most difficult phases of our law to understand, and it is even more difficult to define it and to place it within any bounds."); Legarre, *supra* note 117, at 747 ("The police power suffers from a surprising problem. Though it has been in constant use for many years and has proved important in the vocabulary of American constitutional law . . . [t]he meaning and implications of the term are far from clear.")

119. Police Power, Black's Law Dictionary (defining police power as "[t]he inherent and plenary power of a sovereign to make all laws necessary and proper to preserve the public security, order, health, morality, and justice").

120. 4 Blackstone's Commentaries 162 (Police power is "the due regulation and domestic order of the kingdom, whereby the inhabitants of a State, like members of a well-governed family, are bound to conform their general behavior to the rules of propriety, good neighborhood and good manners, and to be decent, industrious and inoffensive in their respective stations."); Ernst Freund, The Police Power, Public Policy, and Constitutional Rights 3 (1904) ("It is possible to evolve at least two main attributes or characteristics which differentiate the police power: it aims to directly secure and promote the public welfare, and it does so by restraint and compulsion.").

121. *Nebbia v. People of New York*, 291 U.S. 502, 524-25 (1934) ("[W]hat are the police powers of a State? They are nothing more or less than the powers of government inherent in every sovereignty to the extent of its dominions.").

122. Berman v. Parker, 348 U.S. 26, 32-33 (1954):

> Public safety, public health, morality, peace and quiet, law and order--these are some of the more conspicuous examples of the traditional application of the police power to municipal affairs. Yet they merely illustrate the scope of the power and do not delimit it . . . . The concept of the public welfare is broad and inclusive . . . . The values it represents are spiritual as well as physical, aesthetic as well as monetary. It is within the power of the legislature to determine that the community should be beautiful as well as healthy, spacious as well as clean, well-balanced as well as carefully patrolled.

interpreted the police power.[123] The extent of the police power, however, seems to resist delineation, for it depends on shifting social, economic, and political winds.[124]

Using their reserved police power, state legislatures could give the power to regulate land development and mitigate its adverse impacts on water quality to state agencies. State legislation in most states, including New York, however, does not give state agencies authority to regulate land development that contribute to groundwater contamination and nonpoint source pollution. The New York model, perhaps more aggressive in creating and empowering water-related state agencies than most states, demonstrates the statutory limits of state agencies to control the sources of water pollution and watershed degradation.[125]

The New York Department of Health (DoH), for example, has the statutory authority to regulate the operation and design of private and some public groundwater wells.[126] This is done in partnership with EPA.[127] Such wells must meet DoH established water quality standards, but failure to meet them simply defeats the well permit application; it does not give the DoH the authority to prevent water pollution through land use regulation or other means.

The DoH does prevent water pollution by establishing requirements for small, residential onsite wastewater treatment systems (OWTS), also through

123. *See, e.g.*, Wulfsohn v. Burden, 150 N.E. 120, 122 (N.Y. 1925):

> The [police] powers [are] not limited to regulations designed to promote public health, public morals, or public safety, or to the suppression of what is offensive, disorderly, or unsanitary, but extend to so dealing with conditions which exist as to bring out of them the greatest welfare of the people by promoting public convenience or general prosperity.

Spann v. City of Dallas, 235 S.W. 513, 515 (Tex. 1921) ("[t]he police power is a grant of authority from the people to their governmental agents for the protection of the health, the safety, the comfort and the welfare of the public. In its nature it is broad and comprehensive"); *see also* Ohm, *supra* note 118, at 632-35.

124. Freund, *supra* note 121, at 3 (It is "only by a detailed examination of statutes and decisions that the [police] power can fully understood and defined." Such an examination will "reveal the police power not as a fixed quantity, but as the expression of social, economic and political conditions As long as these conditions vary, the police power must continue to be elastic.").

125. *See* ECL, art. 15, tit. 15, which authorizes DEC to govern allocation of limited water sources among users. The State's Water Resources Law, Title 11 of Article 15, ECL, authorizes the DEC to undertake comprehensive planning for the protection, conservation, and beneficial utilization of the water resources of the state. Although seldom employed, Title 11 allows local governments to receive comprehensive planning assistance. Title 27 of Article 15 of the ECL in New York provides for the management and protection of certain wild, scenic, and recreational rivers which can affect the scope of local land use regulations. A little-used provision of state law, Article 11, §1100 of the Public Health Law allows the DoH to issue watershed rules and regulations, which can unite upstream and downstream municipalities in collaborative efforts to limit contamination of downstream public water supplies.

126. N.Y. Pub. Health Law, art. 11.

127. Under the Safe Drinking Water Act, EPA must establish maximum levels for contamination to protect public health. 42 U.S.C. §330g-1. States may obtain primary responsibility enforcing these federal standards by adopting standards that are no less stringent than those of EPA. *See id.* §300g-2.

a permitting system.[128] OWTS facilities must be designed to meet DoH water quality standards. Its authority to manage this permitting function, however, does not give the state agency authority to limit, shape, or prevent land development on private property. It does not reach the issue of nonpoint source pollution.

State statutes in New York give the Department of Environmental Conservation (DEC) primary authority for comprehensive management of the state's water resources.129 DEC also collaborates with EPA to identify and list water bodies that qualify as "impaired waters" under §303(d) of the CWA. The Act encourages states to classify such waters and develop TMDLs of a large number of contaminants for them.130 The DEC has developed an elaborate system for classifying waterbodies in the state by best uses, but the lack enforcement and penalties for failing to meet TMDL standards renders this federal-state initiative relatively impotent concerning land use regulation and non-point source pollution prevention.

IV. The Police Power in Practice: Local Solutions

A. *Local Government Initiatives*

Many local governments understand that they need to use their delegated land use authority to respond to the threats to their water bodies and watersheds. This part describes a number of traditional land use techniques and several innovative measures municipalities use to protect and conserve water.[131] Included are land use plan components, zoning provisions, site plan regulations, water conserving landscape and building features, water supply permits, public nuisance laws, well testing, and stormwater remediation fees. These examples are models that can be adopted by other localities and illus-

128. 10 NYCRR Appendix 75-A. *See also* 6 NYCRR pt. 750 giving the DEC authority to create design standards for residential wastewater systems with flows of over 1,000 gpd and other private, commercial, and institutional systems.

129. The Water Resources Protection Act, Article 15, Title 29, ECL, in New York gives its DEC primary responsibility for comprehensive management of the state's water resources including establishing a permit system for private user water withdrawals from wells and surface waters.

130. *See supra* notes 105-11 and accompanying text.

131. Not included in this part is comprehensive treatment of the methods that local governments use to regulate settlement patterns to conserve and protect water indirectly by shaping settlement patterns: strategies referred to as smart growth, sustainable development, or, more recently, climate change mitigation and adaption, all of which tend to increase water conservation and protect its quality. For an example of the water conserving potential of sustainable development, *see* John R. Nolon, *Low Carbon Land Use: Paris, Pittsburgh, and the IPCC*, 40 Univ. of Ark. at Little Rock L. Rev. 661, 692 (2018). "As a sustainable development . . . Hudson Park . . . reduced average per household impervious coverage by 92%, lowered per capita water use by 60%, and avoided developing wetlands and watercourse environments." *See also infra* the town of New Paltz growth zone, notes 133-34.

trate the wide range of actions that they can adopt by analogy. They demonstrate how local governments can fill the gaps in state and federal regulations to create a more holistic system of water protection. These laws, and their many counterparts, are part of our national system of water law.

B. Comprehensive and Topical Land Use Plans

Comprehensive and topical land use plans establish goals for land use planning and define strategies to achieve those goals. They are not regulatory but guide the adoption of zoning and other land use regulations. Plans require citizen participation, which educates the public and secures strategic support for their goals and proposed implementation measures. The process of framing or amending plans provides an opportunity for land use leaders to identify and provide for the resolution of emerging problems such as threats to water quality and supply. Through this process, the community assesses problems and develops techniques to address such concerns in its own way, responsive to its unique circumstances.

The town of New Paltz, New York, for example, adopted a comprehensive plan that encourages water efficient land use patterns; it designates priority areas for growth and others for conservation as a strategy for encouraging water efficient land use patterns. It includes a Future Land Use Plan, the focus of which is an area for future development designated for higher density development while preserving the character, open space, farmlands, and natural resources throughout the rest of the town.[132] This allows the municipality to concentrate water infrastructure in the growth area and adopt lower density, low impact development in the conservation areas.

The growth zone's compact development allows for shorter transmission systems, lessening the cost of water and sewer infrastructure and future maintenance costs. It reduces energy needs for pumping and pressurization. Infill development leverages taxpayers' investment in existing water-delivery systems and other infrastructure. Higher density and mixed-use development increases walkability, reduces vehicle miles travelled, lowers CO_2 emissions, and lowers transportation costs. A smaller building footprint per household reduces polluting and flood-inducing impervious surfaces, minimizing the pollution of surface waters and groundwater recharge areas that receive the runoff. The town created a preservation and investment fund and a Clean Water and Open Space Commission to pay for the acquisition of open space

132. Town of New Paltz, New York, Comprehensive Plan 36-40 (February 2010) https://www.villageofnewpaltz.org/download/archives/master_plans/Town-of-New-Paltz-Comprehensive-Plan-Feb-2010.pdf.

and to set priorities for purchase of title or development rights. The designation of priority conservation areas guided the town's acquisition of open space program. [133]

The village of Bannockburn, Illinois, adopted a comprehensive plan that committed the village to being a "pioneer in environmentally friendly practices" and adopted a variety of best management practices.[134] The strategies are designed to minimize flooding, reduce pollution, protect natural resources, and wisely manage stormwater. To implement the plan, the village began a Rain Garden Public Participation Program that encourages residents to install and maintain rain gardens on their own private properties, and such rain gardens may be eligible for a village cash grant. Bannockburn's rain garden program aims to help with stormwater detention to offset the adverse effects of increased development and impervious surfaces. Standards for this voluntary program could be written into the zoning code as requirements for new or renovated buildings.

Leesburg, Virginia, adopted an Urban Tree Canopy Plan (UTCP) that establishes a goal of increasing its city-wide tree canopy from 20% to 40% of the community. A UTCP typically measures the total leaf cover of a city from a bird's-eye view, the species composition of the urban forest, and the distribution of tree cover throughout the municipality. A well-balanced tree canopy correlates positively with water quality, biodiversity, socioeconomic stability, and mental health.[135] It mitigates stormwater runoff, reduces energy consumption, provides habitat for wildlife, promotes species diversity, reduces air pollution, is aesthetically pleasing, increases mental health, and tends to increase property values.

Under its city management plan, Crystal Lake, Illinois, adopted a *Watershed Stormwater Management Design Manual* to guide and control construction projects.[136] Under the plan, the city created an ad hoc technical advisory committee to examine watershed regulations to increase water quality in its watershed. The regulations control the use of fertilizers, herbicides, and pesticides[137] and reduce the use of salt for snow removal. Reducing fertilizer use leads to less phosphorus in the watershed and consequently less algae

133. Town of New Paltz, N.Y., ch. 44, Agriculture and Open Space Preservation and Acquisition (2007), https://ecode360.com/9166301.

134. Comprehensive Plan for the Village of Bannockburn 3 (Dec. 8, 2014) https://bannockburn.org/wp-content/uploads/2014/05/Approved-Comprehensive-Master-Plan-2014.pdf.

135. Charles J. Fausold & Robert J. Lilieholm, *The Economic Value of Open Space: A Review and Synthesis*, 23 Envtl. Mgmt. 307 (1999) https://doi.org/10.1007/s002679900188.

136. Hey and Associates, Inc., *Crystal Lake Watershed Stormwater Management Design Manual* (Nov. 6, 2007) https://www.crystallake.org/home/showdocument?id=15263.

137. *Id.* at 3-2.

growth. Less salt is critical to the plan's objective of preventing greater acidity of Crystal Lake and promoting ecosystem health. Another objective of the plan is to increase the amount of permeable pavement and associated vegetation on developed property to increase water absorption and reduce runoff and flooding.[138]

C. Zoning

In Cheshire, Connecticut, zoning regulations protect the community's tree canopy by regulating the removal of mature trees, requiring that they be retained on construction sites to the greatest extent possible. Its zoning also encourages tree preservation in areas not disturbed by construction. The application of these provisions prevents sedimentation and erosion, maintains ecological balance, and provides protection from the sun and wind. On sites with limited vegetation, the zoning requires that developers provide vegetative cover, including trees.[139]

Henderson County, Kentucky, uses its zoning code to establish rules and regulations to prevent the adverse impacts of surface mining of coal, such as degradation of water, soils, and agricultural production.[140] The code requires mining operators to control sediment and off-site erosion, aimed at reducing runoff from disturbed areas.[141] The county requires that any surface drainage from disturbed areas must pass through sedimentation ponds before leaving the permit area.[142] These sedimentation ponds are required in all affected drainage areas prior to any mining in order to control sedimentation and protect water quality,[143] and they must be designed by a registered professional engineer.[144] Sediment removal must be done in a manner that minimizes adverse effects on surface waters.[145]

Portland, Oregon, adopted a floating zone called an EcoDistrict to promote water conservation and quality.[146] The city uses a Performance Area Toolkit that provides direction, methods, and processes for assessing performance. These techniques are contained in the floating zone and applied,

138. *Id.* at 3-4, 3-12.
139. Ceshire, Conn., Zoning Regs. ch. 44, art. a, §10 (1993).
140. Henderson Cnty, Ky. Zoning Code, §A-27.01
141. *Id.* §A-27.13(A)
142. *Id.* §A-27.13(A)(2)
143. *Id.* §A-27.13(A)(2)
144. *Id.* §A-27.13(A)(4)
145. *Id.* §A-27.13(A)(3)
146. *See The EcoDistricts Toolkit: Prioritizing Projects in an EcoDistrict*, Portland Sustainability Inst., https://ecodistricts.org/wp-content/uploads/2013/03/4_Toolkit_EcoDistrict_Assessment_v_1.12.pdf.

as appropriate, to areas of the city where water consumption needs to be reduced. They include targets for per capita water consumption, provide for water reclamation and reuse, require water efficient landscaping and on-site wastewater treatment, and control stormwater runoff.

The town of Big Flats, New York, adopted an overlay zoning district to protect its drinking water aquifers. The Aquifer Protection Overlay District (APOD) designates three groundwater areas for protection based on soil types, permeability, and development pressures. Each district is subject to project review processes and standards that apply in addition to the underlying zoning and site plan regulations. The APOD prohibits high-risk land uses and gives the planning board, as it reviews and approves projects, authority to request additional information from professional hydro-geologists or other experts to ensure protection from harmful commercial and industrial uses proposed within the APOD areas.[147]

Similarly, the town of Goshen, also in New York, identified five overlay districts in its comprehensive plan and zoning ordinance to protect specific types of natural resources. Three of the five overlay districts directly address water protection. The Flood Plain and Ponding Area Overlay District controls development within areas subject to periodic inundation and ponding. The Stream Corridor and Reservoir Watershed Overlay District protects the scenic character and water resource values of designated rivers and streams. The Aquifer Overlay District protects groundwater resources that provide both public water supplies and drinking water for private wells.[148]

D. *Site Plan Regulations*

Site plan regulations adopted by the town board in Greenburgh, New York, require its planning board to ensure that new and renovated buildings are water efficient. Under the town's Green Building Initiative and Energy Construction Standards, an applicant seeking site-plan review must submit a Green Building Project Checklist[149] completed by a Leadership in Energy and Environmental Design (LEED) Accredited Professional, and a Green Building Worksheet, and any other documents that may be necessary to

---

147. Town of Big Flats Comprehensive Plan 32 (May 2006) https://www.bigflatsny.gov/sites/g/files/vyhlif2816/f/file/file/big_flats_comprehensive_plan.pdf. Big Flats, N.Y., Code of Ordinances §17.24.020, https://library.municode.com/ny/big_flats/codes/code_of_ordinances?nodeId=TIT17ZO.

148. Town of Goshen Comprehensive Plan 33 (January 2019) http://www.townofgoshen.org/UpdatedCompPlan2009/Comprehensive%20Plan,%201-12-09.pdf; Goshen, N.Y., Zoning Ordinance §§97.25-27.

149. U.S. Green Building Council, *Checklist: LEED v2009 for New Construction* (Apr. 2009), https://www.usgbc.org/resources/new-construction-v2009-checklist-xls.

demonstrate compliance with the town's green building requirements. Site plan approval will not be granted until the designated Green Building Official of the town approves the design and construction plans of the applicant. A building permit and certificate of occupancy will not be issued unless plans and actual construction comply with the checklist and, uniquely, post-occupancy documentation is required to show continuing compliance with the standards.[150]

In Pennsylvania, Lancaster County's Conservation District provides best management practices that constituent localities can use to prevent sedimentation and erosion as they review and approve development proposals.[151] The Rouge River Wet Demonstration Project provides similar guidance. It contains structural elements including artificial wetland creation, detention ponds, swales, pervious pavement, vegetative cover, water quality inlets, and rain gardens.[152] These techniques slow down and reduce the volume of runoff that reaches downstream surface waters.

The Pennsylvania Department of Environmental Protection assists local governments in the state by promulgating and recommending practices to minimize stormwater runoff.[153] They include site planning strategies such as low impact development, conservation design, and cluster development.[154] They also include protecting sensitive environmental features, reducing impervious cover, and disconnecting storm leaders.[155]

E. *Water Conservation*[156]

Water conservation is directly tied to water quality.

> Water quality is fundamentally connected to water quantity by the fact that water of inferior quality effectively reduces the amount of available water for

150. Town of Greenburgh, N.Y., Building Regulations, §233-7 Compliance (2012), https://ecode360.com/13704934?highlight=green#13704934.
151. *Erosion & Sedimentation Best Management Practices*, Lancaster Cnty Conserv. Dist., http://lancasterconservation.org/erosion-sedimentation/earth-disturbance/es-bmps/ (last visited Aug. 4, 2020).
152. *Stormwater Management: Best Management Practices (BMPs)*, Rouge River Nat'l Wet Weather Demonstration Project, https://www.michigan.gov/documents/deq/ess-nps-savvy-bmp_209386_7.pdf (last visited Aug. 4, 2020).
153. *Pennsylvania Stormwater Best Management Practices Manual*, Dep't of Envtl. Prot., (Dec. 30, 2006) http://pecpa.org/wp-content/uploads/Stormwater-BMP-Manual.pdf.
154. *Id.* at 5-1.
155. *Id.* at 5-2.
156. *See* Jennie C. Nolon Blanchard, *Integrating Water Efficiency Into Land Use Planning in the Interior West: A Guidebook for Local Planners*, Land Use L. Ctr. (2018). https://westernresourceadvocates.org/publications/integrating-water-efficiency-into-land-use-planning/. This 300-page manual was published by the Land Use Law Center and Western Resource Advocates to help growing communities throughout the Interior West reduce the water footprint of new development.

> some users (or it can dramatically increase the cost of obtaining available water because of necessary treatment). Despite this important linkage, most investigations that evaluate water stress treat the problems of water quality and water quantity separately.[157]

The efficient use of water reduces waste water, which "may carry nutrients, biological and chemical contaminants, floating wastes, or other pollutants. Upon discharge, wastewater ultimately finds its way into groundwater or surface waters, contributing to their pollution."[158] One strategy for reducing wastewater is simply to use less water. This allows wastewater treatment plants and on-site treatment systems to "more efficiently treat incoming waste."[159] The more efficiently water is used the better water quality will be.

Asheville, North Carolina, incentivizes water conservation through bonus density zoning to increase water efficiency. The city offers more residential units under its zoning code for projects that feature green building amenities, including water efficiency measures for the building and site.[160] Asheville also offers a rebate of fees associated with the installation of stormwater and gray water collection devices.[161]

Dutchess County, New York, developed a Model Water Resource Management Zoning Ordinance for its constituent localities. The model allows as-of-right zoning status to water conserving projects, while requiring other developments to seek special or conditional use permits.[162] Site plan applications where projected water consumption exceeds natural recharge are allowed only by special permit, while projects where consumption is less than or equal to natural recharge are permitted as-of-right. This streamlines the approval process for developers of water conserving projects, reducing soft-costs of the approval process and getting the project to the market in a timely manner. The model contains conditions for the issuance of the special permit, including a requirement that applicants demonstrate how water quality impacts will be mitigated. Applicants must identify the source of the water being used, water quantity required, water-use minimization measures to be

157. David M. Borrok et al., *A Framework for Incorporating the Impact of Water Quality on Water Supply Stress: An Example From Louisiana*, 54 J. Am. Water Res. Ass'n. 134, 134-35 (2017).
158. Trent R. Schneider, Long Island Sound: Water Conservation and Marine Water Quality (2019), http://longislandsoundstudy.net/wp-content/uploads/2010/03/fact14.pdf.
159. *Id.*
160. City of Asheville, N.C., Code of Ordinances, §7-16-1 et seq., Uses by Right, Subject to Special Requirements (2010), https://www.municode.com/library/nc/ asheville/codes/code_of_ordinances?nodeId=PTIICOOR_CH7DE_ARTXVIUSRISUSPRECOUS_S7-16-1USRISUSPRE
161. City of Asheville, N.C., July 1, 2018-June 30, 2019 Development Services Department, Fee Schedule (2018-2019), http://www.ashevillenc.gov/civicax/filebank/blobdload.aspx?BlobID=30664.
162. Water and Wastewater Issues, Model Aquifer Protection Laws, Dutchess County, .Y., https://www.dutchessny.gov/Departments/Planning/planning.htm.

implemented, water recycling measures to be installed, and measures used to enhance on-site recharge.

The town of Wayland, New York, enacted a law establishing a water conservation and permitting program. The Town's primary source of water is an underground aquifer, which is naturally limited in quantity and was experiencing increasing pollution.[163] New development increased groundwater pumping, furthering its pollution.[164] The town found that if water quality and quantity problems were not addressed, and water conservation and permitting programs not instituted, irreparable damage could be done to the local aquifer. In response, the local legislative body enacted Local Law No. 3 to ensure that the quality and quantity of water available meets both present and future demands. The purpose of the law is to promote "the public health, comfort, convenience, safety, welfare and environment of the town of Wayland and its inhabitants, in order to protect the public potable water supply of the town from the possibility of contamination or overuse, to protect the aquifer in the town, and to supplement permit requirements."[165]

Local Law No. 3 requires a permit for the installation of any new water supply system. In order to obtain a permit, the applicant must include a map showing the water supply system, watershed maps showing the watershed or aquifer affected, profiles of the proposed facilities, proposed contracts, an engineer's report, analysis of the water supply, treatment methods, and project justification.[166]

Boulder, Colorado, adopted water conservation measures in its Green Building Program which requires proposed developments to qualify as green buildings.[167] Applicants can earn green points by incorporating into their developments the following improvements: hardscape shading by preserving existing mature trees on site or planting shade trees; xeriscaping methods that conserve water, such as reduced turf areas, wood chip mulching, xeric plants grouped by water needs, and water conserving irrigation systems; high-efficiency automatic irrigation systems; water efficient fixtures, such as low-flow showerheads and toilets; and surface water flow management through the use of permeable surfaces.

163. Town of Wayland Local Law No. 3 (1996) §4.

164. *Id.* (pumping had "resulted in the loss of water, low water, cloudy or muddy water, and bad tasting or smelling water").

165. *Id.* §3.

166. *Id.* §9(B).

167. City of Boulder, Colo., Municipal Code, §10-7.5-1 et seq., Green Building and Green Points Program (2013); Green Building and Green Points Guideline Booklet (2014), https://www-static.bouldercolorado.gov/docs/green-points-guideline-booklet-1-201306271201.pdf.

F. *Local Nuisance Laws*

Local laws that define and regulate nuisances to protect water quality provide an innovative legal option for municipalities to consider. Riparian landowners adversely affected by groundwater or surface water pollution caused by their neighbors may bring an action under common law private nuisance. Under state common law, this typically requires that the plaintiff carry the burden of proving that the neighbor's actions are unreasonable.[168] In many states, case law requires courts to balance multiple factors and provides few clear definitions of reasonable use, which increases the costs of such suits and renders the result uncertain. Local governments can provide some clarity for potential plaintiffs by designating water pollution as a public nuisance broadly targeting activities that harm and diminish water quality. Not incidentally, such laws strengthen and broaden the statutory authority of municipalities to protect local water quality through municipal enforcement.

Common-law causes of action can coexist with civil enforcement under federal, state, and local clean water regulations. In *Merrick v. Diageo Americans Supply, Inc.*, the Sixth Circuit found that the plaintiffs had stated a cause of action for common-law nuisance when a whiskey distillery emitted tons of ethanol emissions, leading to the growth of a particularly harmful fungus. Because ethanol is regulated under the Clean Air Act (CAA), the defendant alleged that the nuisance claim was preempted. The circuit court ruled that the CAA expressly reserves the right of the states to prescribe requirements more stringent than those set under the CAA. Further, those requirements include state common-law claims, such as nuisance.169

Yonkers, New York, adopted a statute prohibiting pollution relating to its separate storm sewer system as part of its obligation to conform to a required state permitting system as a regulated utility.[170] The city is required to regulate the contribution of pollutants to the sewer system, to prohibit illicit connections, activities, and discharges, and to establish legal authority to carry out all inspection, surveillance, and monitoring procedures necessary to ensure compliance.[171]

The Yonkers law states:

168. William B. Stoebuck & Dale A. Whitman, The Law of Property 414-17 (3d ed. 2000).

169. Merrick v. Diageo Am. Supply, Inc., 805 F.3d 685 (6th Cir. 2015); *see also* Little v. Louisville Gas & Electric Co., 805 F.3d 695 (6th Cir. 2015) (holding a coal burning plant operator could not avoid common-law tort claims on grounds that the emissions or airborne dust and coal ash on neighboring properties were solely governed by the plant's CAA permit).

170. *See infra* notes 213-17 and accompanying text.

171. Yonkers, N.Y., Code ch. 96, art. V, §39 (2007).

> In addition to the enforcement processes and penalties provided, any condition caused or permitted to exist in violation of any of the provisions of this article is a threat to public health, safety, and welfare and is declared and deemed a nuisance and may be summarily abated or restored at the violator's expense, and/or a civil action [brought by the city of Yonkers Stormwater Management Officer] to abate, enjoin, or otherwise compel the cessation of such nuisance may be taken.

A law adopted by Pennington, New Jersey, defines a nuisance as:

> Any matter, thing, condition or act which after investigation by the Health Officer or other enforcing official is deemed to be injurious, detrimental or a menace to the public health or environment or is deemed to be an annoyance or interfere with the comfort or well-being of the inhabitants of the Borough is hereby declared to be a nuisance and shall include but not be limited to the following: Pollution or the existence of a condition or discharge or release which causes or threatens pollution of any surface water or subsurface water of the Borough.[172]

Adoption of local nuisance laws that include language defining and prohibiting landowner activities that threaten water quality not only supplements municipal legal authority to protect water quality but provides a statutory backbone to an otherwise circumstantial private nuisance action.

G. *Mandatory Well Testing*

The town of East Fishkill, New York, adopted a law that requires property owners with individual groundwater wells to have the quality of the well water tested prior to the sale of their property.[173] The purpose of the law is to "requir[e] mandatory private well testing for all properties in the town of East Fishkill that rely on a private water supply which is utilized for purposes of human consumption."[174] It also applies to multifamily and nonresidential properties and residential rental properties that are subject to testing under the New York State Sanitary Code.[175]

The required water tests must be filed with the town of East Fishkill Building Department and County Health Department and made available for public inspection and reproduction. All provisions of the mandate are enforced by "[t]he Town of East Fishkill Building Inspector, Code Enforcement Officers, Zoning Administrator, Deputy Zoning Administrator, and

172. Pennington, N.J., Code ch. 136, art.1 §3 (2001).
173. *See* Town of East Fishkill, ch. 189: Wells, art. I, Testing of Private Wells (2007).
174. *Id.* §189-3(B).
175. *Id.* §189-7.

the Fire Inspector. . . ."[176] This legal strategy is particularly effective because the law prohibits the town building department from providing a Certificate of Occupancy to a prospective purchaser who requires it to secure title insurance and a mortgage.[177]

H. Stormwater Remediation Fee

Water quality can be protected by limiting on-site stormwater runoff. This is accomplished through extensive regulation of the construction process by imposing stewardship practices as a condition for receiving municipal approval for the proposed development.[178] This applies only to new developments, not to the existing properties that contribute to stormwater runoff that is the responsibility of the local government to manage. The city of Ithaca, New York, found a way to incentivize the owners of already developed property to reduce stormwater runoff, as well as to pay for the public facilities needed to manage and treat stormwater. Municipalities have the authority to impose fees to pay for the capital costs and administrative expenses related to specific users of municipal services.[179]

Individual developed properties contribute to such stormwater management costs in direct proportion to the amount of impervious coverage they contain. The city used a geographic database of all impervious surface area and determined that the average amount of impervious surface area on a property with a one-, two-, or three-family home is approximately 2,300 square feet. City officials used this metric to calculate an equivalent residential unit (ERU) and to determine the user fee for larger commercial and multifamily properties. Small-scale residential properties pay a flat fee because, according to the database, they have roughly similar amounts of impervious surface area throughout the city. Larger residential properties and commercial and manufacturing properties pay a fee that is based on their ERU.

The city's stormwater remediation fee law includes incentives to encourage less runoff by lowering the fee for owners who reduce the amount of impervious coverage of their properties, such as installing pervious pavers or a green roof. There is also a credit for engaging in certain engineered stormwater practices or structures.

---

176. *Id.* §189-8(A).
177. *Id.* §189-8(B).
178. *See infra* note 180 and accompanying text.
179. N.Y. Municipal Home Rule Law §10(1)(ii)(a)(9-a).

V. Correcting Parochialism Through Collaboration

This chapter argues that local governments must play a central and proactive role in protecting water quality. Municipalities are the locus of the problem and are required by practical circumstance to respond to threats to their water supplies.[180] They are the most decentralized level of government with the legal authority to act effectively and, under the principal of subsidiarity,[181] deserve deference and respect by the other governmental and nongovernmental actors who are invested in watershed health.[182] The examples discussed above demonstrate that local governments can be effective actors in addressing critical resource problems.

Still, local governments are rightly criticized for the multiple barriers they face that obstruct effective action, particularly regarding interjurisdictional problems.[183] The danger in taking this criticism too seriously is that it tends to identify local control as the problem to be cured rather than a foundation on which to build an intergovernmental process that is responsive to state and federal needs. This has been described as an "institutional conundrum whereby the entity with the greatest potential to solve the problem currently lacks the capacity to do so such that efforts to respond to the problem tend to exacerbate it rather than resolve it."[184]

This part provides a partial response to those who are critical of depending on local action to protect natural resources. Building on the remarkable examples of effective action discussed in Part IV, the case studies below illustrate several methods of collaboration that respond to the criticisms of localism and help, first, to explain the principle of "collaborative subsidiarity" developed in the chapter's conclusion, and, secondly, to justify it as a predicate for regional, state, and federal policy and lawmaking.

A. *State-Provided Technical Assistance*

New York's Community Risk and Resiliency Act of 2014 provides local governments critically needed data, maps, and laws to adapt to the consequences of climate change.[185] It expands the technical capacity of municipalities to

180. John R. Nolon, *In Praise of Parochialism: The Advent of Local Environmental Law*, 26 Harv. Envtl. L. Rev. 267 (2002)
181. *See supra* note 16.
182. Nolon, *supra* note 132 (This principle applies to a host of contemporary problems including the mitigation and adaptation to climate change.).
183. *See infra* notes 248-56 and accompanying text.
184. Sarah K. Adams-Schoen, *Beyond Localism: Harnessing State Adaptation Lawmaking to Facilitate Local Climate Resilience*, 8 Mich. J. Envtl. & Admin. L. 185, 220 (2018).
185. Community Risk and Resiliency Act, 2014 N.Y. Laws 1115-19.

respond by requiring the New York Department of State to provide sea-level rise data and maps as well as model laws that they can adapt to projected inundation and flooding associated with global warming. These data, maps, and model laws are not products that most localities have the resources to develop and are properly done at state level where agencies can produce information and model regulations relevant to constituent communities that share vulnerabilities to climate change and the inundation of their coastal neighborhoods. The maps are based on data that reflect various scenarios of sea-level rise and allow localities to choose the scenario that they deem prudent to use for planning. The model laws are drafted so that municipal leaders can adapt them to their local circumstances. These resources and their adaptability to local circumstance are built on the understanding that local circumstances vary, that local officials best understand those circumstances, and that those officials need resources to guide decision making.

B. *State-Mandated Impact Review*

The New York State DEC amended its rules for conducting environmental review under the State Environment Quality Review Act (SEQRA).[186] Under this Act, local governments must conduct environmental impact reviews regarding any decisions they make that might have an adverse environmental impact.[187] The new rules require local agencies to consider the impact of their decisions on climate change and the impact of climate change on projects subject to their review and approval under their land use authority.[188]

The amended regulations require local land use agencies to conduct climate change impact reviews when adopting or amending zoning laws, adopting or amending comprehensive plans, and reviewing local land use applications by developers. This regulatory amendment "may turn out to be one of the most effective features of the state's adaptation regime."[189] It demonstrates that local resistance to taking effective environmental action may be overcome by state requirements that integrate needed strategies into roles currently played by municipal governments. The strategy is effective because it respects the prerogative of local governments to make judgments within the context of a state-required impact review regime. The ability of localities

186. N.Y. Envtl. Conservation Law art. 8; N.Y. STATE DEPT. OF ENVTL. CONSERVATION, STATE ENVIRONMENTAL QUALITY REVIEW ACT: FINDINGS STATEMENT FOR AMENDMENTS TO 6 NYCRR PART 617, at 24 (2018), https://www.dec.ny.gov/docs/permits_ej_operations_pdf/617fnlfindings.pdf.

187. *The SEQR Handbook*, N.Y. State Dept. of Envtl. Conservation 181-94 (4th ed. 2019).

188. 6 NYCRR pt. 617, at 148.

189. Adams-Schoen, *supra* note 185, at 238

to conduct this review is greatly assisted by a policy document published by DEC that contains detailed standards for determining the effect of projects on climate change and adjusting development design to adapt to climate change.[190]

C. *Bottom-Up Intergovernmental Cooperation*

Municipalities can take the initiative to reach out to higher levels of government for needed technical support. The Master Plan of Cannon Township, Michigan, for example, contains a goal of establishing "a working partnership with the Kent County Health Department, Michigan Department of Environmental Quality, and other applicable local, state, and federal environmental agencies to ensure that the quality and quantity of water available to the Township residents is acceptable."[191] The Master Plan recognizes Bear Creek as one of the township's most sensitive environmental features, and one of the most important natural resources that embodies the natural character of the community.[192] The municipality amended its zoning to add a Bear Creek Watershed Protection Overlay District to "preserve and enhance the integrity of certain creeks and their tributaries located within the Bear Creek Watershed,"[193] which includes Bear Creek, Stout Creek, and Armstrong Creek, as well as any flowing tributaries.[194]

The township's zoning ordinance recognizes its creeks and streams as valuable natural resources that contribute to its rural character, provide scenic views, serve as a habitat for fish and wildlife, minimize land erosion, protect water quality, avoid runoff of nutrients into creeks and streams, and maintain water temperature of creeks and streams at natural levels.

The city of Boulder and Boulder County worked together to create an intergovernmental agreement and adopt the Boulder Valley Comprehensive Plan to concentrate urban development in the city as part of a strategy to preserve lands and natural resources beyond the city's limits.[195] The plan's natural environment chapter memorializes the city and county's agreement

190. *See Assessing Energy Use and Greenhouse Gas Emissions in an Environmental Impact Statement*, N.Y. State Dept. of Envtl. Conservation (July 15, 2009). https://www.dec.ny.gov/docs/administration_pdf/eisghgpolicy.pdf.
191. Cannon Twp. Master Plan 4 (2015 Update), https://cannontwp.civicweb.net/document/4739.
192. *Id.* at 6.
193. Cannon Twp. Zoning Ord. §18.01 https://cannontwp.civicweb.net/filepro/documents/3722?preview=4606.
194. *Id.* §18.02
195. City of Boulder, Colo. Boulder Valley Comprehensive Plan (2015), https://www-static.bouldercolorado.gov/docs/BVCP_2015_Update-5-1-19-1-201905011635.pdf?_ga=2.118497034.2072862681.1596563007-449189878.1596563007.

to promote water resource conservation through a combination of regulation, public education, monitoring, and appropriate water usage.

The plan establishes growth boundaries to phase growth and creates compact and sustainable settlement patterns by capitalizing on vacant or underused sites and by carefully considering the expansion of the urban center, reducing the encroachment of city growth upon lands less suitable for development because of their environmental conditions and the high cost of extending infrastructure, and providing public services. Implementation involves the acquisition of open space lands and the purchase of water rights using both county and city resources.[196]

D. State-Created Intermunicipal Initiatives

State legislatures can proactively encourage intermunicipal collaboration by adopting legislation permitting cost-effective joint action. The Greater New Haven Water Pollution Control Authority (GNHWPCA or the Authority) is an intermunicipal mechanism created under a State statute that permits and encourages the creation of regional water pollution control authorities.[197] Four municipalities took advantage of this special state law to create the GNHWPCA: New Haven, Hamden, East Haven, and Woodbridge. The Authority's mission is: "To provide reliable municipal wastewater services in compliance with applicable laws, in a cost efficient and effective method, and with the intent and desire to protect the environment and public health of the constituent municipalities." The Authority was created for the operation of a wastewater sewage treatment plant to collect, transport, treat, and dispose of sewage generated within the cooperating municipalities.[198]

The state of California acted to assist small water supply systems that lack the capacity to operate efficiently.[199] A small water system is one that provides water to fewer than 10,000 customers; such systems make up more

196. Joseph N. de Raismes III, et al., Growth Management in Boulder Colorado: A Case Study 25 (1999), https://livableboulder.org/wp-content/uploads/2015/04/Growth-Management-In-Boulder-Colorado-a-Case-Study-.pdf.

197. GNHWPCA, *About GNHWPCA*, https://gnhwpca.com/about-gnhwpca/about-gnhwpca/ (last visited Aug. 4, 2020)

198. *Id.* C.G.S.A §22a-500(7). The sewer system operated by the GNHWPCA includes 555 miles of pipeline, 30 pumping stations, and a secondary water treatment plant that holds up to 40 million gallons per day. A wastewater system is defined as any device, equipment, appurtenance, plant facility and method receiving, collecting, transporting, reducing, treating, reclaiming, disposing, separating or discharging sewage, or the residue from the treatment of sewage

199. Nathaniel Logar et. al., *Ensuring Safe Drinking Water in Los Angeles County's Small Water Systems* Pritzker Brief No. 11, Pritzer Environmental Law and Policy Briefs, 1, 17 (Dec. 2018).

than 97% of the nation's public water systems (PWS).[200] Because of their lack of resources and technical capacity, they are prone to regulatory lapses and a relatively high rate of groundwater contamination. The state legislature facilitated the ability of the state Water Resources Control Board to integrate struggling PWS through state-aided consolidation.[201] The state assistance includes badly needed capital financing.[202]

E. *Intergovernmental Watershed Planning*

State laws that permit local governments to jointly exercise their land use planning and regulatory authority can be used to create vertically and horizontally integrated mechanisms to protect water supplies. Nearly two dozen New York municipalities in a shared watershed crafted an intermunicipal agreement that includes the county water authority and department of planning, nongovernmental stakeholders, and the New York DEC.[203] Together they formed a council and adopted the Moodna Creek Watershed Conservation and Management Plan.[204] The plan supports source water protection, regional watershed planning, and research and monitoring of water resources. The purpose of the Moodna Creek Watershed Intermunicipal Council is: "To continue to work together across municipal boundaries in order to protect, conserve, and enhance the water resources of the Moodna Creek and its watershed."

This intermunicipal initiative demonstrates how mechanisms can be created that address the criticisms of local governments such as lacking geo-

---

200. *Learn about Small Drinking Water Systems,* U.S. EPA, https://www.epa.gov/dwcapacity/learn-about-small-drinking-water-systems (last visited Aug. 4, 2020).

201. Consolidation is the "joining of two or more public water systems, state small water systems, or affected residences not served by a public water system, into a single public water system." Logar, *Ensuring Safe Drinking Water in Los Angeles County's Small Water Systems,* Dec. 2018, at 18. The benefits of consolidation include "(1) improved economies of scale; (2) increased financial opportunities for water systems; (3) reduced duplication of services; (4) increased reliability; (5) increased system flexibility; and (6) enhanced protection of public health, skill improvement, and service efficiency." *Id.*

202. California's Proposition 1 created a $7.1 billion bond for water improvements, making $520 million available for projects providing clean, safe and reliable drinking water. Cal. Legis. Council, Assemb. B. 1471, Filed with Secretary of the State, August 13, 2014. The Proposition was created after Los Angeles received no funding from an already limited funding pool for small water systems provided by the federal government. The Proposition's bond will be used for two Los Angeles County drinking-water projects, both in water systems serving fewer than 10,000 customers, for wellhead treatment to provide residents with cleaner water. Working within the bounds of Proposition 1, the state government also made organizational changes to help smaller systems with funding and technical support, creating an Office of Sustainable Water Solutions; Logar et al., *supra* note 200.

203. N.Y. Gen. Municipal Law, §190-o(1); N.Y. Gen. City Law, §20-g(1); N.Y. Town Law, §284(1); N.Y. Village Law, §7-741(1).

204. *Moodna Creek Watershed,* Orange County Water Authority (2011), http://waterauthority.orangecountygov.com/moodna.html.

graphical reach and the technical capacity to respond to watershed issues. The compact includes nongovernmental Council Members including fish and gaming clubs, environmentalists, conservationists, and other affected stakeholders. The effect of the intermunicipal agreement is to organize and direct the staff professionals and volunteer technicians, as well as to provide needed data and policy direction to the individual legislative and land use bodies of the constituent localities.

The Council addresses issues that include:

> (A) Securing and sharing the public and private grants available to address issues pertaining to watershed protection and management; (B) Utilizing each undersigned Parties' ability to address issues pertaining to the Creek and its Watershed; (C) Creating an avenue for intermunicipal dialogue for addressing water quality and water quantity issues; (D) Considering implementation of the Moodna Creek Watershed Conservation and Management Plan; (E) Developing educational programs on watershed planning, flooding, pollution prevention, stormwater management, biological resources and other best management practices for individuals and municipalities; (F) Coordinating other organizational efforts in each municipality that impact or benefit the resources of the Moodna Watershed; and (G) Benefitting watershed Municipalities, individually and collectively, by integrating protection of watershed resources with economic and social policies.[205]

Federal and state agencies can themselves encourage local governments to exercise their intermunicipal powers to protect water resources. Years of unchecked pollution and its adverse impact on Manhasset Bay on Long Island led to the signing of an intermunicipal agreement to preserve this shared environmental and economic resource. Signatories included 11 villages, 1 town, and Nassau County. It was the result of several years of work under programs of the U.S. Fish and Wildlife Service and the New York Department of State. The agreement recognized the interdependence of environmental conservation and economic activity across municipal lines and the need to collaborate intermunicipally to protect the Manhasset Bay.[206] Its goals are:

205. *Moodna Creek Watershed Intermunicipal Council: Operating Procedures* §II (Apr. 29, 2013), http://waterauthority.orangecountygov.com/PROJECTS/MOODNA_CREEK_WATERSHED/Operating%20Procedures%20MCWIC.pdf.

206. *See* The Manhasset Bay Protection Committee Agreement, 1995. The parties entered into this Intermunicipal Agreement upon:

> recogniz[ing] the importance of Manhasset Bay as a vital coastal ecosystem essential to the environmental and economic well-being of the people in the surrounding communities and as a . . significant coastal fish and wildlife habitat as noted by the U.S. Fish & Wildlife Service (1991) and the New York Department of State (1987); and the [Town of North Hempstead] and the Municipalities are deeply concerned with the existing degradation of

> [To] improve the water quality Manhasset Bay so that all waters of the Bay will consistently meet water quality standards for bathing, swimming, and fishing; improve the water quality of Manhasset Bay so it will once again be classified as an area suitable for the harvesting of shellfish for human consumption; restore and enhance the surrounding tidal wetlands that serve to cleanse ecosystems; provide marine food production and wildlife habitat; offer opportunities for education, research and recreation; provide flood and storm control . . . open space and aesthetic appreciation; control and reduce point and nonpoint source pollution affecting the Bay and its environs; and coordinate local coastal regulations so as to maximize protection and enhancement efforts to improve the quality of Manhasset Bay, its tributaries and wetlands.[207]

The agreement establishes the Manhasset Bay Protection Committee to coordinate efforts to protect and enhance the quality of the Bay and its watershed. The Committee's function is to coordinate the involvement not only of the constituent municipalities, but to work with the relevant county, state, and federal agencies. Representatives of each municipality serve on the Committee. It is empowered to act for these municipalities to secure New York State Department of State grant funds, hire environmental consultants, and jointly fund and implement the Manhasset Bay Local Waterfront Revitalization Program.[208]

F. *Larger Regional Networks*

At the larger regional level, intergovernmental agreements can provide significant help to watershed stakeholders. The Chesapeake Bay Program, for example, is an interstate watershed partnership created to address watershed pollution issues in the multi-state Chesapeake Bay.[209] The program has a rich history of federal, state, and local effort and coordination, culminating with the Chesapeake Bay Watershed Agreement signed on June 16, 2014.

The partnership consists of the states of Delaware, Maryland, New York, Pennsylvania, Virginia, and West Virginia; the District of Columbia; the Chesapeake Bay Commission, a tristate legislative body; and EPA, representing the federal government.[210] Local governments have played a key role in

---

Manhasset Bay and the potential for further degradation due to the variety of pollutant sources, including but not limited to stormwater runoff, petroleum spills, industrial effluent, illegal dumping, floatable debris and boat waste.

207. *Id.* para. 1

208. *Id.* para. 6, §2.

209. *Bay Program History*, Chesapeake Bay Program (2019), https://www.chesapeakebay.net/who/bay_program_history

210. *About the Chesapeake Bay Program Office*, U.S. EPA (Jan. 23, 2018), https://www.epa.gov/aboutepa/about-chesapeake-bay-program-office.

the success of the program because of the program's commitment to involve, coordinate, and connect them with federal- and state-level actors through Local Government Engagement Initiative.

The Chesapeake Bay Program illustrates how federal and state actors can equip local governments with the tools and capacity they need to address water pollution concerns in large regional watersheds. The Chesapeake Bay Watershed Agreement includes a commitment to proper stewardship of the bay and its tributaries focusing on education regarding the nature of the threats to water quality and strategies for addressing those threats. It sees the involved local governments acting as stewards, assisting with necessary conservation and restoration efforts to achieve a healthy bay. The stewardship goal is achieved through training and leadership programs for local officials to transfer knowledge from one another and from the involved civic organizations and state and federal agencies.

G. *Top-Down Required Collaboration*

Federal legislation and agency regulations can operate from the top down to harness the resources of states while recognizing and guiding local governments to use their land use power to protect surface water quality. Under the authority of the CWA, EPA adopted the Stormwater Management Program.[211] Its goal is to improve water quality in surface waters that receive stormwater runoff from discrete point sources.[212] Localities that operate Municipal Separate Stormwater Sewer Systems (MS4s) must get a national pollution elimination discharge system (NPDES) permit to discharge the effluent from their MS4s (a point source of pollution) into surface waters. States are encouraged to manage the required permitting system by adopting a state pollution discharge elimination system permit to operate in lieu of its federal counterpart.

EPA's promulgation of the Stormwater Phase II Final Rule in 1999 expanded significantly the number of municipalities required to comply with stormwater control measures.[213] To meet their MS4 general permit requirements under the CWA, MS4s must implement six minimum controls to reduce pollution caused by diffuse surface runoff. The controls include the following: (1) public education and outreach; (2) public participation and

211. *Stormwater Discharges From Municipal Sources*, U.S. EPA, https://www.epa.gov/npdes/stormwater-discharges-municipal-sources (last visited on Aug. 4, 2020).
212. *Evaluating the Effectiveness of Municipal Stormwater Programs*, U.S. EPA (2008), https://www3.epa.gov/npdes/pubs/region3_factsheet_swmp.pdf.
213. Stormwater Phase II, 64 Fed. Reg. 68722 (Dec. 8, 1999).

involvement; (3) illicit discharge detection and elimination; (4) construction site runoff control; (5) post-construction runoff control; and (6) pollution prevention and good housekeeping.[214]

The requirements to control construction site runoff and post-construction runoff require local governments that operate MS4s to exercise their land use authority through zoning and site plan regulation to comply with the controls required by the permitting system. EPA and state environmental agencies provide guidelines and materials to help municipalities comply. A key focus of this program is to improve water quality by minimizing erosion and sediment pollution during and after soil disturbance activities, i.e., construction.[215] Localities can adopt practices to restrict the volume of water flow and slow the speed of water runoff to reduce soil erosion and other surface water pollution.[216]

H. *Lessons Learned in Using Local Land Use Power*

There are several lessons taught by these examples.

1. Local governments often know their own limitations. Canon Township reached out to its county for assistance in watershed management, and the city of Boulder preserved threatened natural resources in cooperation with Boulder County.
2. Localities are willing to collaborate with a variety of partners, including county and state agencies, their municipal neighbors, and nongovernmental stakeholders.
3. States use a number of methods of filling jurisdictional, political, and technical gaps at the local level by encouraging intermunicipal cooperation, providing data, maps, and model laws, adopting new enabling statutes, and requiring local action to achieve state objectives like climate change mitigation. The Manhasset Bay example shows how state and federal agencies can operate in partnership to encourage localities to use their authority to protect a shared water resource.
4. Municipalities can integrate their actions vertically and horizontally; in the Moodna Creek watershed, two dozen local governments reached

214. *Stormwater Phase II Final Rule, An Overview: Why Is the Phase II Stormwater Program Necessary?* U.S. EPA (Dec. 2005), https://www.epa.gov/sites/production/files/2015-11/documents/fact1-0.pdf.
215. *Erosion & Sedimentation Best Management Practices, supra* note 152.
216. *See Stormwater Management: Best Management Practices (BMPs), supra* note 153.

across municipal and sectoral lines and up to higher levels of government for support and technical assistance.

5. Using many of the mechanisms employed at smaller scales, interstate networks of governmental and other sectoral agencies can be created that operate effectively at much larger regional levels, such as the Chesapeake Bay Program.
6. The federal government can create nested hierarchies where federal standards are incorporated into state regulations that govern permits needed by local governments that then use their land use power to manage stormwater.

It is notable that in most of these examples, the collaborations succeed because they are bottomed on local action, buoyed by respect for local governments, and strengthened by the knowledge and commitment of municipal leaders who are closest to and most immediately affected by threats to water quality and other natural resources.

VI. Conclusion—Toward a Principle of Collaborative Subsidiarity

A. De Facto *Localism and Its Theoretical Supporters*

Despite its critics, land use control remains firmly in the hands of local governments.[217] Through land planning, zoning, and other land use regulations, they determine the use of the land within their jurisdictions. "[U]nder localism, the crucial power center is at the tip of the shovel, where the actual work is being done. Expertise is not in the think tanks but among those who have local knowledge, those with a feel for how things work in a specific place and an awareness of who gets stuff done."[218] "[L]ocalized governments will have a better grasp of local conditions and issues."[219] "With broad authority for local decision-making delegated to the local level, such municipal governments

217. *See e.g.*, Craig Anthony Arnold, *The Structure of the Land Use System in the United States*, 22 J. of Land Use & Envtl L. 441, 486 (2007) ("The land use regulatory system is located primarily at the local level of governance and decision making in the United States, despite the rise of federal and state statutes and regulations that govern certain aspects of land use."); Ashira Pelman Ostrow, *Land Law Federalism*, 61 Emory L.J. 1397, 1397 (2012) ("the dominant descriptive and normative account of land-use law is premised upon local control").

218. *See* David Brooks, *The Localist Revolution*, N.Y. Times, July 20, 2018, https://www.nytimes.com/2018/07/19/opinion/national-politics-localism-populism.html.

219. David Owen, *Cooperative Subfederalism*, 9 UC Irvine L. Rev. 177, 213 (2018) (quoting a land use attorney in Oregon saying that the city council, planning commission, and city staff are the ones who community members see at the Rotary Club meetings, in church, and at the store).

often 'play a vital governance role,' with responsibility for 'drinking water . . . .'"[220] In addition, "[l]ocal land use and zoning laws offer one of the most effective opportunities to create more resilient patterns of development."[221]

Chapter Twelve of the Intergovernmental Panel on Climate Change's (IPCC's) Fifth Assessment Report addresses the relationship between the shape of human settlements and climate change mitigation.[222] To mitigate climate change, the IPCC focuses heavily on urban form, infrastructure, and land use mix. The chapter discusses many of the land use strategies that local governments are using to mitigate climate change. It notes that mixed-use neighborhoods shape development so as to reduce the amount of CO_2 through the efficient use of energy and the reduction of vehicle trips and auto emissions. Additional strategies mentioned include density regulations, urban containment instruments, building codes, parking regulations, design regulations, and affordable housing mandates. The chapter discusses land acquisition and management through the transfer of development rights and increasing green space and urban carbon sinks. The IPCC recognized the grass-roots theories upon which its Chapter Twelve is based.[223]

The Paris Agreement on combating climate change also endorsed the role of local governments in mitigating climate change and invited their participation in the international agreement by memorializing bottom-up strategies as Nationally Determined Contributions to climate change mitigation.[224] This approach broadened international climate policy by including state and local government actors and inviting them to demonstrate how they can contribute.[225]

Scholars in several disciplines endorse land use localism, that is, grass-roots strategies for responding to societal problems related to the use of the

220. Adams-Schoen, *supra* note 185, at 192 (describing "The Essential Local Role in Creating Climate Resilient Communities").

221. *Id.*

222. Climate Change 2014: Mitigation of Climate Change, IPCC Fifth Assessment Report xiii (2014), https://www.ipcc.ch/site/assets/uploads/2018/02/ipcc_wg3_ar5_full.pdf.

223. *Id.*

> We dedicate this report to the memory of Elinor Ostrom, Professor of Political Science at Indiana University and Nobel Laureate in Economics. Her work provided a fundamental contribution to the understanding of collective action, trust, and cooperation in the management of common pool resources, including the atmosphere. She launched a research agenda that has encouraged scientists to explore how a variety of overlapping policies at city, national, regional, and international levels can enable humankind to manage the climate problem. The assessment of climate change mitigation across different levels of governance, sectors and regions has been a new focus of the Working Group III contribution to AR5. We have benefited greatly from the vision and intellectual leadership of Elinor Ostrom.

224. Conference of the Parties' Twenty-First Session, U.N. Framework Convention on Climate Change, *Paris Agreement*, U.N. Doc. FCCC/CP/2015/L.9/Rev.1 (Dec. 12, 2015).

225. Nolon, *supra* note 132.

land.[226] Yale law professor Robert C. Ellickson, for example, warns against the "Yale disease," which he calls the propensity of his law school students to look entirely to federal laws and federal courts for solutions, causing them to ignore or not understand state and local solutions.[227] He refers to the principle of subsidiarity, which "holds that responsibility for dealing with a problem should be delegated to the most decentralized institution capable of handling that problem."[228] Dr. Elinor Ostrom advanced a polycentric approach to governance, and warned against the "panacea trap,"[229] which is akin to the Yale disease. A panacea trap occurs where responsible actors believe there is a cure-all solution applicable to every environmental issue, regardless of the local circumstances.[230] She too would assign key decision-making responsibility to those who are as close as possible to the scene of relevant events.

All change related to land use manifests itself at the local level, and it is there that land use plans and regulations need to be changed to reorder human settlements. Sociologists study how change happens. One term for what they observe is the "diffusion of innovation," a term which was popularized by Dr. Everett Rogers.[231] Diffusion, he notes, includes the planned and spontaneous spread of new ideas, such as methods of containing sprawl, or implementing measures to mitigate climate change, or to protect water quality. Scholars who study diffusion theory observe how change happens in social systems and document the processes by which successful change occurs.[232] Their focus is on connectivity.[233] They observe that outside change agents, perhaps state or federal officials, are most successful when they place new tools in the hands of respected local leaders. With respect to land use

226. This chapter focuses on scholarship regarding "land use localism," limiting itself to the role of local government as it exercises its delegated authority to control private land development and protect the physical environment under its police power. In the field of localism generally, context matters. How broadly municipal powers are interpreted and what powers are likely to be preempted by state legislation, for example, depends on the context. With respect to land use, municipal governments depend on their land use authority to create land uses that they are authorized to tax to raise revenue to discharge their obligations to provide public services and infrastructure. In this context, there is more deference to local legislative and administrative acts than in others such as regulating paper bags, Styrofoam containers, communications systems, firearms, soda beverages, or tobacco, for example. Schragger, *supra* note 115.

227. Ellickson, *supra* note 16, at 275.

228. *Id.* at 274; Brooks, *supra* note 219 ("Localism is the belief that power should be wielded as much as possible at the neighborhood, city and state levels.").

229. Elinor Ostrom et al., *Going Beyond Panaceas*, 104 PNAS 15176, 15176 (2007).

230. *Id.* at 15177

231. Everett M. Rogers, Diffusion of Innovation 6 (5th ed. 2003).

232. *See, e.g.*, David E. Booher & Judith E. Innes, *Network Power in Collaborative Planning*, J. of Plan. Educ. & Res. 221, 225 (2002).

233. *See* John R. Nolon, *Champions of Change: Reinventing Democracy Through Land Law Reform*, 30 Harv. Envtl. L. Rev. 1, 12 (2006).

localism, most supportive theorists recognize the need for collaboration with higher levels of government, neighboring communities, and the civic and private sectors. Diffusion theorists, in addition to emphasizing the role of outside idea sources, note that as successful change occurs in one community it tends to spread to nearby places confronting similar problems.[234]

In the study of urban planning, researchers describe how local and regional planning networks can be created to link local responses to address common, transboundary problems. Urban planning scholars reference the behavior of complex adaptive systems and the field of diffusion of innovations to define how regional planning networks can work to rationalize land use planning and control. According to David E. Booher and Judith E. Innes:

> Network power emerges from communication and collaboration among individuals, agencies, and businesses in a society. Network power emerges as diverse participants in a network focus on a common task and develop shared meanings and common heuristics for action. It grows as these players identify and build on their interdependencies to create new potential. In the process, innovations and novel responses to environmental stresses can emerge. These innovations, in turn, make possible adaptive change and constructive action of the whole.[235]

David Barron argues that

> local autonomy is more complex than we often acknowledge. . . . The baseline problem arises because no city or state is an island jurisdiction. The ability of each locality to make effective decisions on its own is inevitably shaped by its relation to other cities and states, and its relation to broader, private market forces and, most importantly, by the way the central power structures these relations. . . .[236]

He states that "the role of central government should not be to supplant local decisionmaking so much as to encourage local jurisdictions to understand their role as components of a larger coordinated system that benefits from cooperative interlocal behavior."[237]

Barron, joined by Gerald Frug argue that regionalists should aim "to enable cities and towns to participate in the resolution of regional problems. In this way, regionalism could offer an attractive—even empowering—alter-

234. *Id.*; *see supra* note 232.

235. Booher & Innes, *supra* note 233 ("Like a complex adaptive system, [the planning network] as a whole is more capable of learning and adaptation in the face of fragmentation and rapid change than a set of disconnected agents.").

236. *See* David J. Barron, *A Localist Critique of the New Federalism*, 51 Duke L.J. 377, 379 (2001).

237. *Id.* at 432.

native to the form of local power that now exists."[238] "The main point we wish to underline, therefore, is a conceptual one. Local autonomy is not the problem. . . ." "Opportunities may arise, therefore, for collective efforts to seek increased local power that the state need not fear. In return, the state need ask only that these new powers be exercised with regional interests in mind."[239] Baron and Frug argue that advocates for regional solutions to governmental problems "should take the desire for local control more seriously, not less."[240]

David Owen focuses his support for local control one rung up on the governmental ladder, what he calls subfederalism targeting state agencies as preferred collaborators. Under this approach, he writes "state and local governments can work together in ways that bring the benefits of local knowledge up to state levels."[241] His research rejects the idea of intergovernmental separation where each one—local, state, and federal—operates in its carved out autonomous space. Instead, as he learns from state-local case studies participants who credit success to "robust and continuous systems of interaction, to . . . major state investments in both empowering and supporting—as well as demanding—local governance."[242]

Ashira Pelman Ostrow observes that "[i]n contrast to federal bureaucrats, local officials are literally on the ground. Local officials, who are part of the local community and are politically accountable to it, have the nuanced knowledge and local sensibilities necessary to regulate land."[243] In his article

238. *See* David J. Barron and Gerald E. Frug, *Defensive Localism: A View of the Field From the Field*, 21 J.L. & Pol. 261, 262 (2005). To explain, the authors note that municipalities pursue local economic development because it "is the only interest municipalities can plausibly pursue given the state-designed structure of local power and the reality of inter-local competition for private investment." *Id.* at 265. They define "defensive localism" as follows: "Our findings suggest that many local residents are practicing what we call 'defensive localism,' a form of local power that arises as much from being constrained as from being empowered." *Id.* at 270. It is "a form of active engagement that is spurred by a feeling of not being in control." *Id.* at 271.

239. *Id.* at 290.

240. *Id.* at 262.

241. Owen, *supra* note 220, at 226.

242. *Id.*, at 218. This reference by Owen to state "demanding" is important. Despite this Article's deference to localism, there are instances in which state and federal governments must assert their overriding interests and take action to effectively influence local behavior. This is the case with respect to the nation's housing affordability and fair housing crisis. In this highly inflamed context, local decision-makers need cover and guidance, at a minimum, to approve affordable housing projects. States or the federal government must assess housing needs and take steps toward allocating responsibility to localities for their proportionate share of those needs. Financial incentives to offset the local costs of needed infrastructure and public services are also needed. This type of robust intervention in local decision making is not required to encourage local governments preserve and protect their drinking water, for example. Context matters.

243. Ostrow, *supra* note 218, at 1446.

on *Cooperative Localism*, Nestor Davidson reinforces Ostrow's emphasis on the local-federal connection.

> [He] proposes a new framework for conceptualizing federal empowerment of local governments. . . . The Court in its modern federalism jurisprudence has built a largely instrumental case for devolving and decentralizing governmental power. . . . . These core instrumental concerns are served even more forcefully by enhancing the autonomy of local governments. Thus, the very values of federalism that the Court invokes to enhance state sovereignty provide a compelling case for the particular exercise of federal authority represented by cooperative localism—in essence, a localist grounding for federal power.[244]

He continues: "Direct federal-local relations merit continued judicial respect."[245] Finally, Davidson notes: "Given the critical importance and ubiquitous practice of local government involvement in national policies, it is well past time for a firmly grounded jurisprudence of cooperative localism."[246]

B. *Opposition to Exclusive Localism*

Despite *de facto* local control of land use and its supportive theories, untethered land use localism has many critics. In addition to pointing to the limited technical capacity, resources, and geographical reach of local governments, critics note that municipal governments are susceptible to collective action problems[247] and neglect to take into account the external impacts of their actions.[248] Others lament the lack of local government accountability for the effect of local actions on larger scale contexts.[249] Negative views of local autonomy in land use matters arise in the context of climate change

244. Nestor M. Davidson, Cooperative Localism: Federal-Local Collaboration in an Era of State Sovereignty, 93 Va. L. Rev. 959, 961-962 (2007).
245. *Id.* at 963.
246. *Id.* at 964.
247. Alice Kaswan, *Climate Adaptation and Land Use: The Vertical Axis*, 39 Columbia J. of Envtl L. 390, 429-32 (2014) (arguing that local governments fail to overcome the collective action barrier because of inadequate information, insufficient funding, a "race to the bottom mentality," and to benefit from their free-rider status).
248. *Id.* at 432-36.
249. *See* Nestor M. Davidson, *The Dilemma of Localism in an Era of Polarization*, 128 Yale L.J. 954, 977 (2019) ("And local policies often generate externalities and spillover effects not fully accounted for by local governments. Davidson labels these "pathologies of localism").

adaptation,[250] watershed management,[251] and species and habitat loss, among others.[252] These lead some scholars to the conclusion that transboundary land use issues require control of local actions by higher levels of government.

Ostrow notes that "[i]n a world where capital and information pass freely across increasingly porous jurisdictional boundaries, few regulatory matters can be cabined within the borders of a single state, let alone a single locality."[253] Viewed from the federal level, local land use functions can be seen as woven into a thickening national law fabric. She argues that there is a "substantial body of existing federal land law," describing the role of local officials in this context as that of "federal agents."[254]

Sarah J. Adams-Schoen is particularly critical of the inability of local governments to adapt to climate change. "However, because of various intractable technical and socio-political obstacles—which could also be characterized as 'super wicked' attributes of this policy problem—robust resilience lawmaking is largely unrealized at the local level. Moreover, many local governments continue to allow or even encourage patterns of development that magnify the risks."[255]

C. *Support for Collaborative Localism*

Despite this relatively harsh criticism, there is a discernable movement toward taking a polycentric approach to solving shared environmental problems—even climate change—that requires the involvement of actors at all levels of government, including municipalities.[256] Even advocates of top-down

250. Robert Glicksman, *Climate Change Adaptation: A Collective Action Perspective on Federalism Constraints*, 40 Envtl. L. 1159, 1174-78 (2010); Kaswan, *supra* note 248, at 392-93, 418-19, 436-39, 460 (arguing that local governments are ill-equipped to address the climate change and instead advocates for a multilevel governance structure in which local land use regulations are augmented by state and federal regimes).
251. A. Dan Tarlock, *The Potential Role of Local Governments in Watershed Management*, 20 Pace Envtl. L. Rev. 149 (2002).
252. John Harte, *Land Use, Biodiversity, and Ecosystem Integrity: The Challenge of Preserving Earth's Life Support System*, 27 Ecology L.Q. 929 (2001).
253. Ostrow, *supra* note 218, at 1397.
254. "Finally, the Article applies principles of federalism theory to outline a 'local-official-as-federal agent' mode of land use law that harnesses the relative regulatory capacities of each level of government. *Id.* at 101.
255. Adams-Schoen, *supra* note 185, at 191.
256. Elinor Ostrom, *A Polycentric Approach for Coping with Climate Change*, 15-1 Annals of Eco. & Finance 97, 124 (2014):

> Given the complexity and changing nature of the problems involved in coping with climate change, there are no "optimal" solutions that can be used to make substantial reductions in the level of greenhouse gases emitted into the atmosphere. A major reduction in emissions is, however, needed. The advantage of a polycentric approach is that it encourages experimental efforts at multiple levels, as well as the development of methods for assessing the benefits and costs of particular strategies adopted in one type of ecosystem and comparing these with

solutions support robust local involvement in land use control. Ostrow, for example, espouses a theory of land law federalism within which federal law and agencies provide the support local officials need. She notes that states are relatively absent in land use law, inviting "federalism theorists to explore the boundaries of a federal-local relationship."[257] She is highly critical of the inadequate jurisdictional reach of local governments yet recognizes that local officials "have detailed knowledge of the land and are politically accountable to the local community, to implement land-use policy at the local level."[258]

Cooperative subfederalism, advocated by Owen, on the other hand, suggests that states have distinct and powerful potential to support local land use policy and programs.[259] Among the advantages he sees are that a state-local partnership "provides promising mechanisms for facilitating inter-local collaboration, countering interest group influence, and bolstering the financial resources available to local government, all the while retaining key benefits of localism."[260] Based on his extensive interviews with practitioners involved in state-local collaborations he concludes "experienced practitioners of cooperative subfederalism agreed, almost unanimously, that it offers a promising balance of state and local authority."[261]

Adams-Schoen agrees. She advocates for a strong state-local partnership, referencing Richard Briffault's scholarly work which urges scholars "to give greater attention to the state as a political and legal focal point in the system of local governments."[262] Adams-Schoen reviews recent New York statutes and regulations and concludes that "state lawmaking can and should help local governments use local lawmaking authority to comprehensively and

results obtained in other ecosystems. A strong commitment to finding ways of reducing individual emissions is an important element for coping with climate change. Building such a commitment, and the trust that others are also taking responsibility, can be more effectively undertaken in small- to medium-scale governance units that are linked through information networks and monitoring at all levels.

257. Ostrow, *supra* note 218, at 1403.

258. *Id.* at 1404. ("Local implementation of a federal land-use policy is likely to produce individual decisions that are consistent with national priorities but sensitive to the local context.").

259. Owen, *supra* note 220, at 177 ("A review of three long-established, state-local programs . . . demonstrates that their cooperative subfederalism arrangements can succeed."); Owen is concerned about traditional federalism theory which tends to recommend carving out "spaces in which states can act without federal interference. It is in that autonomous space, both the Court and commentators often opine, that allows states to serve as democracy's laboratories, check the power of the center, and compete for mobile citizens." *Id.* at 217.

260. *Id.* at 216.

261. *Id.* at 216 (State agencies are needed to mediate inter-local disputes, provide local officials with guidance and cover, offer funding, and make technical support available to staff. His extensive interviews with officials involved in state-local programs "identified state support for local decision-making as an essential element of a successful program.").

262. Adams-Schoen *supra* note 185, at 187, n. 1.

proactively adapt communities to climate- and weather-related risks."[263] Her work adds a fourth case study to the three that Owen examined.

She explains how the New York Community Risk and Resiliency Act of 2014 is helping local governments overcome the barriers to effective action.[264] The Act requires state agencies to provide sea-level rise inundation data and maps to coastal communities so that they can track and assess risks in particularly vulnerable neighborhoods; it also required that state agencies provide model laws to help them retreat from or accommodate those risks.[265] She refers with favor the state's amendment of its environmental impact review regulations to require local governments to review the impact of climate change on land use projects that it approves as well as to assess the impact of those projects on climate change.[266] Because New York's environmental impact review law applies to local governments and requires them to mitigate the adverse environmental impacts of their actions, these regulatory amendments "may turn out to be one of the most effective features of the state's adaptation regime."[267]

Alice Kaswan, the author of many of the critiques of localism, understands the key role that local governments play. Her concern focuses on local governments acting in isolation such that their unassisted initiatives "are unlikely to provide a sufficient national response to the dramatic risks ahead."[268] She recommends that "by creating links between local, federal (and state) programs, multilevel governance provides an opportunity for dynamic engagements among levels of government. Such engagement could prompt federal, state, and local dialogue, dialogue that could lead to more carefully considered and effective regulatory outcomes."[269]

Kaswan opposes exclusive local control while demonstrating the benefits of her multilevel framework. "Shared governance can best serve the range of values informing government structures. They demonstrate that, whatever the limitation of exclusive local control, a continued and substantial local role remains critical."[270] Kaswan continues: "While local governments are unlikely to give up their autonomy easily, federal involvement could provide

263. *Id.* at 215
264. *Id.*
265. New York's Model Laws to Increase Resilience can be accessed at www.dos.ny.gov/opd.
266. Adams-Schoen, *supra* note 185, at 216-220.
267. *Id.* at 238.
268. *See* Kaswan, *supra* note 248, at 393.
269. *Id.* at 438.
270. *Id.* at 474.

local governments with real benefits: coordination, financial and technical assistance, and even some alleviation of responsibility."[271]

D. *The Principle of Collaborative Subsidiarity*

There is general consensus among the theorists discussed above that, with respect to land law localism:

- local governments play an essential role in land use problem solving;
- they must be meaningfully involved in strategic planning and implementation;
- there are several limitations to their ability to solve problems;
- to solve complex land use problems, they need assistance, guidance, and direction;
- the assistance should be responsive to local needs; and that
- for this to happen, higher levels of government at the regional, state, or federal level must collaborate in solving larger scale land use problems.

There is little consensus, however, about who, precisely, the preferred collaborators are and how collaborations should be structured. The possibilities range from intermunicipal partnerships, to collaborations with regional, state, or federal agencies, or a combination of them.

The principle of subsidiarity "holds that responsibility for dealing with a problem should be delegated to the most decentralized institution capable of handling that problem."[272] There is a single actor implication in this phrasing, and it begs a question regarding the capacity of the decentralized institution. Complex land use issues like the protection of water quality always engage local people and their governments since that is where the problems manifest themselves. Nearly all local governments have been delegated significant legal authority from their state legislatures to adopt the types of strategies reviewed in Part IV of this chapter. Even with that capacity and numerous model actions to choose from, they regularly form partnerships with one or more regional, state, or federal agencies to supplement their ability to deal with the problem.[273] In other words, they reject the single actor implication of the principle and routinely collaborate with other agencies to supplement

271. *Id.* at 476.
272. Marshall, *supra* note 16, at 93.
273. *See generally supra* Part V. "The capacity at a given level to perform a task satisfactorily can often be enhanced through strategies seeking to strengthen access to the requisite capacities. Subsidiarity obliges

their parochial capacity. In so doing, they embrace a principle of collaborative subsidiarity.

Further, they chose various partners depending on the circumstances of the land use problem they confront and the resources that each can provide. The theorists of collaborative subsidiarity, if we can call them that tend to favor one collaborator over others. Advocates of intermunicipal cooperation look to neighboring communities, regionalists lean toward regional entities, subfederalists chose the state, while federal-local cooperation proponents orient toward agencies of the national government. Evidence of multilevel intergovernmental collaboration abounds, with localities working with partners up and down the vertical axis.[274]

Why scholars focus on, even advocate for, particular collaborators rather than embrace the flexibility evident in the wide variety of extant intergovernmental efforts to solve land use problems is a bit of a mystery.[275] This is especially true when one observes the changing policies of the courts and executive leadership at the state and federal level from one decade to another. In some states in some periods, state agencies might be extraordinarily helpful in providing needed assistance, while in other times federal players might stand closer to the bar. When serious water quality problems occur, local officials are required to respond, and they will search out and engage help where it exists in the moment.

This is a long answer to the question that Margaret asked. She is the watershed leader we encountered in Part I.[276] Margaret wanted to know why we were training land use leaders in her jurisdiction to initiate strategies to prevent public health problems by protecting water quality. Why, she wondered, isn't this the responsibility of a state or federal agency?

Our training method is guided by the principle of collaborative subsidiarity. We taught her and her fellow leaders not just about local powers, but also about the partnerships they might form with neighboring communities, the powers and resources of the state departments of health and environmental

---

actors at higher levels to explore such opportunities before ruling out the possibility of decentralizing tasks to lower levels." See Marshall, *supra* note 16, at 93.

274. *See* Kaswan, *supra* note 248; Davidson, *supra* note 245, at 963-64 ("A pragmatic judicial approach to intergovernmental relations that does not give priority to any particular alignment of governmental collaboration allows the political branches at all levels of government to craft approaches most appropriate to modern exigencies).

275. *See* Ostrom, *supra* notes 230 and 257; *See also* Marshall, *supra* note 16, at 75 (exploring "how Elinor Ostrom's 'nesting principle' for robust common property governance of large-scale common-pool resources might inform future upscaling efforts. In particular, I consider how the design of nested governance systems for large-scale environmental problems might be guided by the principle of subsidiarity.")

276. *See supra* Part I(A).

conservation, and the role of EPA in protecting some sources of drinking water. The leaders in the program hailed from adjacent watershed communities and learned from one another how they might share resources through intermunicipal collaboration. We involved representatives of potential partner agencies in the training so that they could explain what they had to offer. We did not tell Margaret which collaborators to choose or how to organize a collaboration but rather trusted her and the others in the room to craft their own partnerships based on the problem at hand, case studies from peer communities, and the resources available.[277]

277. *See supra* notes 232-38 and accompanying text on the theory of diffusion of innovation.

Chapter Seven
Societies Choosing to Succeed

The local land use toolbox is full. At hand are countless strategies to manage climate change at the local level. Change happens where crises appear, and the climate change crisis manifests itself most dramatically at the local level. The legal system, too, changes to respond to the needs of society. Local legal authority is losing its historical shackles and embracing innovative partnerships with state and federal agencies causing them to adjust to meet conditions on the ground. This chapter explores the theories of change that explain this movement in the law, tracks as an example the disappearance of Dillon's Rule of narrow construction of local power, and explains that these changes enable municipalities to adopt innovative and effective strategies for managing climate change.

I. Bubbles as Agents of Change

Chapter Five explored the structure of federal disaster planning law and its embrace of the state and local land use system: a collaborative process uniting all levels of government. The warnings flagged by disaster events are clear and inescapable: the bubbles are everywhere, and people at the local level are aware that change is needed for survival. These bubbles are grass-roots perturbations, and they lead to discrete changes in the legal system and society. Just as early common-law courts discovered legal norms in people's customs, local communities today discern challenges and adopt responsive local laws. In responding to grass-roots impulses, state and federal laws become better ordered, coordinated, and integrated.

Local governments, reacting to ground-level influences, have adopted numerous innovative land use laws that achieve sustainable development.[1]

1. *See* John R. Nolon, *Golden and Its Emanations: The Surprising Origins of Smart Growth*, 35 Urb. Law. 15, 30-54 (2003). For a survey of local efforts to achieve sustainable development, *see* Robert R.M. Verichick, *Why the Global Environment Needs Local Government: Lessons from the Johannesburg Summit*, 35 Urb. Law. 471 (2003).

They have encouraged "the most appropriate use of land"[2] by discovering a field of sustainable development law, designating priority growth districts in developing suburban areas, and providing for the expansion and redevelopment of sustainable cities and urban settlements. Local legislatures have virtually invented a new field properly called local environmental law and clarified their focus on preserving large and critical environmental areas.[3] They are at work infusing equity in human settlements by legislating to develop affordable housing.[4] When viewed as an organic whole, these local laws and practices demonstrate remarkable adaptation to contemporary needs and challenges. This burst of political reform in land use planning and law merits careful examination.[5] How and why did it occur? In considering this question, we may discover the strategic path to reform at the state and federal level as well.

Instructive is the adoption of local environmental laws over the past two decades. Although certain types of local environmental protection laws were

---

2. U.S. Dep't of Com., A Standard State Zoning Enabling Act §3 (1924, reprinted 1926). The phrase "encouraging the most appropriate use of land" was incorporated into most state laws that authorize local governments to adopt zoning laws. It explains the essential purpose to be achieved through the adoption of local land use laws. The text of the Standard Act can be found on the American Planning Association website at https://planning-org-uploaded-media.s3.amazonaws.com/legacy_resources/growingsmart/pdf/SZEnablingAct1926.pdf.
3. *See* John R. Nolon, *In Praise of Parochialism: The Advent of Local Environmental Law*, 26 Harv. Envtl. L. Rev. 365 (2002) [hereinafter Nolon, *In Praise of Parochialism*]. *See also* James M. McElfish, Nature-Friendly Ordinances: Local Measures to Conserve Biodiversity (2004); American Plan. Ass'n., Growing Smart Legislative Guidebook: Model Statutes for Planning and the Management of Change (Stuart Meck ed., 2002); John R. Nolon, Open Ground: Effective Local Strategies for Protecting Natural Resources (2003).
4. Alice Kaswan, *Environmental Justice: Bridging the Gap Between Environmental Laws and "Justice,"* 47 Am. U. L. Rev. 221, 226-27 (1997). *See also* Verichick, *supra* note 1, at 475-76:

   > Local governments have the greatest potential for democratic participation and social equity . . . . In democracies, elected officials tend to be more responsive to voter demands because it is easier for members of the public to monitor politicians and it is easier for new politicians to challenge unpopular incumbents . . . . Politics on a small scale also enables less affluent grassroots organizations to promote their interests through marches, speeches, and creative forms of activism that would not work on a national or regional scale. For this reason, some American environmental justice organizations have proved remarkably effective in fighting local environmental battles on behalf of the poor or people of color. Indeed, some environmental justice advocates have warned against emphasizing national solutions to environmental discrimination, out of the belief that national forums like the Congress or the federal courts favor the business elite over the common citizen.

   The current concerns with the lack of affordable housing and an increase in homelessness, combined with an increase of evictions in many quarters, has raised questions about the need for state legislatures to impose affordable housing obligations on municipalities, particularly by requiring them to allow the construction of small-scale multiple-family structures in neighborhoods zoned for single-family housing.
5. This movement is anything but ubiquitous. Citing impressive evidence of local reform is not the same as asserting that all is well in the American land use system. The rapid spread of innovative land use laws in the past few decades parallels the rapid adoption of zoning enabling laws by state legislatures and the adoption of zoning as the preferred method of land use control in the 1920s.

adopted previously, the new laws emerging expanded in scope and expressly focused on protecting critical natural resources and habitats, rather than just benefitting the human species.[6] Similarly, with respect to local sustainable development law, there has been a recent increase in the adoption of priority growth district laws in developing suburban areas and a reinvention of 1970s urban redevelopment law in cities and urban villages.

New York's Hudson River Valley region, located in the epicenter of the sprawl occurring in the New York metropolitan area, is the laboratory for the Land Use Law Center at Pace Law School. There, the Land Use Law Center has trained and assisted hundreds of local land use leaders and has taken a closer look at the challenges, influences, and processes of local land use reform and innovation. By learning from this extended exposure to change over a period of years in the Hudson River Valley and interviewing local leaders responsible for land use innovations throughout the country, the Land Use Law Center has gleaned some understanding of how such positive reform happens and how state and federal action can encourage it.[7]

When local leaders are asked why they adopt particular land use law reforms,[8] the most frequent response is that they were faced with a crisis and had no choice but to respond. This can be called the "perturbation effect." Local officials have much to attend to other than land use law reform; it is when the ill effects of sprawl, the decay of their neighborhoods, a particular environmental crisis, or the adverse impacts of outside land use decisions get their attention that they act. In the absence of a perturbing crisis, some local leaders adopt innovative land use plans and laws because of citizen agitation or through the intervention of their advisors or higher levels of government.

---

6. *See* Nolon, *In Praise of Parochialism*, *supra* note 3, at 376 ("The gradual evolution toward environmental sensitivity in local land use controls has proceeded far enough that a distinct environmental ethic, as opposed to an incidental one, is evident.").
7. The author founded the Land Use Law Center in 1993 after conducting a study on the sustainability of land development patterns in the Hudson River Valley for the President's Council on Sustainable Development. This study indicated that training local land use leaders was essential if current unsustainable development trends in the region were to be reversed. With funding from Congress and various additional sources, the Land Use Law Center created and has conducted extensive multi-day training programs for local land use leaders from over 200 towns, villages, and cities in the valley. The program, known as the Local Land Use Leadership Alliance Training Program (LULA), has educated over 2,500 local leaders in six states. The curriculum of the training program includes in-depth exposure to embodying land use strategies in local law and consensus-based decision-making techniques to effect change responsive to unique local crises and circumstances.
8. Students in the author's classes at the Yale School of Forestry and Environmental Studies conducted research on local environmental and smart growth laws adopted by municipalities in all 50 states, identifying well-crafted and exemplary laws and interviewing the local land use leaders involved in drafting and securing the adoption of these laws. *See* YALE SCHOOL OF FORESTRY & ENVIRONMENTAL STUDIES, REPORT NUMBER 2: GAINING GROUND INFORMATION DATABASE (John R. Nolon et al. eds., 2004) (describing the methodology and conclusions of this research).

This can be called the "anticipatory effect." When anticipating future land use challenges, local leaders can be motivated to act when faced with change, armed with good ideas, and encouraged by technical assistance or grants. In other words, local land use change can be spontaneous or planned: a reaction to a crisis or a considered response to anticipated, adverse change in community character.

In their perturbation and anticipatory postures, municipal leaders are often helped in adapting to change by land use lawyers, professional planners, environmental advocates, citizens, and state and federal agency personnel. These "change agents" are armed with data, technical information, guidebooks, best management protocols, case studies of successful innovations, persuasive policies, and economic incentives. These tools, properly used, can alert local leaders and guide them as they evaluate local circumstances and adapt solutions to their particular circumstances.

II. Complex Adaptive Systems and the Process of Societal Change

Nobel Laureate Murray Gell-Mann describes biological evolution, the behavior of organisms in ecological systems, learning and thinking in human beings, the evolution of human societies, and the behavior of investors in financial markets as "processes." Within each process, he asserts:

> A complex adaptive system acquires information about its environment and its own interaction with that environment, identifying regularities in that information, condensing those regularities into a kind of "schema"or model, and acting in the real world on the basis of that schema. In each case, there are various competing schemata, and the results of the action in the real world feedback to influence the competition among those schemata.

Until perhaps the late 1950s, traditional zoning techniques sufficed to order the external development pressures on communities in the United States. As development pressures mounted, this model of land use control failed many communities whose leaders then reacted to this feedback of failure by adopting new land use techniques. This process evolves within and spreads among communities through what Gell-Mann describes as a complex adaptive system.

Two areas of academic theory and research are particularly useful in understanding the dynamic interactions within local land use law: the scholarship of scientists, like Gell-Mann, who examine the behavior of "complex adaptive systems"[9] and a field called the "diffusion of innovation."[10] These descriptions parallel descriptions of change within and among communities that the Land Use Law Center staff have seen from their experience working directly with local governments. What follows is an outline of the process of adoption of land use innovations and an explanation of why and how state and federal influences can help further positive local change.

In the fields of physics and ecological studies, scientists have studied complex adaptive systems that exist in nature and how they successfully adapt when challenged by change. Their theories gradually migrated to the study of business associations, governmental entities, and public law. Broadly defined, a complex adaptive system is an organized entity comprising various components: niches in ecosystems, divisions in corporations, departments in governments, and stakeholder groups in localities, to name a few.[11] Diffusion theorists refer to "social systems" and observe and describe the diffusion of innovations as they are communicated and adapted through defined processes over time by members within a system.[12] Urban planning scholars reference the behavior of complex adaptive systems and the field of diffusion

9. *See* Murray Gell-Mann, The Quark and the Jaguar: Adventures in the Simple and the Complex (1994). Murray Gell-Mann describes biological evolution, the behavior of organisms in ecological systems, learning and thinking in human beings, the evolution of human societies, and the behavior of investors in financial markets as "processes." Within each process, he asserts:

> A complex adaptive system acquires information about its environment and its own interaction with that environment, identifying regularities in that information, condensing those regularities into a kind of "schema" or model, and acting in the real world on the basis of that schema. In each case, there are various competing schemata, and the results of the action in the real world feedback to influence the competition among those schemata.

Id. at 17. Until perhaps the late 1950s, traditional zoning techniques sufficed to order the external development pressures on communities in the United States. As development pressures mounted, this model of land use control failed many communities whose leaders then reacted to this feedback of failure by adopting new land use techniques, a process that evolves within and spreads among communities through the process Gell-Mann describes as a complex adaptive system. *See generally* Mitchell M. Waldrop, Complexity: The Emerging Science at the Edge of Order and Chaos (1992) (providing details of the work conducted by the Santa Fe Institute on the science of complexity).

10. *See* Everett M. Rogers, Diffusion of Innovations 6-7 (5th ed. 2003) ("Diffusion is a kind of social change, defined as the process by which alteration occurs in the structure and function of a social system. . . . In this book, we use the word 'diffusion' to include both the planned and spontaneous spread of new ideas.").

11. *See* Gell-Mann, *supra* note 9, at 9:

> Complex adaptive systems include a human child learning his or her native language, a strain of bacteria becoming resistant to an antibiotic, the scientific community testing out new theories, an artist getting a creative idea, a society developing new customs or adopting a new set of superstitions, a computer programmed to evolve new strategies for winning at chess, and the human race evolving ways of living in greater harmony with itself and with the other organisms that share the planet Earth.

12. *See* Rogers, *supra* note 10, at 5 ("Diffusion is the process in which an innovation is communicated through certain channels over time among the members of a social system.").

of innovations to define how regional planning networks can work to rationalize land use planning and control.[13]

Regarding grass-roots change in land use law and practices, the relevant system is the community and its formal decision-makers, local legislature members, and those who influence their actions. At this level, land use innovations[14] include laws that provide for the transfer of development rights (TDRs) or the protection of wildlife habitat, for example. The larger system relevant to land use reform comprises the locality, constituent civic and private-sector stakeholders, state and federal legislatures, and their land use agencies. In nature and human organizations, the systems that thrive are those that have established effective mechanisms for exchanging, evaluating, and reacting to information among their component parts. As stress occurs, information is gathered at the lowest level of the system and relayed to higher levels that digest and synthesize it. Then, through continued communication, system behaviors are reordered to react and adapt to change.[15]

Connectivity among components is the key to successful adaptation. In a fully connected system, the components can be described as nested into one another, forming a loose network of interdependent parts. They constitute a hierarchical form that enables the system to self-regulate, adapting organically as stresses occur. This process of change is not necessarily orderly, nor does the nested hierarchy necessarily exhibit consistently rational behavior; however, through continued and effective communication, the system adapts in unpredictable but generally successful ways as it deals with external events.[16]

---

13. *See* David E. Booher & Judith E. Innes, *Network Power in Collaborative Planning,* 21 J. Plan. Educ. & Res. 221, 225 (2002):

    > Network power emerges from communication and collaboration among individuals, agencies, and businesses in a society. Network power emerges as diverse participants in a network focus on a common task and develop shared meanings and common heuristics for action. It grows as these players identify and build on their interdependencies to create new potential. In the process, innovations and novel responses to environmental stresses can emerge. These innovations, in turn, make possible adaptive change and constructive action of the whole.

    See also id. ("Like a complex adaptive system, [the planning network] as a whole is more capable of learning and adaptation in the face of fragmentation and rapid change than a set of disconnected agents.").

14. *See* Rogers, *supra* note 10, at 12 ("An innovation is an idea, practice, or object that is perceived as new by an individual or other unit of adoption.").

15. *See* Gell-Mann, *supra* note 9, at 17:

    > The common feature of all these processes is that in each one a complex adaptive system acquires information about its environment and its own interaction with that environment, identifying regularities in that information, condensing those regularities into a kind of "schema" or model, and acting in the real world on the basis of that schema. In each case, there are various competing schemata, and the results of the action in the real world feedback to influence the competition among those schemata.

16. *See* Rogers, *supra* note 10, at 404-35.

III. The Expansion of Municipal Land Use Authority

As local bubbles have grown, as perturbations have become more serious and frequent, the legal system has changed profoundly by giving governments at the local level more and more power to respond. For municipal governments to promote sustainable and green development, create safe densities and open spaces in response to the pandemic, protect lives and property in areas vulnerable to natural disasters, and manage climate change, they must be able to influence the development and preservation of privately owned land. For them to control the negative impacts of oil and gas facilities, they must find power to regulate matters that are typically the prerogative of state agencies. To legalize emerging renewable energy technologies, they must have authority to make them permitted uses in their zoning ordinances and to innovate by creating solar-ready homes in subdivisions and provide for solar easements.

To all of these, Dillon's Rule has been an obstacle. It was handed down in 1868 by then-Iowa Supreme Court Justice Forrest Dillon. In December 1869, Justice Dillon became a judge for the U.S. Court of Appeals for the Eighth Circuit. The rule holds that municipalities are not sovereign entities but merely instrumentalities of states and that the legal powers delegated to them by state legislatures are to be narrowly construed.[17] The opinions of the Supreme Court of Iowa are not precedential in other states, but Dillon's Rule was incorporated into Judge Dillon's influential treatise on the *Law of Municipal Corporations*.[18] It held surprising sway over judges in other jurisdictions and became and remained a major hurdle to municipalities using their charter and delegated powers innovatively to confront changing conditions. Slowly, over the past 150+ years, it has been repealed or eroded in the vast majority of states through court decisions that broadly interpret delegated land use authority, amendments to state constitutions, or acts of state legislatures. As often happens in the American legal system, the law has evolved to meet society's changing needs; as bubbles formed and perturba-

17. *See* City of Clinton v. Cedar Rapids & Mo. River R.R. Co., 24 Iowa 455, 475 (Iowa 1868).

> It is a general and undisputed proposition of law that *a municipal corporation possesses and can exercise the following powers, and no others*: First, those granted in *express words*; second, those *necessarily or fairly implied* in or *incident* to the powers expressly granted; third, those *essential* to the accomplishment of the declared objects and purposes of the corporation.—not simply convenient, but indispensable. Any fair, reasonable, substantial doubt concerning the existence of power is resolved by the courts against the corporation, and the power is denied. . . . All acts beyond the scope of the powers granted are void.

18. John Forrest Dillon, 1 Commentaries on the Law of Municipal Corporations §237(89) (5th ed. 1911).

tions mounted at the local level, the law has given local governments increasing authority to meet serious emerging challenges.

Under land use enabling acts of state legislatures in all 50 states, for example, municipalities are delegated the power to adopt zoning provisions that regulate land use and the structure, location, and configuration of buildings. The model for these state acts, the Standard State Zoning Enabling Act, stated that "[s]uch regulations shall be made with reasonable consideration, among other things, to the character of the district and its peculiar suitability for particular uses, and with a view to conserving the value of buildings and encouraging the most appropriate use of land throughout such municipality."[19]

The relevance of Dillon's Rule of narrow construction of municipal powers is that it might prevent localities from including green building requirements in zoning, adopting provisions that mitigate climate change, regulating the location of oil and gas facilities, or adopting standards that protect ecosystem services or promote renewable energy facilities. In Virginia, one of a few remaining Dillon's Rule states, a local government's attempt to enlarge a resource protection area within its geographical boundaries under the Chesapeake Bay Preservation Act, for example, was declared void.[20]

In contrast, broadly construed, the "suitability for particular uses" and "most appropriate use of the land" language of the Standard State Zoning Enabling Act allows local governments to incorporate provisions that apply to emerging technologies such as renewable energy or emerging exigencies such as climate change or pandemics. If narrowly construed, local governments could only enact these laws if the state legislatures provide them with specific enabling legislation. Given the unique challenges, opportunities, and highly diverse conditions among states' many municipalities, the system's impracticality is obvious.

With respect to this delegated local land use control, many state courts have abandoned Dillon's Rule in favor of a broad interpretation of local power. In Idaho, a court noted that "in enacting the Local Planning Act of 1975, the legislature obviously intended to give local governing boards . . . broad powers in the area of planning and zoning."[21] In Texas, "[t]he power of local governments to zone and control land use is undoubtedly broad and

19. U.S. Dep't of Com., *supra* note 2.
20. Marble Techs. v. City of Hampton, 279 Va. 409, 412-15 (Va. 2010). (The issue in the circuit court was "whether the City acted ultra vires in passing this amendment to the zoning ordinance.").
21. Worley Highway Dist. v. Kootenai Cnty., 663 P.2d 1135, 1137 (Idaho Ct. App. 1983).

its proper exercise is an essential aspect of achieving a satisfactory quality of life in both urban and rural communities."[22]

Some state legislatures have adopted statutes that explicitly repeal Dillon's Rule. The state of Arkansas repealed Dillon's Rule in this way in 2011.[23] "The rule of decision known as 'Dillon's Rule' is inapplicable to the municipal affairs of municipalities."[24] The statute defines "municipal affairs" as "all matters and affairs of government germane to, affecting, or concerning the municipality or its government except" certain state affairs "subject to the general laws of the State of Arkansas."[25] States have incorporated self-executing provisions related to home-rule authority in their state constitutions; such amendments can greatly diminish the scope of Dillon's Rule or eliminate it altogether.[26]

The National League of Cities recently published *Principles of Home Rule for the Twenty-First Century*, a detailed analysis of the 130-year history and evolution of local home-rule authority that also contains a Model Home Rule Law.[27] The report states that "the principles are a hopeful vision for the future of state-local relations, grounded in the lessons of more than 130 years of experience with home rule. They make clear that cities, towns, and villages are fully capable of governing, and that states must have a healthy respect for the institutions of local democracy."

The importance of the adoption of home-rule provisions is evident in Tennessee. The Tennessee Constitution was amended in 1953 to permit municipal governments to operate under home-rule authority.[28]

---

22. Barr v. City of Sinton, 295 S.W.3d 287, 297 (Tex. 2009) (quoting Schad v. Borough of Mount Ephraim, 452 U.S. 61, 68 (1981)).
23. 2011 Ark. Act 1187 (codified at Ark. Code Ann. §14-43-602(b) (2011)).
24. *Id.*
25. Ark. Code Ann. §14-43-601(a)(1) (2011).
26. Hon. John D. Russell & Aaron Bostrom, *White Paper: Federalism, Dillon's Rule, and Home Rule*, Am. City Cnty. Exch., Jan. 2016, at 6.
27. National League Of Cities, Principles of Home Rule for the 21st Century 5 (2020):

    > [The report] represents the culmination of a year-long process of research, drafting, outreach, and refinement. The principles are a hopeful vision for the future of state-local relations, grounded in the lessons of more than 130 years of experience with home rule. They make clear that cities, towns, and villages are fully capable of governing, and that states must have a healthy respect for the institutions of local democracy.

    For a critical assessment of the NLC's publication, see David Schleicher, *Constitutional Law for NIMBYs: A Review of "Principles of Home Rule for the 21st Century" by the National League of Cities*, Ohio St. L.J. (forthcoming March 2020). ("Unfortunately, the Model Article is severely flawed. Rather than systematically addressing and responding to the various contemporary problems of local governance, it is laser-focused on . . . the spate of preemptive laws passed by politically-conservative state legislatures . . . .").
28. Tenn. Const. art. XI, §9 (1953).

> [A]n exception to Dillon's Rule necessarily arises when the issue concerns the authority of home rule municipalities . . . . The effect of the home rule amendments was to fundamentally change the relationship between the General Assembly and these types of municipalities, because such entities now derive their power from sources other than the prerogative of the legislature. Consequently, because the critical assumption underlying application of Dillon's Rule is no longer valid as to home rule municipalities, Dillon's Rule simply cannot be applied to limit any authority exercised by them.[29]

As stated by the Supreme Court of Tennessee, "the whole purpose of the Home Rule Amendment was to vest control of local affairs in local governments . . . ."[30]

"Home rule, in effect, reverses Dillon's Rule because a local unit of government may exercise wide-ranging powers despite a lack of specific statutory authority."[31] In 1972, South Carolina amended its constitution, adding a home-rule provision that repeals Dillon's Rule altogether.[32] The legislature subsequently passed the Home Rule Act[33] and in doing so, "intended to abolish the application of Dillon's Rule in South Carolina and restore autonomy to local government."[34] Some states have given home-rule authority to municipalities either directly through self-executing constitutional provisions or by authorizing the state legislature to adopt home-rule legislation.[35]

A self-executing provision directly grants local governments power.[36] The Arizona Constitution states, for example, that "[t]he provisions of §§5 through 8 of this [home-rule] article are self-executing, and no further legislation is required to make them effective."[37] "Any city containing, now or hereafter, a population of more than three thousand five hundred may frame a charter for its own government consistent with, and subject to, the Constitution and the laws of the state . . . ."[38]

29. Southern Constructors Inc. v. Loudon Cnty. Bd. of Educ., 58 S.W.3d 706, 713-14 (Tenn. 2001).
30. Farris v. Blanton, 528 S.W.2d 549, 551 (Tenn. 1975).
31. Louis V. Csoka, *The Dream of Greater Municipal Autonomy: Should the Legislature or the Courts Modify Dillon's Rule, a Common Law Restraint on Municipal Power?*, 29 N.C. Cent. L.J. 194, 201 (2007).
32. S.C. Const. art. VIII, §§7-17 (1895).
33. S.C. Code Ann. §§5-7-10 to -310 (1976).
34. 19 S.C. Jur. Const. Law §12.1.
35. Russell & Bostrom, *supra* note 26, at 6.
36. *See* John Martinez, 1 Local Government Law §4:6 (2020).
37. Ariz. Const. art. XII, §9 (2018).
38. *Id.* art. XIII, §2.

IV. Choosing to Succeed

It would be easy to despair at the time of this book's publication. We face a perfect storm: the combination of inescapable evidence of racial hostility and systemic segregation, worse and more frequent natural disasters, mounting evidence of devastating climate change, and a runaway pandemic calling for transformational change. Like climate change bubbles, the warnings are everywhere, and people at the local level are aware that change is needed for survival.

It is a sign of hope, and a potential strategy for success, that these bubbles are grass-roots perturbations, and they lead to discrete changes in the legal system and society. The tools that the law gives local leaders to employ against the consequences of climate change are many and readily available. The reach of these tools is explored in Chapter Five, where a land use stabilization wedge is described as a potentially powerful tool to mitigate and adapt to climate change. The effective use of these tools by serious, committed people will send signals to state and federal leaders that the problem is present and real, that it must and can be confronted, and that these local efforts need effective leadership and help. Powerful signals from the grass-roots level can realign and strengthen top-down policies and programs. Most transformative change in our country has started locally and then built into significant national movements.[39]

Societies that have ignored such signals have not fared well. In his book *Collapse: How Societies Choose to Fail or Succeed*, Jared Diamond reflects on the costs to society caused by ignoring early warnings of long-term problems, such as those caused by major natural disasters.[40] He describes how ancient and contemporary societies either disappeared or were damaged severely by rigid adherence to cultural values in the face of drastic environmental change. His paradigmatic story is that of the Norse colonies in Greenland that lasted for 450 years and then vanished.[41] They simply and fatally assumed that Greenland's ecosystem would perpetually support their approach to livestock-based agriculture. They cleared meadows, pastured cattle, grew hay to

39. *See* James Fallows, *The Reinvention of America*, ATLANTIC, May 2018, https://www.theatlantic.com/magazine/archive/2018/05/reinventing-america/556856/:

> The more we traveled, the more parallels and resonances we saw. . . . Every place had its local features, but together those efforts formed a pattern whose sweep and power can be hard to discern from any single instance. . . . And the evidence of past waves of reform, from the labor-rights and women's-suffrage movements of the early 1900s through the civil-rights and environmental movements of mid-century, suggests that national transformations must start from local roots.

40. JARED DIAMOND, COLLAPSE: HOW SOCIETIES CHOOSE TO FAIL OR SUCCEED (2005).

41. *Id.* at 178-276.

feed their livestock during long winters, dug sod to build comfortable houses, and ate beef as their principal staple. They continued these practices even after evidence of environmental catastrophe was upon them.[42] In this and many other stories, Diamond provides sobering evidence that human beings, pursuing their self-interests, are not rational actors, and in the normal course of events, their unmediated interactions do not insulate societies from environmental devastation. Societies that choose to succeed engage in effective long-term planning that according to Diamond, "characterizes some governments and some political leaders, some of the time."[43]

Local governments and local leaders can choose to succeed and catalyze a movement to change, reassess, realign, and employ our considerable resources more intelligently and effectively.[44] What is evident in climate change bubbles is equally visible in the contagious movement toward racial justice and our growing commitment to confront the pandemic. Signals from the bottom of the legal system have a talismanic effect on state and national leaders. Past legal reforms have sprung up at the local level, risen in the state and national consciousness, and produced positive change regarding civil rights, voting equity, and environmental protection.[45] Individual local advocates, elected and appointed local leaders, and their political representatives in the statehouse and the halls of Congress have significant legal power. Their work provides abundant evidence of successful strategies to employ. They can, and we must hope that they will choose to succeed.

---

42. Diamond describes the work of anthropologists who explored these abandoned settlements and found the bones of newborn calves, mother cows, and pets consumed during the final winter. From this he concludes that until the bitter end, the Norse clung to their environmentally destructive diet despite the abundance of seals and fish which were consumed by the Inuits who inhabited the same environment. Hunting seal, consuming the meat, and burning the blubber for heat and light were anathema to the Norse. Their commitment to European agriculture and the raising and consumption of beef was a cultural value too dear to be abandoned. Diamond discusses the "landscape amnesia" that must have beset the Norse. As a result, they forgot to pay attention to what they were doing to their environment. In the end, they starved to death. *Id.* at 425-26.

43. *Id.* at 523.

44. David Brooks, *The Localist Revolution*, N.Y. Times, July 19, 2018, https://www.nytimes.com/2018/07/19/opinion/national-politics-localism-populism.html:

> Under localism, the crucial power center is at the tip of the shovel, where the actual work is being done. Expertise is not in the think tanks but among those who have local knowledge, those with a feel for how things work in a specific place and an awareness of who gets stuff done.

45. *See* Fallows, *supra* note 39.

V. Conclusion: An Agenda for the Future of Land Use Planning and Regulation

This agenda is a work in progress and an invitation for others to comment on, add to or subtract from, update, or disagree with these matters. Proponents of effective land use planning and regulation and others searching for meaningful strategies have a major challenge to face as the world turns and heightens our appreciation for the evolution of the law to meet changing conditions. Here is a list of issues:

1. **Reduced carbon emissions**. The 2015 Conference of the Parties to the International Convention on Climate Change in Paris called on participating nations to list the strategies they will use to mitigate climate change. These are called nationally determined contributions (NDCs), and they are to be submitted to the United Nations so that it can evaluate their cumulative results. We must realign with the global movement and rejoin the Paris Accord; meanwhile, local governments are adopting innovative NDCs, such as land use strategies that reduce vehicle miles traveled and energy consumption by reshaping settlement patterns and revising building construction protocols. Whether we are in or out of the formal international structure, municipalities are developing a long menu of NDCs, and these can be positive examples for other nations as they confront climate change.

2. **Retreat and resilience**. Much of our population is settled along coastal waterways and floodplains. Many more are in the drought-prone Southwest where the summer's heat threatens livability and sparks wildfires. Retreating from the most dangerous of these areas is highly controversial, but an inevitable result of the changing climate. Land use law is evolving to plan for and manage the gradual retreat from some of these danger zones and to make others resilient through proper placement and construction of buildings and infrastructure. The loose confederacy of strategies now being developed must become a clear blueprint of best practices for states and localities to adopt.

3. **Reduced liability for preventing dangerous development**. Over a quarter of a century ago, the U.S. Supreme Court, in *Lucas v. South Carolina Coastal Council*,[46] held that land use regulations that prevent all economic development are takings that require full compensation

46. 505 U.S. 1003 (1992).

for the affected owner. Justice Antonin Scalia, writing for the majority, noted that changed circumstances and changed knowledge could be used to soften this rigid total takings rule. Properly constructed no-build regulations in climate change's danger zones must be validated by the use of this dictum to liberate regulators from the liability that has stifled common-sense adaptation strategies.

4. **Creating livable neighborhoods, safe buildings, and safe densities for the new demographics**. Land use regulations can create livable neighborhoods for the nation's emerging households: young individuals and couples (millennials), immigrants, and seniors who are leaving single-family neighborhoods. Most prefer urban living, but only in safe neighborhoods with a proper mix of services, entertainment, restaurants, and transportation alternatives. Density makes cheaper mass transportation and affordable housing possible, supports large public hospitals, and a broader safety net. The many solid innovations already in place must be shaped into a common agenda for implementing this objective. These places are where society has invested in infrastructure and where per capita carbon emissions are less than half the national average, mitigating a public health and environmental justice problem of serious concern.

    This recent movement is challenged by the pandemic, which is causing some urban residents to relocate to presumably safer suburbs and discouraging investors from building in urban places. There is a fear of sharing doors, elevators, crowded subways, busy playgrounds, and traditional sidewalks. The command to socially distance and permission to work from home compound the situation. This reaction to COVID-19 risks recreating the flight from and disinvestment in urban places that originally caused sprawl and its crippling effects on the economy, environment, and particularly on global warming. Urban planners and lawyers must revisit building codes and land use plans and regulations to create safe homes, businesses, parks, and neighborhoods. Public health must become a driving concern in urban planning and design.

    Codes can require that buildings have better internal ventilation, ultraviolet light to disinfect indoor air, high-efficiency air filters, health screening technology in buildings, wider corridors, work-at-home spaces, more elevators, voice-activated elevators, automatic doors, spatial distance metrics for indoor service, and redesigned interior amenity spaces. City agencies can provide for spatial distancing in urban parks and open space, broader sidewalks and promenades, expanded capacity for outdoor service for retailers, and curbside management to facilitate pick-ups.

5. **Creating transportation alternatives**. Technology is making cities smarter. They are using new media, communication, and transportation software to lower the costs and increase the amenities of urban living. Foremost among these is transit-oriented development (TOD) that connects mixed-use buildings with transportation services in transit station areas and makes the connections obvious and accessible to residents and workers through smart technologies. Transportation alternatives such as walking, bicycling, and buses must be used in addition to, or in lieu of, TOD. All forms of transit and movement must also keep their eye on public health imperatives.

6. **Managing neighborhood transitions**. Urban redevelopment can result in gentrification—the displacement of low- and moderate-income residents and small businesses—a result clearly counter to the basic precepts of sustainability. The faint outlines of a strategy for managing this transition without displacement are becoming visible. They involve job development and training for current residents, remediating distressed properties (while keeping them affordable), including affordable units in new housing projects, and paying close attention to the quality of education and public safety, among other initiatives. Small businesses are critical to the viability of urban living. The predicted loss of small businesses due to the pandemic requires a rethink: enhancing their ability to serve customers with takeout services, pop-up capacity, and use of parking spaces and streets. Curbside management, initiated in anticipation of ride-sharing efficiencies, will become a priority for recovering small businesses.

7. **Resolving the fair housing/systemic racism dilemma**. The *Inclusive Communities Project*[47] case, decided by the Supreme Court in 2015, determined that zoning that disparately impacts racial minorities may be invalid under the Fair Housing Act. This determination requires careful thought and action by affluent communities where whites and single-family zoning predominate. How to create an inclusive community through land use regulations is an elusive objective. Equally challenging is the issue of distributing limited federal and state housing dollars and tax credits. Historically, these resources have been

47. Texas Dep't of Hous. & Cmty. Affairs v. Inclusive Communities Project, 576 U.S. 519 (2015).

allocated to communities with low- and moderate-income populations: where the need is, as they say. The Court indicated that this kind of steering may violate the Fair Housing Act because it perpetuates segregation. To the extent that limited subsidies are allocated to more affluent areas, they are less available to mitigate gentrification in revitalizing urban neighborhoods. This is a public policy quandary of critical importance.

In addition, single-family zoning and the housing it creates are barriers to housing affordability for those long excluded from many communities: groups including middle- and low-income households, but disproportionately families of color. Reforms achieved in Minneapolis and Oregon require single-family zones to allow small-scale multiple-unit structures. This reform provides a powerful new source of housing; as traditional single-family homes become less affordable in many parts of the country, particularly in successful urban communities, this new housing source can reduce the barriers to housing affordability.

Climate change is causing deadly conditions in many low- and moderate-income neighborhoods, the most obvious of which is the heat island effect. Temperatures in lower income neighborhoods are higher, as is the percentage of residents who die from heat exposure. These neighborhoods, with a few exceptions, have limited tree canopies and extensive impervious surfaces such as sidewalks, streets, parking lots, and even treeless city parks, all of which absorb and reflect the heat. Zoning is complicit. It must be changed to allow for on-site vegetation and other green infrastructure. Racial equity is emerging as an element of climate action planning, and that concern—as well as the strategies that address it—must find their way into comprehensive land use planning and zoning.

8. **Protecting urban food sheds**. The local food movement is inherently sustainable, and innovative farmers are producing crops close to urban centers: a gain for public health and mitigation of climate change. Critical to the success of this strategy is the preservation of high-quality farmland in defined food sheds. Land use laws must be adjusted to permit farmers in critical areas great flexibility to use farmland to meet market needs, diversify their on-site land uses, and provide zoning incentives to do so. Zoning that permits residential development of farmland must be reformed to protect the most fertile soils and farms.

9. **Reducing water demand and protecting water quality**. As the domestic population expands, water consumption will increase in areas with limited potable water supplies. Land use regulations can foster settlement patterns that reduce per capita water use by emphasizing smaller lots and higher density development. Combined with regulations that require water-smart facilities and water-conserving landscapes, this can reduce per capita consumption by half or more. At the same time, development that serves the nation's growing population must be governed by local land use laws that protect groundwater and surface water nonpoint source pollution. These are not strategies that federal agencies are empowered to employ under the Clean Water Act. This requires more communities to adopt the innovative water pollution controls developed over the past two decades as local environmental law has matured.

10. **Making local land use strategies an intentional objective of state and federal initiatives**. The power of local governments to control land use may be guided or marginally controlled by higher levels of government, but it is not likely to be taken away. State and federal legislatures represent local constituencies and are sensitive to maintaining local control and home rule. This power and its proper use must be harnessed for the sustainable development agenda to be realized; integrating local land use authority must become an intentional objective of state and federal policy. The principle of collaborative subsidiarity—that is of building on local control but shaping and assisting it at the state and federal level—must guide the agendas of higher levels of government. Thinking globally is critical; it must be informed by acting locally.

Chapter Eight
Pandemic Postscript

Here, the book changes course, moving from heavily footnoted chapters with abundant case studies to an undocumented look ahead as land use law confronts climate change and the recent pandemic. The chapter builds on what we know from earlier chapters about the breadth of local land use power and how municipalities leverage that power by creating partnerships with state and federal governments. But the chapter also draws from techniques that cities have used to confront other serious problems and creates a menu of strategies for local officials, stakeholders, and land use professionals to consider. The chapter includes a discussion of systemic racism and how zoning and other governmental actions are complicit in causing environmental injustice. Noting that these public health and welfare threats have been with us for decades, it suggests several actions that cities can take to deal fairly with low-income neighborhoods in rethinking how to protect public health comprehensively. The chapter ends by examining whether and to what extent the U.S. Constitution limits the scope of state and local emergency orders that protect the public health. Efforts to respond to climate change and pandemics will inevitably limit what property and business owners can do with what they own. How far can this power be stretched?

I. Yet Another Beginning for Land Use Law: The Pandemic

The chapters of this book chart the journey of local land use law from its inception in 1916 through the end of its first century. It is a story of new beginnings: first to shed its Euclidean straight jacket, then to protect natural resources, further on to embrace smart growth, eventually to mature into sustainable development, and then recently to manage climate change. Its story, fully explored in Chapter Two, is replete with new beginnings. The book ends with this chapter's exploration of the critical challenge to urban places caused by the pandemic.

As this book goes to press, the evolving land use system in the United States is confronting the pandemic and the fear of crowding that it begot. This is an essay supported by only a few footnotes and fewer case studies because it is too early to write knowingly about this challenge to land use law. It may be a momentary phenomenon, a lingering annoyance, or a permanent tear in the fabric of urban settlements. Chapter Eight can only squint ahead, looking into a cloudy crystal ball and ruminating about what will happen. It can only speculate about what denser cities will do to stop the contagious fear that they are unsafe places. They will soon teach us what they can do to stem and reverse the incipient flight of largely affluent households, attempting to avert a repeat of the white flight that occurred in the middle of the 20th century.

This book's chapters have demonstrated that land use regulations can create livable neighborhoods for the nation's emerging households: young millennials; immigrants needed for urban jobs; and seniors who are leaving single-family neighborhoods. Until the pandemic, most of these households preferred urban living in neighborhoods with a dynamic mix of services, entertainment, restaurants, and transportation alternatives. Density makes mass transportation cheaper and affordable housing possible, supports large public hospitals, and affords a broad safety net. It is also associated with greater environmental preservation, economic productivity, innovation, traffic safety, air quality, social capital, and opportunities for upward mobility, as well as less likelihood of some chronic diseases and increased overall life expectancy.[1] In short, it makes neighborhoods lively, walkable, and efficient.

In the wake of COVID-19, it may also reduce disease contagion and mortality rates. In a recent study, researchers analyzed the COVID-19 infection and mortality rates in 913 U.S. metropolitan counties. When they took factors such as race, education, and metropolitan size into account, the researchers found that "county density is not significantly related to the infection rate." Further, "counties with higher densities have significantly lower virus-related mortality rates than do counties with lower densities."

One possible reason for such a lower mortality rate in higher-density areas is the availability and quality of health care. In one survey, almost all low-income respondents who live in suburban and rural areas cited transportation as "a significant barrier to obtaining health care services."[2] Not only do suburban and rural residents travel farther to medical facilities, but many

1. Shima Hamidi et al., *Does Density Aggravate the COVID-19 Pandemic?*, 86 J. Am. Plan. Ass'n 495, 496 (2020).
2. Laurie E. Felland et al., Suburban Poverty and the Health Care Safety Net 6 (2009).

people in these car-dependent areas do not own cars. Since public transportation seldom serves these areas, many are left without a reliable means of obtaining medical care. To make matters worse, "a substantial portion of the US population residing in [these areas] lack[] health insurance," and their medical providers are "less likely to receive public funds" to support care for the uninsured.[3]

In contrast, dense urban areas provide more medical care options (including free or low-cost alternatives). Also, the options provided in denser communities are often more accessible. Since high-density areas can support public transportation, many people living in these areas need not rely on cars to obtain medical care. These factors can reduce disease mortality. Regarding disease contagion, research indicates that connectivity between areas "matters more than density in the spread of the COVID-19 pandemic."[4] By itself, density may even work to reduce infection rates since high-density areas have the infrastructure to more effectively implement measures that promote social distancing.[5] In addition, high-density makes it easier to provide services to people most in need while social distancing orders are in place.

These findings suggest that density can play a critical role in promoting public health and building a more sustainable future. The many solid land use planning, regulatory, and financial innovations already in place are an accepted and beneficial part of the urban agenda, guiding the shape of human settlements. These high-density places are where society has invested in infrastructure and where per capita carbon emissions are less than half the national average, mitigating climate change: a public health problem that dwarfs COVID-19. Chapter Three contains a detailed description of these tools and how they are being used to create low-carbon human settlements. Low-carbon urban places are being challenged by the pandemic. There is a fear of sharing doors, elevators, crowded subways, busy playgrounds, and traditional sidewalks. The command to socially distance and permission to work from home compound the situation. This reaction to COVID-19 risks recreating the flight from and disinvestment in urban places that originally caused sprawl and its crippling effects on the cities and their tax base, revenues, and physical environment. To this, add the per capita increase of car-

3. Alina S. Schnake-Mahl & Benjamin D. Sommers, *Health Care In The Suburbs: An Analysis Of Suburban Poverty And Health Care Access*, 36 Health Affs. 1777, 1777; Felland, *supra* note 2, at 5.

4. Shima Hamidi et al., *Longitudinal analyses of the relationship between development density and the COVID-19 morbidity and mortality rates: Early evidence from 1,165 metropolitan counties in the United States*, 64 Health & Place 1, 1 (2020).

5. *Id.* at 2.

bon emissions caused by the urban residents' resettlement to car-dependent suburbs.

To illustrate, anecdotally, Yorktown, a car-dependent suburb north of New York City, has branded itself Destination Y. The news coverage on August 1, 2020, read: "Town markets itself as a place to build, live after the pandemic is over." The next day, the same newspaper featured a headline regarding development in cities just south of Yorktown that read: "Developers take a step back, economic slowdown cools fervor for big downtown projects."

Policymakers and scholars will have to wait for real data to determine the extent and duration of this trend. In the New York metropolitan area, the available evidence abounds in media headlines. Here are a few of the many that appeared in various news sources between March and August 2020:

- Foreign buyers take a step back from New York real estate;
- Residential vacancies double;
- Subway ridership down 75%;
- Metropolitan Transit Authority faces fiscal tsunami without federal aid;
- City leaders fear urban flight gaining momentum;
- New Yorkers ditching city for elbow room fuel housing boom upstate;
- Goodbye city life: Litchfield housing booming due to city flight;
- City dwellers are looking to move to suburbs as more work from home;
- Real estate prices fall sharply in New York;
- Retail chains abandon Manhattan: "It's Unsustainable"; and
- Residential contracts and closings surged last month in Fairfield and Westchester counties.

Testimonials in the press from real estate brokers confirm this exodus: "[T]he unprecedented sales growth [which was also seen throughout Connecticut and in the Berkshires] is driven by a continuation of New York City buyers relocating to the suburbs amidst the ongoing pandemic." Paul Breunich, president and CEO of William Pitt-Julia B. Fee Sotheby's International Realty, stated that

> buyer demand will remain unparalleled in the months to come . . . . The level of buyer interest in our markets is unmatched in recent memory, and it serves

as an enormous incentive for potential sellers to list their properties. In my 30 years in the real estate industry, I have never seen a market like the one we're in now.[6]

A broker in Madison, Connecticut, confirmed this sentiment:

I've been selling largely second and third homes . . . for 30 years. What is happening now is different . . . . Buyers who have no connection to this area are discovering it for the first time . . . . Most quietly share that they no longer want to have New York as their base, they are done with that life.[7]

Outside the New York metropolitan area, the evidence is equally anecdotal. Moving companies reported that several large cities had more people leave than move in during the six months following the outbreak of the pandemic: San Francisco—80%; Los Angeles—70%; Washington, D.C.—58%; Miami—53%; Alexandria, Va.—63%; and Arlington, Va.—78%. Idaho saw 194% more people moving into the state than out, while Illinois, Washington, D.C., New Jersey, and Connecticut were among states where departures outnumbered arrivals by 50% or more.

In mid-summer 2020, Prof. Richard Florida wrote in the Bloomberg press about the pull of the suburbs:

There is no doubt that the current crises have impelled some, particularly families with young children and also the old and the vulnerable, to decamp to the suburbs or even rural communities. For families, fear of Covid-19 has put a premium on private amenities like backyards and home offices, while reducing the appeal of more public amenities like parks or even restaurants, theaters, galleries and museums found in urban centers . . . . Working out of a spare bedroom is much safer than heading to a downtown office building or co-working space. All of these desires can be far more easily satisfied in the suburbs, and almost always for a lot less money than in urban neighborhoods like Tribeca, Park Slope, Nob Hill, Georgetown or Beacon Hill. There is likely to be an uptick in rural gentrification as well, especially to smaller cities like Hudson, New York, that have lots of natural amenities and lovely main streets, but are still within a few hours of driving from a major urban center.[8]

Jerry Seinfeld, an unlikely match for Professor Florida as an observer of urbanism, pushed back as a valued representative of his cohort in an August opinion piece in the *New York Times*:

6. Press Release, Andrew Wood, Contracts and Sales Surge in July, Reports William Pitt-Julia B. Fee Sotheby's International Realty: Buyers in New York Suburban Markets Still Out in Record Numbers (Aug. 11, 2020).

7. Duo Dickinson, *Are Cities Over? Not So Fast*, ArchDaily (Sept. 20, 2020), https://www.archdaily.com/947845/are-cities-over-not-so-fast.

8. Richard Florida, *The Forces That Will Reshape American Cities*, Bloomberg CityLab (July 2, 2020).

> But one thing I know for sure: The last thing we need in the thick of so many challenges is some putz on LinkedIn wailing and whimpering, "Everyone's gone! I want 2019 back!" He says he knows people who have left New York for Maine, Vermont, Tennessee, Indiana. I have been to all of these places many, many, many times over many decades. And with all due respect and affection, Are . . . You . . . Kidding . . . Me?! . . . . There's some other stupid thing in the article about "bandwidth" and how New York is over because everybody will "remote everything." Guess what: Everyone hates to do this. Everyone. Hates. You know why? There's no energy. Energy, attitude and personality cannot be "remoted" through even the best fiber optic lines. That's the whole reason many of us moved to New York in the first place.[9]

There are studies that back Seinfeld's view. *Crain's New York Business* newsletter reports that

> the pandemic has shown us just how essential the office is to our personal and professional lives. Working remotely has serious drawbacks, starting with the fact that it isolates employees. According to Buffer's *2020 State of Remote Work Survey*, before the outbreak, 20% of remote workers said they struggled most with collaboration and communication, while another 20% said loneliness. Today those feelings of isolation have been amplified. What 74% of workers miss most about the office, according to Gensler's new *U.S. Work From Home Survey*, is other people.[10]

Other headlines note the threat to small businesses—in some areas of the country, more than one-third have closed permanently. They are the delis, caterers, coffee shops, barbers, bookstores, nail and hair salons, bars, service establishments, cafes, and restaurants that make urban life vibrant, walkable, and entertaining. Executive orders closed them and prevented landlords from evicting commercial tenants for non-payment of rent, at least for a time. As the curve levels and they are allowed to reopen, how many will return, will they be profitable, can landlords hang on, and how many vacancies will remain? In retail shops, everything is connected to demand, so reversing the exodus of residents to the suburbs is a retail recovery strategy. Cities have been helping small businesses become profitable for many years. Can they redouble those efforts, find resources, and help businesses adjust to a new business environment before street-level properties stop paying their taxes? Moody's Investors Service reported in August 2020 that commercial mortgage debt in distress surged 320%, attributing much of the delinquency to

9. Jerry Seinfeld, Opinion, *So You Think New York Is "Dead": (It's Not.)*, N.Y. Times, Aug. 24, 2020.
10. *Coronavirus May Be the Best Thing for the Office Life*, Crain's N.Y. Bus., Aug. 21, 2020.

the pandemic, including distress in large-scale retail, office buildings, and hotels.

So, who knows? Does Professor Florida or Seinfeld win the debate? So much is not known. How long will this pandemic last? Will there be others? How long will the fear of them last? How long will the new allure of suburbs last? Will the appeal of city life return? Will cities become more affordable and suburbs less so? Or will the loss of the affluent and small businesses cause cities to further disinvest in low-income neighborhoods and become even further segregated? Will suburbs become more segregated, compounding the nation's failure to provide fair housing?

The future of our post-pandemic world is uncertain. However, one thing is clear: cities must continue striving to become healthier. While recovery from COVID-19 poses many challenges and questions, it also presents an opportunity—one that involves not just returning to "normal" but developing into a more resilient, equitable, and sustainable society.[11]

II. What Can Be Done?

The simple answer is much. If you want to know how, read this book. What is certain is that cities will need to become safer for a variety of reasons, including this stubborn pandemic, future pandemics that are equally fearsome, and the certain consequences of climate change. Cities must continue to make density palatable. Their planners and lawyers have known this for years as their populations increased and developers responded by building mixed-use, transit-oriented developments and other buildings that need to feel and be safe. There now needs to be an acceleration of these efforts, with a clear focus on public health.

What follows is a beginning menu of what cities can do with their plans, codes, regulations, capital, and operating budgets.

Comprehensive Plan: Public health must become a driving concern in urban planning and design. Comprehensive plans are road maps for the future. They involve stakeholders in their formulation and, in the process, build support for their strategies. They direct land use regulations, infrastructure, and city budgets. Public health components need to be drafted

11. The Global Mayors Covid-19 Recovery Task Force have united to do just this. One of their guiding principles for recovery is to not "return to 'business as usual'—because that is a world on track for 3° C or more of over-heating." Another is that we "must be guided by an adherence to public health and scientific expertise," and further that "[t]he recovery must address issues of equity that have been laid bare by the impact of the crisis . . . ." *Global Mayors Covid-19 Recovery Task Force*, C40 Cities, https://www.c40.org/other/covid-task-force (last visited Nov. 8, 2020).

by experts and stakeholders and approved by legislative bodies. These health components must specify how safe buildings and densities are to be achieved. What are the goals, objectives, strategies, and implementation techniques to create safe homes, businesses, parks, and neighborhoods?

The DNA has been there for more than a century. The Standard City Planning Enabling Act (1928) provided that plans will, "in accordance with present and future needs, best promote health, safety, morals, order, convenience, prosperity, and general welfare, as well as efficiency and economy in the process of development . . . ." The purposes of planning were broad. Zoning had to conform. The stage was set for the adoption of flexible zoning and land use strategies that moved beyond the rigid contours of Euclidean zoning. This system is rising to the challenge of climate change. Now, the health of the people needs to move center stage as this current new beginning unfolds.

Building Codes: Codes can be amended so that all new and substantially rehabilitated buildings have better internal ventilation, ultraviolet light to disinfect indoor air, high-efficiency particulate air (HEPA) filters (like those used in hospitals and airplanes), health screening technology in buildings, wider corridors, work-at-home spaces, more elevators, voice-activated elevators, automatic doors, spatial distance metrics for indoor service, and redesigned interior amenity spaces.

Capital Investments in Infrastructure: City budgets can provide for "creative place-making," spatial distancing in urban parks and open space, tree canopies, broader sidewalks, expanded capacity for outdoor service for retailers, streets with more bicycle lanes, "slow" and "dining" streets, and curbside management to facilitate retail pick-ups.

Zoning and Land Use Regulations: Short-term permits can be given for new uses and expansion, particularly for small businesses. Temporary use permits can be offered quickly to commercial tenants adjusting to the changing economy. Emergency variances from set-back requirements can be awarded, parking lots and spaces used for commerce, and required parking reduced. Office zone standards can be amended to allow creative interior arrangements and flexible residential uses. Where retail is not feasible, requirements for on-street retail use can be eliminated. Permits for all small business applications can be expedited by bringing together regulatory agencies, authorities, and government departments to review projects simultaneously. Pre-application meetings with developers can include health professionals as well as architects and engineers to assure the health of future occupants.

Existing Buildings: Techniques used to encourage owners of existing buildings to retrofit their properties to reduce potential contagion can be adapted from the green building and carbon emission reduction experiences of cities. Green buildings with low-carbon footprints are more marketable than their competitors. Safe buildings will be too. Property owners can follow prescriptions for safe buildings and safe sites; cities can work with public health experts to create the standards for them and offer incentives for compliance. Emerging ratings such as the WELL Health Safety Rating and Fitwell Viral Response Module Financial incentives can be recommended and become prerequisites for qualifying for incentives such as tax abatements. Some of these standards can be added to property maintenance codes, which apply to existing buildings.

Small Business Recovery: City staff and their consultants are following the rapid transitions for small businesses from traditional models, to transitional approaches, to post-pandemic strategies. While streets become dining streets and parking lots host outdoor dining and pop-up retail, businesses will need to learn digital strategies and accommodate their customers' changing service needs. This transition will require modernization of software and digital equipment and adequate internet capacity to attract and hold customers. All this requires grants and affordable loans that governments provide. Small business development corporations will be challenged to bring recovery strategies and resources to vulnerable commercial districts. The U.S. Conference of Mayors Partner America Program and Small Business Assistance Program will be in high demand. Tutorials for volunteer lawyers, landlords, and tenants on how to mediate nonpayment evictions and enter into economically feasible recovery leases are needed. Courts can refer eviction proceedings to city-supported mediation clinics to search for win-win solutions where the bottom lines of both commercial tenants and landlords are considered.

III. Who Is in Charge? Emergency Powers and Property Rights

Most of the chapters in this book have vaunted the role of local governments, but always in the context of the nation's federal system of laws. During the first six months of response to the pandemic, it was difficult to understand who was in charge. The post-pandemic response in this chapter has again focused on what cities, as municipal corporations, can do through their land use laws. With this effort, they clearly need help. With small business recovery, they need grants and loans for their small businesses, and with transportation, they need state and federal dollars; with all the recovery strategies, they need technical assistance.

Chapters Five and Six devoted considerable space to this topic. In Chapter Five, we saw how the national program of hazard mitigation planning reaches down and respectfully includes local comprehensive planning. In Chapter Six, we saw local planning and regulation fill in gaps in federal and state water law and witnessed the natural tendencies of municipalities to reach up and partner with state and federal agencies. In the process, we discussed cooperative federalism, reflexive law, framework laws, complex adaptive systems, and the diffusion of innovation—leading to a new principle of collaborative subsidiary. These are all theories that stitch together the separate powers within our federal governmental system.

As we embrace public health as a central focus of land use planning, regulation, building codes, and open space management, it is essential to pay attention to aligning federal and state efforts with local initiatives. State public health agencies and councils, and federal health agencies need to provide help in integrating health planning and action into the municipal land use planning and regulatory system. How else can we ensure safe buildings and safe densities?

Our response to COVID-19 has been anything but coordinated. National cohesion can only be accomplished through the federal government. Its powers and resources must be used in a collaborative process with the states and local governments. The states possess the police power to protect public health and, consequently, have broad powers to declare emergencies and enforce compliance with mask orders, business closings, and eviction moratoria. On the ground, localities have broad powers to regulate building uses and construction through their state delegated land use control. They can also legislate to abate public nuisances and other public health emergencies. Lawsuits by the governor of Alabama against the mayor and the city council of Atlanta are ill-advised. Intergovernmental powers must be linked; collaboration is essential; resources must be leveraged; strategies must be consistent.

Collaboration has been emphasized throughout this book. A clear understanding of federal, state, and local powers, prerogatives, and imitations is required. Some consensus about how the actions of each level of government can be integrated into a cohesive response to pandemics and other emergencies is essential.

This is a book on climate change and land use law. Missing are two important topics. The first is systemic racism, and the second is property rights. With trepidation and apologies for addressing them only in closing, this essay offers a brief exploration of these climate change issues. They are both ideologically charged and much disputed, but essential climate change-related topics. Formerly redlined, racially segregated neighborhoods experience elevated temperatures and heat-related deaths than white neighborhoods in the same city. Aggressive regulations designed to create safe buildings and safe densities limit property rights, which are defended by equally aggressive litigation.

IV. Racial Justice and Public Health

The public health concerns of urban residents who can afford to move is a new challenge caused by the recent pandemic. The public health threats to lower income neighborhoods where households of color predominate have existed for decades. Those fleeing COVID-19 are largely on the top rungs of the economic ladder, so statistically more are white than minority households. If they move to mostly white suburbs, they increase segregation there as well as the cities they leave behind. If they move to small cities with affordable housing, they can increase housing prices, causing displacement and homelessness. Disproportionately, those displaced will be households of color.

In cities, climate change is causing deadly conditions, the most obvious of which is the heat island effect. Temperatures in lower income neighborhoods are higher, as is the percentage of residents who die from heat exposure. These neighborhoods, with exceptions, have limited tree canopies and extensive impervious surfaces such as sidewalks, streets, parking lots, and even treeless city parks, all of which absorb and reflect the heat.

Zoning is complicit. Multi-family housing is allowed in these zoning districts, and developers can cover most of the lot with buildings and asphalt. Policies that apply to buildings in other areas such as green roofs and on-site landscaping don't apply. Comprehensive plans, to which zoning must conform, only recently have been amended to comply with climate action plans. Largely, these plans have not targeted low-income neighborhoods for relief from heat or the other obvious consequences of climate change. Zoning and site plan regulations, as a result, have been similarly mute on the topic. Trees and bushes absorb water and sequester carbon. They reduce soil erosion and cool nearby buildings. Racial equity is emerging as an element of climate action planning, and that concern—as well as the strategies that address it—must find their way into comprehensive land use planning and zoning. This imperative clearly marks another new beginning for land use law.

Redlining—federal mapping designating neighborhoods safe or unsafe for investment—labeled many of today's low-income neighborhoods "hazardous," effectively denying residents access to mortgages and other financial resources. Summer temperatures in such hazardous neighborhoods are from 5 to 10 degrees higher than other residential neighborhoods in the same communities. Predictably, life expectancies are lower—from 10 to 20 years. In Portland, Oregon, neighborhoods rated "best" on federal investment maps today are 8 degrees cooler than the city-wide average, while those rated "hazardous" are nearly 5 degrees hotter. This disparity is similar in many metropolitan areas across the country.

As with the pandemic and city attempts to stem residents' movement to the suburbs, planning and zoning can set the stage by properly regulating land use. Similarly, city budgets and aid from higher levels of government are critical complements. Targeting poorer neighborhoods to receive a fair share of city expenditures dedicated to tree planting, greener parks, flood reduction, green roofs, and green infrastructure is a necessary component of broader economic policies. Many of the essential workers during the pandemic—and many of those who work in the shops that city dwellers count on—live in these formerly redlined areas. Keeping them healthy is not only a humanitarian mandate; it is a necessary part of local, state, and federal economic recovery policies.

V. The Police Power and Property Rights

Dealing with the pandemic and its effect on business and property owners requires an understanding of property rights and the power of government to limit those rights. At a recent webinar on "emergency and police power: property claims in times of crisis," a panel deliberated on this topic. The program description read as follows:

> On the eve of the centennial of *Pennsylvania Coal Co. v. Mahon* (U.S. 1922), this panel will revisit the question: How far can the police power be stretched to protect the public against dangers? The panel will evaluate the scope of state and local authority to respond to emergencies and the implications for private property rights—asking, how far is too far? What is the scope of

> implied limitations on private property rights in times of crisis? When does the diminution of existing property rights require compensation? Can local governments respond to a crisis without delegated authority or in defiance of state mandates? What rights do property owners/landlords/tenants have to privately respond in times of crisis?[12]

As a member of this panel, I gave the following overview of property rights and the case law regarding due process and regulatory takings. It is fitting to end this chapter and the book with this exploration of the U.S. Supreme Court's clear and consistent view that property is held subject to reasonable laws and limitations. In view of pandemics and climate change, what is reasonable to protect the public health is clearly a central issue.

After reviewing property rights under English common law, I will mention the contributions to today's topic of several U.S. Supreme Court opinions ranging from 1906 to 2002: a century's worth of balancing property rights and the public interest. This will set the stage for a discussion of state law and executive orders that require the pubic to stay at home, wear masks, close or limit their businesses, suspend the right to evict tenants, and other mandates imposed to respond to the pandemic.

The legal power to protect the public in a time of emergencies is called the police power. The concept of the police power—that is, of the government's power to regulate behavior and property, is derived from the Greek word *polis* for city or *polity*, and from the Latin word *polita*, meaning citizenship, and from the French *police*, which means government.

William Blackstone's *Commentaries on the Common Law of England* demonstrate that personal liberties were limitable by government regulation. In 1769, he reported that the state's police power gave the enforcement authorities of the Crown the right to exercise the means by which "the individuals of the state, like members of a well-governed family, are bound to conform their general behavior to the rules of propriety, good neighbourhood, and good manners; and to be decent, industrious, and inoffensive in their respective stations." This offers some historical perspective on the notions of some, during this pandemic period, who object to governors, in lieu of kings, exercising the police power to direct the public to shelter in place, wear masks, and forgo trips to the movies and bars in modern neighborhoods. Kevin Stitt, the governor of Oklahoma, said that he is opposed to

12. West Legal Ed Ctr. & American Bar Ass'n, *Emergency and Police Power: Property Claims in Times of Crisis* (July 22, 2020) (webinar), https://westlegaledcenter.com/program_guide/course_detail.jsf?courseId=100288767 (*Pennsylvania Coal Co. v. Mahon* was the first decision of the U.S. Supreme Court to hold that the regulation of private property could go "too far" and become a regulatory taking, the equivalent of an actual governmental taking of property. Justice Oliver Wendell Holmes wrote the majority opinion)

ordering masks because "you can't pick and choose what freedoms you are going to give people."

More to the point of *Penn Coal* and the regulation of property, Blackstone commented that property "consists in the free use, enjoyment, and disposal of all his acquisitions, without any control or diminution, save only the laws of the land."

1922 *Pennsylvania Coal Co. v. Mahon*[13]: This nearly century-old case involved coal mining regulation by the laws of the land—that is, the state of Pennsylvania. The case was initiated, not by the coal industry against a state statute that regulated mining, but by a bill in equity brought by a property owner asking the court to enjoin coal mining under his house.

One hundred-fifty years after Blackstone's definition of property rights, *Penn Coal* dealt with Pennsylvania's laws, adopted by its legislature. Pennsylvania's constitution granted its legislature the police power to adopt legislation to protect the health, safety, welfare, and morals of the people of the state. The legislature was concerned about the subsidence of streets, homes, and businesses caused by the extraction of coal from the support estate, a separate estate from the surface and subsurface estates as defined by Pennsylvania common law. The Kohler Act restricted mining companies from extracting coal from the support estate, thus preventing subsidence to protect public safety.

We did not know in 1922 when the case was decided that a police power regulation could be a regulatory taking. Challenges to property regulations prior to that time were based on the deprivation of due process—that is, the claim that the law did not achieve a valid public objective. We do not hold our land, from Blackstone forward, subject to irrational and arbitrary laws—only laws that protect the public health, safety, welfare, or morals. The Fifth Amendment, applied to the states by the Fourteenth Amendment, prevented the deprivation of property without due process. By showing that a law did not reasonably protect the public, one could win a due process claim. The remedy was invalidation of the law by the court, freeing the property owner from its constraints.

The taking of property is an altogether different thing. As Justice Holmes declared in the *Penn Coal* case, when a regulation goes too far, it can be the equivalent of a physical taking, which is also prevented by the Fifth and Fourteenth Amendments, unless it is for a public purpose and accompanied by just compensation.

The Court held that the Kohler Act cannot be sustained as an exercise of the police power. "The general rule at least is that while property may be regulated to a certain extent, if regulation goes too far it will be recognized

13. 260 U.S. 393 (1922).

as a taking." It noted that the Act cannot be justified as a protection of public safety, which is secured by notice requirements to affected owners prior to the commencement of mining.

Holmes understood that the plaintiff, Mahon, had either sold the support estate to the defendant coal company or had bought only the surface estate from it. "As applied to this case," he noted: "The statute is admitted to destroy previously existing rights of property and contract. The question is whether the police power can be stretched so far." He wrote that the Act

> purports to abolish what is recognized in Pennsylvania as an estate in land—a very valuable estate—and what is declared by the Court below to be a contract hitherto binding the plaintiffs. If we were called upon to deal with the plaintiffs' position alone we should think it clear that the statute does not disclose a public interest sufficient to warrant so extensive a destruction of the defendant's constitutionally protected rights.

Holmes further noted:

> This is the case of a single private house . . . . A source of damage to such a house is not a public nuisance even if similar damage is inflicted on others in different places. The damage is not common or public . . . . So far as private persons or communities have seen fit to take the risk of acquiring only surface rights, we cannot see that the fact that their risk has become a danger warrants the giving to them greater rights than they bought.

So the Court denied the bill of equity, asking the court below to enjoin the mining of the support estate. The holding was not that it was a taking, but rather that the Mahon should not be awarded an injunction as a remedy; to do so might have constituted a taking. The Court held that the police power could not be stretched this far. The effect of the holding was to invalidate the Kohler Act as it applied to the plaintiff's property. It was not a valid exercise of the police power. It does reflect on takings by noting: "To make it commercially impracticable to mine certain coal has very nearly the same effect for constitutional purposes as appropriating or destroying it. This we think that we are warranted in assuming that the statute does." The remedy was invalidation of the law as applied to *Mahon* and, by extension, others who might challenge it; this is a due process remedy.

1906 *Strickley v. Highland Boy Gold Mining Co.*[14]: Justice Holmes wrote the opinion in *Strickley* 16 years before *Mahon*. In this case, the rights of a private owner to enjoin a police power law in Utah were similarly limited. In *Strickley*, an easement over the plaintiff's property was condemned by the state and conveyed to his neighbor, a private mining company. The complaint was that this was done solely for private benefit and was not, therefore, a

14. 200 U.S. 527 (1906).

public use under the Fifth and Fourteenth Amendments. The condemnation was done under a Utah statute that asserted that the state's public welfare demanded that mining operations in the mountains have access to rail lines in its valleys. Justice Holmes wrote:

> In the opinion of the legislature and the supreme court of Utah the public welfare of that state demands that aerial lines between the mines upon its mountain sides and the railways in the valleys below should not be made impossible by the refusal of a private owner to sell the right to cross his land. The Constitution of the United States does not require us to say that they are wrong.

Thus, the taking of private property and conveyance of it to another private party is not unconstitutional.

1915 *Hadacheck v. Sebastian*[15] and *Reinman v. City of Little Rock*[16]: These cases considered the legitimacy of using the police power to prevent property use that constitutes a nuisance or that simply might cause injury to others. In 1915, seven years before *Penn Coal*, the Court decided two cases that bear on this point: *Hadacheck v. Sebastian* and *Reinman v. City of Little Rock*. In *Penn Coal*, by declaring that the mining of Mahon's support estate did not prove a public nuisance, the Court could not sustain the regulation as a valid exercise of the police power.

However, in these two 1915 cases, the court validated property restrictions of land uses that it found injurious to the public. In *Hadacheck*, the city prohibited the operation of a brick kiln in a three-square-mile area and in *Reinman*, a livery stable in certain parts of the city. The owners attacked the laws on numerous grounds, including that they were arbitrary and unreasonable. Justice [Joseph] McKenna wrote for the majority in *Hadacheck*:

> It is to be remembered that we are dealing with one of the most essential powers of government,—one that is the least limitable. It may, indeed, seem harsh in its exercise, usually is on some individual, but the imperative necessity for its existence precludes any limitation upon it when not exerted arbitrarily. A vested interest cannot be asserted against it because of conditions once obtaining.

The *Hadacheck* Court commented on its earlier ruling that year in *Reinman*:

> The circumstances of the case were very much like those of the case at bar, and give reply to the contentions of petitioner, especially that which asserts that a necessary and lawful occupation that is not a nuisance per se cannot be made so by legislative declaration. There was a like investment in property, encouraged by the then conditions; a like reduction of value and deprivation of

15. 239 U.S. 394 (1915).
16. 237 U.S. 171 (1915).

> property was asserted against the validity of the ordinance there considered; a like assertion of an arbitrary exercise of the power of prohibition. Against all of these contentions, and causing the rejection of them all, was adduced the police power. There was a prohibition of a business, lawful in itself, there as here. It was a livery stable there; a brickyard here. They differ in particulars, but they are alike in that which cause and justify prohibition in defined localities,—that is, the effect upon the health and comfort of the community.

In *Reinman*, the Court wrote:

> Granting that [the business] is not a nuisance per se, it is clearly within the police power of the state to regulate the business, and to that end to declare that in particular circumstances and in particular localities a livery stable shall be deemed a nuisance in fact and in law.

The only stated limitation upon the power was that it could not be exerted arbitrarily or with unjust discrimination. Blackstone had a commentary on this matter as well:

> And by consequence it follows, that if one does any other act, in itself lawful, which yet being done in that place necessarily to the damage of another's property, it is a nuisance: for it is incumbent on him to find some other place to do that act, where it will be less offensive.

1928 *Miller v. Schoene*[17]: Six years after *Penn Coal*, the Supreme Court took up this issue of limiting the use of property because of its damaging effect on one's neighbor. In *Miller v. Schoene*, the Court held that the Takings Clause did not require the state of Virginia to compensate the owner of cedar trees for the value of the trees that the state had ordered destroyed under the Cedar Rust Act. The trees needed to be destroyed to prevent a disease from spreading to nearby apple orchards, which represented a far more valuable resource. In upholding the state action, the Court held:

> We need not weigh with nicety the question whether the infected cedars constitute a nuisance according to the common law; or whether they may be so declared by statute. (Citing *Hadacheck*.) For where, as here, the choice is unavoidable, we cannot say that its exercise, controlled by considerations of social policy which are not unreasonable, involves any denial of due process. The injury to property here is no more serious, nor the public interest less, than in *Hadacheck* . . . .

The *Miller v. Schoene* Court continued: "Here the public interest is involved preferment of that interest over the property interest of the individual, to the extent even of its destruction, is one of the distinguishing characteristics of every exercise of the police power which affects property." (Citing *Mugler*

17. 276 U.S. 272 (1928).

v. Kansas, Hadacheck v. Los Angeles; Village of Euclid v. Ambler Realty Co.; and *Reinman v. Little Rock.)*

1926 *Village of Euclid v. Ambler Realty Co.*[18]: These cases make it easier to understand the famous 1926 case of *Village of Euclid v. Ambler Realty Co.*, which sustained the constitutional validity of zoning. The Court noted:

> The matter of zoning has received much attention at the hands of commissions and experts, and the results of their investigations have been set forth in comprehensive reports. These reports which bear every evidence of painstaking consideration, concur in the view that the segregation of residential, business and industrial buildings will make it easier to provide fire apparatus suitable for the character and intensity of the development in each section; that it will increase the safety and security of home life, greatly tend to prevent street accidents, especially to children, by reducing the traffic and resulting confusion in residential sections, decrease noise and other conditions which produce or intensify nervous disorders, preserve a more favorable environment in which to rear children, etc.

In *Euclid*, another due process claim was defeated. "[I]t is enough for us to determine, as we do, that the ordinance in its general scope and dominant features, so far as its provisions are here involved, is a valid exercise of authority."

The case articulated the Court's presumption of validity of police power enactments and the heavy burden of proof on challengers: "The reasons [offered by the village] are sufficiently cogent to preclude us from saying, as it must be said before the ordinance can be declared unconstitutional, that such provisions are clearly arbitrary and unreasonable, having no substantial relation to the public health, safety, morals, or general welfare."

Euclid also demonstrates that the scope of constitutional principles expands and contracts in a changing world:

> [W]hile the meaning of constitutional guaranties never varies, the scope of their application must expand or contract to meet the new and different conditions which are constantly coming within the field of their operation. In a changing world it is impossible that it should be otherwise. But although a degree of elasticity is thus imparted, not to the meaning, but to the application of constitutional principles, statutes and ordinances, which, after giving due weight to the new conditions, are found clearly not to conform to the Constitution, of course, must fall.

"Regulations, the wisdom, necessity, and validity of which, as applied to existing conditions, are so apparent that they are now uniformly sustained, a century ago, or even half a century ago, probably would have been rejected as arbitrary and oppressive."

18. 272 U.S. 365 (1926).

1988 *Pennell v. San Jose*[19]: The city of San Jose enacted a rent-control ordinance to alleviate skyrocketing rent prices due to the growing shortage of housing. The issue was whether the ordinance violated the Fourteenth Amendment's Due Process Clause. The Court held that the ordinance was rationally crafted to protect landlords' financial investments while simultaneously preventing tenants from becoming victims of burdensome rent increases. The ordinance's purpose of preventing unreasonable rent increases caused by the city's housing shortage is a legitimate exercise of appellees' police powers. The Takings Claim was deemed to be premature.

2002 *Tahoe-Sierra Preservation Council v. Tahoe Regional Planning Agency*[20]: In *Tahoe-Sierra Preservation Council*, the Court held that a 32-month moratorium on all development was not a regulatory taking. The moratorium's purpose was to give the Agency time to deal with the threat posed by land development to the clarity of Lake Tahoe, which had begun to cloud as early as the late 1950s. This case bears on the issue of whether pandemic-related moratoria on evictions, for example, or even on temporary closings constitute a regulatory taking.

VI. Conclusion

Recall that San Jose adopted a rent control ordinance. Little Rock and Los Angeles, in *Reinman* and *Hadacheck*, adopted nuisance prevention ordinances. The village of Euclid adopted a comprehensive zoning ordinance that mandated the separation of land uses. In most states, local governments have the authority to govern local property and affairs and to regulate and prevent nuisance-like activity. In all states, they have been delegated the power to adopt zoning and other land use ordinances. A recent study demonstrates that at least 40 states have repealed Dillon's Rule, which required that the power delegated to municipalities to control land use is to be narrowly construed.

In its journey, land use law has shed many of the shackles that would have reduced its ability to adjust as times change. As climate change worsens, pandemics come and go, and systemic racism is better understood and confronted, it is important to recall that the law changes, in application if not principle, to meet society's needs. To repeat what the Court noted in *Village of Euclid v. Ambler Realty Co.*: "[W]hile the meaning of constitutional guaranties never varies, the scope of their application must expand or contract to meet the new and different conditions which are constantly coming within the field of their operation. In a changing world it is impossible that it should be otherwise."

19. 485 U.S. 1 (1988).
20. 535 U.S. 302 (2002).

Table of Cases

Index

O

Q

R

T

Notes